THE AGE OF
RECONSTRUCTION

AMERICA IN THE WORLD

Sven Beckert and Jeremi Suri, Series Editors

For a full list of titles in the series, go to https://press.princeton.edu/series/america-in-the-world

Mary Bridges, *Dollars and Dominion: US Bankers and the Making of a Superpower*

Don H. Doyle, *The Age of Reconstruction: How Lincoln's New Birth of Freedom Remade the World*

Jeffrey A. Engel, Mark Atwood Lawrence, and Andrew Preston, editors, *America in the World: A History in Documents since 1898, Revised and Updated*

Mark Atwood Lawrence, *The End of Ambition: The United States and the Third World in the Vietnam Era*

Roberto Saba, *American Mirror: The United States and Brazil in the Age of Emancipation*

Dorothy Sue Cobble, *For the Many: American Feminists and the Global Fight for Democratic Equality*

Stefan J. Link, *Forging Global Fordism: Nazi Germany, Soviet Russia, and the Contest over the Industrial Order*

Katy Hull, *The Machine Has a Soul: American Sympathy with Italian Fascism*

Sara Lorenzini, *Global Development: A Cold War History*

Michael Cotey Morgan, *The Final Act: The Helsinki Accords and the Transformation of the Cold War*

A. G. Hopkins, *American Empire: A Global History*

Tore C. Olsson, *Agrarian Crossings: Reformers and the Remaking of the US and Mexican Countryside*

Kiran Klaus Patel, *The New Deal: A Global History*

Adam Ewing, *The Age of Garvey: How a Jamaican Activist Created a Mass Movement and Changed Global Black Politics*

THE AGE OF RECONSTRUCTION

HOW LINCOLN'S NEW BIRTH OF FREEDOM REMADE THE WORLD

DON H. DOYLE

PRINCETON UNIVERSITY PRESS

PRINCETON & OXFORD

Published by Princeton University Press
41 William Street, Princeton, New Jersey 08540
99 Banbury Road, Oxford OX2 6JX

press.princeton.edu

Library of Congress Cataloging-in-Publication Data

Names: Doyle, Don H., 1946– author.
Title: The age of Reconstruction: how Lincoln's new birth of freedom remade
    the world / Don H. Doyle.
Other titles: How Lincoln's new birth of freedom remade the world
Description: Princeton, New Jersey: Princeton University Press, 2024 | Series:
    America in the world | Includes bibliographical references and index.
Identifiers: LCCN 2023036187 (print) | LCCN 2023036188 (ebook) |
    ISBN 9780691256092 | ISBN 9780691256115 (ebook)
Subjects: LCSH: Europe—Politics and government—1848–1871. |
    Democratization—Europe—History—19th century. | United States—
    History—Civil War, 1861–1865—Foreign public opinion. | Reconstruction
    (U.S. history, 1865–1877)—Public opinion. | Lincoln, Abraham, 1809–1865—
    Influence. | United States—Foreign relations—Europe. | Europe—Foreign
    relations—United States. | BISAC: HISTORY / United States / Civil War Period
    (1850–1877) | PHILOSOPHY / Political
Classification: LCC D392.D69 2024 (print) | LCC D392 (ebook) |
    DDC 940.2/86—dc23/eng/20240116
LC record available at https://lccn.loc.gov/2023036187
LC ebook record available at https://lccn.loc.gov/2023036188

British Library Cataloging-in-Publication Data is available

Editorial: Priya Nelson, Morgan Spehar, and Emma Wagh
Production Editorial: Theresa Liu
Production: Danielle Amatucci
Publicity: Alyssa Sanford and Carmen Jimenez

Jacket image: C. Schultz. *Fraternité Universelle, Schultz work of Lincoln and other famous men.* Lemercier & Co. Paris, France, 1865. Photograph. Rare Book and Special Collections Division / Library of Congress.

This book has been composed in Arno.

Printed in the United States of America

10 9 8 7 6 5 4 3 2 1

For all my sons

Matt Baker
Ned DeWitt
Scott Wheeler
Jesse Wheeler

The power of the United States, not only in the great American Continent, but Europe, is—since the war and abolition of slavery—immense. You can now be, and therefore must be, for the good of your own country and of mankind, a leading and initiating Power. . . . Throughout and beyond Europe a mighty battle is fought between States constituted by Kings in the most arbitrary way, and Nationalities pointed out by the wishes and wants of Populations—between a Republican belief and Monarchical interests. You must step forward and take your share in the battle. It is God's battle.

—GIUSEPPE MAZZINI, ITALIAN NATIONALIST,
TO THE FRIENDS OF REPUBLICAN PRINCIPLES IN AMERICA,
DECEMBER, 1865

The working men of Europe feel sure that, as the American War of Independence initiated a new era of ascendancy for the middle class, so the American Anti-Slavery War will do for the working classes. They consider it an earnest of the epoch to come that it fell to the lot of Abraham Lincoln, the single-minded son of the working class, to lead his country through the matchless struggle for the rescue of an enchained race and the reconstruction of a social world.

—KARL MARX, LETTER OF THE FIRST INTERNATIONAL TO
ABRAHAM LINCOLN, LONDON, NOVEMBER 1864

Everything which has occurred in America, from all which is to follow in the future, grave teachings will result for us, lessons of which it is indispensable to keep an account; for, in spite of ourselves, we belong to a society irrevocably democratic.

—CHARLES FORBES MONTALEMBERT, FRENCH LIBERAL
CATHOLIC, *LA VICTOIRE DU NORD AUX ÉTATS-UNIS,* 1865

CONTENTS

List of Illustrations   xi

Timeline of Key Events   xv

Introduction: Reconstruction and World Democracy   1

PART I. MARTYRDOM

1   Tributes of the Nations   15

2   Retribution   42

PART II. AMERICA FOR AMERICANS

3   The Mexican Lesson   69

4   Russia Exits   99

5   Home Rule for Canada   121

6   Avanza Lincoln   147

PART III. EUROPE'S DEMOCRATIC REVEILLE

7   British Democracy   175

8   Spain's Democratic Moment   202

9   The Last Monarch of France   231

10   The Fall of Rome   263

Coda: The Undoing   284

Acknowledgments   299
List of Abbreviations   303
Notes   305
Index   357

ILLUSTRATIONS

1. *Fraternité Universelle*   13

2. "Britannia Sympathises with Columbia"   20

3. News of Lincoln's Death in London   21

4. The French Medal   30

5. George Bancroft   44

6. "About the Size of It"   56

7. Giuseppe Mazzini   58

8. *The Execution of Maximilian*   67

9. Matías Romero   71

10. "Get Out of Mexico"   81

11. The Bagdad Raid   88

12. "Letting Him Slide"   93

13. Abraham Lincoln, Benito Juárez, and Simón Bolívar   96

14. "Emperor Maximilian's Firing Squad"   97

15. The Gustavus Fox Expedition to Russia   109

16. "The *Miantonomoh* Galop"   110

17. Banquet in Moscow Honoring the Fox Expedition   111

18. *Signing the Alaska Treaty*   117

19. The St. Albans Raid   125

20. *The Fathers of Confederation*   129

21. Fenian Brotherhood   132

22. "The Fenian Pest" 134

23. Fenian Picnic at Jones's Wood, New York 136

24. "The Fenian Expedition" 141

25. "The British Lion Disarmed" 145

26. The Bombardment of Valparaíso 149

27. "Cuban Patriots Rallying Round Their Flag" 166

28. "Under a Palm-Tree, Waiting for a Sail" 168

29. "The War in Cuba" 169

30. *Manhood Suffrage Riots in Hyde Park* 173

31. "The Mob Pulling down the Railings in Park Lane" 189

32. "The Brummagem Frankenstein" 193

33. "Mill's Logic" 199

34. Queen Isabella II in Exile 210

35. Spain's Revolutionary Provisional Government 211

36. "Allegory of Spain's Glorious Revolution, 1868" 213

37. "Republican Demonstration in Madrid" 216

38. "Effect of Mediation" 222

39. Emilio Castelar y Ripoll 224

40. "The Slaves Will Be Free" 226

41. "Napoleon III Receives the Sovereigns at Universal Exhibition of 1867" 235

42. Napoleon III 238

43. Georges Clemenceau 242

44. Napoleon III Surrenders to Bismarck 249

45. Léon Gambetta Proclaims the Third Republic 251

46. The Barricade at Chaussée Ménilmontant 255

47. The Pope Bans Protestant Worship from Rome 271

48. Giuseppe Garibaldi at Mentana 274

49. The Ecumenical Council of the Vatican   275

50. "I am now infallible"   277

51. United Italy   279

52. "Rome, Funeral Oration over the Bust of Mazzini"   282

TIMELINE OF KEY EVENTS

1865

February 23: British Reform League founded to expand voting rights

March 3: Queen Isabella II signs law annulling Spain's annexation of the Dominican Republic

March 11: British North American delegation proposes Canadian Confederation to British Parliament

April 2: Spanish Abolitionist Society formally constituted

April 14–15: Assassination of President Abraham Lincoln

April 23: News of Confederate surrender at Appomattox reaches Europe

April 26: News of Lincoln's assassination reaches Europe

May 17: General U. S. Grant orders General Philip Sheridan and 50,000 troops to Mexican border

May 29: News of Lincoln's assassination reaches Peru, Chile, later China, Japan

July 15: Spain completes evacuation of the Dominican Republic

September 24: Spain declares war against Chile for refusing to salute the Spanish flag

October 3: Maximilian issues Black Decree against Mexican republican resistance

October 11: Morant Bay, Jamaica, British troops massacre Black protesters

October 21: Fenian National Congress meets in Philadelphia

December: U.S. State Department publishes foreign condolence messages honoring Lincoln

December 5: Peru and Chile form alliance against Spain; Ecuador and Bolivia join later

December 6: Thirteenth Amendment prohibiting slavery ratified

1866

January 4: Spain's Juan Prim instigates a failed barracks revolt and flees to exile in Europe

January 5: U.S. Colored Troops raid Bagdad, Mexico

January 22: Napoleon III announces French will withdraw from Mexico

February 1: British government begins mass arrests of Irish and Irish American Fenians

February 12: George Bancroft gives controversial eulogy to Lincoln before U.S. Congress

March 12: William Gladstone introduces Reform Bill to expand British suffrage

March 31: Spanish naval fleet bombards Valparaíso, Chile

April 17: Fenian Brotherhood raids Campobello Island, New Brunswick

May 2: Battle of Callao, Peru, Spanish naval squadron repulsed

May 31: Napoleon III announces plan for staged withdrawal from Mexico

June 1, 2: Fenian Brotherhood raids Canada West resulting in the Battle of Ridgeway

June 13: Congress passes Fourteenth Amendment

June 14–July 26: Austro-Prussian War, Austria loses territory to Prussia and Italy

June 16: Mexican Republican Army defeats French in Battle of Santa Gertrudis

June 18: Gladstone's Reform Bill fails due to reactionary Adullamite faction of Liberal Party

June 22: Spanish military officers lead failed barracks revolt in Madrid against the throne

June 26: British Tories form new government led by Lord Derby and Benjamin Disraeli

June 27: British Reform League stages first mass demonstration in Trafalgar Square, London

July 13: Carlota departs Mexico for Paris, Rome, and Vienna seeking support for Maximilian

July 23: British Reform League demonstration known as the "Hyde Park Riot"

July 27: Transatlantic telegraph completed

July–December: Mexican Republican Army scores victories against French

August 4: Spanish revolutionary Juan Prim contacts John Bigelow with an offer to sell Cuba

August 6: Gustavus Fox mission arrives in Russia

August 16: Spanish revolutionaries sign the Ostend Pact to overthrow the Bourbon monarchy

September 3–8: Geneva Congress of International Working Men's Association, a.k.a. First International

September 14: Karl Marx publishes volume one of *Das Kapital*

October 1: Spain's Infante Montpensier meets with John Bigelow to offer the sale of Cuba to the United States

November 6: U.S. elections give Republicans majorities in both houses of Congress

December 4: London Conference on confederation of British North America begins

1867

February 5: French troops evacuate Mexico City

February 13: Maximilian leaves Mexico City for Querétaro

March 12: France completes withdrawal of its troops from Mexico

March 29: Queen Victoria approves British North America Act and proclaims the Dominion of Canada

March 30: Seward signs treaty with Russia to acquire Alaska; Senate ratifies April 9

April 1: Napoleon III opens the Third Universal Exposition in Paris

May 6: British Reform League defies government ban on mass demonstration in Hyde Park

May 13: Jefferson Davis released from jail; charges of treason dismissed

May 15: Maximilian captured at Querétaro

June 19: Maximilian executed at Querétaro

June 20: Mexico City falls to Republican forces

July 1: Canada Day, the Dominion of Canada begins

July 15: Benito Juárez enters Mexico City

August 5: British Reform League demonstrates again in Hyde Park

August 15: British Reform Act of 1867 signed by Queen Victoria

September 2–8: Lausanne Congress of International Working Men's Association

October 18: Alaska transferred from Russian to U.S. ownership

1868

February 24: U.S. House of Representatives votes to impeach President Andrew Johnson

March: Napoleon III begins the "Liberal Empire" by relaxing censorship

March 30: U.S. Senate begins impeachment trial of President Johnson

May 26: U.S. Senate acquits President Johnson

July 9: U.S. Fourteenth Amendment ratified

September 18: Spain's Glorious Revolution begins six years of democratic government

September 23: Puerto Rican *Grito de Lares* proclaims independent republic

September 30: Spain's Queen Isabella II flees to France

October 9: U.S. recognizes Spain's revolutionary government

October 10: Cuban rebel Carlos Manuel de Céspedes proclaims independence from Spain

November 3: Ulysses S. Grant elected president

November: Spain sends troops to suppress the Cuban rebellion

1869

February 26: U.S. Congress passes Fifteenth Amendment protecting the right to vote

March 4: Ulysses S. Grant inaugurated president, appoints Hamilton Fish secretary of state

March 24: Cuban rebels request meeting with Hamilton Fish

April 10: Cuban rebels meet at Guáimaro, draft constitution, abolish slavery

May: Ex-Confederate general Thomas Jordan arrives in Cuba

May 23–24; June 6–7: French elections give conservatives majority but gains for republicans

June 6: Spain's revolutionary government promulgates democratic constitution

July 21: Daniel Sickles, U.S. minister to Spain, arrives in Madrid with instructions to mediate peace in Cuba

December 8: First Vatican Council meets to condemn liberalism and affirm papal infallibility

1870

February 3: Fifteenth Amendment ratified

May 8: France, plebiscite approves reforms of Liberal Empire

July 3: Spain proposes German monarch; Napoleon III prepares for war with Prussia

July 4: Spain enacts Moret Law freeing children born to enslaved mothers

July 19: Franco-Prussian War commences

August 23: James Bryce, British historian, arrives for his first visit in the United States

September 1–2: France surrenders army at Sedan; Napoleon III taken prisoner

September 4: France's Corps Législatif deposes Napoleon III and proclaims the Third Republic

November 16: Spanish Cortes elects Amadeo of Italy as king of a constitutional monarchy

December 30: Juan Prim, leader of Spain's revolutionary government, assassinated

1871

January 28: Paris falls to Prussian Army and grueling siege ends

March 19: Napoleon III joins Empress Eugénie in exile in England

March 18: Paris Commune seizes control of the city

May 8: United States and Britain sign Treaty of Washington settling *Alabama* Claims

May 10: Franco-Prussian War ends with France ceding Alsace-Lorraine

May 21–29: Paris Commune ends in Bloody Week

July 20: British Columbia becomes province of Canada

September 28: Brazil enacts Rio Branco law freeing children born to enslaved mothers

INTRODUCTION

Reconstruction and World Democracy

It was the greatest and most important step toward world democracy of all men of all races ever taken in the modern world.

—WILLIAM E. B. DU BOIS, *THE GIFT OF BLACK FOLK*, 1924

In April 1865, America's grueling war against the slaveholders' rebellion ended with the Union victorious, slavery on the verge of extinction, and the American experiment in democracy sustained. At home and abroad, supporters celebrated the Union victory as a welcome harbinger of human progress and a "new birth of freedom," in Abraham Lincoln's felicitous words. Days later, John Wilkes Booth, enraged by Lincoln's promise to grant voting rights to Blacks, fired the shot at Ford's Theatre that propelled a wave of horror, grief, and outrage around the world.

News of the assassination traveled to nearly every inhabited part of the globe. In large cities, people poured into the streets, gathered in public halls, and milled outside U.S. diplomatic posts to learn more about what happened in America. Hundreds of public meetings took place in the days, weeks, and even months that followed. Workers, students, women's groups, former slaves, exiled revolutionaries, and people from every social station gathered to listen to tributes to the fallen American leader and endorse resolutions to carry on the cause he died serving. "We are the fellow-citizens of John Brown, of Abraham Lincoln, and of Mr. Seward," a group of students in Paris told John Bigelow, America's minister to France. "We young people, to whom the future belongs, must have the courage to found a true democracy."[1]

A flood of similar messages, eulogies, speeches, condolence letters, and other tributes to Lincoln poured into U.S. diplomatic posts abroad. Bigelow was amazed at the public response and the courage of French students, Masons, republicans, and other opponents of Napoleon III's Second Empire to brave the police and government censors by issuing messages often laced with biting political innuendo. He sent a batch to Secretary of State William H. Seward, who lay bedridden at his home in Washington, recuperating from a terrible carriage accident and a vicious knife attack from one of Booth's fellow assassins. After the assailant's pistol jammed, he lunged at Seward with a Bowie knife and nearly severed his cheek from his jaw. Seward could barely walk without help or speak due to a heavy leather-clad iron brace that stabilized his jaw. But he was eager to return to duty, and when he saw the bundle of condolence messages Bigelow sent from Paris, he realized their value.

Here was the unfiltered voice of the "public mind" politicians and journalists always wrote about, though rarely with reliable evidence. Many messages came from workers and ordinary citizens, handwritten on plain paper. Others came grandly decorated with calligraphic lettering on parchment or even velum, some with heavy black mourning borders, others adorned with colorful ribbons and wax.

The messages of condolence voiced solidarity with America. They proclaimed Lincoln a martyr to the Great American Republic, as admirers called it, and to the universal cause of emancipation of enslaved Africans and "universal emancipation" of the oppressed everywhere. Many letters recounted the story of the humble rail-splitter who, by diligent labor and dedication to learning, prepared himself to become president of a nation at arms, the personification of republican virtue at war with the slaveholding aristocracy.

Seward had the letters translated, published, and bound in handsome, gilt-lettered volumes. He sent them out to every nation in the world and each person and organization contributing to the book. The public response to Lincoln's martyrdom abroad signaled widespread enthusiasm for Lincoln and the American cause. They also transmitted a genuine revival of confidence among reformers and revolutionaries and sounded a reveille for a new birth of freedom abroad.

In Europe, notably Britain, France, and Spain, the resurgence of reform spawned new political organizations promoting the demands of workers for political rights, new antislavery movements, international peace leagues, and the proliferation of progressive political journals. It gave rise to huge public meetings full of speeches and defiant public demonstrations in support of democratic reform. These noisy assemblies also demonstrated awareness of the international connections between the Civil War in America, workers' rights in Britain, the Italian Risorgimento, Giuseppe Garibaldi's march on Rome, the execution of Maximilian in Mexico, and myriad other events, people, and ideas coursing through the Euro-American world.

The story of the new birth of freedom abroad after the Civil War is what this book is about. Most of the action occurs within Reconstruction's usual time frame, about 1865 to 1871, yet it takes readers outside the familiar national boundaries to Mexico, Alaska, Canada, and Cuba and across the Atlantic to Britain, Spain, France, and Rome. Though the international perspective adopted here is novel, the book also focuses on more traditional subjects of politics and foreign policy with the familiar players, such as secretaries of state William Seward and Hamilton Fish, presidents Andrew Johnson and Ulysses Grant, and myriad members of Congress, senators, and diplomats. This is an international history involving matters of state, but it explores the less familiar interconnections between nations and the pervasive transnational influence of ideas, famous heroes, models of government, reform, and revolution.

Whenever possible, I have given the stage to the actors who made this history, allowing readers to hear their voices and sense their passion. They will witness extraordinary oratory rising from foreign parliaments and raucous histrionics from the public squares of many lands. From the Cooper Union in New York City, a favorite venue for political speech, we will hear militant Irish Fenians, Cuban revolutionaries, exiled Mexicans, and others summoning Americans to their cause. From London's St. James Hall, readers will listen to advocates of the working class denouncing the privileged aristocracy and calling for a new birth of democracy in Europe. Out of the streets of Paris will come "Red" republicans chanting *Déchéance! Déchéance!* calling for the overthrow of Napoleon III and his Second Empire. In Madrid is heard the voice of European republicanism, Emilio Castelar, imploring the Spanish Cortes to follow Lincoln's example of immediate emancipation. And we will hear Karl Marx addressing the new International Working Men's Association, aka the Communist First International, congratulating Abraham Lincoln, the "single-minded son of the working class" whose emancipation edict signaled the "reconstruction of a social world."

This book departs from the usual confines of Reconstruction history, which until recently has remained a tightly nation-bound story that requires no attention to the world beyond America. Historians of slavery and emancipation have produced a rich body of comparative studies, but few others have included foreign affairs in their treatment of Reconstruction.[2] Since the 1960s, historians of Reconstruction have been obsessed with discrediting the influential interpretation of the "Dunning School" that became implanted in textbooks and the popular imagination since the end of the nineteenth century, coinciding by no accident with the undoing of Reconstruction. William Archibald Dunning, an eminent historian at Columbia University, propagated an ideologically driven narrative of Reconstruction as a travesty visited on the South by vindictive Radical Republicans who were determined to upend white supremacy by enfranchising former slaves, whom Dunning deemed unfit for democratic governance.[3]

The guiding light for revisionist historians was William E. B. Du Bois, a leading African American scholar and civil rights leader. His book, *Black Reconstruction: An Essay Toward a History of the Part Which Black Folk Played in the Attempt to Reconstruct Democracy in America,*

1860–1880 (1935), was a tour de force of empirical scholarship combined with a passionate denunciation of the Dunning School and the exaltation of African Americans for their unsung role in redeeming America's democracy (as the book's original subtitle underscored). Du Bois's book remained in the shadows of the Dunning School until a new generation of historians rediscovered it during the "Second Reconstruction" and the Black civil rights movement beginning in the 1950s. Du Bois's legacy would guide revisionist scholarship along two major imperatives: Blacks' positive role in Reconstruction's history must be central, and the baleful influence of the Dunning School must be refuted by empirical research and discredited for its underlying racist motivation.

In the new wave of scholarship on Reconstruction since the 1950s, nowhere was the debt to Du Bois more evident and more impressively repaid than by Eric Foner in his revisionary synthesis, *Reconstruction: America's Unfinished Revolution, 1863–1877* (1988). Foner set forth a compelling story of African Americans and white Radical Republicans struggling to build a biracial democracy. He buried the Dunning School, which had no heirs willing to defend the old orthodoxy by this time. Foner's widely acclaimed book was so broad in scope, meticulously researched, and convincing that one admiring reviewer, Michael Perman, dubbed it the "finished revolution." With the Dunning School vanquished, Du Bois redeemed, and a well-defined argument as to the meaning of Reconstruction, the only question remaining, Perman said, was, "What is left to be done?"[4]

Some historians answered Perman by pushing the geographic boundaries of Reconstruction beyond the South to the North and West and expanding its chronological limits toward the end of the nineteenth century. This "Greater Reconstruction," as some called it, was a national story that examined some of the familiar themes of expanding federal authority, racial strife, and white supremacy, but now regarding Indians, Chinese, and Hispanics in the West.[5] Richard White's *The Republic for Which It Stands: The United States during Reconstruction and the Gilded Age, 1865–1896* may do for the Greater Reconstruction what Foner did for Southern Reconstruction: provide a coherent synthesis of a big story.[6]

Still, the reigning narrative of Reconstruction history remains nation bound as though the rest of the world does not exist. Though rarely noticed, Du Bois had framed America's Reconstruction story within the larger context of world history. He was a cosmopolitan who saw America's racial divide as part of a global clash between European whites and the "colored" races, African, Asian, and all non-whites. "The problem of the Twentieth Century is the problem of the color line," he told the Pan-African Congress meeting in London in 1900. Had America's national experiment in biracial democracy succeeded, Du Bois told readers, it might have been a significant advance for world democracy. But Du Bois's hint toward an international approach went unnoticed.[7]

Thirty years after *Black Reconstruction*, in 1965, David Potter wrote a suggestive essay on the impact of the Civil War on the world, particularly the revival and convergence of liberalism and nationalism. It was one of several efforts to expand the horizons of American historians and overcome what Potter complained was their habit of "navel-gazing." But international history and political ideology went against the primary current of the revisionists' attention to African Americans and race.[8]

As we pass through the 150th anniversary of Reconstruction, there are welcome signs that historians are heeding Potter's call. A flurry of conferences, essays, and books seems to herald an exciting new international direction in Reconstruction studies. As usual, the many conference papers and collections of essays often fly in many directions and are necessarily narrow in focus.[9] Several recent monographs and auspicious dissertations develop intriguing links between Latin American countries and America during Reconstruction.[10] At this nascent stage, no single theme or question appears to direct the recent burst of new research, yet it shows the international approach is full of future promise.

What is missing thus far, and what I hope this book provides, is a volume encompassing the panoramic scope of radical change in the 1860s and advancing a coherent interpretation of what it all means. My fundamental premise is that there were *two* Reconstructions, domestic and international, each complementary and grounded in a common republican ideology. Domestic Reconstruction aimed at pacifying the South, abolishing slavery, dethroning the slaveholding aristocracy, and rebuilding the South on a firm republican foundation.

In the American hemisphere, international Reconstruction sought to ensure national security by ridding the Americas of predatory European empires and creating a zone of friendly, independent, ideally republican nations, "buttresses," as William Seward called them, surrounding and supporting the United States. The underlying premise of U.S. foreign policy was that monarchy, aristocracy, and slavery were inherently hostile to republican institutions and that government, by consent of the people, ensured peace within and between nations.

To justify domestic Reconstruction, Radical Republicans employed a once obscure clause in the U.S. Constitution committing the federal government to "guarantee to every State in this Union a Republican Form of Government." The foreign policy equivalent of the "guarantee clause" was a muscular new version of the Monroe Doctrine that emerged, not as formal policy from William Seward and the State Department but from outrage in Congress and the public square against France's sinister design to erect a monarchy on the ruins of the Mexican republic. Initially a warning against further European colonization of the Americas, after 1865, proponents of the Monroe Doctrine propagated the idea that the entire Western Hemisphere must be a haven for republicanism and that monarchy and slavery were no longer welcome. In this meaning, the Monroe Doctrine's new slogan, "America for Americans," became a Pan-American cause.

This book has a different take on William Seward, the principal architect of post–Civil War foreign policy, and his successor, Hamilton Fish. While Charles Sumner and other Radical Republicans focused on rebuilding a republican South, William Seward set out to make the American Continent safe for republicanism by driving out European imperialists, ending slavery, and fostering the spread of republican principles abroad.

The main thrust of international Reconstruction, I argue here, was anti-imperialist, antislavery, and pro-democracy. It played out in two theaters of action. In the American Continent, U.S. foreign policy was the leading force. In Europe, it was the inspiration of the Union victory, Lincoln's martyrdom, and the example of a thriving democracy that effected change.

The most tangible achievement of international Reconstruction was the withdrawal of European empires from the American Continent and the decolonization of British North America. Within days of one another, in the spring of 1867, France pulled its troops out of Mexico, Russia sold Alaska to the United States, Britain proclaimed the Dominion of Canada, an autonomous home-rule state, and Spain agreed to accept U.S. mediation in wars it had provoked with Peru and Chile. Spain had already vacated Santo Domingo, and in October 1868, Cuban rebels fed up with their Spanish rulers proclaimed independence. These European powers had many factors to calculate before deciding to withdraw, but America's proven military prowess and powerful ideological appeal with the European people were foremost among them.

U.S. foreign policy during Reconstruction was anti-imperialist in another sense. Contrary to the familiar claim that Seward and America remained enthralled by Manifest Destiny, the only significant acquisition during this period, indeed during the half century between 1848 and 1898, was the Alaska Purchase. Further to this point, during the Johnson and Grant administrations, the United States spurned several opportunities for annexing new territories. These included outright invitations to annex Santo Domingo (the Dominican Republic), the Danish West Indies (Virgin Islands), and the Spanish Caribbean (Cuba and Puerto Rico).

International Reconstruction also should be credited with hastening the abolition of slavery in the Americas. Seward turned U.S. foreign policy against slavery early in 1862 when he signed a treaty that finally put the United States on the right side of Britain's effort to suppress the African slave trade. The Lyons-Seward Treaty sounded a death knell for slavery in Cuba and signaled the antislavery turn in U.S. foreign policy. Later, Seward forcefully stopped Maximilian's scheme to reintroduce slavery in all but name as part of a plan to colonize northern Mexico with ex-Confederates. Seward also objected strongly to Maximilian's plans to enlist enslaved Sudanese soldiers in Maximilian's imperial army.

"It is settled," Seward let it be known, "that African slavery, in any form, ought henceforth to cease throughout the world."[11]

When Spain failed to deliver on promises to abolish slavery after its democratic revolution in 1868, Seward's successor, Hamilton Fish, used the threat of recognizing Cuban rebels to coerce Spain into passing what they called the Fourth of July Law in 1870. The Moret Law, as it was also known, put in motion a plan for gradual abolition, which Fish protested as disingenuous. He kept up the pressure, and in 1873 Spain abolished slavery outright in Puerto Rico and promised the same for Cuba once the rebels lay down their arms. Brazil, the only remaining slave nation, followed the same path by enacting a "free womb" law in 1871. The final death of slavery came to Cuba in 1886 and Brazil in 1888. After roughly four centuries, the vast and hugely profitable regime of African slavery in the Americas had ended.[12]

Coinciding with their retreat from the American hemisphere after 1865, European powers experienced a wave of reform and revolution that toppled thrones and challenged aristocratic oligarchies. Whatever role the United States had in stirring European reform, it was by inspiration and indirect influence, not foreign policy or government propaganda. The same European powers that withdrew from the Americas after 1865, Britain, France, and Spain, faced restless agitation for democratic reform at home. The American Civil War created rallying points for the opposition in each case.

Britain's workers and middle class had come around to supporting Lincoln and the Union by early 1865. They learned to use America as a benchmark against which to measure their limited political rights and grim standard of living. In 1865 the International Working Men's Association (a.k.a. the First International), cofounded by Karl Marx, launched the Reform League to "conquer political power" for workers. The League mobilized a massive protest movement and took to the streets. When the workers defied a government ban on public meetings in Hyde Park, a pall of fear spread across the country that Britain was on the brink of genuine social revolution. The League's show of strength forced Parliament to pass the Reform Act of 1867, which doubled the number of voters and placed Britain on the road to democracy.

One year later, in September 1868, Spain's Glorious Revolution over-threw the decrepit Bourbon throne of Queen Isabella II and established a democratic government that astonished Europe. Spanish opposition liberals became enchanted with America as a model of modernity and democratic freedom, and the new constitution of 1869 borrowed heavily from the U.S. model. Despite that, Spain, like Britain, sought to democ-ratize within the traditional casing of monarchy rather than risk a pure republican form of government. Spain's democratic experiment did not last long, but it left behind a liberal constitutional monarchy and a com-mitment to end slavery.

Thanks to Napoleon III's disastrous Grand Design for Mexico, France's liberal opposition gained support. Once cynical about America's claims as "the great republic," the French left became enamored of Lin-coln and the Union and embraced America as a standard of liberty it demanded for France. Napoleon III tried to appease the opposition by easing censorship and bowing to limited democratic reform. To rally support for the "liberal empire," Napoleon III led France into a disas-trous war against Prussia that abruptly ended the Second Empire. In Paris, radical republicans and socialists went to the barricades to pro-claim the Paris Commune as the vanguard of a radically new social order.

Though the Papal State of Rome was not among the powers of Europe, its pontiff, Pope Pius IX, exercised enormous moral power, always against the tide of modern secular liberalism in the Americas and Europe. He became the embodiment of Catholic reaction, author of the *Syllabus of Errors*, which denounced religious tolerance and liberalism generally, and host to the Vatican Council, which ratified the syllabus and declared the pope infallible. When France pulled its troops out of Rome to fight the Prussians, the Italian army stormed the gates and proclaimed the city the new capital of united Italy. Liberals everywhere cheered the fall of papal Rome as another sign of the new birth of freedom.

This book illuminates a capacious Age of Revolution that encom-passed the Americas and Europe for a century between the 1770s and 1870s. Fired by ideas of natural rights and human equality coming out of the radical fringe of the Enlightenment, this transatlantic Age of Revolution witnessed a relentless struggle between the advocates and enemies of those ideals. That struggle defined the modern age and continues to do so.

There were disturbing contradictions and sad failings in domestic and international Reconstruction. Woman suffragists, led by Elizabeth Cady Stanton, Susan B. Anthony, and others, had supported emancipation and equality for former slaves and made their claim to the same rights accorded newly freed African Americans but were made to wait for an entire half century.[13] While the United States pursued noble goals at home and abroad during Reconstruction, the government carried out horrific wars and atrocities against Indians in the trans-Mississippi West. In its brutality, racism, and claims to be civilizing its victims, America's Indian policy resembled the most objectionable features of imperialism that lay ahead, even though its purpose was not to wring wealth from Native Americans in the manner typical of imperialist systems. The "Indian Question," according to Commissioner of Indian Affairs Francis A. Walker, was how to remove them as "an obstacle to the national progress" and what to do with them after ceasing to obstruct the extension of railroads and white settlement. Walker's solution was to remove Indians to reservations, out of the way of "national progress." But insofar as Indians continued to resist "national progress," it was left to the Army to deal with them through a brutal campaign of genocidal warfare.

As for Chinese immigrants, whose labor was indispensable to the national progress Walker celebrated, they were also subjected to horrible exploitation and prejudice, then banned altogether from further immigration in 1882. Underlying the nation's treatment of African Americans, women, Indians, and Chinese immigrants was a common thread of "scientific" theories of inherent human differences in their fitness for full citizenship as members of the republic. Racism in its modern "scientific" guise served to justify the undoing of Reconstruction's domestic and international aspirations.[14]

I wrote this book during an unusually perilous time for democracy in America and the world. Nearly every day, some television pundit reminds us of the relevance of Reconstruction, whether about new voter suppression laws, police violence against Black citizens, impeachment, or insurrection. At no time has the history of Reconstruction commanded a more disturbing relevance. On the last page of *Black Reconstruction*, Du Bois lamented, "The unending tragedy of Reconstruction is the utter inability of the American mind to grasp its real significance, its national and worldwide implications."[15] I hope readers will find in this book a bracing reminder of a moment when much of the world looked to the United States not as a perfect model of democratic success but as an inspiration to continue the forever unfinished task of realizing democracy's promise for America and the world.

PART I

Martyrdom

FIGURE 1. *Fraternité Universelle*, by Christian Schultz, a German lithographer. This 1865 print shows Abraham Lincoln surrounded by allegorical figures including Faith, Hope, Charity, Architecture, Wisdom, Harmony, and Force and several historical figures, including George Washington and Socrates. Foreign liberals commonly portrayed Lincoln as a martyr to universal rather than uniquely American ideals, and they exploited his martyrdom to summon others to the duty of propagating those ideals. Library of Congress.

CHAPTER 1

Tributes of the Nations

The thunderclap at Washington has shaken the earth. . . . How frightful a cataclysm! . . . The American people is a colossus of bronze; traitors may scratch its surface, but they cannot overthrow it. . . . America has become the guide among the nations . . . the nation pointing out to its sister nations the granite way to liberty and to universal brotherhood.

—VICTOR HUGO, FRENCH AUTHOR IN EXILE,
APRIL 29, 1865

In April 1865, days after the Union claimed victory against the slaveholders' rebellion, Abraham Lincoln fell victim to assassins whose purpose was to decapitate America's government and military and, amid the chaos and demoralization, reignite the South's will to fight on. Instead, as the Constitution directed, power passed immediately to Vice President Andrew Johnson, and the Union stood firm. As news of the assassination went out to the world in the days and weeks that followed, Lincoln rose in death a global hero and martyr to the cause of human freedom, equality, and government by the people. It was a rare moment of shared emotions—shock, grief, horror, outrage, reverence, and hope. Still more remarkable, tens of thousands of ordinary people felt moved to express their feelings publicly, leaving to history an unusual glimpse into the foreign public mind unobstructed by government censors or the press.[1]

From the moment he took office, Lincoln had been the target of cruel derision in conservative circles abroad. The London *Times*, the voice of the British establishment, marveled at how a "hard-working simple-minded citizen" like Mr. Lincoln could cause such a violent reaction in the South. Conservative foreign journalists characterized America's rough-hewn president as an unqualified rube thrust into leadership of a nation in crisis with duties far beyond his capacity. Some European journals mocked Lincoln's every speech, including the now-celebrated Gettysburg Address and the Second Inaugural Address. To many critics, Lincoln embodied the foibles of America's "extreme democracy." They predicted failure for the president and the entire democratic experiment.

In death, Lincoln became the unimpeachable embodiment of government elected by the common people and the prophet of world democracy. What Victor Hugo called the "thunderclap at Washington" gave a sorely needed jolt of confidence to the democracy of Europe, which had been somnolent since the failed Revolutions of 1848. The public response to that thunderclap set the enemies of popular government on their back feet.

Lincoln's martyrdom did not *cause* the wave of democratic reforms, revolutions, and emancipation movements that swept across the Atlantic world after 1865. Mexico began its radical democratic reform years before Lincoln took office, and Italy's Risorgimento had thrown off foreign rulers and created a new unified liberal state early in 1861. But the Union's victory came as a welcome source of confidence, and Lincoln's death gave occasion for bold public demonstrations of solidarity. The response to Lincoln's death signaled a reveille that awakened people across the Atlantic world to the possibility of a new era for world democracy and what Victor Hugo called "universal brotherhood."

Martyrdom was traditionally associated with religious persecution and sacrifice, and secular heroes in the nineteenth century inspired their followers similarly. In its religious and political idioms, martyrdom required more than reverent devotion; it imposed duties on followers to carry on the cause for which the martyr died and, when necessary, sacrifice their blood to further it. More than mere emotions of grief, demonstrating for Lincoln was an affirmation of solidarity and commitment to the new birth of freedom ahead.

News of Abraham Lincoln's assassination reached nearly every corner of the globe within the hours, days, and weeks that followed that night of horror. The assassin, John Wilkes Booth, fired his fatal shot on the evening of Good Friday, April 14, 1865. Throughout the night, Lincoln lay dying, surrounded by government officials and his frantic wife, Mary Lincoln, in a cramped upstairs bedroom of a boardinghouse across from Ford's Theatre. As the president slowly succumbed, a large crowd gathered on the street outside. Many African Americans, some fearful that Lincoln's death might return them to slavery, prayed aloud, sang spirituals, and stood vigil with the others through the long cold night as an ominous blood moon rose in the sky.[2]

Reports from the press went out through the night. At 1:30 a.m., Secretary of War Edwin M. Stanton issued the first official dispatch confirming that the president had been shot and William Henry Seward, secretary of state, and his son, Frederick, had been brutally attacked by another assailant. Both might not live. The attending physician kept the crowd outside informed with hourly reports. Stanton issued another statement at 3:00 a.m. identifying the actor, John Wilkes Booth, as the assassin and announcing that a massive manhunt was underway.[3]

Early in the morning, people gathered around the stoop of the boardinghouse to hear the announcement that the president had died. Their songs and grief-stricken shouts echoed across continents and oceans in the following days and weeks.[4]

The telegraph was the internet of its day, even more revolutionary given its leap from the physical transmission of print or voice to the speed of electricity. By 1865 a vast network of telegraph wires spanned much of the North American and European continents. The cable lines followed the sinews of commerce that bound the nineteenth-century world, creeping into eastern Europe, the Middle East, South Asia, and more slowly into Latin America. From telegraph offices in Washington City, the staccato clatter of the keys tapped out Morse code one character at a time, 150 characters or 30 words per minute, sentence by sentence, transmitting the grim news. Within hours word of the assassination flashed across the United States, traveling through fifty thousand miles of wire connecting every city and most towns of any size. Chicago learned of the assassination at 4 a.m. Saturday, San Francisco, by 10 a.m. local time.[5]

As word of Lincoln's assassination traveled into Canada and other parts of British North America, U.S. consuls reported a wave of emotion unlike any they had witnessed. In Toronto, the streets filled with men and women stricken by "universal horror," crowding outside newspaper offices to learn more. David Thurston, the U.S. consul there, reported he had never seen Canadians so moved. Many would later cross the river to participate in Detroit's funeral processions. Toronto merchants reported selling out of black crepe. Across the British provinces of North America, U.S. consuls reported similar demonstrations of sympathy. Several Canadians wrote poems on the spot eulogizing Lincoln. "Not in my time," one Canadian remembered, "did I ever know Canada so profoundly stirred."[6]

News of Lincoln's death crossed the Atlantic to Europe weeks before it reached most of Latin America. The transatlantic telegraph was a year away from being completed, but powerful steamships could plow the three thousand miles of ocean to Europe in eleven days. The *Nova Scotian*, a Canadian packet ship designed to carry mail and passengers, sailed out of Halifax on Saturday morning, April 15. It would be the first to bring the news to Europe.[7]

Early Wednesday morning, April 26, the *Nova Scotian* touched land at Greencastle, a small port on the northern tip of Ireland. From there, operators immediately transmitted the news to the telegraph exchange in London. Within hours it exploded across the British Isles and the European Continent, pulsing through wires that went to every city or small town with access to the telegraph. Beyond the telegraph network, the reports spread by sea and land to Constantinople, Turkey, and St. Petersburg, Russia, two days later; Tunis, Africa, the following day; India and South Asia in the days that followed.[8]

"Over the ashes of the President of the American republic the whole of Europe has come to confess her democratic faith," wrote Adolphe Gaiffe, for the Paris *L'Avenir National.* "This movement has been so general, so active, and so spontaneous, that governments have joined with the people in the expression of their sympathies for the United States and their horror at the assassination. The court of Rome alone has remained silent."[9]

The formal obsequies that arrived at U.S. diplomatic posts from foreign governments were primarily standard, predictable, and unremarkable. Outside the marbled courts of power, however, people from all social strata came into the streets to discover what had happened and share mostly half-baked rumors about what would come next. Newspapers published special editions telling what they knew about the details of the assassination and provided capsule summaries of Lincoln's life story. During the spring of 1865, foreigners instinctively gathered and found ways to express their shared joy over the Union's victory and their sorrow and outrage at Lincoln's assassination.

Britain enjoyed a proud tradition of free speech and assembly. Workers and many middle-class Britons may not have had voting rights, but they knew how to exercise their rights as freeborn Englishmen and women. In cities and small villages across the British Isles, tens of thousands of men and women assembled in town halls, lecture rooms, trade union halls, open-air commons, churches, and wherever they could find a place to meet. One journalist recorded what he saw in London the day he learned of the assassination: "No man who walked in the streets of London at noon on Wednesday will readily forget the scene as the news spread throughout the great city. There was one vast, universal sense of horror and dismay; for the act, in truth, seemed an outrage upon humanity itself. . . . from one end of the land to the other there has been a cry of rage at this most foul assassination. . . . National, indeed, was the sorrow and the anger."[10]

Three mass meetings occurred quickly at St. James Hall, London, on April 28, 29, and May 1. The London Emancipation Society sponsored the second and most dramatic one. The hall was draped in black crepe, and three American flags stood "entwined in crepe" at one end. "The

FIGURE 2. "Britannia Sympathises with Columbia." John Tenniel, a cartoonist
for *Punch*, had been merciless in his ridicule of Lincoln, but he recanted with
this illustration and an accompanying poem that apologized and praised the
fallen leader. *Punch*, May 6, 1865.

floor, the balcony, the galleries, and the platform of the great hall were
literally packed with ladies and gentlemen," Benjamin Moran, secretary
to the U.S. legation, told his diary. Surrounded by mildly hostile Britons
for four years, Moran felt consoled by the thought that "we had friends
in England in our day of sorrow." "In all my London experience," he
wrote, "I never saw so much enthusiasm or heard so many good
speeches. The feeling of profound and heartfelt sympathy was deep and
unmistakable."[11]

William E. Forster, Radical MP for Leeds and stalwart friend of the
Union, took the podium to speak of this moment as a "time when the tie
of blood binding Englishmen to Americans was indeed truly felt. A
thrill of grief, horror and indignation, which had passed through the
length and breadth of Europe, and especially possesses the heart of

FIGURE 3. News of Lincoln's Death in London. In large cities across the Atlantic world, the press sprang to serve the public's appetite to learn more about Abraham Lincoln, the assassination, and what it meant for the world beyond America. *Le Monde Illustré*, May 6, 1865. Gallica, Biblioteque Nationale de France.

every Englishman as though some painful calamity had fallen on himself. [Cheers.]"[12]

Thomas Bayley Potter, another Radical MP from Rochdale, a stronghold of support for the Union, linked America's emancipation to the cause of Britain's working class: "Lincoln destroyed slavery in America. It should be their wish to destroy serfdom at home." He "trusted the result of the conflict in America would be to give an impetus to the cause of reform in Europe."[13]

Dozens of similar meetings gave voice to the solidarity of peoples and the universality of causes that Lincoln personified. Most notable were the resounding voices of British workers who, though divided at the beginning of the war, had come around to supporting Lincoln and the Union with impressive loyalty, despite their suffering from the cotton blockade.

The harsh weather in Peterboro' did not discourage some 250–300 townspeople from attending a meeting at their Assembly Hall. Nor did it dampen their enthusiasm as they "rejoiced with joy unfeigned at the over throw of the slaveocracy of the South."[14] The workingmen of Brighton declared how proud they were of "the first president elected from the working classes to the highest position of ruler of one of the mightiest nations of the globe; that he carried successfully the struggle of free against slave labor."[15]

"The name of Abraham Lincoln had already become famous to the working people of England," a speaker at a South London gathering proclaimed. "He appeared as one of themselves, fighting the battle of freedom for all lands; he is now, and for all coming time, the hero martyr of liberty and right." The Bristol Reform Union saw a valuable lesson for democracy in Britain in Lincoln's life. Organized "for the purpose of obtaining political rights for the unenfranchised millions of our own country, we feel the sudden removal of such a man as a loss not only to you, but to ourselves and the world at large," for Lincoln "has endeared himself to all lovers of liberty by his devotion to the great cause of negro emancipation, and by his earnest desire to confer the blessings of equal rights and privileges on all, without distinction of party, creed, or color."[16]

For British workers, mourning Lincoln served as preparation for the reform movement about to advance their claim to a place in the political arena. The Reform League that led it had formed only a few weeks earlier. One eloquent condolence message looked forward with the conviction that "if cruelty and injustice are still potent in many of the affairs touching our personal honor, it is nevertheless easy to see that the idea of *a government of the people for the people* will soon be realized among all the civilized nations of the earth."[17]

The Swiss Republic was the only democratic republic in Europe, and its citizens reveled in their proud assignment as America's "sister republic." George Fogg, U.S. minister to Switzerland, was genuinely moved by the Swiss display of affection for Lincoln and America that spring: "The millions in America who loved Mr. Lincoln as a father and revered him as the purest and greatest of patriotic statesmen, could scarcely have mourned him more profoundly than did the masses in Europe. Especially dear was he to the citizens of this little republic of Switzerland."[18]

Switzerland provided asylum to European revolutionaries and dissidents driven from their homelands. Polish refugees from the failed uprising against their Russian rulers sent a poignant message of outrage and hope: "The Polish emigrants participate in the recent joy and sorrow of the American people; they hail the triumph of the principles of equality and liberty in America, and the expected triumph of those principles in Europe, assuring the regeneration of Poland by putting an end to the rule of brute force and to white slavery, as they have done to black slavery in the New World."[19]

Swiss republicans did not just send letters; they assembled in enormous meetings in each canton, drawing five to six thousand mourners at a time. In Berne, the Swiss capital, citizens rose "with uncovered heads to manifest their sympathy with the American Union to express their support." In one "democratic canton," no less than ninety thousand voters affirmed their sympathy and solidarity with their sister republic.

"The mourning and regret for the death of our President are universal from the old men to the boys in the schools," Fogg wrote. "I am convinced that no other man in any part of the world held such a place in so many millions of hearts." In Berne, the federal government spoke for the republic in a separate note of solidarity: "Free Switzerland, with similar institutions, will not cease to devote all her sympathies to free America."[20]

Reports of Lincoln's death hit France on April 26, the same day as the rest of Europe, with the same *frisson d'horreur* (thrill of horror). The French people enjoyed none of the political liberties of Switzerland or Britain. The Second Empire of Napoleon III banned public gatherings of more than twenty people and censored the press and public, punishing any political expression deemed to be subversive. Precisely because of the government's heavy-handed censorship, defiant French radicals seized the death of Lincoln as an opportunity to rejoice in republican sympathy and challenge the government's determination to muzzle them.[21]

The "martyr's blood was . . . shed to bear fruit," republican dissident Henri Allain-Targé thought. The Civil War had produced "the greatest victory in the world for the republicans of France." With this victory, "the principle of authority, privilege, caste, aristocratic monopolies,—all these things . . . that seemed as necessary to European society as slavery to the Southern aristocracy,—all this will be swept away by egalitarian democracy."[22]

Édouard Laboulaye, professor of history at the Collège de France, had become a celebrity among students in the Latin Quarter thanks to his well-attended lectures on America and democracy. Writing under a pseudonym, in 1863, he published a best-selling satirical novel, *Paris en Amérique*, where the hallucinatory protagonist wakes up in New England, astonished to find the government safeguarding instead of repressing freedom of religion and speech. Laboulaye was in full accord with the French fashion for *Américomanie*, defined by the *Grand Dictionnaire* as the "affected, ridiculous admiration for everything associated with America." In Paris, he became known as *le plus américain de tous les Français* (the most American of all the French).[23]

On April 28, 1865, Professor Laboulaye dragged himself from bed after a dreadful illness and headed to the Conservatoire national des arts et métiers, a monument to the French Enlightenment located in the Marais. The auditorium was packed with people, including Laboulaye's student admirers. Though billed as a lecture on Benjamin Franklin, one of his abiding passions, Laboulaye soon changed course to give a moving eulogy on Lincoln and his meaning to France. "Never in my life as a professor have I found so much sympathy," he later wrote his friend, John Bigelow, U.S. minister to France. "The audience applauded three times with great enthusiasm, not for the speaker, but for the noble victim of a base assassination. You should see how general the excitement is in Paris; it is much greater than I expected."[24]

After his lecture, the students poured out of the auditorium and gathered near the north end of Pont St. Michael. They planned to march en masse, an estimated 1,200 to 3,000 students, out the Champs- Élysées to deliver an address they had prepared to present to Bigelow at the U.S. legation nearly three miles away. As the crowd grew, police swarmed out of the nearby prefecture on Île Saint-Louis and waded into the crowd with swords drawn. They arrested all they could catch. Most of the others scattered, except for an estimated five hundred who evaded the police and ran through the back streets of Paris to deliver their message to John Bigelow.

When they arrived at the U.S. legation, the students met a cordon of police blockading the entrance. They jostled through, and Bigelow welcomed them inside. One of the students, whom Malakoff described as "a handsome, intelligent boy . . . stepped forward to the front of his comrades and read in a steady, clear voice."

> Citizen ambassador. . . . We openly proclaim our sympathy for the brave defender of that great cause of justice called, in America, emancipation of slaves—in Europe, liberation of the oppressed. In President Lincoln we weep for a fellow-citizen, for no country is shut up now; and our country is that where there are neither masters nor slaves; where every man is free, or is fighting to become free. We are the fellow-citizens of John Brown, of Abraham Lincoln, and of Mr. Seward. We young people, to whom the future belongs, must have the courage to found a true democracy; and we will have to look beyond the ocean to learn how a people who have made themselves free can preserve their freedom. . . . The President of the great republic is dead, but the republic itself shall live forever.[25]

Theirs was no sentimental sympathy message for the grieving widow; the students delivered a bold republican polemic. The address deftly joined Lincoln's cause to that of French republicans and transformed Lincoln's martyrdom into a plea to all of France and Europe to answer the call for revolutionary change.[26]

Bigelow was amazed at the defiance and passion the students displayed. "I had no idea that Mr. Lincoln had such a hold upon the heart of the young gentlemen of France, or that his loss would be so properly appreciated," he wrote Seward that evening.[27]

No one had any idea, not until that spring of 1865, when Lincoln's death galvanized the democracy of Europe and gave them an excuse and cause to stand up and speak out.[28] "It is difficult to exaggerate the enthusiasm which [Lincoln's] name inspires among the masses of Europe at this moment," Bigelow wrote Seward later. "I think it is generally conceded that the death of no man has ever occurred that awakened such prompt and universal sympathy at once among his own country people and among foreign nations."[29]

Malakoff, nom de plume for Dr. William Edward Johnson, an American physician and the *New York Times* correspondent in Paris, was an unusually astute monitor of the French political pulse. He was equally astonished by the enthusiastic demonstrations for Lincoln. "Nothing like it has ever before been seen," he reported on May 5. It "almost makes one forget that we ever had any enemies in France. The subject is in every one's mouth; the columns of the newspapers are given up to it. It gives one some hope of the future of European democracy." Even monarchists in France were "in favor of seeing the experiment of a great republic succeed." This moment has given "to the world a shock from which it will not readily recover. . . . it will mark an important epoch in the revival, the strengthening, and perhaps the commencement of the triumph, of the democracy."[30]

"The Democratic party in France," Malakoff continued, "cite with justness the peaceable accession to power of the Vice-President as evidence that the republic is the strongest form of government which exists." This peaceful transfer of power alone, Malakoff predicted, "which will produce an immense effect in Europe in favor of the principles of self-government, cannot avoid vexing beyond measure the monarchists . . . who staked their judgments in the most solemn manner at the commencement of the war, that the great republic was at an end."[31]

From exile in Belgium, French radicals linked their political aspirations to Lincoln and America as "an example to the world" that would illuminate Europe's path forward. "You have done more than reestablish the Union of the American Republic; you have saved the holy ark of the liberties of the world, the world, cradle of the universal republic. We, conquered republicans, salute your victorious republic. . . . We cheer the triumph of your cause, which is ours; we accept your victory as a presage, and your success as a promise."[32]

From the remains of France's West Indian empire, a group of freed people wrote in praise of the Great Emancipator slain in America: "We,

Creoles of Guadeloupe, of African descent, wish to express the profound sorrow we feel at the loss your great republic has suffered in the person of its illustrious President, Abraham Lincoln. This event, which has shocked the civilized world and all the true friends of the northern cause—the cause of the freedom of an oppressed race—cannot find us indifferent. . . . Accept gentlemen, without our regrets, the wishes we express for the prosperity of the American republic, and for the triumph of the great principles of liberty and equality."[33]

Though rid of slavery in their own country in 1848, French intellectuals took the occasion of the Union's victory and Lincoln's martyrdom to spread the cause of emancipation and aid for the newly freed people abroad. They formed the French Committee of Emancipation, whose purpose was to correspond with similar organizations in America, England, and elsewhere "to aid the entire abolition of slavery, the education and assistance of the freed families, and the publication of all facts connected with that great cause of humanity." Among their first acts was to send President Johnson a lengthy eulogy praising Abraham Lincoln. Though drafted only a few days after news of the assassination arrived, it demonstrated an impressive knowledge of Lincoln's life story, his speeches, and what this obscure prairie politician had come to mean for Europeans. Bigelow wrote to Augustin Cochin, a prominent committee officer known as "the Wilberforce of France," assuring him that President Johnson would greatly appreciate their efforts "to popularize the lessons of which the late insurrection in America has been so fruitful."[34]

Some of the more remarkable public campaigns to memorialize Lincoln took place in the provinces, where observers were astonished to find such passion and interest in American affairs. Nantes, a city southwest of Paris on the Loire River, nurtured a vocal coterie of Freemasons and republicans, including a young historian named Charles-Louis Chassin. Earlier in 1865, Chassin had authored a vigorous defense of the French Revolution, *Le génie de la Révolution* (The Genius of the Revolution).[35]

On April 28, 1865, Chassin issued a letter to several newspapers calling for a mass subscription drive to raise money for a gold medal to present to Mary Todd Lincoln, the slain president's bereaved widow. "It is important that European democracy offer American democracy a solemn testimony of intimate brotherhood," he wrote. Donations, Chassin suggested, should be limited to ten centimes or two sous under the old monetary system. This token contribution would ensure it would be a "touching manifestation of the heart of France" involving "all ranks, classes, all members of the French family: men, women, children." The two-sous limit, not incidentally, also ensured that the subscription would irritate the Second Empire for months. Newspapers across France published Chassin's appeal, and interest in the campaign soon went viral. At an annual celebration of Parisian carriage makers, a guest speaker pitched the subscription to the workers, and all seventy-five subscribed on the spot. The *Phare de la Loire* boldly published the names of all the subscribers, whose numbers grew to over eleven thousand within a matter of days.[36]

Napoleon III's Second Empire employed an army of spies and police and a network of provincial Procureurs Généraux (attorneys general) whose duties included reporting subversive activities to the government. Early on the morning of May 24, in Chauvigny, a subscription collector named Rigollet was astonished to find police pounding on his door. They demanded the subscription lists, and when asked why, the officer told him only *les listes sont arrêtées partout* (the lists are stopped everywhere). The government was cracking down on what it had decided was a subversive republican operation to embarrass the emperor, which it was.[37]

The U.S. consul at Nantes, a New Yorker named John de la Montagnie, alerted Bigelow of the incident at Chauvigny. In his efforts to cultivate French public support of the Union cause, Montagnie had worked closely with the *Phare de la Loire* to publicize war news. Bigelow asked him bluntly if he had any role in instigating the subscription. Montagnie assured him, "it is entirely a French matter." Bigelow answered sardonically, "I am sorry that the Commissary of Police . . . did not think it safe for the people of his commune to express two sous' worth of sympathy for the widow of our murdered President; but he knows the danger of such a proceeding better than we do."[38]

The Second Empire exposed its weakness by overreacting to a sincere manifestation of sympathy in response to a distant foreign tragedy, and it played right into the opposition's hands. Immediately after the police intervention, the two-sous subscription escalated to a national cause célèbre among French opposition liberals. Soon, a stellar committee of dissidents, calling themselves "The French Democracy," organized a nationwide subscription in sheer defiance. The committee, limited to twenty members according to the censorship laws, included such prominent figures as Victor Hugo, Louis Blanc, Jules Michelet, Eugène Pelletan, and many others. All were well-known foes of the empire, and several enlisted from exile. By the end of summer, the number of subscribers rose to twenty-five thousand. One enthusiastic republican exclaimed, "the day is not far away when bringing together Europe and America on the common ground of freedom and law, these united democracies will form the United States of the two worlds!"[39]

The government backed off its ham-fisted effort to confiscate subscription money and lists. Still, Napoleon III prohibited further publication of appeals for contributions. He instructed prefects across France to throw every obstacle they could in the way of the subscription, short of outright interdiction. The police went so far as to prohibit the striking of the medal in France.[40] These repressive efforts only prolonged the embarrassment intended. By autumn 1866, some forty thousand subscribers had signed their names and donated two sous to Mrs. Lincoln's medal—and to the cause of French democracy.[41]

The medal, designed by Franky Magniadas, an Italian artist, was struck in Geneva, Switzerland. In its faded purple velvet case, it now resides among the Abraham Lincoln Papers at the Library of Congress, where I held it in gloved hands. Solid gold, over three inches in diameter and a quarter-inch thick, the medal is remarkably hefty. On the obverse side is an iconic profile of Lincoln encircled by the inscription DÉDIE PAR LA DÉMOCRATIE FRANÇAISE A LINCOLN, PRÉSIDENT DEUX FOIX ÉLU DES ÉTATS-UNIS (Dedicated by the French Democracy to Lincoln, twice elected President of the United States). On the reverse side is an image of a tomb flanked by a weeping angel and two African American figures, a shirtless man holding a rifle with a bayonet fixed, and a young shirtless boy holding a large book and laying a palm on the tomb. On the tomb are the words (all scripted from Charles Chassin's original call for the

FIGURE 4. The French Medal. Abraham Lincoln Papers, Library of Congress.

subscription), *LINCOLN L'HONNÊTE HOMME, ABOLIT L'ESCLAVAGE, RETA-BLIT L'UNION, SAUVA LA RÉPUBLIQUE, SANS VOILER LA STATUE DE LA LIB-ERTÉ, IL FUT ASSASSINÉ LE 14 AVRIL, 1865* (Lincoln, the honest man, abolished slavery, reestablished the union, saved the Republic without veiling the statue of liberty. He was assassinated April 14, 1865). Below the tomb were the familiar words *LIBERTÉ–ÉGALITÉ–FRATERNITÉ*, the motto of the French Revolution—and its heirs in France, Europe, and the Americas.[42]

The committee's letter to Mrs. Lincoln, accompanying the medal, did not miss the opportunity to denounce its imperial censors: "If

France possessed the liberties enjoyed by republican America, it is not by thousands, but by millions that would be counted, with us, the admirers of Lincoln, and the partisans of those opinions to which he devoted his life, and which are consecrated by his death." Eugène Pelletan handed the medal, encased in its purple velvet box, to John Bigelow and told him: "Tell Mrs. Lincoln the heart of France is in that little box."[43]

One bold confirmation of the general support for democratic success came from Charles Forbes, Comte de Montalembert, a prominent voice of liberal Catholicism, who spoke out as few others dared about the lessons America had for the world. He was one of the forty *immortels* elected to the prestigious French Academy, part of the Institut de France. In May 1865, he published a sensational essay extolling the victory of the North and what it meant to Europe.

"Everything which has occurred in America," Montalembert wrote, "from all which is to follow in the future, grave teachings will result for us, lessons of which it is indispensable to keep an account; for, in spite of ourselves, we belong to a society irrevocably democratic." Bigelow was ecstatic over Montalembert's endorsement and quickly arranged for the address to be translated and published in America. Here, he later wrote, was "the most comprehensive, intelligent judgment of the crisis through which our country had just passed that has ever come . . . from any foreign pen."[44]

The response to Lincoln's death, the *Avenir National* summarized, showed "how extremely popular the ideas of liberty and equality have become." The newspaper ran a series of articles praising Lincoln and the American republic. Alphonse Peyrat, the newspaper's publisher, exclaimed, "it cannot be too often repeated, in every variety of tone, that the triumph of the North is the triumph of democracy; and we cannot express in too strong a manner to the United States the gratitude we owe them for the examples and lessons they have given us." Among those lessons, of course, was the sad contrast Lincoln and the Union offered to Europe, particularly France. "To conquer liberty, to lose it, . . . to be ignorant of the way to be free—such has been the spectacle afforded more than once by European democracy."[45]

Italy was in the throes of the Risorgimento, the long campaign to expel foreign rulers and create a unified nation founded on liberal, many hoped republican, institutions. Italy was the darling of liberal Europe. When the Revolutions of 1848 failed in one country after another, the Italian Risorgimento remained for the European democracy a beacon of hope and out of it came many of the most progressive visions of the future. Still, the struggle to make Italy one with the universal republic had foundered. Its guiding light, Giuseppe Mazzini, had to flee to exile in London as an outlaw with a price on his head. This left Giuseppe Garibaldi, the Risorgimento's hugely popular man of action, to accept that Italy must be made under the auspices of King Victor Emmanuel II, whose kingdom in Piedmonte would annex provinces into the United Kingdom of Italy proclaimed in 1861.

In 1865, Mazzini sought to merge the Risorgimento with the rising enthusiasm for the Union victory and his idea for a transatlantic "Universal Republic." In a public letter "To Our Friends in the United States," he joyfully greeted the Union victory. He summoned America to its present duty, which, as he saw it, was to lead the way to a new era of republican peace and freedom: "Your triumph is our triumph; the triumph of all, I hope, who are struggling for the advent of a republican era. . . . You have done more for us in four years than fifty years of teaching, preaching and writing, from all your European brothers have been able to do. Complete your work. The United States stand now a leading Power in Europe, too, and power is duty. You are called on by God to enter a new career."[46]

No sooner was the Civil War ended than Mazzini organized a movement to enlist American "Friends of Republican Institutions" in the cause of European liberation. The United States, he told America, is now "summoned by the admiration, the sympathies, and expectations of all of progressive Europe . . . to carry out a service for the general progress of Humanity."[47]

If their messages of condolence to America are any guide, many Italians shared Mazzini's dreams of a transnational "Universal Republic."

Chieti, a small town in the hills of Abruzzo east of Rome, had no less than three public meetings to draft messages of condolence to America. Luigi Preliti presided over a gathering of more than 230 people identified simply as "the Italians of Abruzzo." Their letter revealed the same majestic ideas of universal republicanism and cosmopolitan nationalism that animated Mazzini.

> Your history is the same as ours. From Camillus and Cincinnatus to Franklin and Washington, from Lincoln and Seward to Garibaldi and Mazzini, the tradition of the great struggle between good and evil, liberty and slavery, civilization and barbarism, national autonomy and the rule of foreign despots, has ever been the same. The roar of your battles was borne across the ocean and awaked an echo in our Apennines.[48]

The Democratic Republican Association of Florence wrote, "the democracy of Europe owe your people an eternal debt of gratitude for preserving, intact and pure, their great republic, from the model of which the nations of the old world may yet be formed anew."[49] From Bologna, the Ladies Society informed the American people that "we, the maidens, spouses, and mothers of suffering Italy, are waiting hopefully for the time when America, restored to her former strength and glory, and to her rightful station among the great nations of the earth, will come to our aid and relieve us from foreign oppression."[50] In the spring of 1865, the Italians sounded a rousing chorus of praise for Lincoln, America, and the new birth of freedom in Europe.

Meanwhile, reports of Lincoln's death made their way into Latin America. From Haiti, M. B. Bird, a British Wesleyan missionary, described the grief Haitians felt in *The Victorious: A Small Poem on the Assassination of President Lincoln*. Lincoln's death, he wrote, "filled Hayti with profoundest grief; the soul of the Nation was stirred to its deepest depths . . . from the last to the greatest." Lincoln's "proclamation of liberty" had, naturally, "produced unbounded joy amongst a people who, more than half an age ago, blew the same trumpet to the world." Bird's poem evoked the Christian hope that Lincoln's death would, in time, bring blessings.

Lincoln then lives; his soul
Commands. He fell, but not the fabric which
He built; yea, he went home to God, but left
A host of mighty spirits, that fill well
His place, that caught his spirit, and his plans[51]

The news reached Havana by ship on April 23 with stunning effect. During the war, Blacks—free and enslaved—gathered around the docks whenever mail packets arrived, hoping to glean stories of the great war raging to their north, sensing somehow that it would change their world. U.S. consuls in Cuba reported hearing chants rising among the enslaved: "Avanza Lincoln, Avanza! Tu eres nuestra Esperanza!" (Onward Lincoln, Onward! You are our hope!)[52]

Word of the assassination suddenly gave rise to "an unparalleled demonstration of grief" among all Cubans, one observer noted, "especially among the Negroes." The *luto de Lincoln* (mourning) took on a religious tone of worship for the man and what he stood for in Cuban minds. A letter in Havana's *El Siglo* described April's mood: "Lincoln departed wearing on his head the crown of martyrdom that God reserved in His mysterious ways for the apostles of great causes." Men and women of all colors and classes "wore . . . black ribbons with the eagle of the Union and a picture of the martyr." Spanish authorities were "dismayed" by all the demonstrations of reverence for Lincoln. They were wary that the enslaved might adopt Lincoln as their "martyred political saint" and enlist his spirit in a general uprising. Officials ordered the press to publish no eulogies to Lincoln and never to reference him as El Gran Emancipador or associate him in any way with the dangerous subject of abolition. Young José Martí, the future hero of Cuban independence, a boy of twelve, wore a hemp bracelet as an emblem of mourning. Lincoln became his lifelong hero.[53]

Cuban reverence for Lincoln lasted long after April 1865. Images of Lincoln adorned the walls of homes, the grand houses of progressive Cubans, and the humble huts of workers, Black and white. Three years after the assassination, Cuban rebels rose against their Spanish rulers. Afro-Cubans, enslaved and free, fled to the Liberation Army bearing images of Abraham Lincoln as though to signify this is why we fight.[54]

Reports of Lincoln's death moved slowly into Mexico, which had only a limited telegraph network. It reached Mexico City by ship from New Orleans to Veracruz in early May, then inland by mule-drawn coach. Maximilian, the Austrian archduke, had taken the throne as emperor of Mexico less than a year earlier. He still counted on French armed forces to protect his throne from Mexico's republicans, whose president, Benito Juárez, had fled to northern Mexico. When the United States refused to recognize any but Mexico's republic as the legitimate government of Mexico, Maximilian sided with the Confederates. He invited them to bring their slaves and colonize northern Mexico to create a barrier against U.S. aggression. Maximilian's supporters greeted news of the assassination in Mexico City as good tidings. One account gleefully predicted the entire United States was about to "become the prey of an uncontrollable anarchy."[55]

In contrast, Benito Juárez, president of the Republic of Mexico, ordered all flags to fly at half-mast and all officials to "clothe themselves in mourning during nine days." In a dispatch to his envoy in Washington, Juárez regretted that a leader "who worked with so much earnestness and abnegation for the cause of nationality and freedom, was worthy of a better fate than the poniard of a coward assassin." A condolence message from the republican mayor of Tobasco avowed that "the kindred people of this continent, united in the lovely bonds of democracy, ought to share mutually in its joys and its sorrows." Mexicans, he vowed, "will be worthy members of the great democratic family that people the world of Columbus, in spite of the mean strategy now used to divide us. I make vows to Providence for the happiness of the United States, and pray that the peace the great republic has just conquered at such a great sacrifice may last long, for the good of humanity."[56]

Matías Romero, the Mexican Republic's young ambassador to Washington, for four years had tirelessly propagated the idea that the Union and Mexico were engaged in a common war against the enemies of republican freedom. The Southern slaveholders and Mexico's Church

Party rebelled against the people's will. Each enemy of the republic sought foreign allies to aid them. Both rebellions must be defeated before either republic would be safe.

Romero organized a massive rally at the Cooper Union in New York City in July 1865. Several exiled Mexican republicans spoke, summoning America to avenge Lincoln's death by fulfilling its duty to free the continent of the new European conquistadores: "Americans! on the other side of the Rio Grande is a sister nation whom they are murdering; and that nation need arms to defend themselves," one speaker exclaimed. "Will they be refused by the sons of Washington and Lincoln?"[57]

Reports of Lincoln's death migrated slowly down the Atlantic Coast of South America, and Rio de Janeiro did not learn until May 18, over a month later. Brazilians had watched the crisis in the United States closely, knowing that if it led to the abolition of slavery there, it would portend grave consequences for Brazil, whose enslaved population was second only to America in numbers. As the American war unfolded, the country's officials were terrified that abolitionism and slave insurrections would infect Brazil.[58]

During the war, Brazil's university students, intellectuals, and others saw the conflict in America as a contest between a slaveholding aristocracy defending the past and free-labor liberal proponents of progress. Aureliano Candido Tavares Bastos, a young law student in São Paulo, became enthralled with the American Union as the model for Brazil's progress. He was equally convinced that slavery, wherever it existed, was a drag on human progress and prosperity. Through his publications and political speeches, Tavares Bastos used the American Civil War to stir serious debate on the future of slavery.[59]

When news of Lincoln's assassination arrived in Rio de Janeiro, U.S. minister James Watson Webb reported to Washington "the universal horror and dismay which the melancholy news caused among all classes in this city." An American scientist, Louis Agassiz of Harvard University, was visiting Brazil on a scientific expedition. "At first it seemed absolutely incredible," Agassiz wrote, "and the more sanguine among us persisted in regarding it as a gigantic street rumor, invented perhaps by Secession sympathizers, till on our return to town the next morning our worst fears were confirmed by the French steamer just arrived. The days seemed very long till the next mail."[60]

Brazil's antislavery leaders soon transformed Lincoln's martyrdom into a call for emancipation in Brazil. In June 1865, Francisco Gê Acayaba de Montezuma, Viscount of Jequitinhonha, a senator from Bahia de Salvador, told the Brazilian Senate that it was Brazil's duty to honor Lincoln by removing "the cancer that weakens us." When a conservative senator protested, Jequitinhonha made it clear that the "great cancer" he referred to meant "the institution of slavery."[61]

In a stream of pamphlets and published eulogies, liberal Brazilians elevated Lincoln into a Pan-American hero. Brazilian newspapers advertised the sale of photographic images of Lincoln, and illustrated journals featured images of Lincoln ascending to heaven in the embrace of George Washington. Felix Ferreira, a Brazilian poet, published *A Morte de Lincoln: Canto Elegiaco*. The country's premier Masonic lodge, Grand Oriente do Brazil, lamented the death of "the most energetic, if not the foremost, representative of the cause of progress" and "a benefactor of humanity." The "blood of Abraham Lincoln was the supreme baptism to the Christian idea in the modern era, an idea which he embodied with sublime perseverance and indomitable courage." Brazil's antislavery leaders suggested Dom Pedro II should emulate Lincoln by enlisting slaves in the military and promising them freedom.[62]

Agassiz recorded a conversation with a Brazilian slaveholder, who rather matter-of-factly told him that in light of Lincoln's Emancipation Proclamation, Brazilian slavery was doomed. "It finish with you; and when it finish with you, it finish here, it finish everywhere." "The death-note of slavery in the United States was its death-note every where," Agassiz wrote. "We thought this significant and cheering."[63]

Joaquim Nabuco, Brazil's leading abolitionist, later recalled, "Through what Lincoln did, owing to the great light he kindled for all the world with his Proclamation, we could win our cause without a drop of blood being shed." He added, "We all owe to Lincoln the immense debt of having fixed forever the free character of American civilization."[64]

By late May, after news of Lincoln's death traveled down the coast to Buenos Aires, all the Argentine newspapers appeared in mourning and were "filled with glowing editorials on President Lincoln," reported Robert Kirk, the U.S. minister to Argentina. The president of the Argentine congress expressed regret for "the loss that liberty and democracy have suffered by the death of Abraham Lincoln, the great republican." Senators and deputies wore mourning for three days and ordered the Argentine flag to half-mast. All the newspapers appeared with black borders of mourning. The government agreed to honor Lincoln by naming a town after him. Argentinians were stricken with grief, and many gathered outside the U.S. legation to express their feelings. "It has never been my lot to witness such intense sorrow as this sad event has produced," Kirk wrote Seward.[65]

Meanwhile, along the Pacific coast of South America, the news tricked southward even more slowly. The first signal of the evil tidings was a British steamer that, on May 18, entered Peru's main port, Callao, with an American flag flying at half-mast. Christopher Robinson, U.S. minister to Peru, reported to Seward that news of the assassination "spread with electric rapidity" and "the feeling of indignation . . . was unanimous, pervading all classes." Flags on all government and diplomatic offices immediately dropped to half-mast. The next day in the port, the ships of all nations fired funereal salutes.[66]

It had been an entire month and a half since the assassination when Chileans heard the news, but the lapse of time did not affect their emotional response. "The effect upon the residents of Santiago and Valparaíso was sad beyond description," U.S. minister Thomas Nelson wrote Seward. "Strong men wandered about the streets weeping like children, and foreigners, unable even to speak our language, manifested a grief almost as deep as our own." Nelson watched as Chilean citizens, "overcome by their emotion, sat down upon the very ground and wept; and men whose stoicism had never been affected gave violent course to their grief."

Later, the Chileans conducted a funeral march through the streets of Santiago, led by a Pan-American group styled the Society of the American Union. They were "bearing the flags of the different American republics, also shrouded in crepe, and citizens, most of them dressed in mourning, with crepe upon the left arm," Nelson wrote to Seward. He was moved by what he witnessed, and so were the Chileans. "As the procession passed the legation, . . . I observed tears falling from the eyes of many, and the absolute silence and decorum of the thousands of spectators who filled the streets for squares was in itself a tribute to the memory of the illustrious dead."[67]

Eventually, the letters and tributes that poured into U.S. diplomatic posts worldwide between late April and June 1865 found their way to the State Department in Washington. In Paris, John Bigelow had been the first to recognize the potential propaganda value of the tributes he had received in France. He wrote a friend in New York that Lincoln's death "is destined to work a radical change in the Constitution of France. It is impossible for the government, if disposed, to resist the lesson in political science taught by the United States during the past four years."[68] A master of the fine arts of public diplomacy, Bigelow saw in these popular manifestations for Lincoln and America an irresistible opportunity to educate France and Europe on the strength of democratic republicanism as a practical example in the United States and as a popular ideology in Europe.[69]

Others saw the potential power of the public response to Lincoln's death. George Marsh, U.S. minister to Italy, wrote to Bigelow, "If we bear, as doubtless we shall, this hardest test of stability of our institutions, it will prove the severest blow that European despotism has ever received, and I trust we shall soon be in a position to show our bitterest enemies, the ecclesiastical and lay monarchies of [Europe], that their conduct towards us has been not only a crime, but, what they would more regret, a blunder."[70]

Bigelow began by sending Seward six dozen from "among the manifold testimonials of sympathy," a small sample of sentiment in France. They will show, he told Seward, "how deep a hold he had taken upon the respect and affections of the French people. It is difficult to exaggerate the enthusiasm which his name inspires among the masses of Europe at this moment—an enthusiasm before which the ruling classes, however little disposed to waste compliments upon anything associated with republicanism, are obliged to incline."[71]

Seward was slowly recovering from the wounds his would-be assassin inflicted on April 14, though his face remained braced and bandaged, and he relied on a wheelchair to move about. Eager to get back to the business of statecraft, the ailing secretary immediately realized the testimonies to Lincoln and America Bigelow sent him might play a role in his effort to get the French out of Mexico. To ensure the French government was aware of its people's affection for Lincoln and America, Seward instructed Bigelow to consult with the French foreign minister to determine that "such a publication would be agreeable to the Emperor's government."[72]

As other messages poured in from diplomatic outposts worldwide, Seward decided to translate those not in English and publish the whole bunch, nearly a thousand in all, as a separate volume and appendix to the annual diplomatic correspondence. It was an ingenious means of transmitting what Bigelow called the "lessons" of events in America to the governments, press, and opinion leaders of all nations. Copies of annual diplomatic correspondence went out to all those countries the United States recognized.

Seward was so pleased with the effect of the appendix that he decided to publish an expanded edition in more attractive binding for broader distribution at home and abroad. In 1867 the government printing office came out with a handsome large-format leather-bound volume with two hundred additional pages of letters, newspaper articles, and other communications from abroad. Printed on fine paper, with wide margins and marbled end sheets, it was "bound in full Turkey morocco, full gilt" and included a striking engraved image of a rather handsome President Lincoln as frontispiece. Renamed *Tributes of the Nations to Abraham Lincoln*, copies of the book were sent to every member of Congress, "to each foreign Government, and one copy to each corporation, association, or public body, whose expressions of condolence or sympathy are published in said volume."[73]

Seward's memoirs cast a warm light on this clever exercise in public diplomacy. The "avalanche of letters, and resolutions of condolence and sympathy" had poured into the State Department from kings and workers, students and intellectuals, and people from every walk of life. They "all joined in these manifestations of their horror at the crime, and their sympathy with the American people." Seward added with a flourish, "it was as if an electric touch had brought all the world in unison, and revealed the common brotherhood of all mankind."[74]

Few knew better than Seward that behind the mourning of Lincoln's death, republicans abroad had seized an opportunity to embarrass America's adversaries, revel in the Union's unexpected triumph, praise the wondrous strength of republican institutions, and create in Lincoln a universally admired martyr to the Union cause. Now the leaders of Europe's Great Powers could read in *Tributes of the Nations* testimonies from their people, what they thought about Lincoln, America—and what they thought about their own country's leaders and governments. They would soon realize that the demonstrations for Lincoln and America were symptoms of more profound unrest about to rise.

CHAPTER 2

Retribution

All Europe was opposed to us, they hastened to vest our enemies with the rights of war; they threw open their ports for their privateers; they prepared in their machine shops the materials for breaking our blockade; they prepared the arms with which our enemies fought us. . . . They thought our day of doom was come. . . . they began their work.

—HENRY WINTER DAVIS, RADICAL REPUBLICAN
CONGRESSMAN, FOURTH OF JULY, 1865

The effusive tributes to Lincoln and America coming from sympathizers abroad in the spring of 1865 stood in sharp contrast to the trepidation the governments of Britain, France, and Spain felt. They had calculated that the American republic could not sustain a protracted civil war, and it would be only a matter of time before it accepted separation as inevitable. Meanwhile, they took advantage of America's "distraction" to advance their ambitions in the Americas, invading and taking over Latin American republics and resetting the balance of power in the Americas in favor of European imperialism.

Against the expectations of many, President Lincoln won reelection in November 1864, which was understood as a mandate to carry on the war and emancipate four million African Americans. When the Confederacy collapsed, European powers faced a battle-tested nation at arms that was fully prepared, even eager, they thought, to turn its military might against them.

Britain's Prime Minister Lord Palmerston wrote to Queen Victoria in January 1865, warning that "whenever the Civil War in America shall be ended, the Northern States will . . . either make war against England or make inroads into your Majesty's North American possessions which would lead to war."[1] The only question European observers had was, would the Union seek to redress its grievances against the British in Canada, the French in Mexico, or Spain in the Caribbean? Or maybe all three in time?

There was good reason for the European powers to anticipate retribution. American politicians in both parties rivaled one another in their bellicose defense of the Monroe Doctrine. Popular tunes filled the air promising to "Take the fight to Mexico" and "Go with Grant again" against the French defending Maximilian's so-called Empire of Mexico, and recruiters were busy enlisting veterans as "emigrants" headed south. On the northern border, armed and angry Irish American veterans attended huge "picnics" of the Fenian Brotherhood, a paramilitary organization aiming to attack the British Empire in Canada and liberate Ireland from British rule. Nor was Spain exempted. Mass meetings in New York City denounced its aggression against the Dominican Republic, Mexico, Peru, and Chile. They called on America to stand up for the Monroe Doctrine in defense of its besieged sister republics.

Europeans were startled by the bellicose rhetoric of American politicians and newspapers representing both parties. Nothing was more insulting than the alarming speech by the eminent historian and diplomat George Bancroft before an enthusiastic joint session of Congress on Lincoln's birthday, February 12, 1866.

In the afternoon, the audience gathered in the House of Representatives to witness what they expected to be a eulogy from the dignified, somewhat austere historian George Bancroft. President Andrew Johnson, most of his cabinet, and judges of the Supreme Court took their seats toward the front. Members of the diplomatic corps, ambassadors Sir Frederick Bruce of Britain, Gabriel García Tassara of Spain, Baron Wydenbruck

FIGURE 5. George Bancroft, an eminent historian, statesman, and diplomat, turned a eulogy to Abraham Lincoln presented before Congress into a contentious indictment of European powers for betraying Lincoln and America during the Civil War. Wikimedia Commons.

of Austria, Eduard de Stoeckl of Russia, Edouard Blondeel of Belgium, and several other distinguished European envoys were prominently seated toward the front. The galleries were packed to the top with men and women who had managed to secure tickets; hundreds more were turned away.

Bancroft, the son of a Massachusetts clergyman, had been superbly educated at Exeter Academy, Harvard, and distinguished German universities

in Heidelberg, Göttingen, and Berlin. Remembered as a fervently nationalist historian, he became a true cosmopolitan in outlook and manner after
his years in Europe. Upon returning to Harvard from his European studies,
Bancroft was brimming with Continental affectation, sporting a full
European-style beard and dropping German and French phrases into conversations at every opportunity. He greeted his former professors at Harvard with "moist kisses" Continental style, leaving one irritated faculty
member to swear Bancroft would never get a professorship there. Bancroft's hugely popular ten-volume *History of the United States of America*
(1834–74) chronicled America's passage from its colonial beginnings as the
unfolding of providential destiny. A romantic nationalist in the German
mold, Bancroft portrayed America's historical mission as the advance
guard of democracy and republicanism. His books sold well.[2]

While in diplomatic service Bancroft proved a stout defender of republicanism and staunch adversary of European monarchical presump-
tion. European courts did not receive American envoys as "ambassadors,"
a status reserved strictly for those representing monarchs. American
"minister plenipotentiaries," as they were called, refused to imitate the
archaic plumage ambassadors donned, replete with silk stockings, buck-
led slippers, pantaloons, and colorful brocade coats. They chose instead
to present themselves in court in the simple republican attire of plain
black suits and white shirts. When one haughty British ambassador
asked, "In God's name, Mr. Bancroft, why don't you Yankees send your
representatives to court like Christians, in a proper uniform, instead of
turning them out all dressed in black, like so many undertakers?" "Really,
Lord Augustus," Bancroft coolly replied, "I am surprised that you, as
Ambassador of the Queen of England, and with those keen powers of
penetration for which you are so generally distinguished, should have
failed to perceive that we could not be more appropriately dressed
than we are—at European courts where what we represent is the Burial
of Monarchy."[3]

When he spoke before Congress in February 1866, Bancroft was
sixty-five years old. His face was framed by a full mane of white hair and
a downy mutton-chop beard. That day, he held the podium for over two
and a half hours of classical oratorical style before a rapt audience.

Beginning with the nation's noble founding on republican ideals of equality and liberty, he turned to the South, whose aristocratic leaders defended slavery as a blessing rather than a stain on the republic. As Bancroft saw it, slavery and aristocracy were two sides of the same "hereditary wrong" that contradicted America's republican principles. Wherever slavery exists, he quoted James Madison, "the republican theory becomes fallacious." "Neither hereditary monarchy nor hereditary aristocracy planted itself on our soil," Bancroft noted; "the only hereditary condition that fastened itself upon us was servitude."[4]

About halfway into his address, Bancroft turned to the challenges Lincoln had faced abroad. With Sir Frederick Bruce, the genial British ambassador to Washington, sitting a few yards away, Bancroft issued a sharp attack against Britain's deceitful behavior during the war. The British Empire's "grasping ambition had dotted the world with military posts" and "kept watch over our borders on the northeast, at the Bermudas, in the West Indies." Britain's "aristocracy had gazed with terror on the growth of a commonwealth where freeholders existed by the million, and religion was not in bondage to the state," Bancroft spoke, "and now they could not repress their joy at its perils."

He also picked the scab left from Britain's hasty decision in early May 1861 to accord belligerent rights to the Southern rebels. Britain, Bancroft reminded the audience, abandoned the United States to face enemies of "the gentlest and most beneficent government on earth" for a rebellion "directed against human nature itself for the perpetual enslavement of a race." Then Bancroft turned to criticize Earl Russell, Britain's foreign secretary, who "made haste to send word through the palaces of Europe that the great republic was in its agony; that the republic was no more; that a head stone was all that remained due by the law of nations to 'the late Union.'"

Next, he turned to France, once "so beloved in America," for its aid during the Revolution. France also acted immediately to award belligerent rights to the Confederacy, which Emperor Napoleon III was eager to recognize as an independent nation if only to assist in his shameful usurpation of Mexico. Envoys from the party of slavery in the South and the monarchist Church Party in Mexico made their way to France to seek aid in their dual rebellions against republicanism. France's emperor, "moved by a desire to erect in North America a buttress for imperialism," sought to transform Mexico's republic into a "secundo-geniture for the House of Hapsburg" (Maximilian was the younger brother of Austria's Emperor Franz Joseph).

Nor did Bancroft spare Pope Pius IX, whose public letters to Catholic bishops in the North and South denounced Union atrocities against Catholic churches and urged America's clergy to lend their voice to peace. He "gave counsels for peace at a time when peace meant the victory of secession," Bancroft charged. Confederates brandished the pope's letter to "President Jefferson Davis" as propaganda to discourage Union recruits in Ireland and other parts of Europe from enlisting in the Union's godless war. On his way to Mexico from Trieste, Maximilian won the pope's blessing for his mission to restore Mexico to Catholic moral authority, thus aligning the Church with Napoleon III's imperialist design and against the Union.

Bancroft did not fail to commend "our unwavering friend" Russia, "whose emperor had just accomplished one of the grandest acts in the course of time, by raising twenty millions of bondmen into freeholders." He also praised China, whose foreign secretary Prince Kung "read a lesson to European diplomatists" by closing its ports to "the war-ships and privateers of 'the seditious.'" While America's allies in western Europe turned their backs on the Union, Bancroft seemed to say, distant civilizations remained its friends. So, "the war continued, with all the peoples of the world for anxious spectators."

Bancroft finished with a cruel takedown of Lord Palmerston, Britain's recently deceased prime minister, who had vexed Lincoln with schemes to intervene on behalf of the rebels. Bancroft proceeded at length with invidious comparisons between the aristocratic British leader and the humble American president. Frederick Bruce, Britain's minister to Washington, undoubtedly cringed as Bancroft capped off his indictment by saying, "Palmerston did nothing that will endure; Lincoln finished a work that all time cannot overthrow."[5]

Bancroft knew just what he was doing that February afternoon in Washington. Anticipating that his remarks would offend Britain and

France, he had warned its envoys well in advance should they prefer to stay away. He played the audience like a musical instrument, as he gleefully explained to his wife that evening: "The radicals would applaud vehemently at one part and the friends of Johnson at the other, and so it went on for several sentences . . . it was like touching the different keys of a piano, each sending its note at the touch."[6]

The London *Times* castigated Bancroft and, even more, his cheering audience in Congress and the press. "Americans hate England," the *Times* American correspondent reported, "and love to hear her abused." A *Times* editorial denounced "this mischievous old man" for "slandering two such countries as England and France in the presence of their representative." He set out "to rail at and vilify the country whose language he was speaking and whose authors he had in former times tried his best to imitate."[7]

The French imperialist press was equally incensed. A French translation of Bancroft's address, published in Brussels, appeared later in the year. French journals reported the insults to Maximilian and France but cautiously omitted those hurled at Napoleon III. The conservative *La Presse* denounced *L'incident Bancroft* as a "violent diatribe against the European governments." It even blamed Bancroft for a tumble in the French stock market, coming as it did when tensions ran high between France and America over the Mexico Question.[8] The *Courrier des États-Unis*, a New York publication, denounced Bancroft's lofty address as "the undigested lucubration of a soul without heat and of a pen without direction."[9]

The press in Spain, as in France, operated under strict censorship, and both liberal and conservative journals found it safest to note the reports of other newspapers and dwell on Bancroft's attacks on every country but Spain.[10]

The fulminations abroad over Bancroft's incendiary speech were predictable and must have performed just as Seward hoped. Bancroft had presented a summary indictment against Europe while heralding a "new era of republicanism" about to dawn. His statement was the unofficial view of a private citizen. Yet, everyone understood the speaker's authority, having been invited by President Johnson and Secretary Seward and enthusiastically applauded by both political parties in the Capitol.

William Seward gave the disgruntled diplomats no satisfaction: "When they send legions to this side of the Atlantic to overthrow republics, they necessarily submit themselves to the censure of all free States." In case any European monarchs might be mistaken into thinking Bancroft was out of favor, Johnson and Seward rewarded him with an appointment as U.S. minister to his beloved Berlin.[11]

Though it made only a glancing reference to the "policy . . . known commonly as the doctrine of Monroe," the Bancroft address went beyond objecting to further European colonization in the American Continent. European emperors and the pontiff of Rome had taken advantage of the crisis in the United States not to further colonization of the American Continent. Their deeper purpose was to suppress the infectious spread of American republicanism, restore the orderly rule of Church and Crown in Latin America, and dismember and weaken the capacity of the United States to defend the American Continent against such designs. Henceforth, Bancroft's message made clear that the United States would protect Pan-American republicanism, armed with a powerful military and encouraged by a Monroe Doctrine that vilified European empires as the enemies of peace in the American hemisphere.[12]

Before the Civil War, "Monroe's doctrine," as it was known, was a principle rather than an active policy, a warning—and a toothless one—against further European colonization of the American hemisphere. In December 1823, a short passage in President James Monroe's annual message, authored by Secretary of State John Quincy Adams, stated, "the American continents, by the free and independent condition which they have assumed and maintain, are henceforth not to be considered as subjects for future colonization by any European powers." It added, "we should consider any attempt on their part to extend their system [meaning monarchy and colonization] to any portion of this hemisphere as dangerous to our peace and safety" and a "manifestation of an unfriendly disposition toward the United States." By "unfriendly," it was meant to say an act of war.[13]

During the Civil War, the "Monroe Doctrine," as it was now routinely called, emerged as a muscular, pro-republican version of the 1823 edition.

It became commonplace in America's political vocabulary and was the central plank in U.S. foreign policy after the Civil War. Joshua Leavitt, a clergyman and abolitionist from Massachusetts, authored *The Monroe Doctrine* in 1863, a pamphlet that set forth its new meaning in light of recent European interventions. Leavitt sharpened the distinction between the European "system" of monarchical imperialism and American republicanism.[14]

Leavitt explained that European hostility to American republicanism had crystallized in the Holy Alliance, a league formed in 1815 after the defeat of Napoleon I by Austria, Prussia, and Russia, representing the Catholic, Protestant, and Orthodox Christian branches of the Church. It was devoted to restoring the divine right of kings and opposing liberalism and revolution in all its manifestations. Having consolidated its control over the European Continent, the Holy Alliance turned to the Americas. In 1823 Spain launched a failed attempt to "resubjugate the colonies of Spain" by sending a flotilla to Mexico. The United States, Leavitt explained, took the bold step of recognizing the former Spanish colonies as sovereign nations and found itself "at the head of a glorious sisterhood of free and independent states." Except for Britain, the American Continent was now free of European imperialism. Monroe's declaration of 1823 forbade further colonization in the Americas, and it warned the United States would "consider any attempt on the part of the European powers to extend their political system to any portion of this hemisphere as 'dangerous to our peace and safety.'"[15]

During the Civil War, the Union repurposed the Monroe Doctrine to oppose European intervention. In response to those who argued the 1823 policy was a dead letter, a temporary mandate to answer a passing threat, Leavitt answered with a robust defense of Monroe as an enduring principle guiding U.S. foreign policy. It was grounded in an understanding that the American and European "systems of government" (borrowing from William Seward's language on the North-South conflict) "cannot exist together in the Western Hemisphere without creating a constant and irrepressible conflict of irreconcilable ideas."[16]

Leavitt took his message public with additional publications and speeches. In an alarming article published in July 1864, "The Key of a

Continent," Leavitt reminded American statesmen and business leaders that Napoleon III's Grand Design was not limited to imposing monarchy and Catholic domination on Latin America. His ultimate purpose was to make France the master of global commerce by building a canal across Mexico or Central America to control trade between Europe, the Americas, and Asia.[17]

At a rally for Mexican exiles held at New York's Cooper Union in July 1865, Leavitt delivered a fiery speech. "Both the invasion and the rebellion were parts of one grand conspiracy of the upholders of absolutism in Europe and the upholders of slavery in the United States, to make common cause and strike a united blow against republican liberty on the American continent, in the hope of rendering arbitrary power more secure in both hemispheres." He urged Americans to take up the strenuous defense of the Monroe Doctrine. By this doctrine, the people of the United States "make common cause and cherish a common sympathy with the American republics, and welcome them to the common platform of national independence." The United States will be "greater, stronger, and richer in proportion to the elevation of our sister Republic in the South."[18]

The Monroe Doctrine was one of the few policy issues on which many Republicans, Radicals and moderates alike, and Democrats from South and North could find common ground after 1865. President Andrew Johnson clarified in his first presidential message to Congress that he would defend Monroe's declaration, even if he avoided invoking it by name.[19]

"From the moment of the establishment of our free Constitution," Johnson stated, "the civilized world has been convulsed by revolutions in the interests of democracy or of monarchy, but through all those revolutions the United States have wisely and firmly refused to become propagandists of republicanism" (one of Seward's favorite points). "It is the only government suited to our condition . . . we have never sought to impose it on others." America has preferred to "leave the nations of Europe to choose their own dynasties and form their own systems of government." In doing so, it "may justly demand a corresponding moderation." Then to the point: "We should regard it as a great calamity to ourselves, to the cause of good government, and to the peace of the world should any European power challenge the American people, as it were, to the defense of republicanism against foreign interference."[20]

By "interference," Johnson obliquely alluded to France's effort in Mexico to impose a European monarchy on the ruins of Mexico's hard-earned republic. The intervention in Mexico was part of Emperor Napoleon III's *gran pensée* or "Grand Design" for regenerating the Latin race in the Americas under French tutelage. The Grand Design was to create a stable Catholic monarchy on the European model that would safeguard the projected inter-ocean canal and ensure France's preeminent role in world commerce.[21]

Since splitting from Spain in 1821, Mexico had gone through countless cycles of democratic elections, *pronunciamientos*, military dictatorships, and civil wars until the liberal Constitution of 1857 opened the way to the creation of the Estados Unidos Mexicanos. This liberal, secular, democratic republic proved able to defend itself against the violent rebellion of Conservatives spearheaded by Catholic clergy and wealthy landowners. After the Liberals finally prevailed in the War of the Reform, Mexico's Conservatives would not accept defeat at the ballot box nor on the battlefield. They turned to European Catholic monarchies and the Church in Rome, seeking intervention to rescue Mexico from "the revolution."[22]

Emperor Napoleon III was sympathetic. He believed republicanism was a product of the Anglo-Saxon culture encroaching from the United States. Democracy and republican institutions were wholly unsuited to the "Latin race," which required a hereditary monarchy and Catholic moral discipline to ensure order, Napoleon III reasoned. France's mission was not to colonize Mexico, nor to expand the French Empire, and therefore not in violation of the Monroe Doctrine. France's mission was, instead, to "regenerate" the American branch of the Latin race. Far from imposing an alien and unwelcome form of government, he insisted Mexican monarchists had invited France to Mexico and ratified Maximilian's throne by popular plebiscite.[23]

Though Seward was furious at the sight of Spain, Britain, and France preying like vultures on helpless Latin American neighbors, he and President Lincoln feared that any move to thwart such aggression might push European powers into the welcome arms of the Southern rebels. The French intervention in Mexico and Spain's incursions in the Dominican Republic, Peru, and Chile reified the Union's message that its struggle against the Southern rebels was not just about secession or slavery and did not concern only the United States. America's Civil War was part of the contest between monarchy and republicanism, aristocracy and democratic self-rule, and slavery and freedom that Monroe addressed in 1823.[24]

The Union narrative of a world divided between monarchists and republicans found continued nourishment in the rhetoric of the new Monroe Doctrine. The American hemisphere was to be the asylum of republicanism, protected from European imperialists that threatened the peace and well-being of American republics. The old doctrine had posed a shield against European efforts to reclaim or expand their American empires. By 1865 the Monroe Doctrine became a weapon against European imperialist designs backed by U.S. military prowess and a new sense of duty to defend the republican experiment in the Americas. The celebrated poet and publisher William Cullen Bryant explained to a New York audience gathered to support Mexico in 1864, "We of the United States have constituted ourselves a sort of police of this New World."[25]

During the last year of the Civil War, fears of a European alliance with the Confederacy gave way to outspoken resentment of European aggression, especially in Mexico. Democrats and Radical Republicans took turns lambasting Seward and Lincoln for failing to defend the Monroe Doctrine. As the war drew to a close, this impatient anger came to a boil in Congress and the press. Behind the scenes, Matías Romero worked diligently with members of Congress who planned to issue resolutions condemning French intervention and threatening Maximilian's throne. Maximilian was on his way from Trieste to Mexico, with stops in Rome and Paris, to be crowned emperor of Mexico in the spring of 1864. Romero hoped a bold resolution from Congress might stop him in his tracks.[26]

Henry Winter Davis, a Radical Republican representing Maryland, issued a resolution in Congress expressing the new spirit of the Monroe Doctrine and made it clear that the United States would not stand by as

France and other European monarchies established a regime hostile to American republicanism next door.

> Resolved, That the Congress of the United States are unwilling by si-
> lence to have the nations of the world under the impression that they
> are indifferent spectators of the deplorable events now transpiring in
> the Republic of Mexico, and that they think fit to declare that it does
> not accord with the policy of the United States to acknowledge any
> monarchical government erected on the ruins of any republican gov-
> ernment in America under the auspices of any European power.

Our party, Davis told the Senate, wishes "to cultivate friendship with our republican brethren of Mexico and South America, to aid in con-solidating republican principles, to retain popular government in all this continent from the fangs of monarchical or aristocratic power, and to lead the sisterhood of American republics in the paths of peace, prosper-ity, and power."[27]

From Paris, Malakoff reported that the congressional resolution "fell like a bomb in time of peace." French government newspapers had mis-led the public into thinking the United States would acquiesce in ac-cepting Mexico's "choice" of Maximilian as emperor. "Government people were horrified at any man calling those events 'deplorable,'" Malakoff told his *New York Times* readers, "even the opposition were astonished at the audacity of the word."[28]

Two months later, the Republican Party's 1864 campaign platform endorsed the congressional resolution and added pointedly that the United States "will view with extreme jealousy, as menacing to the peace and independence of their own country, the efforts of any such power to obtain new footholds for Monarchical Government, sustained by foreign military force, in near proximity to the United States."[29]

The aggressive tone of the new Monroe Doctrine surfaced again during the supposed peace talks between Confederate and Union representatives at Hampton Roads, Virginia, in February 1865. Rumors circulated that North and South might cease their war with one another and join forces in an invasion of Mexico to vindicate the Monroe Doctrine. The peace talks failed, but the prospect of war in Mexico sent alarm bells off in Europe.[30]

When Lincoln and Seward met with the Confederate commission, Alexander Stephens, vice president of the Confederacy, was keen on the idea and kept trying to steer the discussion back to upholding what he called the "sacred" principles of the Monroe Doctrine. Stephens seemed to think the Monroe Doctrine sustained the principle of self-determination for Mexico—and the Confederacy. After the peace talks failed, Confederate diplomats tried to turn the rumors of invasion to advantage by warning European powers that the South was "fighting the battles of France and England" and that Lincoln's plan for "one war at a time" meant France would be next.[31] The "rumor of the Monroe Doctrine being made the basis of union" had caused a minor "panic" in Paris. The French consul in New York wrote the home office in Paris, "it might be better . . . if the war were to continue for some time to come."[32]

Europeans watched the steam rising from postwar America with a mix of contempt and apprehension. In April 1865, the United States stood before the world boasting a massive citizen army of more than one million battle-tested soldiers still enlisted, not counting the hundreds of thousands of Confederate and Union veterans who had served earlier. In late May 1865, the Union staged a Grand Review of the Armies at Washington, featuring two days of soldiers passing in review down Pennsylvania Avenue. As William Seward watched the review from a window in the State Department offices, the European diplomats sat toward the front of the presidential reviewing stand where they could take in the parade of military might. Seward's wife, Frances, no doubt spoke for her husband, still recovering from the attempt on his life, after watching the review: "Until I saw these immense armies, I never had any adequate conception of the power of masses of human beings." This army "seems to me invincible," she added, "I am glad to know that the representatives of foreign governments are looking at this wonderful exhibition." So was her husband.[33]

Since the beginning of the Civil War, the British worried that if the Union lost the South, it would take over Canada in compensation. Now,

FIGURE 6. "About the Size of It." This cartoon in *Harper's Weekly*, May 16, 1865, appeared at a time when politicians and the press in Europe were enthralled by rumors, partly true, that the victorious Union was bent on expansion at the expense of European empires in the Americas. Hathitrust.

the talk was of a victorious Union turning northward in revenge. "Monadnock," the pseudonym of Dr. Nicholas, London correspondent to the *New York Times*, summarized what influential Britons were saying. A democracy, they understood, "must rest upon the good will of a people," and "to secure that good will" and forget "past conflicts and humiliations . . . North and South shall join in enterprises which will give them mutual advantages and a common glory." Whatever might happen, there would be no time to waste, for the financial burden of America's large army would compel quick action. "The temptations to this policy of aggrandizement are so great," Monadnock continued, "its advantages so apparent, its necessity even so evident, that the employment of the united armies of the North and South to carry out the Monroe doctrine at once" seemed likely to British observers.[34]

The French were probably more nervous than the British, given all the bluster from Congress and the press about vindicating the Monroe Doctrine in Mexico. Malakoff reported that a speech by Seward at his home in Auburn, New York, made it appear that he was about to move against France in Mexico, causing a rapid dive in the Paris stock exchange. Once the full text of the speech arrived in Paris, it gave "the timid a little more confidence, but does not tranquilize them entirely."[35]

The bellicose rhetoric from America was not all that gave Europe reason to worry. European revolutionaries encouraged the United States to lead the march toward the "Universal Republic" and attack European imperialists in North America. In June 1865, Giuseppe Mazzini, the exiled Italian nationalist, issued a public appeal to America to lead what he called the "Universal Republican Alliance," an international army that would begin by assaulting the "outpost of Caesarism" France was building in Mexico. In a widely circulated public letter, Mazzini told Americans, "you are summoned by the admiration, the sympathies, and expectations of all progressive Europe to affirm yourselves before kings and people, and to carry out a service for the general progress of Humanity." Mazzini and his European revolutionaries wanted, in effect, to globalize the Monroe Doctrine and build a transatlantic republican offensive against autocratic monarchies in the Old and New World.[36]

American enthusiasm for defending the Monroe Doctrine made it a winning message for politicians in both parties. Henry Winter Davis made American retribution the theme of a spread-eagle Fourth of July address in 1865. "We stand to-day, before the nations of the world, as the

FIGURE 7. Giuseppe Mazzini, the intellectual architect of the Italian Risorgimento and international champion of revolutionary republicanism, called on the victorious Union in 1865 to take up its duty to the world by leading what he called the Universal Republican Alliance into war against the "outpost of Caesarism" France and other European powers had erected in Mexico. Wikimedia Commons.

American people never stood before," Davis told a cheering crowd in Chicago. "All Europe was opposed to us. . . . They thought our day of doom was come." "They preyed on helpless neighboring republics in San Domingo, Peru, and Mexico." Now that our trial is over, Davis warned, the American "people have not forgotten the insult, nor ceased to appreciate the greatness of the danger to republican institutions involved in allowing the example of an imperial throne standing on the ruins of an American republic supported by European bayonets."[37]

Montgomery Blair of Maryland, a former member of Lincoln's cabinet, defected from the Republican Party to the Democrats in 1865 and made militant support of the Monroe Doctrine his adopted party's leading issue. Democrats learned that Seward's minister to France, John Bigelow, had told the French government that, while the United States would "prefer" a republican government in Mexico, it "would not go to war" if the Mexican people wished to have a monarchy. For Blair this was blasphemy, a betrayal of the Monroe Doctrine, and part of a pattern of Republican weakness on the issue. "All the world knows that republican institutions were put down in Mexico by French bayonets," Blair thundered. At the same time, "our American Minister is made [by Seward] to say that they were put down by the people themselves!" "What can be more humbling to the pride of our country?"[38]

"America for Americans!" became the slogan of the new Monroe Doctrine, now signifying a Pan-American reproach to European imperialism. The French in Mexico were not the only targets of wrath among what the *New York Times* called the "Crusaders of St. Monroe." In January 1866, the newspaper gave full coverage to an impressive public rally at the Cooper Institute, which had been convened "with the purpose of reaffirming the spirit of the Monroe Doctrine." A banner across the stage exclaimed, "Heroic Santo Domingo, Chile, Peru, Mexico. If they have not conquered, they will conquer." William Cullen Bryant, the voice of Radical Republicanism, presided, and another speaker read letters to a cheering crowd from a string of illustrious political and military figures who could not attend. Montgomery Blair's letter captured the crowd's major grievance against Europe: "The late rebellion was the work of these European Powers. . . . By their money and intrigue it was inaugurated. They fomented, encouraged, and recognized it, with a view to suppress the growth of republicanism in Europe, and to resume their sway over this continent."[39]

The featured speaker was Benjamín Vicuña Mackenna, an eloquent Chilean intellectual whose compatriots in South America faced Spanish naval commanders bent on bullying them into submission. Vicuña Mackenna delivered a rousing speech, pleading for Pan-American solidarity in the face of European aggression. "I am here not officially," he began, "but as a member of the great brotherhood of men—as a friend of liberty and Republican Democracy." All Chileans "learn in the laps of their mothers" the names of George Washington and Abraham Lincoln, the "greatest redeemer that ages have seen since our savior." "Your country is very great and powerful," he told the American audience, "but I tell you that there is another America, your sister.... That sister you have forgotten and forsaken." Vicuña Mackenna went on to make the Monroe Doctrine a Pan-American cause: "We have a Monroe Doctrine of our own.... We understand the Monroe Doctrine to mean not invasion, but protection ... the Kings and Emperors of Europe will not be permitted to interfere with republican institutions on this continent." His rousing speech closed to a "perfect storm of applause."[40]

Vicuña Mackenna put his finger on the new meaning assigned to the Monroe Doctrine. It was now a pact among American republics that would protect the whole hemisphere from the European enemies of republicanism. Another corollary to the Monroe Doctrine also took form in the public mind after 1865. Besides warning against *further* European intervention in the Americas, the new understanding of the Monroe Doctrine seemed to imply that *existing* European colonies were no longer welcome and that it was the duty of the United States to hasten their departure.[41]

The belligerent rhetoric and saber-rattling from America alarmed European observers because they believed America's wild democracy might be stampeded into war before sober minds could calculate the genuine national interest at stake. William Seward had long since earned a reputation for reckless, vindictive remarks against foreign adversaries to win favor with voters. During the Civil War, he loved entertaining foreign diplomats and journalists in a free-wheeling conversation of an evening after brandy and cigars. Full of bluster and boasting, he threatened to "wrap the world in fire" if any European power dared to aid the rebellion. Britain's Prime Minister Lord Palmerston called him a "vapourizing, blustering, ignorant Man" full of "foolish and uncalculating arrogance." Perhaps so, but it left European leaders wondering how Seward's penchant for retribution would play out once the war ended.[42]

Much of Seward's wartime posturing was a calculated strategy to thwart European intervention in favor of the Confederacy. His foreign policy had been defined by the harrowing experience of watching the Union become surrounded by European adversaries, either aiding the Confederacy or invading and subjugating America's defenseless Latin American neighbors. He came out of four years of diplomatic intrigue a master of statecraft. His overriding goal after the war was national security and peace, not territorial aggrandizement or imperialist conquest.

To that end, Seward sought to rid North America of European empires and create a zone of independent, stable, ideally republican nations surrounding the United States. The Caribbean had been especially troublesome during the war, when most ports were in the hands of Union adversaries, Spain, Britain, and France. All had recognized the Confederacy as a belligerent and provided safe harbor to its warships, piratical raiders, and blockade runners. The United States had no Caribbean possessions, no ports to which it might have towed captured Confederate ships, blockade runners, or the captured British mail ship *Trent*, which carried Confederate diplomats to Europe. Seward did not "set out to obtain clear title" of the Caribbean, as the historian Walter LaFeber claimed. He wanted naval bases to sustain a U.S. maritime presence in the region, provide coal, protect merchant vessels, and establish a prize court where the U.S. Navy could bring captured enemy ships. The United States needed naval bases, and Seward sought them energetically, but he repeatedly spurned invitations to acquire and govern Caribbean islands.[43]

Nonetheless, European powers had reason to fear U.S. aggression. It was entirely in keeping with European traditions of warfare for the victors to take possession of enemy territory as reparations to defray the cost of war. The war had left the United States with an enormous debt, a nation of war-weary citizens, and experienced leaders who knew better than to take on another war. No sooner did the Union Army finish the Grand

Review in Washington than the volunteer army melted away almost overnight. The government reduced the regular army to less than 55,000 men, deployed to Reconstruction in the South, suppressing Indians in the West, and clerical duties in Washington (including the massive task of creating an official record of the *War of the Rebellion*). The Navy scrapped most of its 700 ships, including 65 ironclads, and reduced the number of sailors proportionally. Postwar America prepared for peace, not imperialist aggression.[44]

John Bigelow wrote from Paris that news of the Union's disarmament caused a sensation in Europe. "It was to Europeans the most incomprehensible step imaginable. It showed how falsely we had been accused of intending to profit by the peace to adopt an aggressive foreign policy," and above all, "it showed the folly of standing armies in a light in which it had never before been presented." Instead of turning its massive army on Canada, Mexico, or the Caribbean, the United States laid down its arms, discharged its military, and turned to the enormous task of fostering republican institutions at home and creating republican peace in the Americas.[45]

There were periodic bursts of enthusiasm in the press or political circles for acquiring northern Mexico, British Columbia, British North America at large, or, in the Caribbean, Santo Domingo (Dominican Republic), Cuba, and the Danish West Indies (St. Thomas, St. John, and St. Croix). Some initiatives came from the Caribbean territories. The people of Santo Domingo demonstrated great enthusiasm for joining the United States. Cuban revolutionaries invited President Grant to aid their insurrection and annex their island as the only means of ensuring independence from Spain. The colonists of St. Thomas held a plebiscite on the annexation question, during which the "colored people" sported American cockades and spoke warmly of "the liberty and advantages they were to enjoy under the Yankee flag." A few years earlier, Caribbean people of all colors were terrified at the prospect of filibustering expeditions from the United States. With the defeat of the Confederacy and the abolition of slavery, many welcomed the idea of joining a reconstructed United States.[46]

Ultimately, the only significant territorial acquisition on Seward's or Hamilton Fish's watch (1861–73) was Alaska, which faced considerable opposition from Congress and the press. Another accidental acquisition during Seward's term was later known as Midway Island. This tiny Pacific atoll was worthless as a colony, but it came to play a vital role nearly a century later in America's war against fascism.

Some of America's distaste for expansion was rooted in republican ideology. Conquering non-adjacent territory and subjugating alien peoples was the stuff of monarchy and empire. Republics were based on voluntary consent. Territories previously acquired by the United States, Louisiana, Florida, Texas, Oregon, and the Mexican Cession, had all been put on a fast track to statehood with equality of citizenship and representation under the Constitution. Was the Great Republic of America now to assume governance of colonies transferred from European empires?

The aversion to absorbing Latin American colonies and nations was also rooted in racial and cultural antipathy toward the idea of absorbing mixed-race peoples whose language, religion, and historical inexperience with democratic self-government made statesmen like Hamilton Fish think they were unfit for membership in a predominantly Anglo-Saxon nation. The idea of taking on another war-torn former slave society must have seemed unwelcome to a government enduring the violence and turmoil of Reconstruction. "Anybody who . . . with even a faint conception of the magnitude of the problems now awaiting solutions," E. L. Godkin wrote in *The Nation*, "still desires the speedy annexation of Cuba and St. Domingo, with their semi-barbarous populations, to the United States, is a person with whom there is not much use in arguing."[47]

Seward was keen on establishing a U.S. naval base in Samana Bay, a deep, well-protected port in the Dominican Republic. The purpose was to provide a coaling station for U.S. merchant and naval ships and prevent European adversaries from seizing control of this valuable harbor and threatening America's national security. Control of the port at Samana had been the primary purpose of Spain's seizure of the Dominican Republic in 1861.[48] Early in 1865, Seward quietly explored the purchase of Denmark's

West Indian colonies, now known as the U.S. Virgin Islands since acquisition in 1917. Though the United States was willing to pay up to ten million dollars, Denmark wanted fifteen, and when word got out, the press blasted Seward's obsession with "outlandish possession." The controversy over the Alaska Purchase and Republican animosity toward President Johnson and Seward sunk any hope of a deal with Denmark. Seward explained America's indifferent mood in instructions to the U.S. minister to Denmark. America's "desire for the acquisition of territory has sensibly abated" after the Alaska Purchase. "In short, we have come to value dollars more, and dominion less. . . . No absolute need for a naval station in the West Indies is now experienced."[49]

Seward was disappointed that Americans seemed indifferent to the dangers European powers had posed so recently, but he understood which way the wind was blowing. Congress and the public turned against the Johnson administration and did not want to give Seward, the president's staunch defender, any feathers in his cap. Seward also understood the significant disadvantages of governing and defending distant territories and alien peoples that burdened European empires. Rebellious indigenous colonists from Algeria to New Zealand besieged the French and British empires. The French experiment in Mexico was another prime example of the difficulties imperialism entailed. Instead of controlling and governing distant territories, Seward realized that America's Manifest Destiny might arrive through the informal influence of commerce, migration, and information by which America's example of success would spread.

In early 1866, while visiting the Dominican Republic, Seward explained his vision of America's role in the hemisphere in a brief address to the country's president, Buenaventura Baez.

We have built up in the northern part of the American continent a republic. We have laid for it a broad foundation. It has grown up on our hands to be an imposing, possibly a majestic empire. Like every other structure of large proportions, it requires outward buttresses. Those buttresses will arise in the development of civilization in this hemisphere. They will consist of republics like our own, founded in adjacent countries and islands, upon the principle of the equal rights of men. To us, it matters not of what race or lineage these republics shall be. They are necessary for our security against external forces, and, perhaps, for the security of our internal peace. We desire those buttresses to be multiplied, and strengthened, as fast as it can be done, without the exercise of fraud or force on our own part.[50]

Here was Seward's optimistic vision of a United States surrounded by friendly neighbors bound by common republican principles and shared enmity toward European monarchy. The "buttresses" supporting his "majestic empire" would consist of independent, liberal nations, not colonial appendages of predatory European empires and not colonies of the United States. They would coexist in democratic peace in a hemisphere free of monarchy and slavery, the natural enemies of American republicanism.[51]

PART II

America for Americans

FIGURE 8. *The Execution of Maximilian*, painting by Edouard Manet, 1867. The failure of Napoleon III's Grand Design for Mexico created a rallying point for opposition to the Second Empire. France banned Manet's painting, including drawings of it, from public exhibition in France, not least because the soldier on the far right, loading his rifle for the coup de grâce, resembled the French monarch. Maximilian's execution was an alarming message to European empires that they were not welcome in the American hemisphere. Wikimedia Commons.

CHAPTER 3

The Mexican Lesson

The Mexican question involves the fate of the continent. In it is to be decided the antagonism which exists between despotism and liberty, between monarchy and republicanism, and therefore it is a continental question, an American question, which no people in the New World can contemplate with indifference without being false to their destiny.

—FRANCISCO ZARCO, MEXICAN POLITICIAN EXILED TO
NEW YORK CITY, JULY 19, 1865

Two rebellions against liberal republicanism raged simultaneously in North America during the 1860s and were deeply intertwined. In Mexico, the Church Party or Conservatives refused to accept the Constitution of 1857 that governed the Republic of Mexico. After they failed to defeat the Liberals at the ballot box, they plunged Mexico into civil war. Mexico's Reform War (1858–60) ended in Liberal victory just as the United States descended into civil war after Southern slaveholders refused to accept the election of Abraham Lincoln and the Republican Party because it opposed the expansion of slavery. Both rebellions sought allies abroad. Mexico's Conservatives lobbied the crowned heads of Europe to aid them. They welcomed Napoleon III's offer to install Maximilian, the younger brother of Austria's Hapsburg emperor, as the emperor of Mexico. The Confederacy sent envoys to Europe simultaneously, offering inducements of discounted cotton in exchange for aid and a chance to strike a blow against their common enemy, the so-called Great Republic of America.[1]

The Union's distraction during the Civil War made it possible for the French to conquer Mexico with little more than impotent protests from the Lincoln administration. In April 1865, that was about to change. France's intervention in Mexico presented a formidable challenge to the whole future of republicanism in the American hemisphere. According to Napoleon III's Grand Design, Mexico was to become the showcase for the "regeneration" of the Latin race in the New World, a model of monarchical order and Catholic moral authority. It would draw other troubled Latin American republics within its protective shield and create a bulwark against the spread of Anglo-Saxon republicanism from the United States. The expression "French intervention" should not obscure the crucial role of Mexico's Conservatives who enabled it. Composed of ultra-conservative Catholic clergy, the military high command, wealthy landowners, and others, they were entirely in accord with the Grand Design to restore the government of Church and Crown.[2]

Matías Romero, Juárez's young ambassador to Washington, never tired of telling Americans that the two wars raging in Mexico and the United States were part of a far greater contest between aristocracy and democracy, slavery and freedom, that spanned the Atlantic Ocean. Above all, Romero wanted Americans to understand that both insurgencies must be crushed before either republic would be safe.[3]

As Maximilian prepared to take the throne in the spring of 1864, a smoldering mood of resentment across the Union ignited. Congress grew impatient with Seward and Lincoln, who feared that any aggressive response to the French in Mexico would give the Confederates an ally. Congress wanted more than just polite diplomatic protests, and, in a stunning show of bipartisan spirit, both houses unanimously passed a joint resolution stating the United States would never recognize Maximilian's regime.[4]

At the same time, Romero stoked outrage through the clubs he and others helped organize in support of Mexico. He also staged well-publicized banquets in New York, inviting dozens of prominent public

FIGURE 9. Matías Romero began his diplomatic career in the Republic of Mexico's Washington legation in 1861 at the age of twenty-four. He rushed to meet president-elect Abraham Lincoln early in 1861 to press the idea that the two rebellions in North America, Mexico's Conservative Church Party against Benito Juárez's liberal republic and America's Slave Power against Lincoln's Republican government, were integrally connected and both must be crushed before either nation would be secure. Wikimedia Commons.

figures to speak. In speeches, pamphlets, and even popular songs, Americans and Mexicans denounced France and vented their impatience with the Lincoln administration for not standing up for Mexico and America's Monroe Doctrine.

The rumors from the peace conference in Hampton Roads in February 1865 that the peace terms might involve the two armies joining forces to invade Mexico and topple Maximilian from his throne lit up the international press and caused consternation in Paris.[5]

The following month, Seward responded to France's "apprehension of aggression" from the United States, assuring the government that the "executive government" had no plans to take action in Mexico. There might be reasonable cause for concern, he added, that "the national will, under high excitement, may overrule the peaceful purposes of the executive government." In plain language, if France did not peacefully withdraw from Mexico, there is no telling what Congress and the American public might get up to. It would be for France to decide.[6]

In April 1865, events conspired to upset Seward's plan for a peaceful solution in Mexico. He suffered a terrible carriage accident on April 5, leaving him lying in bed with a broken arm and jaw and a leather-covered iron brace protecting his jaw. Nine days later, the night Lincoln was shot, one of John Wilkes Booth's gang of assassins burst into Seward's bedroom with his pistol drawn. After his gun jammed, the assailant lunged at Seward with a Bowie knife, gashing his face and neck. Seward's right cheek had been nearly severed from his face, but the jaw brace saved his life from more fatal cuts. To add to Seward's misery, his son Frederick suffered severe injuries while shielding his father, and his beloved wife, Fanny, was so traumatized she fell seriously ill and died weeks later. Many expected Seward to retire from office, yet he was determined to return to duty. During this crucial interlude, rivals plotted a different course on the Mexico Question.[7]

Days after taking office, President Andrew Johnson summoned Matías Romero to the White House for a private meeting. Romero had long been frustrated with Lincoln and Seward because of their caution about challenging the French in Mexico, and he had high hopes for Johnson. "Suddenly," he wrote to the Juárez government in Chihuahua, "a change of administration has occurred from which Mexico will sup-posedly be among those able to draw the most advantage."

Johnson began their meeting by asking if Secretary of State William Seward knew they were meeting. Romero was not entirely honest, assuring the president that he had brought his concerns "repeatedly to Seward's attention." That was true, but Romero avoided telling the president that Seward, bedridden at his home a few doors from the White House, knew nothing about this meeting and would be furious once he found out.[8]

Romero saw in Andrew Johnson a strong advocate for Mexico and the Monroe Doctrine. During the 1864 election, Johnson gave a bom-bastic speech in Nashville that elevated his reputation as a fearless champion of Mexico and the Monroe Doctrine, a popular gesture with both parties. "The day of reckoning is approaching," he told the boister-ous crowd. "It will not be long before the Rebellion is put down. . . . and then we will attend to this Mexican affair, and say to Louis Napoleon, 'You cannot found a monarchy on this Continent.'" The crowd roared its applause, and it no doubt helped the bipartisan ticket Johnson and Lincoln rode to victory that fall.[9]

Romero flattered Johnson, telling him he thought so much of his Nashville speech that he had translated it for President Juárez. Johnson "listened very attentively and without interrupting," except to ask ques-tions about the military needs of Mexico's republican army. Romero gushed that he "had rejoiced with all my heart at his accession to power." Mexico, he added, also rejoiced. President Johnson, he told his government, "could not hide his pleasure upon learning of my report on these matters." Romero came away from the White House that day highly satisfied that in Andrew Johnson, Mexico finally had a U.S. presi-dent willing to defend the Monroe Doctrine.[10]

Six days later, Romero met General Ulysses S. Grant, commander of the Union Army, at his home in Washington. Grant felt he owed Mexico something for his part in the regrettable war against Mexico almost twenty years earlier. He wrote in his memoirs that war was "one of the most unjust ever waged by a stronger against a weaker nation" and a shameful "instance of a republic following the bad example of European monarchies."[11]

Grant was also keenly alert to the national security threat Maximilian's regime posed. During the war, the French intervention had allowed Confederates to circumvent the Union blockade by allowing cotton exports and essential imports to come in at Matamoros, a border town near the mouth of the Rio Grande with a deep-water port on the Gulf of Mexico dubbed "Bagdad." The Matamoros "back door" was a lifeline for the rebellion, and without it, the Civil War would have ended much sooner.[12]

Maximilian's threat to national security did not end there. As the war ended, he was actively recruiting Confederate refugees to colonize northern Mexico and bring their slaves with them. Grant foresaw that Maximilian was creating a base from which diehard rebels would carry on a revanchist war against the United States and create an obstacle protecting Maximilian's empire against invasion by U.S. forces. The day after General Lee surrendered, Grant allegedly rose from his desk at headquarters in City Point and announced, "Now for Mexico!"[13]

Romero came away from his first meeting with Grant altogether thrilled by the general's "upright intentions and love of justice" and, not least, his "Americanism," meaning his spirit of Pan-American republican solidarity. "I believe we can already count him as one of the best friends of our country," he wrote the foreign office in June 1865. Grant "could not do more if he were a Mexican." Romero and Grant forged a close collaboration whose purpose was to carry out what amounted to an unofficial, covert foreign policy for Mexico.[14]

While Seward convalesced, Grant took full advantage of President Johnson's cooperative spirit on Mexico. For General Grant, a man of action, the Mexico Question was a military problem that required a military solution. On May 17, 1865, he ordered General Philip Sheridan, a celebrated Union general, to go immediately to the Texas border and take command of some 52,000 troops assembled there. Grant ordered Sheridan to apprehend Confederate holdouts under the command of Confederate general Kirby Smith and crush whatever other resistance he met. Grant also ordered Sheridan to shut down the stream of Confederates taking refuge in Mexico.[15]

Sheridan was fully in tune with Grant and Romero regarding the purpose and meaning of his mission on the border of America's "sister republic." The very "appearance of our troops, and the knowledge that friends were on the border, went like electricity to the homes and hearts of the Mexican people. . . . this hardy people, without money, without arms and munitions of war, and without supplies" would decide "the destiny of imperialism." Sheridan always felt that "the occupation of Mexico was a part of the rebellion; and knowing that the contest in our own country was for the vindication of republicanism, I did not think that vindication would be complete until Maximilian was driven out of Mexico."[16]

Once Sheridan took command, Grant issued oblique instructions for Sheridan to move surplus weapons to the Mexican army: "Place them convenient to be permitted to go into Mexico if they can be got into the hands of the defenders of the only Government we recognize in that country." Grant had a talent for lacing political grievances against France into the otherwise brusque military orders he sent to Sheridan. "We want then to aid the Mexicans without giving cause of War between the United States and France. Between the would-be Empire of Maximilian and the United States all difficulty can easily be settled by observing the same sort of neutrality that has been observed towards us for the last four years."

Mexico needed men also, and Grant devised an ingenious scheme to supply them. He ordered Sheridan "to discharge all the men you think can be spared" and allow them to return home or go where they pleased. "You are aware," he reminded Sheridan, "that existing orders permit discharged soldiers to retain their arms and accouterments at low rates, fixed in orders?" Though careful to avoid blatant violation of U.S. neutrality laws, Grant authorized armed and willing U.S. volunteers to join the Mexican republicans in their war against the French occupation.[17]

Grant and Romero took this a step further. They secretly worked out an elaborate ruse whereby Union general John M. Schofield, whom Grant put on official leave, would conduct an "inspection tour" of U.S. forces along the Rio Grande. He would then cross into Mexico, taking any officers and soldiers who wished to follow. Once in Mexico, they would enlist in the Mexican republican army and pay their salaries out of funds loaned to Mexico by the United States.[18] President Johnson gave Grant free rein, though he urged caution when it came to any action that might provoke war with France. "In all that relates to the Mexican Affairs," Grant wrote Sheridan in July 1865, Johnson "agrees in the duty we owe to ourselves to maintain the Monroe Doctrine."[19]

Meanwhile, as he returned to duty in Washington, Seward was furious to learn of Grant and Romero's secretive foreign policy scheme. Probably at Seward's insistence, President Johnson called Grant to the White House cabinet meeting on June 16 to explain what he had in mind for Mexico. Seward was frail, in severe pain, his face still encased in an iron brace, and he could barely speak, yet he attended with a firm resolve to stop Grant's dangerous game on the border.

The president asked Grant to lead off, and he launched into his view that Mexico was an integral component of the yet-unfinished war. "The act of attempting to establish a Monarchy on this continent, was an act of known hostility to the Government of the United States," Grant told the cabinet. Such aggression "would not have been undertaken but for the great war which was raging, at the time and which it was supposed by all the great powers of Europe, except possibly Russia, would result in the dismemberment of the country and the overthrow of Republican institutions."

During the war, Grant continued, the imperialists in France and Mexico had violated all pretense of neutrality by allowing a massive stream of commerce through Matamoros to sustain the rebellion. More was at stake than settling scores with France or Maximilian; there were ominous signs that diehard Confederates were planning to carry on a war of revenge against the United States under the protection of Maximilian and France. "I see nothing before us but a long, expensive and bloody war; one in which the enemies of this country will be joined by tens of thousands of disciplined soldiers embittered against their government by the experience of the last four years. . . . Rebel immigrants will go with arms in their hands. . . . their leaders will espouse the cause of the Empire, purely out of hostility to this [U.S.] government." In short, the U.S. Civil War was not yet over and would not be until Mexico's civil war ended.[20]

After Grant concluded, Seward gathered his strength to take the floor. Speaking barely above a whisper, Seward conceded the main point: France must leave Mexico. However, he warned there were grave dangers in provoking war with France, which Grant's military aggression would surely do.

Seward proposed an alternative diplomatic solution. Napoleon III would pull out of Mexico once he understood that the United States would never recognize Maximilian's regime and would never tolerate a European monarch imposed upon a neighboring country. Seward was aligning himself with the congressional resolution of the previous year. He knew from his minister in Paris, John Bigelow, that France's liberal opposition was embarrassing Napoleon III over the Mexico Question. Jules Favre, a leading voice of the opposition, had recently issued a withering attack before the Corps Législatif on the exorbitant expense of the Mexico venture that left the imperialist deputies sitting in dour silence. The opposition exposed the excessive cost and corruption involved with the Mexican expedition. Worse, they also made it a prime example of the failings of Napoleon III's "personal government," a polite term for dictatorship.[21]

Seward understood the vital connections between domestic politics and foreign policy as few others did. He warned the cabinet that U.S. aggression in Mexico would rally the French public behind the emperor and shame the liberal opposition into silence. France would pull the United States into a war neither nation could afford. Seward also spoke of the possibility that Britain, Belgium, and Austria might enter the fray in a show of European solidarity. Worse still, if the United States became tied down in such a war, diehard Southerners might decide to make common cause with the French and raise the banner of secession again. He gave the cabinet plenty to ponder.[22]

Seward then raised an unexpected argument against U.S. military intervention. It might lead to the exchange of French for American occupation. Bigelow had warned Seward that the French would love nothing more than to "find some adequate pretext for taking Mexico off the end of their spear, with our own." The "on to Mexico" enthusiasm whipped up in the American press and Mexican recruitment drives promising boundless riches to U.S. "immigrants" were reminiscent of Southern filibusterism in the 1850s. Elaborate schemes to annex Mexico's silver mining district in Sonora were also in the wind. Seward warned that U.S. troops might invade Mexico to drive out the French, only to find "we could not get out ourselves." To America's shame, an army of liberation would become an army of occupation.[23]

Secretary of the Navy Gideon Welles watched Seward explain the dangers of Grant's plan while presenting his measured advice with all the wisdom and statecraft he commanded. That evening, Welles confided to his diary: "Seward acts from intelligence; Grant from impulse."[24]

As Seward reasserted his control of foreign policy at the cabinet meeting in June, a few days later, his reasoned diplomatic solution ran into a hailstorm of public outrage. At the end of the month, the French minister of state, Eugène Rouher, leaked a private conversation with John Bigelow, in which the U.S. diplomat candidly told him the United States would not go to war over the form of government the Mexican people preferred, whether monarchical or republican. Bigelow added honestly, "The success of republican institutions in Spanish America had not been such as to justify us becoming their armed propagandists."

Bigelow's concession was sheer heresy in the minds of many Americans. He contradicted the fundamental creed underlying the postwar Monroe Doctrine, that republican government was the default choice of all American nations, indeed people everywhere, if only they were free to choose. Monarchies and dictatorships always imposed their arbitrary power against the people's will, most thought, so they could never result from free and fair elections. That, after all, is why autocratic states required standing armies, police, and censors to silence the people's voice.[25]

It was a classic political gaffe, an official carelessly saying out loud what he (and, by implication, Seward) truly believed. In a private letter to Seward, Bigelow confessed doubt about Mexico's capacity for self-government. They "belong to a different race from ours, . . . speak a different language, . . . possess a different religion" and have no experience with self-government. America cannot "propagate republicanism by the sword." Furthermore, he wrote, "no action of the Latin Race has succeeded in establishing a government worthy of being called Republican."[26]

Bigelow's gaffe brought American outrage to a boil. Montgomery Blair, a Maryland Democrat, went after Bigelow for saying the United States "can understand how Mexico" having been under a monarchy for so long "would like to return to that form of government." Blair wondered if he could not say the same for the people of "our country," who also lived under an English monarchy for generations.[27]

John Jay, a prominent New York Republican and namesake of his illustrious grandfather, gave Bigelow a public tongue-lashing at a Fourth of July celebration in Paris. Not satisfied, Jay followed with a published pamphlet whose title said it all: *An Imperial Policy Not Fitted for an American Minister*. He came after Bigelow again in a published lecture to the New York Union League Club. Blair's and Jay's harsh responses to Seward and Bigelow's soft stance on the Monroe Doctrine indicated broad bipartisan support for an aggressive, pro-republican Monroe Doctrine after 1865.[28]

Later, in July 1865, Matías Romero organized a meeting at the Cooper Union in New York City designed to answer Bigelow's doubts about Mexico's commitment to republicanism. The meeting was "the first of its kind ever held," featuring distinguished exiled Mexican leaders who vigorously supported the Monroe Doctrine and called on Americans to defend it in Mexico. Among the Mexican speakers were José Rivera, a novelist and soldier who escaped capture by the French; Francisco Zarco, a politician and journalist; Manuel Balbontin, a military officer; and Joaquín Villalobos, a fiery editor. Reverend Joshua Leavitt, the author of an influential pamphlet on the Monroe Doctrine, acted as chair and welcomed the Mexican speakers as "members of the general American brotherhood."[29]

Though mainly delivered in Spanish, with English translation, the speeches were in the common idiom of Pan-American republicanism. They spoke of the Manichean contest between the forces of monarchy against republicanism and religious dogma against secular freedom. They held up the Monroe Doctrine as a shield protecting all American republics. It was as if they had all been schooled in the same romantic language and ideas of the nineteenth century.

In one of the more flamboyant speeches, Joaquín Villalobos blasted the *New York Times* for its betrayal of the Monroe Doctrine in a recent anonymous article defending the French intervention and questioning the capacity of Mexicans to govern themselves. A paper "that applauds the abolition of slavery at home" yet "approves the enslavement of a whole nation—can that be the organ of free men?" "Let us then march forward," he implored the audience, "let the American people see only the common enemy, and come to the rescue; let the torches of civil war in the United States and in Mexico be extinguished in the blood of the minions of Napoleon. . . . The destinies of the new world hang on your decisions . . . you can make the world respect American institutions, or, neglecting this duty, expose them to the scorn and aggression of tyranny and fraud."[30]

The enthusiasm for "On to Mexico" inspired a flurry of popular tunes and sheet music adorned with comical cartoons that captured the popular mood toward Maximilian. The irreverent cartoon on the cover of "Maxy" showed the emperor of Mexico sitting on the mouth of a cannon about to be ignited by a Black Union soldier. "Get Out of Mexico!" "Oh! I Vants to Go Home," "How Are You Maximilian, or Off for Mexico," and "We'll Go with Grant Again: Song of the Sons of Monroe" were among the dozens of songs that cheered the American public. The lyrics from the last jingle give some indication of the martial spirit of the moment:

> Napoleon, down in Mexico, is fighting rather shy
> But Uncle Sam has let him know that he had better quit;
> We're slow to take offence, my boys, but "mighty hard" to hit;
> We'll take the old familiar guns and go with Grant again.[31]

Running through the lyrics were familiar themes of North and South reuniting in defense of the Monroe Doctrine and a pronounced Pan-American spirit favoring the rescue of a "sister republic" from the tyranny of European despotism. The cover of "Get Out of Mexico" showed

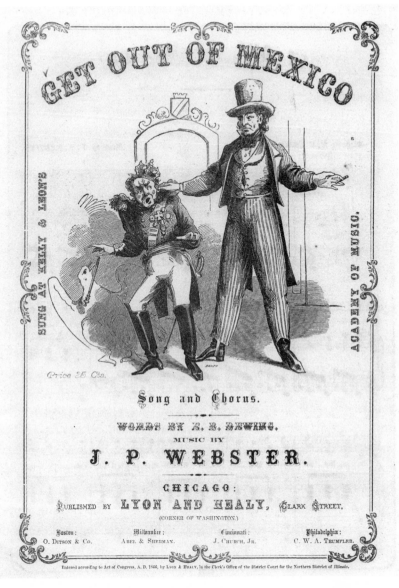

FIGURE 10. "Get Out of Mexico." Sheet music for one of dozens of popular songs that whipped up popular indignation toward the French and Maximilian while Civil War veterans were volunteering for service in Mexico. More than any other European incursion in the Americas, the French intervention and Maximilian's Catholic monarchical regime fueled a new spirit for the Monroe Doctrine and its motto, "America for Americans." Library of Congress.

a stout Uncle Sam taking a boyish Maximilian by the ear. The lyrics went:

> Now, political tradition,
> Since the time of James Monroe,
> Had prevented interference
> In affairs of Mexico
> By the crowned heads of Europe
> Until just the moment when
> Uncle Sam had both his hands full
> With some desperate naughty men.[32]

These militant tunes accompanied the recruitment drive for American volunteers to join the Mexican republicans in arms. Colonel William H. Allen, a veteran who served in two Ohio infantry units, operated as an agent of Mexican general Jesús Gonzáles Ortega, a political rival of Juárez. Allen advertised in several New York papers in May 1865, calling for recruits to join the "Mexican Emigration Company." One of his posters had "MEXICO, MAXIMILIAN, AND MONROE DOCTRINE" across the top. "All persons who desire joining a company soon starting 'to make a strike' for fame and fortune in the land of golden ores and luscious fruits." Recruits were promised $1,000 cash bounties and 800 acres of land in Mexico. The response was strong. Allen claimed, likely with exaggeration, that within a month and a half, he had enlisted 109,000 "emigrants," including several thousand from Southern states.[33]

The *New York Herald* envisioned the American volunteers as an army of liberation for Cuba as well as Mexico. "There are a hundred thousand of these tried men now ready to be off to the land of the Montezuma at a moment's notice. If these men once became possessed of the idea nothing could prevent them from dropping in at the island of Cuba by the way ... the armed visitors would be heartily welcomed by the mass of the people of Cuba, and the emancipation question, about which there is so much fear and trouble, would be decided without much further delay."[34]

At most, a few thousand of the "Crusaders for Saint Monroe," the *New York Times* nickname, ever made it to Mexico. French diplomats in

New York and Washington protested Ortega and Allen's recruitment scheme as a clear violation of U.S. neutrality. Then it fell apart for want of funds. Allen tried to sue Ortega but was left holding the bag. The recruitment drive failed but not for want of American volunteers willing to "take the fight to Mexico."[35]

Matías Romero estimated that no more than three thousand American volunteers fought with the Mexican republican army. Another two thousand, primarily Confederate veterans, volunteered to fight for Maximilian. The requirements of secrecy, Mexican national pride, and the fog of war made precise numbers hard to come by.[36]

The new militant spirit caught fire among American citizens, particularly Union veterans. The Monroe League, a new group in San Francisco, staged banquets and torchlight parades to raise money and men for Mexico. The Defenders of the Monroe Doctrine organized units in New Orleans and Brownsville, Texas. Several pro-Mexico clubs, fostered by Matías Romero and others during the war, also spawned interest among veterans in joining arms with the Republic of Mexico. Letters from volunteers poured into the Mexican legation in Washington, and large crowds of men gathered outside its doors. Mexican agents secretly sponsored much of the recruitment and paid handsome bounties in cash and land to foreigners willing to fight for Juárez and the republic. The Mexican agents, in turn, hired veteran Union officers to recruit "emigrants" to Mexico as a ploy to avoid outright violation of neutrality laws.[37]

In Mexico, French forces pressed Juárez's Republican Army hard, forcing it to retreat northward from San Luis de Potosi to Chihuahua. Then in August 1865, as French troops advanced, Juárez moved to El Paso del Norte (Ciudad Juárez), just south of the border. If necessary, he was prepared to seek refuge in the United States if necessary. Sheridan was disgusted by Seward's inaction as he watched Juárez's republic nearly succumb.[38]

Seeing the republican enemy in retreat, Maximilian put aside efforts at reconciliation and, in early October 1865, issued a stunning imperial edict known as the Black Decree. The decree declared victory and falsely claimed that Juárez's republican government "has left the country" for the United States. "From now on, the struggle will be between honorable men of the nation and bands of criminals and brigands. The time of indulgence has passed." The Black Decree warned that further armed resistance would meet with summary executions. Maximilian later claimed he only planned to terrorize the opposition, but his imperial army slew tens of thousands of republican officers and men. At the end of 1865, Juárez and the republicans stood with their backs to the wall facing a war to the death. The United States faced hard decisions as well.[39]

Sheridan had no illusions that a trickle of volunteers crossing into Mexico would be sufficient, or come soon enough, to turn the tide. He wrote to Grant that the Rio Grande border was a desert, and American soldiers could not live as Mexicans did on a diet of "frijolis and tortas." For U.S. volunteers to be supplied, a port of entry must be established at Matamoros, which could be easily taken with a force of six thousand troops, but quick action was imperative, Sheridan thought. Louis Napoleon waited too long to solidify control of Mexico. "Had he anticipated the rapidity with which the bottom fell out of the [Confederate] rebellion," he wrote Grant, "we would have had much work on our hands; therefore let us not imitate his example and wait too long in this Mexican affair lest we make a mistake."[40]

By this time, General Jo Shelby and his Confederate veterans had joined the imperial forces along the border. William Gwin, a Mississippi planter who served California as a U.S. senator, met with Napoleon III in Paris and enlisted his interest in a plan to colonize Mexico's rich northern mining district. He then went to Mexico to meet with Marshal Bazaine and officials in Maximilian's government to promote the scheme. Soon rumors of "Gwin's Dukedom" raced through the international press. Other prominent Confederates were collaborating with Maximilian's government to colonize some of the most fertile portions of Mexico. Seward's optimistic assurances that time would be on the side of Mexico's republic did little to assuage Sheridan as he watched French troops and Confederate reinforcements assemble across the Rio Grande in the autumn of 1865.[41]

In late July 1865, Seward had John Bigelow deliver a strong protest to the French foreign minister, Drouyn de Lhuys, that included a veiled threat of war. Bigelow objected to ex-Confederates, officers, and soldiers, two thousand in all, entering Mexico to serve in Maximilian's imperial army. He also reiterated Seward's earlier instructions to Sheridan that he was to engage in "no aggressive action" in Mexico "unless under special instructions" which may be "rendered necessary by a condition of affairs not now anticipated."[42]

Napoleon III was sufficiently alarmed to write a confidential letter alerting Marshal Bazaine, commander of French forces in Mexico, to the growing danger of U.S. intervention in Mexico: "Our relations with the United States are not bad; however, they take on a character that could become serious." He warned that a U.S. invasion might be imminent and urged Bazaine to concentrate his forces around the capital.[43]

Shortly after Bigelow delivered Seward's threatening message, Sheridan staged a startling demonstration of force on the Rio Grande. It began with Sheridan reviewing U.S. troops stationed at San Antonio, apparently to ready them for battle. Then he conspicuously opened communications with Juárez asking questions about forage for his army and ordering pontoons to bridge the river. Rumors were "spreading like wildfire" on both sides of the river that Sheridan was about to invade.

In obedience to Seward's carefully worded instructions, Sheridan never crossed into Mexican territory. Still, his feint was enough to compel the French to withdraw from Matamoros and northern Mexico south to Monterrey, as Napoleon III had instructed Bazaine. The French retreat presented a "golden opportunity," so Sheridan thought, to cross over, run the French down, and bring the war to an end. Seward remained fixed on the diplomatic path and issued strict orders against any "active sympathy" with the Mexican republicans. In his memoirs, Sheridan blasted Seward's "slow and poky methods," which he blamed for exposing Mexico's republican army to another year and a half of unnecessary bloodletting. In truth, Seward was using the threat of military intervention to pressure France into taking the diplomatic route he advised. The combination worked in the end.[44]

Seward might use the threat of military action, but he did not trust Grant's scheme to send General Schofield into Mexico to command an army of American volunteers. Immediately after learning about Grant's plan, Seward enticed Schofield to accept a plum assignment in Paris as his special agent. Though he had no experience in diplomacy or politics, Schofield was happy to go to Paris with a handsome purse and the able assistance of John Bigelow. Seward wanted Schofield to say "in language that could not be misunderstood," in a manner "perhaps impossible, to express . . . in official diplomatic language that an emperor could afford to receive from a friendly power." More to the point, he instructed Schofield, "Get your legs under Napoleon's mahogany, and tell him he must get out of Mexico."[45]

Unlike Grant and Romero, Seward did not see the French intervention in Mexico integrally tied to resolving America's Civil War. It was a diplomatic problem, and Seward realized the French were beginning to crack. Time was on his side. Seward delayed for months before sending Schofield over. It was not until mid-November 1865 that Schofield sailed for France. Whether or not by design, the delay increased tensions in France, where the press was stoking apprehension over the arrival of the mysterious Union general, and Napoleon's court was buzzing with rumors of war.[46]

Schofield began his bizarre mission in Paris with a promising performance at the American Thanksgiving dinner at the Grand Hotel, a spectacular new hotel that, incidentally, had been headquarters for John Slidell and his Confederate legation during the war. The crowd and the Parisian press were eager to hear Schofield, who sat at the front table with all eyes upon him.

A toast in Schofield's honor set off rousing applause while the band struck up "Yankee Doodle Dandy." In reply, Schofield spoke of the marvels of America's democracy at war. Among "the great lessons taught by the American war," he said to the hushed crowd, was that its government, though almost invisible in peace, in time of war quickly became "one of the strongest in the world [cheers], raising and maintaining armies and navies vaster than any ever before known [cheers]." Schofield closed with a soothing toast to "the old friendship between France and the United States: may it be strengthened and perpetuated." No one in the room could have missed the warning. Of course, he was playing to a primarily American audience, but reports of his Paris debut ran in the French press.[47]

A few days later, Bigelow reported to Seward that General Schofield's presence in Paris "still engrosses public attention." Many believe "he has been instructed to make some peremptory communication to the French government about Mexico." Our relation with France, he told Seward, "preoccupies the attention of all journals, of all classes and of all interests . . . the feeling here is intense. It alarms the government." Bigelow expected "an important crisis in our relations with France" would erupt in the coming week. In light of the "universal unpopularity" of the Mexican expedition, Bigelow thought the emperor would "take a step backwards" before braving the disapproval of his people, "and ours," he wrote to Seward.[48]

Schofield never did get his legs under the emperor's mahogany, and there was no need to do so. His mere presence in Paris had the effect of arousing the public mind of France. Without bluster or threats, the modest American general amplified Seward's message that time was running out and France must get out of Mexico.[49]

Seward continued ramping up pressure on France through President Johnson's first annual message to Congress in December 1865. Seward drafted the portion on foreign policy, which reviewed the struggle between American republicanism and European monarchism. Though it never mentioned the Monroe Doctrine or the French intervention in Mexico, both were present in nearly every sentence Seward drafted. It would be a "great calamity . . . to the peace of the world," Johnson's address concluded, "should any European power challenge the American people, as it were, to the defense of republicanism against foreign interference."[50]

Immediately after Johnson's address, Seward instructed Bigelow to issue what amounted to a firm ultimatum on December 16, 1865. France must "desist from the prosecution of armed intervention in Mexico, to overthrow the domestic republican government existing there, and

FIGURE 11. The Bagdad Raid. In early January 1866, Black U.S. soldiers, with uniform insignia removed, joined a clandestine raid on Bagdad and Matamoros and U.S. troops then crossed the Rio Grande to restore order. The U.S. willingness to cross the border alarmed French diplomats, and Napoleon III chose to hasten the withdrawal of occupation forces. *Harper's Weekly*, January 5, 1867. Hathitrust.

to establish upon its ruins the foreign monarchy which has been attempted to be inaugurated in that country's capital."[51]

Emperor Napoleon III felt the pressure to get out of Mexico coming from all directions. Across the Rhine River, Prussia was rising as a formidable Continental rival. France's liberal opposition was having a field day with the Mexican imbroglio, making it a prime example of imperial failure. Some in the French press were turning against Napoleon III. One author in the prestigious *Revue des Deux Mondes* despaired, "How long shall we prosecute this gigantic folly?"[52]

Then, alarming news arrived from Mexico. In January 1866, a band of U.S. soldiers, mostly "colored troops" wearing Union uniforms with all insignia removed, crossed the border near Brownsville, Texas, to raid Bagdad, the bustling port for Matamoros at the mouth of the Rio Grande. The raid was organized by a former Confederate colonel,

R. Clay Crawford, who was part of General Lew Wallace's clandestine Mexico operations. The attack contradicted Wallace's explicit instructions not to cross into Mexico, lest France have an excuse to strike back. Though Seward and other U.S. officials dismissed the raid as a rogue filibuster operation with no official sanction, an account by one of Maximilian's imperial army officers described something far more formidable. Over six hundred Black soldiers in "full uniform" and "led by their officers" came across the Rio Grande, the French forces fleeing before them. They pillaged the town, murdering citizens and raping women, then returned across the river with their loot. France protested the Bagdad Raid but nothing more. The Bagdad raid demonstrated that France was unlikely to engage U.S. forces, even if they crossed into Mexico. Napoleon III also realized that France could not effectively defend Maximilian's empire without risking war with the United States.[53]

On January 22, 1866, during his annual address to the Corps Législatif, Napoleon III made a long-awaited yet startling announcement. France's mission in Mexico was *touche à son terme* (coming to an end). In a series of falsehoods, the emperor stated the Mexican Empire, "founded by the will of the people, is being consolidated; the non-contents [republicans] vanquished and dispersed, have no longer any leader." He said he was "coming to an understanding with the Emperor Maximilian for fixing the period for recalling our troops." At this, opposition deputies burst into loud cheers, clearly intending to embarrass the government.[54]

In the January speech, Napoleon III echoed the same fabulist narrative Mexico's Conservatives had propagated earlier, that the Mexican people welcomed Maximilian as their savior and thanked France for freeing them from republican anarchy. No one familiar with the scene in Mexico believed that Maximilian would last long without the French to defend his throne. He was forced to resort to foreign mercenaries because the Mexican imperial army was weak and untrustworthy. There was little popular support, even among his Conservative Mexican sponsors, the Catholic clergy and landed aristocracy. They felt alienated by his refusal to restore the Catholic Church's control of education and land and his fruitless efforts to reach out to bring republicans into the imperial government. Maximilian proved too liberal for Mexico's Church Party and too monarchical and foreign for Mexico's republicans.

The emperor's January speech also addressed the United States. He began by issuing "sincere wishes for the prosperity of the great American Republic, and for the maintenance of amicable relations, now of nearly a century's duration." He also alluded to Lincoln's assassination for the first and only time, noting the French public's manifestations of grief (he might have added republican sympathy) as proof of France's goodwill toward America. Referring to the recent tensions over Mexico, the French emperor promised that "the emotion produced in the United States by the presence of the French army on Mexican soil will be appeased by the frankness of our declarations."[55]

The exact schedule for the French withdrawal was left unclear. It was not until early April 1866 that Le Moniteur, the government organ, explained that Napoleon III had in mind a staged withdrawal of French forces from Mexico that would begin in November 1866 and end in November 1867. Many speculated Napoleon III was buying time, almost two years, for Maximilian to build an imperial army and rally support from the Mexican people. Under growing pressure from Congress and the press, Seward stepped up the pressure as the first withdrawal stage in November neared.[56]

Meanwhile, the covert traffic in arms was moving in greater volume across the U.S. border to Juárez's desperate army. During the winter and spring of 1866, Sheridan stepped up shipments, supplying an estimated 30,000 guns from the Baton Rouge arsenal alone.[57] More and better weapons were coming through new U.S. channels, thanks to Lew Wallace, an ardent Republican from Indiana who had served at Grant's side during the war. Wallace worked closely with General José Carvajal, who led Mexico's republican forces in northern Mexico. Wallace also enlisted Herman Sturm, a German immigrant in Indiana with a deep commitment to Pan-American republicanism and valuable contacts with European arms suppliers. Sturm procured armament for an estimated 40,000 infantry, 3,000 cavalry, 15 artillery batteries, 2,000 engineers, one million rations, and a sizable collection of medical supplies.[58]

Before this influx of arms, the Mexican republican army engaged in asymmetrical warfare against far better-armed and more numerous troops. Wallace was astonished to learn that General Carvajal's men were reduced to using bows and arrows against the French. With U.S. help, the republican army was prepared to meet the imperialists on more equal terms with modern weaponry.

At Santa Gertrudis, about ninety miles west of Matamoros, on June 16, 1866, republicans under the command of General Mariano Escobedo intercepted a massive caravan of two hundred wagons transporting $3 million in silver and other valuable merchandise from Matamoros to Monterrey. One-quarter of the thousand men with Escobedo that day were veterans of North America's other civil war, including many from U.S. Colored regiments. In one hour of fierce fighting, the republicans cut the imperialist forces to ribbons, confiscated the entire cargo, and captured one thousand prisoners.[59]

In glorious triumph, General Escobedo called on his soldiers to fight on. The "border will be truly free from the hateful presence of the invaders and their accomplices; we will carry the war to the interior of the Republic and we will help our brothers to fight, until expelling from our territory the slaves of Napoleon III."[60]

The Battle of Santa Gertrudis became known as the "Waterloo of the Mexican Empire." Soon after, the French abandoned Matamoros and evacuated northern Mexico. Mexican soldiers in the imperial army laid down their arms and defected to the Liberals before they would fight for Maximilian. Within a short time, republicans took possession of the entire length of the Rio Grande and most of the territory down to San Louis Potosi. As the French retreated from Matamoros, rumors circulated that they might pull out of Mexico ahead of schedule.[61] Mexican soldiers did most of the fighting, to be sure, but American arms and men played a vital part in the war. So did Lew Wallace and Herman Sturm, two unsung heroes in Mexico's Second War for Independence.[62]

By the summer of 1866, with French troops in retreat from a reinvigorated republican army, Maximilian was desperate to save his Mexican empire. Empress Carlota took desperate measures in desperate times.

She sailed to Europe in August 1866 to beg Napoleon III not to abandon Mexico and her husband's imperiled throne. She met with the emperor and Empress Eugénie in Paris, only to learn that they were unwilling to do anything more to defend the empire France had created in Mexico.

Even as they met, Napoleon III decided to move up the last stage of withdrawal by eight months, from November to March 1867. He cabled Maximillian to explain, "We are in fact approaching a decisive moment for Mexico. . . . It is henceforward impossible for me to give Mexico another écu or another soldier." Carlota confirmed the sad news with a terse telegram to her husband, "Todo es inútil" (All is useless).[63]

While Emperor Napoleon III accelerated the withdrawal in the summer of 1866, his military commander in Mexico, Marshal Bazaine, seemed intent on dragging it out. He gave excuses about various difficulties in the evacuation plan and promised to begin in November 1866. Some suspected the delay was to provide Maximilian time to establish his regime with the Mexicans, train his imperial army, and advance the Confederate colonization scheme. Others thought Marshal Bazaine had fallen under the spell of his young and ambitious Mexican wife and was contemplating staying on in Mexico.[64]

Maximilian was desperate to strengthen his imperial army, which Bazaine recognized was ill-prepared to defend the empire. Maximilian turned to Belgian and Austrian mercenaries to serve in its Foreign Legion, but there were never enough. Then he turned to Egypt with plans to bring in hundreds of enslaved Sudanese men. The Sudanese were said to be naturally adapted to the hot climate of Mexico, able to resist *el vomito* (yellow fever), ride on the tops of trains in the blistering heat, and march across the arid deserts exposed to the withering sun, such as no European soldiers possibly could.[65]

When Seward caught wind of the Sudanese scheme in November 1866, he made it clear to the Egyptian government that it had to stop. Because the United States did not recognize Maximilian's government, Seward directed all diplomatic communication to his sponsor, Napoleon III of France. Seward made the Sudanese matter about slavery and made America's hostility to slavery a corollary to the Monroe Doctrine. "The safety of free Republican institutions on this continent," he instructed

FIGURE 12. "Letting Him Slide." French emperor Napoleon III, facing a threat of war from the United States and mounting opposition at home, tells Mexico's putative emperor, Maximilian, "I'm really very sorry, but I must let you go, or you might pull me over!" *Fun*, September 22, 1866.

his overseas ministers in September 1865, required "the abolition of every form of compulsory civil or military servitude in this hemisphere."[66]

Seward accused the French of enabling the reintroduction of African slavery in Mexico and made it clear the United States objected to "slavery in any form replanted . . . on our borders." Recruiting enslaved conscripts was an offense to all the world. "If European opinion can be regarded as established in reference to any one political question," Seward told France, "it is settled that African slavery, in any form, ought henceforth to cease throughout the world."[67]

Coinciding with his attack on Maximilian's efforts to bring in mercenaries, in November 1866, Seward tightened the vise on France. France was still trying to exchange an agreement to withdraw for an American promise to recognize Maximilian's empire. On November 23, 1866, he sent unusually blunt instructions to Bigelow in a lengthy encrypted and exorbitantly expensive ($13,000) telegram. In it, Seward stated the United States expected the evacuation of Mexico to proceed as promised and had no intention of recognizing any but the Mexican Republican government. The delay of French withdrawal was "in every way inconvenient and exceptionable. We cannot acquiesce."[68]

Seward's November telegram also announced that he was sending Lewis Campbell as minister to the Juárez government, accompanied by General William Tecumseh Sherman. The very name of the latter, Seward had to know, would send chills through Napoleon III's court in Paris. It seemed designed to imply the United States was prepared to dispense with any pretense of neutrality and send in armed forces.[69]

Seward was grandstanding, probably to win favor with Congress and the public for his militant defense of Monroe but, above all, to get France's attention. It worked. On December 3, 1866, Bigelow cabled him from Paris that the French "corps of occupation is to embark in the month of March next."[70]

While Napoleon III quietly abandoned any delusions about his Grand Design for the Latin race in Mexico, Maximilian continued to cherish the fantasy that he would be Mexico's enlightened savior. Bazaine implored him to leave with the French troops, which Maximilian initially agreed to do. Then he vacillated back and forth almost daily until it was too late. To abandon the throne would dishonor the Hapsburg dynasty. Besides, he thoroughly distrusted Bazaine and Napoleon III and was determined to decide his own destiny.[71]

From his quarters in the National Palace, on February 5, 1867, Maximilian watched the French troops march out of Mexico City, with Bazaine leading the procession, along with Mexican officials who had served the imperial government. Drums beat, flags flew, yet the streets were eerily empty. "At last, I'm free," Maximilian remarked to his remaining staff.[72]

Soon after the French evacuation, Maximilian and a portion of his imperial army left the capital to take their stand at Querétaro, a more defensible city one hundred miles northwest of the capital. Republican forces soon surrounded and laid siege to Querétaro for over seventy days. On May 15, 1867, after one of Maximilian's Mexican officers betrayed him and opened the city's gates, Republican forces took control of the city with no resistance.

George Green, commander of the American Legion of Honor, volunteer soldiers who fought with the Juaristas, dined out for years on his story of Maximilian's surrender that day. The emperor came down the hill carrying a riding whip with a white handkerchief sufficing as a flag of surrender. "His lips were trembling, he looked ill and wan," as Green told it. Mexico's Republican general Ramón Corona approached, and Maximilian walked up to him to announce, "I am Maximilian, Emperor of Mexico," and then drew his sword to surrender it. "No, Maximilian," Corona replied, "you are not now Emperor, and never were!" Corona escorted Maximilian to the commanding officer, General Escobedo, who accepted the Hapsburg prince's surrender.[73]

Republican officials promptly put Maximilian on trial in the local theater and quickly arrived at a death sentence by firing squad. Humanitarian pleas to spare Maximilian's life came to President Juárez from all the crowned heads of Europe and such celebrities as Victor Hugo and Giuseppe Garibaldi. William Seward also earnestly sought to persuade Juárez not to execute the emperor, if only to prevent European retaliation.[74]

Juárez stood fast. He wanted to send a message to European monarchs. In a public manifesto, he denounced "those who dared to assault the nation

FIGURE 13. Abraham Lincoln, Benito Juárez, and Simón Bolívar. This panel from a mural painted in the 1950s by Aarón Piña Mora in Chihuahua, Mexico, honors three American national heroes and celebrates the Pan-American spirit of the 1860s. Wikimedia Commons.

of Anáhuac; those who led the frightful crime of fettering their independence, felling, burning and slaughtering, no longer exist; Triumphant Mexico used its rights." Anáhuac was the Aztec name for its capital, Tenochtitlàn ("Cem Anáhuac"). It was as though the execution was to avenge Mexico's earlier conquest at the hands of Maximilian's Hapsburg ancestor, the Holy Roman Emperor Charles V. The reference to the Aztecs was all the more poignant because the firing squad was composed of dark-skinned Indian or *mestizo* soldiers whose deadly shots punished the crimes of another Hapsburg monarch. "We inherit the indigenous nationality of the Aztecs," Juárez announced, "we recognize no foreign sovereigns."[75]

Nor was this the time to thank the United States for its supply of arms and men, to say nothing of its forceful diplomacy in Europe. "The good sons of Mexico have achieved [victory] fighting alone, without the help of anyone, without resources, without the necessary elements for war."[76]

Juárez and the Mexican Republic taught an essential lesson to the European world at Querétaro. Mexico and, by extension, all the American republics, whatever their political and economic travails, wanted to govern themselves, for better or worse, without European intervention, and

FIGURE 14. "Emperor Maximilian's Firing Squad," photograph by François Aubert, June 1867. Instead of the European-looking soldiers in Manet's famous painting, the soldiers who executed Maximilian represented the indigenous people that Benito Juárez said had exacted revenge on their European conquerors. Wikimedia Commons.

certainly not European-style monarchy. To the Monroe Doctrine's axiom, "America for Americans," Juárez added, "Mexico for Mexicans."[77]

Two years after the execution, Albert Evans, a colorful journalist from San Francisco, visited the execution site, commemorated by nothing more than three unadorned wood crosses. Evans let his imagination play with the executioners' shots that morning in June. "Those echoes rolled across the broad Atlantic and shook every throne in Europe," he wrote, and Napoleon III "grew pale as he listened. The ominous sound rolled over the Pyrenees, and the throne of Isabella began to crumble; over the Alps, and every monarch from Italy to the farthest East heard in them the rumblings of the coming earthquake—the prelude of the fall of empires."[78]

Evans was there to cover William Seward's remarkable tour through Mexico. The aging statesman retired after serving two presidents as chief diplomat. He looked older than his sixty-eight years, his face still ravaged by the scars from that night in April 1865. He rode in a carriage part of the way, but across Mexico's more rugged terrains his unsteady legs required him to ride in a shaded sedan chair slung between two mules. The spectacle gave an imperial aura to the man presenting himself as the champion of Pan-American republicanism.

The Mexican government honored Seward at a lavish banquet at the National Palace with some four hundred guests, including George Green and his fellow American volunteers.[79] Evans described the enormous banquet hall, still littered with the detritus of Maximilian's wasted empire. Evans gazed at where the throne once stood, "the crimson canopy of rich silk brocade which surmounted it still stands, as if in mockery of the past."[80] Their Mexican hosts took Seward and his entourage into an adjacent room "piled full of the dusty, mouldering relics of the dead Empire—scarlet canopies, laced liveries, jeweled swords, gold and silver cups and vases," and the like. "It was like the property-room of a theater. . . . No sermon on the vanity of human greatness, was ever preached, half so eloquent as that silent room!"[81]

The toasts that evening celebrated Mexican-American friendship forged in common cause against similar enemies. President Juarez took the occasion to pay "high and eloquent tribute to the American people and Government for their sympathy and moral and material support, in the trying hours of the foreign invasion of Mexico." He gave a special nod to Seward's help. In its civil war, spoke Thomas Nelson, U.S. minister to Mexico, the United States "fought not only for the preservation of the American Union but also for the American system of Government. Our victories were, therefore, your victories—our defeats your defeats." Two republics, imperiled by rebellion and foreign intrigue, had endured. They stood as testament to the Pan-American commitment to independent republics in solidarity against European imperialism.[82]

CHAPTER 4

Russia Exits

The present Treaty is a visible step in the occupation of the whole
North American continent. As such it will be recognized by the
world and accepted by the American people. But the Treaty involves
something more. By it we dismiss one more monarch from this continent.
One by one they have retired; first France; then Spain; then France
again; and now Russia; all giving way to that absorbing Unity which is
declared in the national motto, *E pluribus unum*.

—CHARLES SUMNER, RADICAL REPUBLICAN SENATOR
FROM MASSACHUSETTS, 1867

Within days of the French evacuation from Mexico in March 1867, the
Russian Empire agreed to sell its colony, Russian America, to the United
States. That October, what Americans called Alaska became U.S. terri-
tory, and the Russian Empire left the American hemisphere. The Russian
claim went back to 1732 and extended along the Pacific Coast from the
Bering Straits south almost to San Francisco. Russia's ambitions in North
America were part of what prompted the Monroe Doctrine in 1823.

Unlike France, Britain, or Spain, Russia posed no threat to the Union
during the Civil War. On the contrary, both countries fostered a legend
of genuine friendship, which astonished European powers in light of
the significant differences between "semi-feudal" Russia and America's

robust democracy. Their amicable relationship grew partly from the understanding that they faced common adversaries, Britain and France, Russia's enemies in the Crimean War (1853–56) and America's adversaries during the Civil War. What the press and political leaders of both countries put before the public, however, was that they shared a commitment to the emancipation of unfree labor. This began with Tsar Alexander II's emancipation edict in February 1861 and President Lincoln's proclamation the following year. Radical Republicans emphasized that the tsar's declaration of freedom was only the first step. What followed in Russia were plans for the allocation of land, public education, and political enfranchisement so that former serfs could become citizens and participants in what Americans saw as a modern democratic Russia in the making.

"In our American struggle against a barbarous aristocracy," one *New York Times* editorial reminded readers in early 1865, "we are in danger of forgetting the great contest . . . between the last relics of a feudal caste and the representative of the progressive ideas of this century" in distant Russia. "The act of emancipation there, as here, has nearly destroyed a class," the editorial continued, while "the American bastard aristocracy, resting like the Russian, on slaves, is in its dying and desperate struggles." The *New York Times* felt Russia "is on a sure, steady career of progress and reform . . . she will soon educate a mass of intelligent and orderly citizens who will be fully capable of governing themselves."[1]

Many Americans heralded the retreat of another European monarchy from North America as an essential step toward the "new republican era" George Bancroft saw unfolding after the Civil War. But more than the geopolitical map, it was the emancipation and enfranchisement of twenty million serfs and four million slaves that heralded the new birth of freedom in the 1860s. The idea that this was a shared endeavor naturally animated a close bond between the two countries and played an essential role in setting the stage for the Alaska Purchase in 1867.

During the 1850s, while most of his fellow Republicans concentrated on thwarting the spread of slavery in the West, Seward promoted the idea of expanding republican principles of free labor and popular government abroad. It was America's mission, he believed, to thwart despotism and end slavery, not by military force but by the example of republican success and the influence of commerce. As secretary of state under Lincoln, Seward was forced to watch European imperialists encroach on helpless American republics. Under Johnson, Seward was determined to reverse that course. The purchase of Alaska promised to end the Russian presence in North America and possibly throw British North America into play.[2]

Russia's decision to sell its languishing American colony to the United States had been in the works since the end of the Crimean War, but it stalled during the Civil War. The Russian America colony never attracted many settlers, and after Russia's defeat in Crimea, it had to weigh the possibility that Britain might be tempted to take it over. Defending such a distant colony would be costly, and Russia's treasury had been strained since the Crimean War. The Russians might have sold their American colony to Britain, whose North American possessions surrounded it. Instead, they decided to sell to the enemy of their enemy and Russia's new friend, America.

The traditional account of the Alaska Purchase depicts it as something of a lark. William Seward, the story goes, made an impulsive decision to pay Russia over seven million dollars for what skeptics ridiculed as a frozen wasteland. "Seward's Folly" and "Seward's Icebox" were epithets employed to defeat the purchase treaty.

Seward knew what he was doing with the Alaska Purchase, and it fit perfectly within the overarching foreign policy objectives he pursued in Mexico and Canada. Seward named America's new possession "Alaska," an Inuit word the Russians had adopted to refer to the mainland. His ambition went beyond territorial aggrandizement. He wanted to drive European imperialism from North America, support independent liberal nations in their place, and foster the spread of republican institutions throughout the Americas. Should the Alaska Purchase lead to the U.S. annexation of British Columbia and closing off the Pacific Coast to Britain, so much the sweeter it would make a deal with Russia.[3]

On the day Seward signed the Alaska Purchase Treaty with Russia, John Bigelow, who had recently arrived from Paris, joined him at his Washington home on Lafayette Square for a celebratory dinner party.

As they sat down to eat, Seward mused, "the same day that Russia retires from the American continent, the last French soldier sails from Vera Cruz." It was, he thought, "the most remarkable coincidence of this half century, and it will produce a corresponding sensation."[4]

Seward also recognized Alaska as a strategic gateway to Asia. Some view this as Seward laying the foundations for America's "new empire" in the Pacific, including the takeover of Hawai'i and the Philippines. That lay far ahead, and the conquest and subjugation of distant territory contradicted everything Seward had come to believe after the Civil War about the gradual, peaceful spread of republican institutions through commerce, migration, and cultural amalgamation. The Alaska Purchase may have turned America's sight westward to the Pacific. Its more immediate advantage, however, was the possibility of acquiring some or all of Britain's North American colonies and creating a new Anglo-North American Republic.[5]

The lead-up to the Alaska Purchase began more than a decade earlier and a continent away. Russia had been expanding southward into the Ottoman Turkish Empire, a declining power derided as the "sick man of Europe." When the Turks pushed back, France and Britain entered the war on their side and delivered a painful defeat to the Russians in the Crimean War. The disaster in Crimea drained Russia's treasury, weakened its military, and reduced its influence in Europe.

Tsar Nicholas I died during the Crimean War, and his son Alexander II, thirty-seven years old, ascended to the throne determined to restore Russia's stature among the powers of Europe and the world. One account described him as "stoutly built and of an exquisite figure. Very handsome, rather a round face, eyes a beautiful light blue" and fine mustache, he "looks and walks and is every inch a king." According to legend, Abraham Lincoln's election inspired the tsar to emancipate Russia's serfs in 1861. Plans for emancipation had been in the works even before the Crimean War, but it was not until February 1861 that Alexander II announced it to the world. Unlike the other monarchs of Europe, during the Civil War, Tsar Alexander II made his high regard for Lincoln and the United States widely known at every opportunity. "Russia alone," he wrote Lincoln, "has stood by you from the first, and will continue to stand by you. . . . We desire above all things the maintenance of the American Union as one 'indivisible nation.'" Despite vast differences in history and political principles, Russia and America created an entente that caused other European rivals to take notice.[6]

Alexander's foreign minister, Prince Alexander Gorchakov, played a crucial role in the decision to evacuate North America. Born in 1798, he was of medium size with short, grayish hair, a man described as shrewd and agreeable. Gorchakov followed his noble family's footsteps into a distinguished career in diplomacy, serving at several European embassies. After the Crimean War, which Gorchakov opposed, Alexander II appointed him foreign minister, and he soon became a trusted confidant of the young tsar. "Russia is not sulking," Gorchakov announced after the defeat in Crimea, "she is collecting herself."[7]

The sale of its North American colony, Gorchakov believed, was essential to the post-Crimean resurgence of Russia. Apart from the money, the sale of Alaska would achieve two desirable ends: strengthening friendly relations with the United States and increasing the chances of a disagreement between America and Britain. Once it acquired Russia's colony, Russia surmised, the United States would want British Columbia and perhaps Baja California, giving it exclusive control over the entire North American west coast. That would shut the coast off to Britain, thus protecting Russia's plans for expanding into Asia. Gorchakov admitted to Emperor Alexander II that frustrating Britain "is perhaps a motive for us to cede our colonies to the United States. It is certainly a motive for the Americans to acquire them."[8]

Russia's minister in the United States, Baron Eduard de Stoeckl, played a crucial role in the Alaska sale. He epitomized Russia's aristocratic, professional diplomatic corps. Like his father, he was bred to a career in statecraft. He had been in Washington since 1841 and became chargé d'affaires of the Russian legation in 1850. Four years later, he became Russia's minister to the United States. Stoeckl was a master courtier, a handsome man with an aristocratic bearing that impressed Americans.

He married an American woman, Elisa Howard, and they became glittering ornaments in Washington's social circle. The Stoeckls were well-practiced in the art of dispensing small favors among the capital's power elite and gaining access to them when needed. Stoeckl endeared himself to William Seward during his early days on the job. He often dispensed valuable intelligence and advice based on his long experience and inside knowledge of Washington diplomatic circles.[9]

Stoeckl disdained the "revolutionary and socialist spirit" of America's volatile democracy, which he blamed entirely on radical European immigrants. He was, nonetheless, sincerely alarmed that the breakup of the American Union would render the Monroe Doctrine powerless and open the American hemisphere to predatory European empires. The Union's defeat, he thought, would disadvantage Russia and its North American colony. Stoeckl and his government also saw the United States as an essential counterpoise to the British Empire in North America against whatever schemes it might have to thwart Russia's colony there. In one dispatch to the home office in St. Petersburg, Baron de Stoeckl neatly summarized Russia's purpose: "We must never lose an opportunity to fan the flames of hatred" between London and Washington.[10]

Unlike other European powers, Russia publicly demonstrated solidarity with the United States during the Civil War. In the autumn of 1863, when Britain and France were scheming to intervene against the Union, Russia refused their invitation to participate in a multilateral offer to mediate peace between North and South, equivalent to granting Confederate independence. Instead, Russia made a welcome gesture of friendship to the United States by sending naval squadrons to visit New York, Boston, and San Francisco. The Russian navy was feted and toasted at every port as though they were visiting heroes. Thus began an informal alliance between two outliers opposing the Great Powers of western Europe. The memory of Russia's singular act of friendship during the Union's time of peril would be celebrated endlessly during the debate over Alaska.[11]

The legend of this unique friendship was helpful, and both countries continued cultivating the notion of a special relationship between them. The parallels between Abraham Lincoln and Tsar Alexander II as emancipators were an important part of this narration. At every opportunity, Americans referred to "our friends," the Russians, who stood by the Union during the war when other European nations forsook them. After

Lincoln's assassination, images of him were prominently displayed across Russia, often beside those of the tsar's oldest son, Grand Duke Nicolas, who died about the same time.[12]

Russian officials and the press mourned Lincoln's assassination with genuine emotion. "The blow which has struck Mr. Lincoln," Gorchakov wrote, "at the very moment when he seemed about to harvest the fruits of his energy and perseverance, has been deeply felt in Russia."[13] The Russian press took the occasion to reaffirm the special relationship between the two countries. An editorial in the *St. Petersburg Journal* said it "will be felt throughout the whole world, and nowhere will it be felt more keenly than in Russia. The sentiments which unite the two nations are so profound, that one cannot suffer without the sympathy of the other. . . . May this exchange of cordial sympathy draw together still more closely the bonds of friendship." Russian enthusiasm for America was not limited to the government or elite press. Several radical revolutionaries, including Alexander Herzen, Mikhail Bakunin, and Nicholas Chernyshevski, viewed the American republic as the trailblazer toward a democratic future. Judging from a stream of condolence letters coming into U.S. diplomatic posts, the Russian people also felt a genuine affinity for Lincoln and America. A letter, written in English, from Abraham Nadich, a Russian Jew, to the U.S. consul in Odessa was typical of many such messages from the Russian people: "Poor America! Poor Abraham Lincoln! Thou shouldest have been invulnerable to iron and fire; the blood should not have flown when iron cut thee, for thou belongest not to thyself and America only, but to the whole world!"[14]

These sentiments of shared destiny took on even greater meaning one year later. On April 4, 1866, almost one year after Lincoln's assassination, a Russian named Dmitry Karakozov rushed toward the tsar at the gate of his Summer Garden. As he raised his revolver and was about to pull the trigger, a bystander lunged at Karakozov, and the shot went amiss. The assassination attempt aroused extraordinary demonstrations among the Russian people celebrating the miraculous salvation of their tsar. People filled the streets everywhere, forming processions and singing the national hymn, "God Save the Tsar."[15]

Alexander II's narrow escape also aroused sympathy in the United States, and the press was alive with comparisons between Lincoln and Alexander II, their assassins, and their common role as emancipators. Thaddeus Stevens rose in Congress to congratulate Tsar Alexander on his miraculous escape, and he moved that both houses of Congress send a message expressing so. We have learned, he began, "with deep regret of the attempt made upon the life of the Emperor of Russia by an enemy of emancipation. The Congress sends greeting to his Imperial Majesty, and to the Russian Nation, and congratulates the twenty million of serfs upon the providential escape from danger of the sovereign to whose head and heart they owe the blessings of their freedom."[16]

The idea that Karakozov was an "enemy of emancipation," a Russian John Wilkes Booth, was untrue, and Democrats protested Stevens's effort to characterize the incident in such a way as to draw parallels between America and Russia to embarrass them. Karakozov was a radical Nihilist, and he was agitated because he thought the tsar had betrayed his promise of land to the serfs, not because he freed them.[17]

When Stevens's motion reached the Senate, Charles Sumner further obscured matters by explaining that what agitated the assassin was not "the original act of emancipation" so much as the tsar's continued efforts to uplift the emancipated serfs. The tsar, Sumner explained, "has proceeded, by an elaborate system of regulations," to provide for "what have been called the civil rights of all the recent serfs" and to provide their "rights in court, in property, in public education. Added to all these, he has secured to them also political rights, giving to everyone the right to vote for all local officers." In short, Tsar Alexander II was carrying out a program of Radical Reconstruction by elevating twenty million serfs to full citizenship. It was, Sumner concluded, the "very thoroughness with which he has carried out his decree of emancipation that has aroused against him the ancient partisans of slavery."[18]

Once the motion passed both houses, Seward and others in Johnson's cabinet, along with Sumner and others in Congress, thought the occasion called for more than an official letter sent over in a diplomatic pouch. Congress then ordered that the resolution be personally delivered to the tsar. It was an extraordinary signal of the high regard American politicians wished to bestow on their Russian friends before the world. To lead the delegation, Congress selected Gustavus Vasa Fox, the assistant secretary of the navy. Fox had gone to great lengths three years earlier in welcoming the Russians to New York. He was a tall, balding New Englander, about forty-five in 1866, with a full beard. He also played an essential role in building the Union's mighty navy during the war. A thorough republican, Fox also shared Seward's vision of safeguarding the American hemisphere against European incursions.[19]

Fox's expedition entailed much more than carrying a message to Tsar Alexander. The mission was a highly publicized demonstration of Russian-American friendship and America's military power. Fox chose to cross the Atlantic in the USS *Miantonomoh*, one of the new ironclad monitors whose prowess in battle had caused great excitement abroad during the Civil War. Secretary of the Navy Gideon Welles instructed Fox to visit France and Britain on the way to Russia, ostensibly to inspect ship construction but with the unstated purpose of drawing European attention to the American warship and U.S.-Russian friendship.[20]

The USS *Miantonomoh* had a double turret, one armed with an enormous Dahlgren cannon. The ship was designed solely for coastal operations, and this would be the first time any vessel of this kind had crossed the Atlantic. For a good reason, it appeared. When fully loaded, the boat barely cleared two feet above the water. Though Europeans were none the wiser, the *Miantonomoh* was towed across the Atlantic by a side-wheel steamer, then entered European ports unassisted.[21]

Fox's first stop was in Cherbourg, France, at the end of June 1866. In Paris, he met with Napoleon III, who, at that time was worried about getting French troops out of Mexico and Prussia's stunning victory over Austria at the Battle of Sadowa, news of which had arrived recently. After a banquet with French dignitaries, Fox, smarting from the display of French aristocratic disdain for America, wrote Welles: "I think it is a matter of small concern what these Governments think of us or our people. Our superiority in everything excepting tinsel, epaulets, and medals can only be felt by coming over here."[22]

John Bigelow introduced Fox to Prince Jerome Napoleon, the emperor's nephew. The prince warned him against being too friendly with the Russians, who were untrustworthy. Fox replied sharply, reminding Jerome that "when it was doubtful whether we should ever stand again, at a time when the most powerful nations menaced us, Russia felt and expressed her sympathy for us, and America never will forget it." Prince Jerome answered, "Russia is for herself alone." They dropped the subject.[23]

One French journal, *La Presse,* belittled the *Miantonomoh,* saying the French ironclad could "with one stroke of her ram, pierce, run down, and annihilate such a tortoise as the *Miantonomoh.*" The British were more impressed.[24] When Fox arrived in London in early July 1866, the British press took great interest in this strange-looking ship that entered the Thames River. Visitors "came in large numbers" and, according to a generous account in the *Army and Navy Gazette,* they expressed high regard for the "kind attentions and perfect urbanity of the American seamen." In London, the *Miantonomoh* docked right beside the British ironclad *Lord Warren.* Some observers speculated this American iron monster could sink any of Her Majesty's fleet in a few minutes. "The wolf is in the fold," the London *Times* noted gravely, "and the whole flock was at its mercy."[25]

In early August, the Americans arrived at St. Petersburg to the hearty welcome of the Russians. An unostentatious naval officer at home, Fox became an international celebrity when he landed in Russia. Bands played "Yankee Doodle Dandy" and "The Star-Spangled Banner." Everywhere crowds of Russians cheered the Americans with thundering *ooras.* The Russians treated Fox and his entourage to a series of lavish banquets where Russian dignitaries toasted their friendship with effusive emotion. The toasts and speeches frequently alluded to Abraham Lincoln's affinities with Alexander II. At a dinner given by the Royal Navy, on one wall was a colossal shield with portraits of Washington, Lincoln, and Johnson encircled in wreaths.[26] At another lavish banquet in St. Petersburg, a Russian band played "The *Miantonomoh* Galop," a fast-paced tune "composed and respectfully dedicated to . . . Hon. G. V. Fox" by Heinrich Fürstnow, director of music at the royal palace outside St. Petersburg.[27]

FIGURE 15. The Gustavus Fox Expedition to Russia. As a demonstration of sympathy with Russia, after an attempted assassination of Tsar Alexander II, the U.S. Senate commissioned Fox (fourth from left, middle row), assistant secretary of the U.S. Navy, to deliver a message of sympathy and solidarity to Russia. It became an extraordinary celebration of Russo-American friendship and helped set the stage for the sale of Russian America in March 1867. Naval History and Heritage Command.

The U.S. State Department translated and published every word from Russian accounts of the Fox tour, complete with banquet menus, speeches, toasts, songs, band performances, and poetry recitals.[28] A recurring theme in the remarks dwelled on Russia and America's shared destiny as defenders of two "New Worlds" against the declining powers of the "Old World" in western Europe.[29] "I cannot help feeling," Fox wrote Charles Sumner from St. Petersburg, "that God has permitted two great experiments . . . an autocracy in the East and a republic in the West and . . . will surely judge that nation which fails in the trust reposed by Him."[30]

At the banquet in Moscow, Fox recited a poem Oliver Wendell Holmes had given him for the occasion, which alluded to the Russo-American romance:

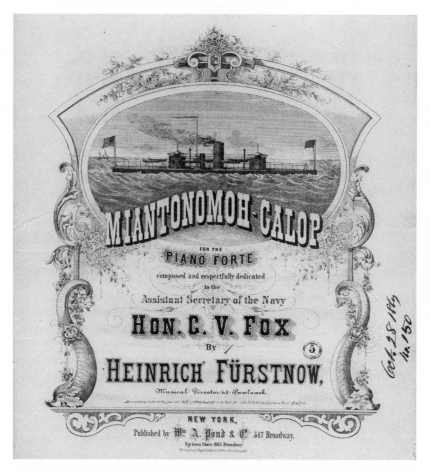

FIGURE 16. "The *Miantonomoh* Galop," a sprightly tune, composed for the occasion by Heinrich Fürstnow, director of music at the royal palace, St. Petersburg. The *Miantonomoh* was one of several Union ironclad ships that had caused a stir during the Civil War. Though it was not suited to ocean crossings, Fox ensured that France and Britain got a good look at this modern naval weapon. Library of Congress.

Though watery deserts hold apart
    The worlds of East and West,
Still beats the self-same human heart
    In each proud nation's breast.
A nation's love in tears and smiles
    We bear across the sea;

FIGURE 17. Banquet in Moscow Honoring the Fox Expedition. The Russians celebrated Fox's visit in numerous lavish events, this one by the Society of the City of Moscow. Prince Sherbatoff is shown speaking, in front of a portrait of Tsar Alexander II, with Assistant Secretary of the Navy Gustavus V. Fox seated on his right. Naval History and Heritage Command.

> O Neva of the hundred isles
>   We moor our hearts in thee![31]

Fox was supremely impressed by the size and emotion of public demonstrations from the Russian people. Enormous crowds of former serfs greeted him at every stop in his forty-one-day tour of Russia with gifts of bread and salt, a traditional welcome usually reserved for visiting royalty. As he came up the bank of the Volga River at Kostroma, one man threw his overcoat in Fox's path, a gesture of reverence usually reserved for the emperor. Fox, ever the republican, was embarrassed by such deference. He stepped over the coat, only to find dozens of others thrown in his path. His Russian host "motioned to me to proceed, and we walked to our carriages, up the high bank of the river, upon the clothing which the people of the country threw down in our path." The Russian government wanted America as its friend, and it was clear to Fox that the Russian people also held America in high regard. "They are a great people," Fox wrote, and "are our friends from the highest to the lowest."[32]

During Fox's celebrated visit to Russia, no word was spoken or written about the sale of Alaska to the United States. However, Russian officials undoubtedly had it firmly in mind. Shortly after Fox left for America, Gorchakov put the negotiations in motion and organized a meeting on December 16, 1866, to decide on terms.[33] Tsar Alexander II presided, and around the table were Prince Gorchakov, Grand Duke Constantine, Minister of Finance Mikhail de Reutern, Vice Admiral Krabbe, and Eduard de Stoeckl, who came over from Washington for the occasion. Within a short time, they agreed on the sale. Reutern advised, "monetary compensation must be not less than five million."[34]

Stoeckl returned to the United States in February 1867 with instructions to quietly sound out political support and offer any bribes needed to induce favorable press coverage or win approval in Congress. Though he had sometimes judged Seward to be a poor statesman, the two men had a long and amicable relationship that had endured four years of international intrigue during the Civil War. Both men were approaching the end of long careers and were interested in their legacies. Stoeckl had another motivation; while in Russia, he worked out terms for a handsome commission on the sale.[35]

It was essential to Russia's imperial pride that Seward should take the initiative, lest it appear Russia was desperately peddling its colonies abroad. While still in New York recovering from a foot injury during a rough crossing, Stoeckl went through an intermediary, probably Seward's trusted advisor, Thurlow Weed, to apprise Seward of the rules of engagement. However, when Stoeckl called on Seward in Washington on March 11, Seward seemed surprisingly slow on the uptake. Either word of the ground rules had not gotten to him, or Seward was playing coy, in any case acting as if he did not know he was to initiate the offer.

After Seward kept running on about leasing and fishing rights, Stoeckl finally had to come out with it. The Russian government had agreed to sell its American colony, he told Seward, and he was there to negotiate terms. Seward acted surprised and sputtered that he would have to consult the president and cabinet before further negotiations. President Johnson was cool to the idea but made no objections, leaving it to Seward to convince the cabinet at the coming Friday meeting.

Before that, Seward called Stoeckl in again, and the two men began an informal discussion on the matter of price. Seward proposed $5 million, a figure mentioned back in 1860 during preliminary talks. Stoeckl kept silent, thinking to himself that Seward had already met Russia's bottom offer. Seward raised his bid, suggesting he might get $5.5 million, "but no more." Stoeckl said nothing except that it might be best to discuss the price later after Seward met with the cabinet. Stoeckl was delighted. Seward was bidding against himself, which made Russia's shrewd ambassador consider going for $6.5 million.[36]

That Friday, when Seward presented the idea of buying Alaska to the cabinet meeting, no one voiced opposition, nor did they show much interest. Still, they ought to have been more surprised since nobody knew anything about the negotiations except Johnson, who sat back and kept silent. The only one who seemed to care about Alaska was Seward, who asked for approval of an offer of up to $7 million and got it without further discussion.[37]

He returned to Stoeckl grumbling about cabinet opposition and various conditions they wanted to impose, all routine bluffing. Then he offered $6.5 million, a whole million dollars above his last offer. Stoeckl could hardly lay down his hand at this point; he decided to bargain for more. When Seward asked to include the buildings and other fixed improvements on-site, Stoeckl said that would cost $7 million. Seward promptly agreed, eager not to haggle so long as he kept inside the authorized limit. On March 25, Stoeckl sent St. Petersburg the complete text of the treaty by telegram, on Seward's account, of course. "This whole affair has been managed in the go-ahead way of the Americans," he told St. Petersburg, all because Seward was in a great rush to get approval from Congress before it adjourned.[38]

Four days later, on March 29, Stoeckl walked over to Seward's home on Lafayette Square to tell him the tsar had approved the treaty with only minor changes. Among them was a provision that the payment be issued immediately in London, and Seward could not accommodate that, so he threw in another $200,000.

By that time, it was late in the evening. Stoeckl said he would return the following day to complete everything. Why wait? Seward responded. "Let's make the treaty tonight." Seward woke up his staff and met them at the State Department, where Stoeckl and his team would join them. The treaty was finally concluded at four o'clock Saturday morning. Seward, sleepless but amazingly chipper, walked it over to President Johnson for his signature later that morning.[39]

Next, it would be for the Senate to ratify a treaty that it had no clue of even being in the works, let alone completed and signed by the president. Seward had informed Charles Sumner, the influential chair of the Senate Foreign Relations Committee, but only at the final hour. The treaty immediately stirred debate and a surprising measure of ridicule in Congress and the press. "Seward's Folly," they called it, a waste of money on frozen land that produced nothing but icebergs and polar bears. "Walrussia," "Seward's Icebox," "Johnson's Polar Bear Garden," a forsaken land uninhabitable by humans, except the "wretched Exquimaux."

Seward took all the ridicule in stride. He arranged the publication of similarly cruel remarks hurled at Thomas Jefferson's Louisiana Purchase. These scurrilous attacks had characterized Jefferson's vaunted "Empire for Liberty" as "a malarial swamp" whose "prairies were destitute of trees or vegetation . . . a territory so worthless and pestilential that it could never be inhabited or put to any possible use."[40]

Opposition to the Alaska Purchase was partly due to resentment among Republicans toward Seward for remaining loyal to President Johnson and toward Johnson for undermining Radical Reconstruction. More than party politics was at stake, however. As the Alaska debate played out in the press, it opened discussion of America's overall territorial ambitions.[41]

More often than not, the leading newspapers favored expansion of America's boundaries, commercial aggrandizement abroad, and the spread of republicanism abroad, especially when these came at the expense of European adversaries. Americans also praised Russia as a friend in time of need and an enemy of America's European enemies.[42]

The *New York Herald*, a reliable proponent of American expansion, celebrated the prospect of "the young giants of the Old and New Worlds" standing on two continents, "one the impersonation of absolutism, the other of republicanism." As Russia will become the "mistress of Europe," "the United States do not define their aspirations, but look quietly forward to the time when the 'whole boundless continent' will form one unbroken republic."[43] Americans, a Philadelphia newspaper proclaimed, "are eager to stretch our empire from Darien to the Arctic ocean, so that the republic shall become in fact, as well as in name, the United States of North America."[44]

Charles Sumner may have resented Seward's secrecy and grandstanding on the Russian treaty. Still, he believed in expanding America's republican institutions and saw the Alaska Purchase as an opening to fulfilling his long-held hope to "squeeze England out of the continent." When the treaty came before the Senate, Sumner carried the day with a magnificent stem-winder speech that went on for three and a half hours. He began by reviewing the practical benefits of Alaska, its land and resources, the future advantages of extending America's boundary along the Pacific Coast, and the expansion of the national domain.[45]

Beyond the material benefits Alaska would give the United States, Sumner pointed to the vital ideological principles and geopolitical strategies in play: "More than the extension of dominion is the extension of republican institutions. . . . It was in this spirit that Independence was achieved. In the name of Human Rights our fathers overthrew the kingly power . . . and offered their example to mankind." Moreover, the purchase of Alaska was "a visible step in the occupation of the whole North American continent. . . . By it we dismiss one more monarch from this continent. One by one they have retired; first France; then Spain; then France again [from Mexico]; and now Russia; all giving way to that absorbing Unity which is declared in the national motto, *E pluribus unum*."[46]

The Senate ratified the treaty on April 9 by an astounding vote of 73 to 2. The United States took possession of Alaska later in October. *Lincoln*, a U.S. Navy ship, carried troops from San Francisco to Sitka, the new capital of Alaska Territory, arriving on October 18, 1867. Russian troops lowered their flag a few hours after landing while the United States fired a twenty-one-gun salute. What had been a remote Russian colony for a century and a half was now part of the American Republic.[47]

Seward commissioned Emanuel Leutze, a German American painter, to do a large-scale painting, *Signing the Alaska Treaty*. Leutze had painted several patriotic scenes that graced the walls of federal buildings in Washington, and he understood his assignment. The painting depicts the moment of signing early on the morning of March 30. Eduard de Stoeckl stands by an enormous globe of the world, his hand framing Alaska. Seward is seated, holding a large map in one hand and signing the treaty with the other. Other government officials surround them, including Charles Sumner, an appreciative nod to his winning speech in support of the treaty.[48]

America's acquisition of Alaska was part of a grand geopolitical chess game in the spring of 1867 with France and Russia taking leave of North America and Britain pulling back. The British government first heard about the sale in the London *Times* on April 1, 1867. So secret were the negotiations that it had to send a telegram to St. Petersburg to confirm the news. In Parliament, the MPs tried to brush it off as though it was of no real consequence to the British Empire, which became the party line with *The Times*, the voice of Conservative England.[49]

Others in the British press showed irritation with the "unscrupulous enemies" of the empire conspiring in secrecy to "insult" Britain. The *Diplomatic Review*, a prestigious London publication, complained that "the two Governments have taken a hostile step toward England" and "in an offensive manner." While the British government refuses to protest, "public feeling" conveys "either a deep sense of humiliation or disingenuous reasons of assent."[50]

Some British pundits noted that if all Russia wanted were money, it would have invited Britain to bid if only to drive up the price. The

FIGURE 18. *Signing the Alaska Treaty*, painting by Emanuel Leutze. The artist imagined Russia's ambassador, Baron de Stoeckl, standing before the globe with William Seward, maps in hand, looking on. As a gesture of goodwill, the painting included a crucial supporter of the treaty, Charles Sumner (second from right). Wikimedia Commons.

whole thing looked to the British press and political leaders like an American plot to take over British Columbia if not all of British North America. Lord Stanley, a Tory leader, wrote privately to Lord Lyons, "the Americans . . . have bought a large amount of worthless territory. . . . Their motive is probably twofold: to establish a sort of claim in the future to British North America, lying as it does between their old and new possessions; and to gain a victory over us by doing without our knowledge an act which they probably think will annoy England."[51]

Not all British officials were so indifferent. From his post in Washington, British ambassador Frederick Bruce warned London of a growing enthusiasm in the western United States for taking over British Columbia and the Red River Valley above the boundary established in 1818. Bruce sent another dispatch warning that Seward was negotiating with Denmark over the sale of Greenland and Iceland. Bruce warned that if the United States made good on these acquisitions, it "would flank British America on the North and West, as they have already done so on the Arctic and Pacific by the acquisition of Alaska." Should that come to pass, he feared, the Canadians might "peacefully and cheerfully" enter the United States.[52]

Seward poured salt on Bruce's wounds by issuing a press release designed to whip up support for the treaty: "The English representatives here are deeply chagrined, and it is said that Sir Frederick Bruce will telegraph to Earl Derby for instructions to protest its acceptance by our Government." The acquisition, Seward's press release continued, "more than doubles the United States coast on the Pacific, which now extends from Lower California to Behring's Straits, with the exception of the comparatively narrow strip comprising British Columbia." Alaska "will influence in our favor the vast trade of the Pacific."[53]

The *Pall Mall Gazette*, a Conservative evening paper in London, admitted the Alaska Purchase had profound implications for British North America's future: "The ultimate hope of America is to fill the Continent of America with great republican States, all governed under the stars and stripes." This acquisition, the *Gazette* went on, was a timely answer to Britain's confederation of its North American colonies, which had been in the works since 1863. The Americans seem to see the confederation of Canada not as a benign movement toward better government but as the creation of military power behind "a strong monarchical State at our doors." The Americans are telling Britain, "We do not intend that any such State shall exist. The time must come when the British possessions in America shall be ours."[54]

The acquisition of Alaska added to the pressure on Britain to follow suit by ceding part, or perhaps all, of its British North American colonies. The idea had support in the American press. "The trouble and anxiety we have had from having such neighbors as England in Canada, France in Mexico, and Spain in Cuba," one Philadelphia editor wrote, "ought to convince the most skeptical that our aim should be to have no neighbors at all."[55]

British Columbia was foremost in consideration among Americans. The sale of Alaska left Britain's western colony like a "sandwich" between two "jaws" of the United States, a favorite metaphor at the time. British Columbia was isolated, stagnating, and fed up with paying heavy taxes to Britain for no real benefit. Separated by thousands of miles of largely unsettled territory and no transportation or telegraph lines connecting them to the East, British Columbia's links to California were more robust than those to Canada and Britain. In addition, thanks to a short-lived gold rush, British Columbia was filled with American immigrants who felt no loyalty to the British Crown. It seemed like ripe fruit ready to drop into America's lap.[56]

Seward commissioned Elias H. Derby, a scion of a wealthy New England mercantile family, to gather relevant facts about the fisheries along the Pacific Coast, including the possessions of Russia, Britain, and the United States. Derby submitted his over three-hundred-page "letter" to Seward, who presented it to Congress in February 1867, just before the Russian offer came to its notice. After endless pages of tedious trade statistics, Derby's report interjected a bold plan that linked Russia's cession of Alaska to his proposal that Britain settle the dispute over its aid to the Confederacy, known as the *Alabama* Claims, by ceding Vancouver Island and British Columbia. "Is not America designed for Americans?" Derby asked. Let "this continent be occupied by one republic, *'una e libera.'*"[57]

The people of British Columbia were of mixed opinions. Their numbers had declined dramatically, from under 14,000 in 1861 to under 9,000 five years later. The gold rush had petered out, and the miners, many veterans of the California gold fields, returned home. Separated from the rest of British North America by thousands of miles of wasteland, their commercial and communication ties were mainly with the United States. More than 60 percent of imports came from San Francisco, and half of their exports went there. Indebted, isolated, and woefully neglected by the Crown, a sullen people faced a "bleak and desolate" future.

Upon hearing news of the treaty, resident Americans in British Columbia flew the Stars and Stripes and signed a petition to the U.S. State Department expressing enthusiasm for annexation. Irish and German inhabitants were enthusiastic about annexation, while English and Scottish residents were careful not to appear disloyal to the queen. Still, an American observer felt confident they would vote for annexation if given a chance. Then came news that Seward wished to make British Columbia the price for settling the long-festering *Alabama* Claims. A steady drumbeat of enthusiasm for annexation arose from the press in British Columbia and a torrent of complaints about British failure and neglect. The *Nanaimo Tribune* asserted Great Britain was a "fast sinking ship" and the United States a "gallant new craft, good and strong, close alongside, inviting us to safety and success."[58]

In July 1867, U.S. consul in Victoria, Allen Francis, received another petition for annexation. This one was from Her Majesty's "Most loyal subjects" begging the queen to either relieve them of their debts, encourage shipping and immigration, or "graciously permit the Colony to become a portion of the United States." Francis forwarded it to the State Department with a comment: "I have no doubt but it will receive the signatures of three-fourths of the loyal citizens of the Colony."[59]

British Columbia's enthusiasm for joining the American republic faded as 1867 wore on, and U.S. interest in absorbing British North America also dwindled. The "sandwich" between the jaws of the United States had its own destiny to contemplate as part of the Dominion of Canada.

CHAPTER 5

Home Rule for Canada

The union of the Canadian Provinces . . . instead of rendering them more dependent on the Mother country, . . . will have the very contrary effect, and "Canada" will be . . . a self-governing community, with a strong resemblance to the neighbouring States of the Union.

—*THE TIMES* OF LONDON, APRIL 12, 1867

For nearly a century, many Americans dreamed that Britain's North American colonies would one day become part of the United States. One of the American revolutionary army's first campaigns aimed at making Quebec the fourteenth colony. That dream was defeated on the Plains of Abraham in December 1775 but did not die. During the War of 1812, American forces invaded Canada West to enlist Canadians as allies and throw off the yoke of British tyranny. They were promptly driven back to Detroit in humiliation.

Still, the idea of a unified Anglo-American nation in North America sprang to life again during and after the U.S. Civil War. British and Canadian officials and pundits feared that, win or lose, the United States might turn its massive army northward and take revenge on Britain for aiding the Confederacy. Such fears were also heightened by American efforts to pressure Britain into considering ceding its North American colonies to settle the *Alabama* Claims. In a bombastic speech before the

Senate, Charles Sumner reckoned that the Confederacy's British-built warships had doubled the cost of the war and therefore put Britain two billion dollars in debt to the United States. Some saw the Alaska Purchase as part of Seward's strategy to peel off British Columbia from Canada and shut Britain off from the Pacific Coast. Then there were the series of raids by Irish American Fenians. Made up mainly of Civil War veterans, the Fenians aimed to incite rebellion in Canada, forcing Britain to defend its colonies on American soil, then draw the United States into the war and make Irish emancipation the price of peace. In any case, they counted on help from America, which was now free to settle scores with Britain for the transgressions it perpetrated during the Civil War. British and Canadian politicians were well aware of the danger that loomed ahead once the Americans finished fighting one another.[1]

Canadians ginned up their own militant spirit, using the threat of U.S. aggression to unite the British American colonies. John A. Macdonald, the revered founding father of the Canadian Confederation, put the matter plainly: if British North American colonists did not want to become American, they must become Canadian.[2]

The making of Canada was a top-down affair and not the culmination of some revolutionary nationalist movement to throw off the yoke of British rule and proclaim independence. On the contrary, it was antipathy toward America and its radical democracy that energized the leaders of the confederation movement. Politicians and British colonial officials hammered out the terms of confederation in Quebec and London out of public sight. When finished, they resisted calls for a plebiscite to confirm public support. Canadians chose union and autonomy not to be rid of their British rulers but to ward off absorption into America's violent democracy. None were more supportive of Canadian home rule than its British rulers, who seemed glad to be rid of any responsibility for governing and defending their North American colonies. Whereas the American Revolution, in Tom Paine's famous rendering, was like rebellious youth breaking from their tyrannical parent, Mother Britannia all but kicked her dependent Canadian children out of the nest.[3]

On March 29, 1867, within days of the French evacuation from Mexico and one day before Seward and Stoeckl agreed to the Alaska Purchase,

Queen Victoria signed the British North America Act, which proclaimed the union of the Dominion of Canada. The new confederation would remain part of the United Kingdom of Great Britain and Ireland, and its government would be on the British model, with a strong bicameral Parliament. The Dominion of Canada was not quite an independent nation, nor was it any longer a disconnected collection of colonies. Though founded in reaction against the United States and its bumptious democracy, Canada was practically more democratic than its British model and grew into one of the world's more vibrant democracies. Its long, undefended border with the United States remains an enduring testament to the idea of democratic peace that shaped the American hemisphere after 1865.[4]

Britain's unfriendly actions during the Civil War strained relations between the United States and its former "mother country." The British government was the first to accord belligerent rights to the rebel South, and members of Parliament openly expressed pleasure at the prospect of America's dismemberment. When a Union naval officer apprehended Confederate diplomats onboard HMS *Trent*, the press and influential leaders beat the drums of war as though they welcomed an excuse to go to war. The British press ridiculed Lincoln and excoriated his Emancipation Proclamation as a resort to barbarous servile warfare. Britain tried to lead France and other European powers to intervene in the Civil War by offering to mediate peace, but on terms that would allow secession. More damaging still was Britain's lax enforcement of its neutrality declaration, which allowed the construction of Confederate warships and blockade runners in British shipyards. These offenses left the Union with scores to settle and left Britain with a long, unfortified border separating its North American empire from a powerful and reunited America.

Few things the British did to harm the Union aggravated Americans quite so much as Canada's role in harboring Confederate terrorists and assassins. The most infamous example occurred in October 1864 as part of a campaign to terrorize Americans a few days before the presidential election. The townspeople of St. Albans, Vermont, a railway center across the St. Lawrence River from Montreal, were carrying on a typical day when a young Confederate agent named Bennett Young stepped onto the porch of a hotel, pulled out a revolver, fired it in the air, and announced: "This city is now in the possession of the Confederate States of America!"[5]

"We are Confederate soldiers and you are my prisoner," one of the raiders announced to an astonished teller at the bank he was holding up. "We have come to give you a taste of Sherman's idea of war."[6] They robbed three banks of some $200,000 and even held up individual citizens on the street. Before fleeing town, they hurled explosive bottles of Greek Fire (similar to Molotov cocktails) at buildings, intending to set the whole village on fire. They fired randomly at townspeople who were giving chase, killing one and wounding two others. They thought they were safe once they made it back to Canada until an American posse, heedless of any diplomatic niceties about international borders, came hell for leather in pursuit and captured several raiders. "We don't give a damn for your neutrality," one of the Americans told a British major. Then they backed down and handed the culprits over to British officials, who promised justice would prevail.[7] Arrested in Montreal, the townspeople treated the St. Albans raiders as local heroes. They stayed comfortably at the jailer's home, where their comrades brought them excellent food, wine, and prostitutes.[8]

The St. Albans raid lit the American press on fire. Editorials screamed for retribution against the British, who turned a blind eye to rebels making war on the United States—just as they had before when British shipyards constructed Confederate raiders. U.S. officials had every right to expect the St. Albans raiders to be turned over for trial in the United States. Then in December, Americans were appalled to learn that the Canadian magistrate hearing the case decided to release them based on some arcane legal technicality. The judge even allowed the culprits to keep the money they had stolen from the good people of St. Albans.[9]

This shocking leniency caused a swift reaction from Washington. Seward ordered all persons from Canada coming to the United States to show passports, an abrupt departure from previous practice. He instructed Charles Francis Adams, his minister in London, to serve notice

FIGURE 19. The St. Albans Raid. In October 1864 Confederate terrorists operating openly in Montreal conducted a violent raid on St. Albans, Vermont, killed innocent civilians, set fire to the town, then escaped back across the border where, in the eyes of Americans, British officials coddled them. This added to American resentment of British actions during the war and caused Britain to fear U.S. aggression against its North American colonies once the Civil War ended. *Frank Leslie's Illustrated Newspaper*, November 12, 1864. Hathitrust.

that the Rush-Bagot Treaty, by which Britain and the United States had agreed to demilitarize the Great Lakes, would be repealed. The American press and politicians howled in protest against the raid. The *Chicago Tribune* called on Union general John Dix, U.S. commander on the northern border, to "take Canada as a St. Bernard would throttle a poodle pup." The *New York Times* asserted, "Canadian territory must be respected no more than Virginia or South Carolina territory. The guerrillas which attack us at the North must be hunted down with the same vigor of pursuit as when they attack at the South." Admitting this might mean war with Britain, it brazenly added that "we were never in better condition for a war with England."[10] The *New York Herald* warned that the next raid would be against whatever Canadian village sheltered the Confederate villains.[11] Canada's governor, Lord Monck, allotted money to strengthen the militia and made plans to fortify Montreal and Quebec with help from Britain.[12]

The St. Albans raid and the coddling of its perpetrators rekindled long-standing grievances against Britain as the sinister enemy of America. It also fed the new enthusiasm for the Monroe Doctrine and its portrayal of belligerent European imperialists abusing peaceful American republicans. Furthermore, it provided another reason the United States might turn its armed might to the north and take over Canada.

The specter of American aggression against British North America found new life as the war ended. William Howard Russell, the famous correspondent for *The Times* of London, in early 1865 published *Canada: Its Defences, Condition, and Resources*, a sequel to his influential reports on the Civil War for the London *Times*. He believed the Canadian enthusiasm for annexation from before the war had cooled considerably. They "see with sorrow the ills which afflict their neighbors" and feel "naturally indignant at being spoken of as if they were a mere chattel, which could be taken away by the United States from Great Britain in order to spite her." Nonetheless, Russell warned that Canada was vulnerable to military aggression and gave Britain a sobering warning: "At some day, near or remote, Canada must become either independent in whole or in part, or a portion of a foreign state."[13]

British North America had failed to prosper like its southern neighbor, and many blamed its British rulers. The steady stream of migration southward to the United States was constant proof of the region's lack of opportunity. In a book written for immigrants in 1864, Thomas Rawlings complained that Canada ought to have been as attractive to the immigrant as the United States, and with better government, it would have been. Rawlings warned that Canada might go the way of the Thirteen Colonies if that did not change.[14]

The British press and political leaders in 1865 seemed almost resigned to losing Canada, not by invasion but as a way of settling claims the United States made for British violation of neutrality laws during the Civil War. The *New York Times* correspondent in London reported that once the *Alabama* Claims were settled, "the British American provinces will be sending Senators and Representatives to Washington as soon as they choose to do so." British officials and the press seemed willing to abandon Canada. Rather than go to war, he thought England would say, "Perverse daughter, go in peace. Join yourself to Brother Jonathan."[15]

The British government, however, was not passively allowing its North American colonies to drift into the possession of the United States. Since 1863, it had been exploring a path that would avoid war with the United States, take the governance and defense of Canada off its hands, and avert annexation. The plan was to combine the North American colonies into a new confederation capable of funding military defense and carrying out badly needed improvements, such as a railroad connecting the Province of Canada with the Maritime provinces.

In the autumn of 1864, with the Union driving into the Deep South and Lincoln about to win reelection, the confederation movement gained momentum. More than just a pact for the common defense, "confederation" now meant the creation of a semiautonomous nation within the British Empire.

What became the Dominion of Canada was nothing more than disconnected colonies, each ruled by the British Empire, yet with no formal ties to one another. The name "Canada," though commonly applied collectively to all of British North America, correctly referred only to the United Province of Canada. It was created in 1841 by merging Anglophone Canada West and Francophone Canada East (today's Ontario and Quebec). The Canadians who led the confederation movement imagined the union of British North America to be something like the United Province of Canada writ large.[16]

John A. Macdonald, a Conservative Party leader in Canada West, was fed up with the deadlock over confederation. In May 1864 reached out to Liberal Party leader George Brown to form what became known as the Great Coalition. They brought in George-Étienne Cartier, a Conservative French Quebec politician, and together created the leadership necessary to make Canada. For Macdonald, the American Civil War heightened the possibility of U.S. annexation and provided an object lesson in the need for a strong Canadian union. British North America's provincial governments, he believed, must be limited and subordinate to a strong central government, or Canada would go the way of its neighbor.[17]

The movement for a united British North America began with the Province of Canada practically annexing the Maritime provinces of Nova Scotia and New Brunswick. It started in September 1864, when Macdonald and the Canadian delegates more or less crashed a convention in Charlottetown, Prince Edward Island, organized to consider a union of the Maritime provinces.

Macdonald and the Canadians dominated the Charlottetown conference, pushing the idea for a Maritime union offstage and making union with Canada the question at hand. Some Maritime delegates were cool to the idea of giving up their local autonomy to the presumptuous and far more numerous Canadians. Yet, they were enthusiastic about the plan for an intercolonial railroad connecting them to the Province of Canada. Nova Scotia and New Brunswick went along with the united Canada project but with reservations about the terms and methods of confederation. Newfoundland stayed out for the time being, and Prince Edward Island pulled out later. Nonetheless, the idea of a British North American union was born in Charlottetown.[18]

Losing no time, delegates from Canada and some of the Maritime provinces (Nova Scotia, New Brunswick, and Prince Edward Island) met in Quebec the following month to draw up the main framework for the confederation government. The government was organized mainly on the British model of responsible government, which meant the real executive power resided in the majority party in Parliament, not the monarch in England, whose duties were more symbolic.

Canada's new government would be decidedly more democratic than Britain's, which at this time was making its first conflicted step toward democracy in the lead-up to the Second Reform Act of 1867 (the subject of chapter 7). The 1867 act would double the number of British voters, from about one-sixth to one-third of adult males. Property qualifications restricted the right to vote in the Dominion of Canada, but not as much as in Britain. Though the property qualification varied from province to province, about half of adult males met the requirement and possessed the right to vote. More notably, Canada did not have the kind

FIGURE 20. *The Fathers of Confederation*, representing what became Ontario, Quebec, Nova Scotia, and New Brunswick, components of the Dominion of Canada, founded in March 1867. They were generally conservative monarchists who saw confederation as the best means of fending off American-style democracy and annexation. This painting by Robert Harris depicts confederation leaders at the Quebec Conference, which laid out the basic terms of the new polity. John A. Macdonald is standing at the center. Wikimedia Commons.

of aristocratic governing class able to win seats in Parliament from small constituencies, as in Britain. Parliamentary constituencies in the new Canadian Parliament would be based on population and revised every ten years based on the census, thus eliminating the feudal legacy of inherited seats and "rotten boroughs" that sustained the British aristocracy's power. Canada's bow to aristocratic governance came in the upper house, or Senate, which was to be appointed for life by the provincial governments. Senate seats would be allotted in three equal shares to Ontario, Quebec, and the Maritime provinces. All the numbers guaranteed the dominance of the former Province of Canada.[19]

The confederation movement acted quickly to create an aura of united Canada as a fait accompli. Unlike other nationalist movements of the nineteenth century, Canada was not born amid the usual passion of popular outrage against the tyranny of foreign rulers. Nor did the Enlightenment theories of natural rights, human equality, and popular sovereignty play a prominent role in the debates on confederation. Confederation, one historian summarized, "was not . . . what is usually referred to as a popular movement. It was imposed on British North America."[20]

While Canadians were working out a plan to keep out of the United States, William Seward was exerting pressure in the other direction. Soon after the St. Albans raid, Seward announced that the United States would not renew the Reciprocity Treaty, ratified in 1854, to allow free trade across the border. The treaty was a boon to the British colonists and an undeniable benefit to the United States, especially during the Civil War when Canadian foodstuffs were vital to sustaining the Union.[21]

Seward's decision, by no coincidence, was announced amid the uproar over the St. Albans raid, and it looked like a deliberate act of retaliation. It was no accident that the U.S. House of Representatives voted to end the treaty the same day Canada's court released the St. Albans raiders. The Senate followed soon after, and on March 17, 1865, Seward issued a formal notice that the treaty would terminate one year hence. At the same time, Seward informed the British that he planned to rescind the Rush-Bagot Convention of 1817, by which the two countries had agreed to demilitarize the Great Lakes following the War of 1812. A border that had been among the most peaceful in the modern world was suddenly hardening, and tensions across it were fast mounting.[22]

Seward's moves were seen as retaliation against Britain, but more was in play than revenge. Some saw in his scheme a design to pressure Britain to consider ceding all or part of their North American empire. John Fox Potter, a Wisconsin politician serving as U.S. consul to Montreal, reported to Seward in January 1865 that he sensed a new enthusiasm among Canadians for joining the United States. Montreal's leading citizens, he said, were concerned that the end of the Reciprocity Treaty would doom their economic future.[23]

In July 1865, with Seward's approval, Potter attended a conference of Canadian and American business leaders held in Detroit to discuss the future commercial situation. Potter told Seward he would "quietly represent" his views but only "as a spectator" with no official standing. Both men knew better.[24]

Potter, never shy about attracting publicity, took it upon himself to issue an explosive speech in Detroit. He began by heartily commending the end of the Reciprocity Treaty as the first step toward annexation. "I believe that in two years from the abrogation of the Reciprocity Treaty the people of Canada themselves will apply for admission to the United States."[25]

"No! No!" Canadians in the audience shouted. The Canadian press was livid that a U.S. consul had the nerve to propose such a thing, and a movement arose calling for the United States to censure Potter. The *New York Times* haughtily advised Canadians to "Keep Cool." "We will not and would not annex you. We should not, in fact, know that such a thing was ever thought of by anybody, if we did not from time to time learn of it from the Canadian papers." The reaction to Potter's speech drove Canadian annexation sentiment underground, and though it was in bad odor among loyalists, it would resurface during the confederation movement.[26]

Into this tense scene on America's northern border appeared a raucous army of Irish American Fenians, mostly Union veterans ready to fight for their own new birth of freedom. The Fenian Brotherhood, named after mythic Celtic warriors, had emerged in the United States in 1858 as the American branch of the Irish Republican Brotherhood (a forerunner of the Irish Republican Army that wrested Ireland from British rule more than a half century later). American Fenians were mainly refugees from the Great Famine that struck Ireland in 1845 and dragged on for seven horrific years. The famine sent more than one million Irish to their graves and forced twice that many to leave Ireland. It set off a sustained diaspora that continued long after the famine subsided and created a transnational nationalist movement seeking the emancipation of the Irish homeland. Wherever they went, the memory of the famine sustained Irish hatred of the British, the most potent element of Irish revolutionary nationalism. "The Almighty . . . sent the potato blight," Irish nationalist John Mitchel famously wrote, "but the English created the Famine."[27]

The American Civil War gave the Fenians an extraordinary opportunity. For one, it produced a large pool of disciplined, battle-tested Irish

FIGURE 21. Fenian Brotherhood. The Fenians took their name from a legendary band of Irish warriors. Their impetus came from the American Irish who fought in the U.S. Civil War. They broke from the tradition of Daniel O'Connell and Catholic emancipation and become a durable secular republican movement on both sides of the Atlantic dedicated to the revolutionary overthrow of British rule. *The Fenians' Progress: A Vision* (New York: John Bradburn, 1865).

American veterans and four years to recruit them. Irish immigrants and their American-born sons constituted the largest ethnic group in the Union Army, totaling 234,000 men.[28] Many consciously enlisted to prepare for the struggle to liberate Ireland from British rule. Several Fenian "circles" (eight hundred men) joined and fought as a unit.[29]

The Fenians tapped the same postwar spirit of revenge that inspired others to "take the fight to Mexico." However, the Fenians' plans for Canada were far more complicated and ambitious. Their strategy was to conduct raids into Canada, incite an uprising against the British, and possibly draw Britain and the United States into war. The plans were vague, and the operations poorly executed, but there was no question that the Fenian raids irritated the already tense relations between America and Britain.

Canada was not the primary Fenian target. Their ultimate goal was to liberate Ireland from its British oppressors. At Seward's instruction, his minister to Britain, Charles Adams, toured Ireland in the late summer of 1865. His report was grim. "The sense of oppression is aggravated by the distinction of religious faith which marks the Roman Catholics as of the servile class almost as distinctly as the negroes are marked by difference of color with us." Adams reported that Fenians gained followers in the southern and western counties where massive emigration to America left behind "a great and festering sore of discontent." The Fenians in Ireland, he told Seward, were busy organizing clubs and took to drilling secretly at night, "preparing for some violent outbreak." Adams thought the disaffected class was large but "poor, unarmed, and generally wanting in the elements of moral power." Any Fenian rising, he warned gravely, would provoke slaughter by British armed forces, which were everywhere.[30]

When the American Civil War ended, many American Fenians returned to Ireland. The American and Irish Fenian organizations plotted to make 1865 "the year of action." The Americans would supply money, arms, and military leaders, and the Irish Fenians would carry out the revolution.[31]

Police said they could identify these American Irish merely by the manner they had of walking down the street. They wore square-toed

FIGURE 22. "The Fenian Pest." This cartoon by John Tenniel employs the same imagery of the Irish as ape-like ruffians that the American cartoonist Thomas Nast used in his drawings for *Harper's Weekly*. *Punch*, March 3, 1866. Hathitrust.

boots, double-breasted coats, and broad-brimmed felt hats; they sported mustaches and carried themselves with a certain "Yankee swagger" and some brandished firearms. Though they had no discernible means of income, they dispensed money freely for drinks and food to potential Fenian recruits.[32]

Police began searching passengers arriving from the United States and arrested dozens of suspected revolutionaries. Irish American prisoners from their jail cells in Dublin insisted they were naturalized American citizens and were being held in violation of international law. In February 1866, the British Parliament, responding to Irish officials pleading for "the most stringent measures of repression," pushed through a bill suspending the Habeas Corpus Act, which meant police could jail suspected Fenians without due process or any evidence of criminal behavior. The Fenian madness, British lawmakers and journalists sniffed, was an American disease, the product of a mob of "restless adventurers whom the close of the American war has let loose upon the world."[33]

If the Fenians were not deliberately trying to foment a diplomatic crisis between Britain and the United States, they might as well have been. As arrests mounted, the jail cells at Mountjoy Prison and Kilmainham Gaol in Dublin swelled with Irish American prisoners. All insisted on their rights as American citizens and flooded the offices of U.S. diplomatic legations in Dublin and London with appeals to be released. Back in America, the imprisoned Fenians were hailed as martyrs to the cause, and the American Fenians called on the U.S. government to take action against Britain.[34]

The American Fenians were more than an army; they were a nationalist movement whose purpose was to arouse American support for the cause of Irish independence. The first Fenian convention in Chicago in November 1863 signaled the arrival of a formidable political organization. Speakers emphasized that the Fenians were loyal American citizens obedient to the nation's laws. They also distanced their organization from the Catholic Church, long an object of suspicion among American Protestants. The Fenians envisioned a secular liberal republic independent of Britain and the Catholic Church. More than any other nationalist movement of the nineteenth century, the Fenian Brotherhood constituted a transnational movement, and none endured longer or fought more doggedly to achieve national emancipation.[35]

FIGURE 23. Fenian Picnic at Jones's Wood, New York. The Fenians staged huge conventions and public rallies attended by men, women, and children, sometimes described as "picnics" to avoid violating U.S. neutrality laws. *Harper's Weekly*, June 2, 1866. Hathitrust.

By the time of the second Fenian national convention held in Cincinnati in January 1865, the Fenian Brotherhood had grown to over 300,000 members in nearly 400 circles spread across the North and some in the South. "This Brotherhood is virtually at war with the Oligarchy of Great Britain," John O'Mahony, the Head Centre (chief officer), declared in the opening speech. "While there is no Fenian army as yet *openly* in the field—such an army nevertheless actually exists, preparing and disciplining itself for freedom's battle."[36]

To recruit members and raise money, the Fenians sponsored massive "picnics" in the countryside. They were actually "monster" political rallies full of anti-British rhetoric thinly disguised as family picnics to avoid flagrant violations of U.S. neutrality laws. The first picnic occurred in July 1865 at Jones's Wood on the north end of Manhattan Island. It drew 30,000 men, women, and children to a great day for the Irish, full of dancing, food, drink, and entertainment.[37]

Then, interrupting the frivolity, a procession of Fenians brought their president, a successful merchant and tireless organizer, William R. Roberts, to the stage. "The time has come," Roberts told the crowd, "when every Irishman who loves his country and believes in the ultimate independence of his native land, must take his place beside the Fenian Brotherhood in asserting that Irish liberty can only be won by fighting for it." "The sword shall now be the arbiter of her destinies and her children, and may God defend the right."[38]

By the time the Fenians met in Philadelphia in late October 1865, they had all the trappings of a people ready to claim their place in the family of nations. Their constitution began with familiar language: "We, the Fenians of America, in order to form a more perfect union, establish justice, insure domestic tranquility, and secure the blessings of liberty for the Irish race in Ireland, do ordain and establish this Constitution for the Fenian Brotherhood in the United States and other portions of America" (alluding to chapters in Canada). The self-proclaimed "Republic of Ireland" launched a bond sale and established headquarters in a posh mansion on Union Square in the heart of New York City. Cruelly mocked in the American press as a rowdy gang of pugnacious, drunken Irish, the Fenian Brotherhood, one advocate proclaimed, now "exists as a serious fact."[39]

The Fenian movement suddenly divided the Irish vote between Democrats and Republicans. That produced what one observer described as "a scramble amongst politicians to secure their votes in local elections, to feed their prejudices and passions by an acknowledgment of their wrongs." The New York state elections were coming in November 1865, and many anticipated they would indicate which party would win the Irish vote. Seward was an old New York politico who had learned to attract the Irish vote simply by vilifying Britain. Johnson badly needed to keep the Irish with the Democrats if he was to survive the mounting Republican opposition in Congress.[40]

The Fenians tested their new political leverage by sending Bernard Doran Killian, an Irish American congressman from St. Louis, to meet with Johnson and Seward and plead the case of John Mitchel. Mitchel was an old Irish nationalist hero who had landed in jail for writing incendiary articles. The Fenians were gathered in Philadelphia for another convention when news of Mitchel's release arrived. The hall exploded with joy.[41]

During negotiations over Mitchel's release, Killian confided to Johnson and Seward that the Fenians planned to invade Canada. They were astonished when Killian asked how the government would respond if the Fenians seized Canadian territory and proclaimed a Fenian republic. They answered with a studied lack of detail, yet they told Killian the government would acknowledge it as a fait accompli. Seward declined Killian's later request to have that in writing, which Seward was far too wise to give. Killian nevertheless believed the Johnson administration was on the side of the Fenians.[42]

In the winter of 1865–66, a flurry of reports from detectives and secret service agents on both sides of the border set off alarms in Canada. The British consul in New York reported to the British colonial governor in Canada that the Fenians were growing in strength and increasing their militant demands for action from the leadership: "The fever of this fanaticism is now at its height." The Fenians were preparing for an invasion on St. Patrick's Day, March 17, 1866.[43]

Canadian officials called up ten thousand volunteers and sent them to the border. The Grand Master of the Toronto Orangemen, a group of zealous Protestants from the north of Ireland, summoned its members to arms. Some feared Irish immigrants in Canada would join forces with the Fenians. No one knew where the Fenians might strike along hundreds of miles of the unfortified border.[44]

One reporter described the anxious scene in Montreal: "There are constant drills and reviews, and the commonly quiet streets of this slumberous town are vocal with clanging swords and the rumble of artillery wagons."[45] The Nation mischievously suggested that after taking perverse joy in America's rebellion "it can do the English nation and their provincial dependencies no harm to feel, by experience, that insurrection is not an excellent jest when it raises its head against themselves."[46]

Along the border, Canadian cities experienced a run on their banks. Shops shut down, and the streets filled with the sounds of militia drilling and drums beating. One Canadian marching song exclaimed:

Shout, shout, shout, ye Loyal Britons!
Cheer up, let the rabble come;
For beneath the Union Jack
We will drive the Fenians back
And we'll fight for our beloved Canadian homes.[47]

St. Patrick's Day in 1866 passed without incident. The Fenian Brotherhood had become divided over strategies. The "Men of Action" were determined to incite war in North America, while the other faction wanted to focus solely on fomenting revolution in Ireland. The latter group suddenly lost support among their followers and decided to reverse course. In April 1866, they launched the first Fenian raid into Canada. The plan was to invade Campobello Island in New Brunswick, claim it as U.S. territory, and make it a base for war against Britain, hoping it might pull the United States into an Anglo-American war.[48]

The Campobello campaign was an utter fiasco. Some seven hundred Fenians gathered in Eastport, Maine, close to the New Brunswick border. The British had no trouble infiltrating the Fenians, and their spies had watched their every move for months. Six British warships were waiting near Campobello. Seward had also been alerted and sent Major General George Meade to Eastport, where he took possession of the arms before the Fenians set off an international war.

Bewildered by Seward's betrayal, the Fenians were left to salvage their honor by raiding Indian Island, slightly north of Campobello. A small band of Fenian raiders arrived by boat and demanded that the astonished British customs agent on the island surrender the British flag. The Fenians hurried back with the captured flag, which one Fenian journal crowed would "cause the British lion to shake his sides and lash his tail." The British, Canadian, and American press ridiculed the Fenians as drunken, crazed Irishmen. Now the Men of Action would have to demonstrate that the Fenians could not be dismissed so lightly.[49]

General Thomas Sweeny, a Union veteran and military commander for the Men of Action, devised an ambitious plan for a full-scale invasion of western Canada. It involved several armies attacking simultaneously across the border from St. Albans, Buffalo, and Chicago.[50] On May 31, 1866, about eight hundred Fenian soldiers under the command of Colonel John O'Neill crossed the Niagara River at Buffalo in the dark of night and established a camp near Fort Erie. Only then did they realize they were alone; the other Fenian forces failed to cross into Canada. O'Neill's army advanced to the small town of Ridgeway the next day.[51]

Reports of the invasion spread quickly across Canada West. An officer of the Queens Own Riflemen interrupted an opera performance at the Toronto Music Hall to announce that the Fenians were coming and all militia groups would muster at six the following day. A loud cheer rose from the audience, and the band played a rousing rendition of "God Save the Queen."[52] A battle between British monarchists and Irish republican invaders was about to commence. The Fenian raid, it seemed, was inflaming more Canadian than Irish nationalism.[53]

The Canadian soldiers were young and green; the Fenians were not. When O'Neill pulled his men back to form a line of defense, the Canadians thought they had them on the run and launched a full-out charge. As they advanced, the Fenians raked them with rifle fire, and the startled Canadians broke ranks and ran, flinging weapons and knapsacks aside as they fled, with the Fenians hot on their heels for nearly three miles.[54]

The Fenians claimed the Battle of Ridgeway to be the first Irish victory against the British since the Battle of Fontenoy in 1745. In truth, it was a minor skirmish involving seasoned Union veterans against an amateur militia of students and civilians. Though it lasted two hours, after all the running and wild shooting there were few casualties on either side.[55]

O'Neill soon realized that Canadian militias arriving on the scene were about to encircle his army. Leaving it to local civilians to bury the dead and care for the wounded, he led a hasty retreat to the Niagara River and waited for transportation to take them back across the border. In his official report, O'Neill admitted that about three hundred of his eight hundred men lost their nerve and deserted. He also destroyed three hundred sets of arms lest they fall into the hands of the enemy. The Fenians were down to 317 men and officers by the time they departed. They boarded a miserable scow, were apprehended by a U.S.

FIGURE 24. "The Fenian Expedition." This cartoon lists Britain's numerous unfriendly acts toward the Union during the Civil War, including granting belligerent rights to the Confederacy, protecting Confederate terrorists operating in Canada, and allowing the construction of the *Alabama* and other Confederate raiders that preyed on U.S. ships. The United States, nonetheless, stood on the principle of neutrality and arrested Fenians raiding British North America. *Harper's Weekly*, June 23, 1866. Hathitrust.

vessel, and towed back to the United States, where they faced charges of violating U.S. neutrality laws.[56]

The Fenian raids irritated Benjamin Disraeli, deputy leader of the new Tory government in the House of Commons, but not to the point of wanting to expend Britain's blood and treasure defending Canada. "It can never be our pretence or our policy to defend the Canadian frontier against the United States," Disraeli wrote Prime Minister Lord Derby a few weeks after the first Fenian raids. "If the Colonists can't, as a general rule defend themselves against the Fenians, they can do nothing. They ought to be and must be, strong enough for that." In exasperation, he asked, "what is the use of these Colonial Deadweights?"[57]

Meanwhile, Britain's North American colonists took the lead in preparing for the time when Canada would have to defend itself. The Charlottetown and Quebec conventions in 1864 created a framework for a federal union that would be able to govern and protect the provinces. The next step was to meet with British officials in London.

On December 4, 1866, representatives from Canada and the Maritime provinces met with British officials from the Colonial Office to prepare the British North America Act for presentation to Parliament. They met at the sumptuous Westminster Palace Hotel in London for three months to discuss the details of Canada's new government. The result was little more than ratification of the resolutions devised at the Quebec Conference two years earlier.

Canadian delegates were dismayed at Mother England's indifference to their passage from colony to semiautonomous nation. Alexander Galt, an English-born leader of the confederation movement, wrote his wife from London: "I am more than ever disappointed at the tone of feeling here as to the Colonies. I cannot shut my eyes to the fact that they want to get rid of us. They have a servile fear of the United States and would rather give us up than defend us, or incur the risk of war with that country." Britain's disinterest in holding onto Canada made him "doubt much whether Confederation will save us from Annexation."[58]

As the meetings drew to a close, the final matter of discussion was over a name for the new polity they had fashioned. The trouble came when the Canadian monarchists wanted to name their new nation the "United Kingdom of Canada." One even recommended that the chief executive be called "viceroy" instead of governor general. This language was entirely in keeping with the conservative, anti-democratic, and anti-American spirit that prevailed among the Canadian leaders of the confederation, but it would not do.[59]

British officials thought it pretentious for a dominion of the British Empire to assume nominal equality with the mother country. Canadians would remain subjects of the British monarch and did not have a monarch of their own. Frederick Bruce, the British minister in Washington, also warned London that rumors about the "Kingdom of Canada" had stirred much "unfriendly" sentiment in America. British officials answered immediately with instructions for Bruce to deny the rumors. They, too, were worried that terms like "Kingdom" and "viceroy" might "open a monarchical blister on the side of the United States."[60]

The blister was already forming. News of the London meetings irritated American politicians. Maine's governor announced in January 1867 that the Canadian union, "along with the French Empire in Mexico [is] a part of a great conspiracy against Liberty on this youthful continent." Monarchy was closing in on a continent dedicated to republican freedom.[61]

Republican congressman Nathaniel P. Banks asked whether President Johnson had protested the "consolidation of all the British North American Provinces into a single confederation under the imperial rule of an English prince."[62] A month later, as the London meetings ended, Banks moved a resolution in Congress asserting that "a confederation of states on this continent, extending from ocean to ocean . . . and founded upon monarchical principles" was a threat to "the traditions and constantly declared principles of this government, endangering its most important interests." Banks was turning the new Monroe Doctrine aimed at the monarchy in Mexico to the North against British North America.[63]

Heeding the warnings from America, British and Canadian officials agreed to call confederated Canada the "Dominion of Canada." As one British official explained the matter, instead of calling it the "United Provinces of Canada"—God forbid they call it the "United States of British North America"—the new name was "a tribute to the Monarchical principle which they earnestly desire to uphold."[64]

The Times of London drolly noted that Americans "have always laboured under the delusion that our zeal for the extension of Monarchical or Aristocratic institutions is equal to their own zeal for the extension of Republican or Democratic institutions. . . . they fancy that French Imperialists and English Constitutionalists are in conspiracy with each other to propagate despotic principles in the New World." That might be true with the French in Mexico but not Britain, the *Times* insisted. "The union of the Canadian Provinces . . . will be . . . a self-governing community, with a strong resemblance to the neighbouring States of the Union."[65]

The former United Province of Canada became the provinces of Ontario and Quebec, while New Brunswick and Nova Scotia constituted two other provinces. Prince Edward Island and Newfoundland opted out for the time being, and all the territory west of Ontario, including British Columbia, was not yet part of the new government.[66]

As the British North America Act made its way through Parliament, Radical MP John Bright, a leading champion of American-style democracy, ridiculed the Canadians' fawning "filial piety," even to the point of mimicking Britain's aristocratic House of Lords with a senate "selected not elected" for life by the British governor general. Bright expressed dismay that the plan for confederation had not been put to the people and noted a petition signed by 31,000 Nova Scotians objecting to the lack of any public voice in the decision. Bright also challenged the underlying premise of the act by denying "there is any party in the United States that wishes to commit any aggression upon Canada, or to annex Canada by force to the United States," that is, aside from the Irish Fenians.[67] The bill became law after a debate one historian described as "less lively than that on a dog tax bill which followed." On March 29, 1867, Queen Victoria gave her royal assent. The Dominion of Canada began its national life on July 1, 1867, a subtle Canadian retort to America's annual celebration of independence from Britain on July 4.[68]

The Canadian Confederation dampened American hopes for annexation. So long as the *Alabama* Claims remained unresolved, however, the idea that some cession of British territory might settle them remained alive. Seward made a valiant effort to resolve the claims before he retired, but the Johnson-Clarendon Treaty he hoped would close the dispute met stiff resistance in the Senate.

Charles Sumner complained that Britain had not even admitted, let alone apologized, for its depredations against the Union. As to the

FIGURE 25. "The British Lion Disarmed." The movement toward the confederation of Canada began in earnest after 1865 when tensions between the United
States and Britain heated up over the *Alabama* Claims, which some Americans
proposed might be settled by the cession of British Columbia or all of British
North America to the United States. This Thomas Nast cartoon depicts Columbia
clipping the British lion's nails with scissors labeled "Alabama Claims." *Harper's
Weekly*, August 1, 1868. Hathitrust.

monetary amount, Sumner argued that any settlement must account for
the general loss in trade and the cost of war. He casually estimated that
Britain's "intervention" in favor of the South had doubled the length of
the war. Because the war cost the United States some four billion dollars,
Britain owed an astonishing two billion dollars in reparations. Michigan
senator Zachariah Chandler moved that Britain cede all of Canada as a
down payment on the settlement, adding that Michigan alone could
muster 60,000 troops to invade and hold Canada hostage. The Senate
voted 54 to 1 against the Johnson-Clarendon Treaty, the issue continued
to fester, and it became clear the Dominion of Canada was not for sale.[69]

American expansionists continued to nourish an ancient dream that
Canadians would eventually find their way to joining the American
union peacefully and voluntarily. The bonds of commerce, common

language and customs, and the imagined desire for independence from Old World monarchy would do their work in time.

This dream was not delusionary. Confederation was the project of royalist elites from the Province of Canada who made American annexation a bugaboo and Canadian unification the only path to salvation. The Maritime provinces were impatient with the dominant role of Ontario and Quebec under the new regime. In Nova Scotia, there was talk of secession and annexation by the United States. Newspapers and public speakers came close to treason. Opponents of the confederation won 36 of 38 seats in the provincial assembly and sent only one proconfederation representative to parliament. Some annexationists wrote directly to Washington seeking help with their campaign. Those that did not want annexation wanted to secede from the yoke of the Dominion, and when the British came down hard on the secessionists, the annexation movement gained force.[70]

In 1869 the inhabitants of British Columbia petitioned the Grant administration for admission to the Union. The same year, settlers in the Red River Valley declared independence from Canada.[71] The confederation was failing, so it seemed, and some thought again that Canada might either fall apart or join the United States. The British ambassador to Washington, Sir Edward Thornton, repeatedly assured Hamilton Fish, Grant's secretary of state, that Britain was eager for Canada to go its own way, whether as an independent nation or as part of the United States. As Thornton explained, Canada, not Britain, must first initiate separation.[72]

Fish and Grant held back on settling the *Alabama* Claims, hoping an exchange might come about. But patience finally gave out, and the United States resolved the *Alabama* Claims in 1871–72.[73] Britain paid the United States fifteen million dollars and issued a priceless apology for aiding the Confederacy. Canada, meanwhile, had taken measures to incorporate the western territories into the confederation. The Fenian agitation by this time had gravitated to Ireland. The boundary between the United States began its illustrious career as the longest unfortified border in the world and a celebrated example of democratic peace.

CHAPTER 6

Avanza Lincoln

Avanza Lincoln, Avanza!
Tu eres nuestra Esperanza!

—AFRO-CUBAN CHANT, 1860S

Spain's imperialist ambitions in the American hemisphere were tenacious and fraught with matters of national honor and proslavery interests. Its retreat from the American hemisphere was far more troubled than that of Britain, Russia, or France. Since the 1820s, when it lost its American empire—except for Cuba and Puerto Rico—Spain had been brooding over its unceasing decline as a world power. Britain and France, along with lesser European powers, felt no necessity to consult with Spain before making any foreign policy moves. When civil war broke out in the United States, Spain saw a golden opportunity to reclaim its place in the American sun. "The Union is in agony," Spain's ambassador to Washington, Gabriel García Tassara, wrote to his government with undisguised pleasure in January 1861, "our mission is not to delay its death for a moment." Now is the time to refute the Monroe Doctrine and "give a good lesson to the United States."[1]

During the Civil War, no European power flouted the Monroe Doctrine so brazenly as Spain. Queen Isabella II, the feckless scion of the Bourbon dynasty that had ruled Spain since 1700, was surrounded by military men seeking to win favor through vainglorious overseas conquests. In March 1861, Spain landed troops in the Dominican Republic and proclaimed its return to the Spanish Empire as a colony. Later the same year, Spain joined France and Britain in an allied invasion of

Mexico, ostensibly to recover debts owed to European investors. Many thought Mexico would return to Spanish rule, but when General Juan Prim realized the French had plans for Maximilian, he pulled Spain's forces out of Mexico.[2]

No sooner did Spain abandon Mexico than it launched a "scientific expedition" to strengthen its "moral and material interests" in South America. Spain's sudden interest in scientific matters alarmed skeptics in August 1862 when the expedition launched from Cadiz with the scientists on one ship that met up with no less than four powerful warships as their escort. The purpose of the armed expedition, according to the secret instructions given to commanding officer Rear Admiral Luis H. Pinzón, was to settle scores with its former colonies and teach them to respect Spain's "honor and dignity."[3]

The expedition's destination was Peru, once Spain's most lucrative American colony, whose independence it refused to recognize. Peru's newspapers had irritated Spain by denouncing its aggression in the Dominican Republic and Mexico, and the Spanish squadron headed toward South America to teach its former colonies respect for the leader of Hispanic culture.[4] Further irritation came when Spain demanded reparations for the death of two Spanish immigrants killed in a brawl with Peruvian workers. Peru refused, and in April 1864, Spain imposed a blockade and then seized the Chincha Islands, whose valuable supply of guano was the country's primary source of income. For Spain's imperialist party, it was a welcome chance to humiliate its unruly former colony.[5]

The seizure of the Chincha Islands coincided with the ascent of Maximilian as emperor of Mexico and added to the wave of outrage that erupted across Latin America. Spain's attack on Peru was an assault on all American republics, as most Latin Americans saw things. In November 1864, Peru's government called for delegates from all American nations to meet in Lima to discuss the threat of European aggression. Representatives from seven South American republics (Peru, Chile, Bolivia, Ecuador, Argentina, Colombia, and Venezuela) met in Lima for the Inter-American Congress in November 1864 to discuss the common threat of European aggression and forge an American union or military alliance.

FIGURE 26. The Bombardment of Valparaíso, March 1866. During the American Civil War, Spain sought to exert influence over the "Hispanic race" in America. After provoking war with Peru and seizing its guano-rich Chincha Islands, Spain's fleet bombarded Chile's defenseless port, Valparaíso. Museo de la Marina, Paris, Wikimedia Commons.

Though they invited the United States to Lima, the Lincoln administration felt that any insult to Spain might turn them toward the Confederacy. If the United States was unwilling to defend the Monroe Doctrine, Latin Americans were.[6]

In solidarity with Peru, Chile refused to supply coal to Spain's warships. Spain answered with an imperious demand that Chile issue a formal apology and give a twenty-one-gun salute to the Spanish flag, which Chile proudly refused. Spain imposed a blockade on Chile, and, after months of altercations and negotiations, in March 1866, it launched a horrific bombardment of Valparaíso, Chile's main port. Spanish cannons fired over two thousand shots at government buildings, warehouses, and the railway station. The Chileans did not return fire; they wanted the world to witness the Empire of Spain bombarding a completely defenseless city. The denunciation of "Spanish Barbarism" rang through the international press and cast the assault on Valparaíso as one of the darkest pages in modern Spanish history.[7]

Enthusiasm in the United States for its "sister republics" in Latin America began to run high in response to Spain's outrageous aggression in

Peru and Chile. Even before the bombardment of Valparaíso, Chile sent Benjamín Vicuña Mackenna, a prominent historian and politician, to arouse American sympathy for his country's courageous stand against Spain. He made a passionate appeal to Pan-American solidarity and the Monroe Doctrine at a massive rally at the Cooper Union in New York on January 6, 1866. "Beyond your southern frontier," he addressed the boisterous crowd, "there exists another America, sister to yours, unknown and forgotten to you." He took the audience through the litany of Spanish depredations against Santo Domingo, Mexico, and now Peru and Chile. Chile stood up to Spain to defend "a Monroe Doctrine of our own." The Latin American Monroe Doctrine, he explained, simply meant that "the monarchical Governments of Europe will not be permitted to interfere with republican institutions in the New World." The crowd went wild, "rising to their feet, waving their hats and handkerchiefs for several minutes, shouting vivas and hurrahs for Chili" in "a perfect storm of applause."[8]

Spain's imperialist overreach during the American Civil War ended in defeat and humiliation, weakened support for the government at home, and set the stage for the Glorious Revolution that overthrew Queen Isabella II's throne in 1868. In Santo Domingo, Blacks were fearful that Spain, the last European power permitting slavery, would reenslave them. Together with neighboring Haitians, Dominicans in 1863 launched a fierce War of Restoration against Spanish forces. They inflicted heavy casualties on the occupation forces, many of whom also fell victim to deadly diseases, especially *el vomito* (yellow fever), which plagued whites far more than Africans. Spain refused to withdraw and sent in more soldiers, raising the occupation force from three to twenty-five thousand by early 1865.[9]

Early in 1865, as the shadow of Union victory loomed over the Spanish Caribbean, the Cortes in Madrid began a lengthy debate on the mounting cost in lives and treasure of defending its former colony and the incalculable price of national honor should Spain give up. March 31, 1865, four years after the invasion of Santo Domingo, the Spanish Cortes voted in favor of withdrawal.[10] That summer, thousands of Spanish soldiers evacuated on ships bound for Havana amid a scene of chaos as panicked Dominican "loyalists" scrambled to get onboard rather than fall into the hands of the victorious republicans. Dominican fighters charged into the capital, setting fire to the buildings the Spanish had erected lest they return.[11]

Laurindo Lapuente, a Latin American poet, paid homage to the Dominicans in his collection of poems, *Republicanas* (1865):

> The Spanish army decimated and convinced of
> its impotence to dominate the Dominicans,
> has gathered its flags and has reembarked,
> to return to Spain to say to its mistress the Queen,
> that the children of Santo Domingo do not want to be slaves.[12]

Nor did the children of South America wish to be slaves. Almost a year after the evacuation of Santo Domingo, on May 2, 1866, Spain got its nose bloodied by Peru. It was trying to do for Callao, Peru's main port, what it had done for Valparaíso, Chile: destroy it with a hail of artillery. At the behest of Peru's liberal president and in violation of all diplomatic protocol, former Union general Alvin Hovey, the new U.S. minister to Peru, secretly helped Peru's military construct a barrier of underwater torpedoes. As the Spanish squadron entered the harbor, a skillfully timed series of torpedo explosions sent massive towers of water into the sky and forced the Spanish ships into retreat. Peru's guns punished the Spanish fleet from the hills overlooking the harbor. Every Spanish vessel was damaged, two sank, and the Spanish commanding officer was seriously wounded. Orders from Spain instructed the wounded admiral to sink his ships in the Pacific rather than return home in dishonor.[13]

Somehow, the Spanish fleet managed to limp out of Callao a few days later. Its vainglorious expedition to teach its former colonies a lesson was all but finished. Then in June, Seward received a surprising report that Spain intended to wring reparations out of the Chincha Islands. Seward put his foot down hard, forcefully invoking the Monroe Doctrine in all but name. "Such a seizure and occupation would constitute an act of intervention by a European Monarchial Power in the proper affairs of Republican Sovereignty in America," Seward warned, which would require the United States to abandon its neutrality in the war between Spain and the South American republics.[14]

Seward had offered Spain the good offices of the United States to mediate peace, and his threat of taking sides with Peru and its allies made that offer all the more attractive. Horatio Perry, the able chargé d'affaires at the U.S. legation in Madrid, wrote candidly to Seward in September 1866 that Spain "would jump at such a good excuse for backing out of the Pacific Ocean forever." He added that the South American republics much preferred that the United States, not Britain or France, mediate peace. The U.S. minister to Chile also advised Seward that the United States was "now more highly respected and appreciated by the allied governments [Peru, Chile, Bolivia, Ecuador] than any power on earth" and would welcome its role in bringing peace.[15] Though it took another four years for the parties to sign an armistice, Spain's war against the South American republics effectively ended at Callao. Just as he nudged the French out of Mexico by means of tough diplomacy, Seward preferred statecraft to saber-rattling in convincing Spain to withdraw from South America. Looming over Seward's quiet diplomacy, however, was the ominous shadow of the Monroe Doctrine backed by the military capacity of the United States to defend the principle of "America for Americans!"[16]

Cuba, the "Ever Faithful Isle," had remained loyal to Spain when its other American colonies broke for independence. It was a prosperous sugar plantation economy heavily dependent on enslaved labor and the continued importation of Africans. Slaveholders feared that a war for freedom from Spain might become a struggle for freedom from slavery. A familiar saying held that "when Cuba ceased to be Spanish she would be African." White fears of Black domination sustained slavery in Cuba much as they had in the United States. That was about to change.[17]

Many Cubans saw Abraham Lincoln and the Union's victory over the slaveholders' rebellion as a cause for hope in Cuba's future. Most Cuban Creoles (whites born in Cuba) were weary of Spanish exploitation and fed up with the inferior status Spanish-born *peninsulares* assigned to them. Creoles outnumbered *peninsulares* nine to one, yet they had no role in governing Cuba. Spain imposed exorbitant taxes on Cuba while its officials enriched themselves on the island's thriving sugar economy. Though Cuba sold most of its sugar to the United States, Spain's archaic mercantilist regulations imposed heavy duties on exports not going to Spain. Discontented Cubans watched as Mexico, the Dominican Republic, Peru, Chile, and other Spanish American republics stood up to Spain and asked: why should Cuba remain "ever faithful" to its Spanish masters?[18]

Though Spanish Cubans tended to sympathize with the Confederacy, among the almost 370,000 enslaved Afro-Cubans (nearly 30 percent of Cuba's population in 1861), there was no question their hopes lay with Lincoln and the Union. During the war, Blacks flocked to the port in Havana, waiting for the ships carrying the latest news. They would "exhibit their happiness for the victories of the north whom they rightfully believed were the redeemers of the African race in America."[19] Robert Shufeldt, U.S. consul-general in Havana, reported: "Among the negroes themselves I have no doubt the effect of the war is well canvassed and I am told that they already mingle within their songs the significant refrain 'Avanza Lincoln, Avanza! Tu eres nuestra Esperanza!'" (Onward Lincoln, Onward! You are our Hope!)[20]

Enslaved Cubans seemed to understand the Civil War was going to destroy slavery, and not only in the United States. Shufeldt's successor, Thomas Savage, heard the same chant and connected it to the stirring of slave rebellion. "The colored population are certainly somewhat agitated," he reported to Seward in October 1863. "The words 'Lincoln Advances' are often heard in their songs, and conversations among themselves." Savage wrote again in July 1864 that there "can be no doubt that the seed has been sown [and] broadcast and that the spirit of discontent amongst the negroes is universal and will sooner or later break out with terrible effect."[21]

During the San Juan and San Pedro festival in the summer of 1865, Spanish authorities in Santiago de Cuba arrested a group of Blacks for planning to raise a flag emblazoned with the word "Esperanza." Both parties understood the subversive implications this simple word carried. All the Cubans, "even the slaveholders," Shufeldt reported in October, "can scarcely refrain from manifesting their sympathy" for the Union cause and the new sense of *esperanza* it carried across the water to Cuba.[22]

"In the decree of liberty for its Negroes," one Cuban later observed, "the United States defined also the future of the Creole slaveowners."[23] Above all, whatever that future meant, it pointed to the end of slavery. "The time in which Cuba and Puerto Rico trembled before the thought of becoming African is over," a group of Cuban reformers wrote Queen Isabella II in July 1865. Many Spaniards also seemed to understand the American war's implications for their colonies.[24]

In no part of Latin America did the appeal of Abraham Lincoln and the shock of his assassination register with more emotion among ordinary people than in Cuba. Emeterio Santovenia, a Cuban historian and politician, described a "cult" of Lincoln that took hold across the island. He wrote that portraits of Lincoln adorned the walls of "many mansions on the Island, in almost all those that housed altruistic, philanthropic, humanitarian and progressive men, the emancipator's effigy was a symbol, a flag, a means of expressing deeply felt aspirations in an oppressed colony and a land of slavery."[25]

Lincoln's assassination caused a wave of grief to pass over the island. "Men and women wore, each man on the watch and each woman on the waist, black ribbons with the Union eagle and the portrait of the martyr," Santovenia recorded. Lincoln's death afflicted Creoles and coloreds with equal emotion, for "both had so longed for Lincoln's advance during the civil war, because they considered it their best hope." Among Lincoln's mourners was "a boy, twelve years old, born in Havana [who] trembled and cried upon learning of Lincoln's death, without knowing him, without knowing an iota of his life." The boy was José Martí, the future martyr for Cuban independence.[26]

Mourning Lincoln became a means of defining new allegiances among those Cubans dissatisfied with Spanish rule and ready to end slavery. A stream of citizens came by the U.S. consulate in Havana to express their condolences. The leading Havana newspaper published a translation of a U.S. government report on the assassination, *Causa celebre*, over eight hundred pages describing Lincoln's life and the trial of his assassins. A popular medical doctor in Havana honored Lincoln by paying for the freedom of all Cuban children born in slavery on July 4, 1865. Poets wrote emotion-filled tributes to the fallen hero, and bards composed songs that extolled his virtues. "The Island was excited and waiting for something that nobody was able to express exactly," Santovenia wrote. "It accepted the probability of the abolition of slavery without the terror that until recently the mere mention of such a phenomenon had inspired." Lincoln's feats were more than a foreign leader's good deeds. As an icon of emancipation and government by the Cuban people, Lincoln embodied *nuestra esperanza*.[27]

In 1865, Spain was the last European nation still permitting slavery. Before then, there had been no public voice against slavery in Spain or its colonies apart from translations and dramatic enactments of Harriet Beecher Stowe's renowned novel *La choza del negro Tomás*.[28] In early 1865, a few weeks before news of Lincoln's death coursed through the Spanish Empire, the Spanish Abolitionist Society held its inaugural meeting in Madrid. The society quickly moved into the political mainstream, gaining the support of prominent politicians.[29]

The American Civil War cast a heavy shadow over the future of slavery in the Spanish Caribbean. Historians point to Lincoln's Emancipation Act, enacted in January 1863, and the Thirteenth Amendment, December 1865, as the most significant blows. Still, they often ignore Secretary of State William Seward's bold steps in 1862 to align the United States with Britain's campaign to suppress the African slave trade. Before secession, Southern politicians had refused to allow British ships patrolling the coast of Africa to search ships flying the U.S. flag, and many of the traffickers of African slaves registered their ships in the United States to evade British interference. The Lincoln administration, Seward made clear, would have "none of the squeamishness . . . that characterized their predecessors." His initiative led to a formal treaty with Britain to allow the search and seizure of slavers under the American flag. It marked a decisive turn in U.S. foreign policy toward ridding the American hemisphere of slavery. The Lyons-Seward Treaty, as it was known, doomed slavery in Cuba because it continued to depend on the importation of

enslaved Africans. Within five years of the treaty's enactment, the Atlantic slave trade vanished, according to Seymour Drescher, the premier
historian of international abolition. The traffic between Africa and Cuba
dropped sharply from an estimated 25,000 in 1860 to less than 7,000 by
1864 and down to only 143 in 1865. Facing growing international con-
demnation, Spain finally passed its own law to suppress the slave trade
in 1866. Seward's treaty with Britain and the abolition of slavery in the
United States forced Spain and its Caribbean colonies to reconsider
the future of slavery.[30]

Immediately after the Union's victory, in May 1865, the Spanish Cortes, for the first time since 1837, opened a long-forbidden debate on the
slavery question. Antonio María Fabié, a conservative deputy who opposed slavery, rose before the deputies to announce, "the war in the
United States is finished, and being finished, slavery in the whole American continent can be taken as finished."[31]

In November 1865, Spain's government announced a Colonial Reform
Commission (Junta de Información de Ultramar) intended to address
slavery and colonial governance in light of the new circumstances in the
American hemisphere. Spanish officials invited Cuba and Puerto Rico to
send delegates to the Reform Commission meetings. The commission's
purpose was to consider, quietly and behind closed doors, necessary reforms in light of the demise of the transatlantic slave trade. Not all Cubans
wanted the same thing, but most agreed on economic reforms involving
tariff and trade regulations and political reform of the Spanish government in Cuba. The commission considered home rule over Cuban affairs,
equality of rights between Creoles and *peninsulares*, and representation in
the Cortes. Though not all delegates agreed on the future of slavery, at
least most wanted to end the slave trade. Some, particularly the Puerto
Rican representatives, wanted to abolish slavery altogether.[32]

After long delays, the Reform Commission met for the first time in
October 1866. The discussion on slavery opened with ideas for encouraging natural reproduction among the existing slave populations by
bringing female house slaves in the cities to the primarily male labor
force in the countryside. The commission also considered plans to coerce
the labor of free Blacks and colored vagrants along with ways to induce

European immigration and the importation of Asian coolies as a substi-
tute for slave labor. The "reforms" Spanish officials preferred to consider
would only postpone emancipation.[33]

At the commission's third session, several Puerto Rican delegates announced they had no interest in preserving slavery. Slavery in Puerto
Rico was in steep decline, and its representatives felt the time had come
to end the "ill-fated institution" of slavery altogether. It fell like a bomb-
shell on the other commission members. The Puerto Ricans then issued
a full-scale attack on how slavery had poisoned Spain and its colonies,
debased work, and created a sugar aristocracy "based on injustice and
iniquity." We ask, the Puerto Ricans implored, "in the name of the honor
and the future of our country, the immediate, radical and definitive abolition of slavery."[34]

Proslavery Cuban delegates answered with predictions of a horrific
Haitian-style descent into barbarism. Emancipation, they warned, must
not deny "the right of the white population to defend its existence and
to remain in the country conquered by their forefathers." The rhetoric
and reasoning were reminiscent of America's slaveholders before the
Civil War.[35]

The Reform Commission's report contained much more than the
proposals for emancipation; the commission also laid out necessary
government and economic reforms. Had all the recommendations been
realized, Cuba might have become for Spain like Canada for Britain,
a self-governing, loyal member of a transatlantic empire able to make a
peaceful transition from slavery to a biracial, free-labor society. Instead,
Spain's government buried the Reform Commission's report and refused to enact any reform measures. Rather than a Spanish version of
Canada, Cuba became more like Ireland, an obstinate irritant within the
empire.[36]

Cubans had suffered Spanish misrule for decades without rebelling, but
the spirit of *esperanza* that washed over the island in 1865 made the failure of reform the last straw for many. On October 10, 1868, Carlos Manuel de Céspedes, a Cuban sugar planter and lawyer, raised the flag of
rebellion near his home in Yara, a rural town in the province of Oriente

on the island's eastern side. He promised freedom to any of his enslaved workers, about thirty in number, willing to join the revolution for Cuba Libre. The main grievances outlined in the *Grito de Yara* were not about slavery and abolition; they were about Spain's corrupt government of Cuba and its economic exploitation of the island.[37]

Céspedes was not quite fifty, "a small man with a good deal of iron in his composition," one journalist observed. He had studied law in Barcelona in the 1840s, where he befriended Juan Prim, a fellow student. The two took part in the failed revolution of 1843, after which Spanish officials deported Céspedes to France, where he imbibed more revolutionary ideas before returning to Cuba.[38]

Word of Céspedes's proclamation moved among the enslaved population across the island. William C. Tinker, a New York dentist living in Havana since 1852, had ties by marriage to Spanish officials, but his republican sympathies lay with the insurrection. Tinker described the Afro-Cubans who joined the revolution: "They were as free as any white citizens, to choose what they would do, or where they would go. They understood that they were free, and that their freedom had been given to them by the republic of Cuba, and their former masters, and they understood that their freedom had resulted in some way from the emancipation of slaves in the United States. They had pictures of Abraham Lincoln, and spoke of him familiarly as the *emancipador*, or emancipator."

One named Cintra "had particularly distinguished himself" in two battles against the Spanish, which Tinker had witnessed. He also testified that volunteers were arriving from Mexico, where they had fought the French and Maximilian's forces; others had fought in the U.S. Civil War or the Dominican War of Restoration. They came to Cuba to drive the last European empire back across the Atlantic and emancipate Cuba's enslaved.[39]

The soldiers in what rebels called the Liberation Army became known as the Mambí. It was a name the Spanish had given to the guerilla warriors of Santo Domingo, some of whom were now fighting in Cuba. It may have referred to an African bird that was heard but rarely seen. Cuban revolutionaries embraced this nickname with pride. After all, it commemorated the victorious war in Santo Domingo. The success of the Cuban insurrection would depend on enslaved and free Africans. They constituted between half and two-thirds of the Liberation Army, or between seven and ten thousand of the fifteen thousand total, according to estimates. Whatever the actual numbers, the Afro-Cuban soldiers were indispensable to the struggle for Cuba's freedom and their own.[40]

A reporter for the *New York Herald*, James O'Kelly, gave American readers a vivid view of the Mambí army. O'Kelly was a firebrand Irish Fenian who recognized the rebellion in Cuba as something like Ireland's against Britain. Cubans fought the "cloven foot" Spanish while the Irish Fenians battled draconian English rule, each people rising against their brutal oppressors. He was also fascinated by the racial democracy of the Mambises. "About one-third of the fighting men are white, and the majority of the other two-thirds are of color other than black, all shades of brown predominating." O'Kelly cheerfully noted, "the most perfect equality exists between the white and colored races, the officers taking precedence by rank, and although the majority of the officers are white, a very large proportion are colored."[41]

As the revolution became increasingly dependent on recruiting Afro-Cubans, its leaders realized that some concrete promise of emancipation was essential to hold their loyalty. Céspedes had cast the revolution as Cuba Libre fighting against Spanish *esclavistas* (proslavery), and he freed his enslaved workers but could only promise eventual freedom for the others. Cuba's large slaveholders, prevalent in the western part of the island, had no intention of ending slavery. Therefore, the revolution remained confined to the eastern provinces, where sugar plantations and slavery were less central to the economy.[42]

Spain's colonial officials in Havana treated Céspedes and his untrained army as an isolated rebellion they could squash with little effort. They maintained only a small force of 7,000 in the regular army, supplemented by a citizen militia group known as the Spanish Volunteers. Organized initially to defend Cuba against filibustering expeditions in the 1850s, the Spanish Volunteers drew mainly from the Spanish-born *peninsulares* and *negreros* (large slaveholders). During the revolution, the Volunteers grew to 85,000 men, all well-armed with Remington rifles purchased in the

United States. They also constituted a reactionary political force whose role was not to fight the insurgents so much as "to over awe the sympathisers and supporters of the Rebel party, to ferret out their accomplices, and to do duty as a police, terrorising the cities."[43]

The political power of the Spanish Volunteers was such that they took control of the colonial government, even forcing Governor Domingo Dulce to resign in June 1869 after he made a gesture of appeasement to the rebels. The Volunteers then dictated a war of extermination to wipe out rebel forces, and they saw the insurgency as nothing more than a slave uprising led by white traitors. The Volunteers constitute an *imperium in imperio* (government within government), observed Thomas Jordan, an ex-Confederate who served the Liberation Army. In all things, he noted, the Volunteers do as they choose and in brazen disregard of the home government.[44]

General Valmaseda, the Spanish military commander, described not unfairly as a "fat and cruel" Spanish aristocrat, became infamous for his ruthless brand of warfare in Cuba. In what amounted to a Black Decree issued April 4, 1869, Valmaseda warned: "Every man, from the age of fifteen years, upward, found away from his habitation, and does not prove a justified motive therefor, will be shot; Every habitation unoccupied will be burned by the troops; Every habitation from which does not float a white flag, as a signal that its occupants desire peace, will be reduced to ashes." When Secretary Fish saw Valmaseda's decree, he wrote the Spanish minister in Washington: "In the interest of Christian civilization and common humanity, I hope that this document is a forgery."[45]

Valmaseda's Black Decree was no ruse, and Spanish forces carried it out with ruthless efficiency. In 1871 Cubans published in English, obviously for the American audience, a record of the "carnival of blood" perpetrated by "Modern Spain" against its people. *The Book of Blood* catalogued the carnage based on information from Spanish sources, as the author deftly pointed out. The publication included an English translation of General Valmaseda's proclamation, underscoring its intended audience, the United States.[46]

The Spanish Volunteers were no less cruel than the Spanish regular army. Henry C. Hall, U.S. consul at Matanzas, reported that among the

Spanish Volunteers "are some of the worst elements of the Spanish (pen-insular) part of the population—men of brutal and sanguinary instincts, that would, if left to themselves, riot in fire and blood."[47] In Havana, the Volunteers entered a theater one evening and fired randomly into the crowd because they felt the previous night's performance had excited revolutionary enthusiasm. Also in Havana, they apprehended a group of students at the cemetery, accusing them of having "profaned" the grave of a Spanish officer, and had them executed before dawn the following day. The regular Spanish army was no better. It summarily executed rebel soldiers, slaughtered civilians, pillaged food and property, and razed homes and whole towns at will. Spain seemed bent on an all-out war of extermination that pitted thousands of well-armed soldiers against the ill-equipped and vastly outnumbered Mambí army.[48]

Céspedes and most rebel leaders understood that Spain's huge military advantage meant the Cuban revolution could not succeed without ex-ternal aid, which could only come from the United States. Britain could hardly expect to intervene in Cuba without provoking the wrath of the United States, never mind France. Nor were they inclined to take sides with Spain's colonial rebels without risking intervention in their volatile colonies such as Ireland or Algeria.

Latin American republics offered moral support but little more. Mex-ico, Chile, and Colombia acknowledged the belligerent rights of the Cuban republic; Peru went so far as to recognize Cuba as a sovereign republic. However, none could offer the financial and military aid the Cuban revolution required to succeed, which would have to come from the United States.[49]

From the beginning, Cuba's revolutionary leaders were pleading for recognition and aid from the United States and even going so far as to invite annexation. Two weeks after he issued the *Grito de Yara*, Céspedes appealed to William Seward in language crafted to appeal to America's republican sensibilities. After three centuries of tyranny, the Cuban people "have finally raised in our beautiful and unfortunate land the flag of liberty" and assembled an army of Cubans willing to die for their free-dom. All that is lacking is the recognition of those "civilized and free nations" capable of upholding modern human rights standards against Spain's barbarism.[50] Céspedes also made an oblique invitation to annex Cuba into the United States. With your help in "conquering our liberty," he told Seward, "we will form an integral part of such powerful States, because the peoples of America are called to form a single nation and to be the admiration and amazement of the whole world."[51]

Seward was about to leave office, and he answered with silence. Undaunted, Céspedes turned to the incoming president, Ulysses S. Grant. He hit the same flattering notes as he had with Seward, calling on the United States to carry out its duty of "civilizing . . . the republics of the New World" by recognizing and aiding the Cuban revolution. Receiving no answer, Céspedes wrote again in March. The United States, he wrote to President Grant, "is the civilized nation closest to Cuba, whose institutions meet a sympathetic echo in the hearts of all Cubans. . . . Cuba ardently appeals to its unquestionable right to be recognized."[52]

Though Céspedes and the rebel leadership understood they would have to align with the United States on the emancipation question, they were hesitant about committing to outright abolition. What worried them were the large slaveholders, especially in the western provinces, who would not give up slavery. There was also widespread apprehension among Cuban whites that emancipation might reawaken traditional fears about racial strife and Africanization. On December 27, 1868, Céspedes issued a cautious decree promising "conditional abolition" (*abolición condicionada*), meaning emancipation would occur *after* Cuba won its independence and would be able to compensate owners. He aimed to appease slaveholders and other whites who worried that "violent emancipation" would upset the whole economy and incite racial conflict.[53]

The revolution's caution on emancipation changed suddenly in early 1869. On January 7, 1869, General Valmaseda led his army east from Havana into the heart of the rebellion. His army engaged the rebels at El Saltillo in the Villa Clara district and left more than two thousand Mambises dead, most of them recent Afro-Cuban recruits. On January 15, Valmaseda's army entered Bayamo, the birthplace of the insurrection, only to find the rebels had burned the entire town to the ground and fled. Valmaseda's march of destruction, the Black Decree, and Spain's overwhelming advantages in arms and men left rebel morale devastated. Thousands of the Mambise surrendered out of fear for their families and themselves.[54]

The same day Bayamo went up in flames, Céspedes wrote his appointed envoy to the United States, José Morales Lemus, to urge the United States to come to the aid of the revolution. He instructed Morales Lemus to inform Secretary Fish that the "abolition of slavery is already a *fait accompli*," an exaggerated claim, and "Blacks in great numbers are fighting in our ranks." He once again flung open the door to annexation: "All of us who have arms in hand and the public in general, are convinced that it is necessary to request the annexation of this Island to those important States." Without U.S. aid, he warned, Cuba will fall into "a fatal state of ruins and destruction" and die "victims of our patriotism."[55]

For many rebel leaders, the choice came down to annexation or devastation at the hands of a vengeful Spanish army. At the same time, Céspedes reached out to separate provincial rebel armies inviting them to form a united front under his command. The rebel leaders in Camagüey, a province west of Céspedes's stronghold in Oriente, were unhappy with Céspedes's leadership. They were critical of him for precipitating the conflict before Cubans were ready to equip and field an army, all for his selfish pursuit of glory. Céspedes, his detractors claimed, operated more like a self-appointed *caudillo* or warlord than a republican statesman. Furthermore, his vacillating policy on emancipation made it impossible to win support from the United States or any other civilized nation.

Céspedes planned first to defeat Spain, then deliver on promises of emancipation and republican government. The Camagüey rebels understood that international aid was crucial, and to gain it, they must first create a unified government that could stand before the world as a republic worthy of the name, with a national army subordinate to civil authority. Not least, the Republic of Cuba must begin by abolishing slavery totally and immediately. The Camagüey Revolutionary Committee led the way on February 26, 1869, by declaring the abolition of slavery.[56]

The contagion of liberty that infected much of the Atlantic world in the late 1860s was nowhere more robust than among the young revolutionaries of Camagüey. They were young men in their twenties and early thirties, who came from well-off families, and many had spent time traveling and studying in Europe and the United States. They returned to Cuba brimming with republican ideals, embarrassed by slavery and fed up with Spain's oppressive rule. Among their leaders was Ignacio Agramonte, a fiery lawyer in his late twenties from a wealthy family in Puerto Príncipe who was educated in Barcelona. Another was Antonio Zambrana, a persuasive speaker and ardent republican, who was only twenty-two years old and fresh out of law school in Havana.[57]

The Camagüey rebels called for an assembly of delegates from all provinces in arms against Spain to meet in Guáimaro, a small village in Camagüey, beginning April 10, 1869, exactly six months after the *Grito de Yara*. The Guáimaro Assembly became the Republic of Cuba's constitutional convention. It was also the site of a political revolt against Céspedes. The assembly's opening session began with lavish praise for his vital role in leading the revolution and then elected him president of the republic. However, under the constitution formulated at Guáimaro, the president's powers would be little more than honorific. Real power was vested in the unicameral House of Representatives, whose duties included appointing the president. Had representation in the legislature been based on population, the Oriente would have dominated. Instead, a Camagüey leader denounced the "tyranny of numbers" and proposed that each of the republic's four "states" have equal representation. By this calculation, Céspedes's Oriente province had no more voice in government than Camagüey, despite having four times its population. The new constitution, with twenty-nine articles, was hammered out with lightning speed during the opening session, which began at four in the afternoon. The new provisional government was to "govern the duration of the War of Independence."[58]

After drafting the constitution, the assembly turned to the delicate question of annexation. The ferociousness of the Spanish army and the Volunteers had been so alarming that many delegates felt that they must either seek the protection of the United States or watch Cuba destroyed by war. The Camagüeyans and Céspedes agreed on this point, but others could not accept that a revolution to throw off Spanish oppressors would require begging the United States to take over. Eduardo Machado, the son of a wealthy sugar mill owner from Las Villas province who had spent eight years in the United States and Europe, spoke eloquently against annexation. It amounted to trading one ruler for another. To plead for annexation was an act of "patriotic suicide" in which Cuba would be "begging another people for freedom."[59]

Antonio Zambrana rose to defend annexation in what others described as a "brilliant speech." "The war has been undertaken to carry out the freedom of Cuba, not to ruin the country," Zambrana began, referring to Valmaseda's cruel campaign and the rebel razing of Bayamo. "If we can achieve this object, without ravaging the land, making Cuba become part of the splendid American constellation, we must not continue fighting for an independence that, if realized, would leave the country reduced to rubble, and to the most frightful desolation." Should the United States reject our plea, Zambrana concluded, "before returning to the Spanish yoke, we will request the protectorate of Great Britain."[60] The assembly voted to approve the petition for annexation and commissioned Zambrana with composing what one delegate ruefully admitted was a confession of "the impotence of the nascent republic."[61]

One of the last items of business taken up by the Guáimaro Assembly was adopting a flag for the newborn Cuban Republic. In a final insult to Céspedes, Antonio Zambrana proposed that the new republic abandon the banner Céspedes raised at Yara and adopt instead the flag chosen by the Camagüeyans. Their banner was the same Lone Star flag that Narciso López and his band of filibusters fought beneath in the 1850s. López was a South American revolutionary whose Cuban expeditions were sponsored, at least in part, by Southern slaveholders eager to annex Cuba and expand the Slave Power's Caribbean empire.[62] In Camagüey, Zambrano explained, López had first raised "the flag of 51," a "glorious testimony that Cubans had long been fighting tyranny." No one at Guáimaro protested the flag's imperialist and proslavery origins, nor did anyone seem concerned that Narciso López had so demonstrably failed to arouse support among the Cuban people. His aspirations to be the liberator of Cuba ended with his public garroting in Havana.[63]

FIGURE 27. "Cuban Patriots Rallying Round Their Flag." The flag originated as the banner U.S. filibusters led by Narciso López fought under in 1851. The Guáimaro Assembly adopted it as the flag of the Republic of Cuba in early 1869 and advocated that Cuba's Lone Star be added to the "splendid American constellation" of the United States. *Harper's Weekly*, April 10, 1869. Hathitrust.

For those puzzled by the Cuban revolution's adoption of the López flag, it bears mention that the Lone Star flag had a long future ahead. It eventually served as the national flag of the First Republic of Cuba in 1902 and continued as Cuba's national flag under Castro's revolutionary regime. By then, Cuba's new defenders of the Lone Star flag stood in defiant opposition to the "splendid American constellation" they once wanted to join.[64]

Whatever else Céspedes found disagreeable at Guáimaro, he was fully on board with the idea of annexation to the United States. In June 1869, he issued a presidential circular urging Cubans to contribute to "the consolidation of our government . . . so that tomorrow we can be worthy of becoming part of the Great American Republic."[65]

Despite its often clumsy appeals to the United States, the Cuban revolution enjoyed strong support across party and regional lines in the United States. The press was enthusiastic about welcoming a "sister republic" and advancing the Monroe Doctrine's promise of Pan-American republicanism. Nathaniel Banks, chair of the House Committee on Foreign Affairs, led the charge for the Cuban Republic's recognition: "The people of Cuba . . . fight against Spanish tyranny; against monarchical and aristocratic government; against dignities and titles; . . . against slavery and the slave trade. . . . It has every claim to the sympathy and support of the friends of liberty, equality, and justice."[66]

Inside Grant's cabinet, his close friend and trusted confidante, Secretary of War John Rawlins, was an outspoken proponent of recognition and annexation. He appealed to Grant's deep resentment of Spain's aggression in Latin America during the war. Rawlins had a personal stake in the matter. He was dying of tuberculosis, and to provide for his wife and children, he had invested thousands of dollars in Cuban bonds whose value hinged on the revolution's success. Hamilton Fish worried Grant would succumb to pressure from his friend, but Rawlins died in September 1869. Still, agitation for intervention in Cuba remained alive in the public square with large rallies, impassioned speeches, and financial support for covert support of the Cuban revolution.[67]

None displayed more enthusiasm for recognizing the Cuban republic than Black American leaders who saw the emancipation of Cuba and

FIGURE 28. "Under a Palm-Tree, Waiting for a Sail," depicting the Republic of Cuba looking to the United States for aid in its war against Spain. *Harper's Weekly*, September 4, 1869. Hathitrust.

Cuba's enslaved as America's moral obligation. Frederick Douglass, speaking before the American Anti-Slavery Society in May 1869, hailed the United States as "the freest and mightiest Republic on the globe" and about to be "recognized as the mightiest nation on the globe, the nation that is to dictate the law to the nations of Europe, the nation which more than any other beneath the sky is to give direction to the

FIGURE 29. "The War in Cuba." Spain's well-equipped army carried out a merciless war against the Cuban insurgents who won the sympathy of many Americans but not recognition and aid from the U.S. government. *Harper's Weekly*, May 7, 1870. Hathitrust.

civilization of the next fifty years." He prophesied that the United States was "getting ready" "to reach out its hand to those brave, those heroic and noble Cubans, who are now defending the cause which this Society and all America have sworn to support."[68]

John Mercer Langston, an African American educator, future U.S. congressman, and minister to Haiti, joined Douglass in advocating for America's postwar leadership abroad. "Every nation, whether its home be an island or upon a continent, if oppressed, ought to have, like our own, a 'new birth of freedom.'" He urged support for the "struggling patriots of Cuba" to make them "free from Spanish rule; her slaves all freemen, and herself advancing in her freedom, across the way of national greatness and renown."[69]

Hiram Revels, an African American senator representing Mississippi, also urged an aggressive policy supporting the Cuban revolution. It was "the duty of our powerful, wealthy, and christian nation," he wrote to

Charles Sumner, "to extend its institutions, or various means of enlightenment and intellectual, moral, and religious elevation with which God has blessed us, to the inhabitants of that Republic." Nor did U.S. Black leaders shrink from embracing annexation as a means of extending the blessings of "freedom, knowledge, and progress" to the victims of tyranny.[70]

On Cuba and other foreign policy matters, Grant, in the end, deferred to his astute—and immovable—secretary of state, Hamilton Fish. The conflict in Cuba, Fish understood, was a civil war within the Spanish Empire. To recognize or take sides in any way with the insurgents would violate every principle upon which the Union had made its case against foreign interference in a domestic insurrection during the Civil War. In particular, taking sides with the Cuban rebels would undermine the *Alabama* Claims the United States was making against Britain for aiding the Confederacy. Besides, Spain had just undergone a stunning democratic revolution, and the new liberal government of what Grant called "new Spain" indicated it would end slavery in the Caribbean, reform colonial governance, or let Cuba and Puerto Rico go. Fish wanted to facilitate Cuba's independence and end slavery there, but not by taking sides against the government in Spain the United States had recently welcomed into the fold of liberal democratic nations. Instead, he offered the "good offices" of the United States to mediate peace (the subject of chapter 8). Fish maintained a strict hands-off Cuba policy and refused to negotiate or even communicate officially with the Cuban revolutionaries.[71]

Fish hailed from a venerable New York family whose lineage stretched back to the Dutch Stuyvesants on his mother's side and an esteemed Revolutionary general on the paternal side. He had an honorable but undistinguished career in public service until, at age sixty, he became Grant's most trusted advisor and one of America's more able secretaries of state. While serving as U.S. senator from New York, he learned the ways of diplomacy as a member of the Committee on Foreign Relations. He was a loyal Republican but had little use for the Radicals and worried about their influence on his impulsive president.

Fish's interest in not offending Spain's new liberal government was only part of his concern about Cuba. He harbored grave doubts about the legitimacy and viability of the putative Republic of Cuba. Despite all the trappings of a constitution, president, legislature, and flag conceived at Guáimaro, the government was unable to establish a secure capital or port, let alone a functioning government. Though the Guáimaro constitution conformed to republican principles, the Cuban people had not elected the delegates who drafted it, nor had they ratified it. There was also little sign that the revolution could succeed militarily against the well-armed Spanish forces, not without U.S. aid. Fish was not alone in asking whether the United States should sustain a revolution the Cuban people were not more fully committed to supporting.[72]

Fish also had doubts about the capacity of Cubans and Latin Americans to sustain a stable republican government. Some doubts were rooted in racist prejudice and cultural bias. To Fish's mind, the racial mix of Indian, African, and Spanish blood, the impulsive "temperament" of the "Latin race," and the ill effects of Cuba's tropical climate on the work ethic all bode ill for the country becoming a stable, independent republic, never mind a member of the United States of America.

One of the chief promoters of such prejudice was the French, the self-appointed leader of the modern Latin race in Europe and America. Marquis de Radepont, an influential diplomat and principal architect of Napoleon III's Grand Design in Mexico, promoted the idea that the American branch of the "Latin race" had degenerated under the baleful influence of Anglo-Saxon republicanism. The Latin temperament, so the thinking went, required the firm hand of monarchy and the moral discipline of the Catholic Church. Anglo-Americans like Fish were usually receptive to the idea. Everything about Cuba, its language, religion, history, and racial mixture, made it alien and ill-suited to what he believed to be the nation's Anglo-Saxon traditions.[73]

News of organized opposition among Cubans to annexation to the United States was no less troubling. In March 1870, several revolutionary leaders complained that the enthusiasm for annexation came from only a tiny minority. "What has the United States done for us?" one opponent asked. "Cuba for Cubans and America for the Americans!" was the mood of the anti-annexationists. These dissidents "merit the thanks of every American," a *New York Times* reporter opined. America had enough to deal with during Reconstruction without taking on another war-torn post-emancipation society.[74]

Had Hamilton Fish's policy toward Cuba been inspired more by the ideals of anti-imperialism and Pan-American republicanism, willing or not, Spain might have joined the parade of empires retreating from the Western Hemisphere in the 1860s. Instead, Cuba and Puerto Rico remained among the last colonial vestiges of European imperialism in the Americas. Though it did not become one of William Seward's friendly "buttresses" surrounding the United States, neither did Cuba remain the "Ever-Faithful Isle." The war for independence that erupted in 1868 finally ground to an end ten years later. The revolution continued to smolder, flaring up in the Guerra Chiquita (Little War) of 1879–80 and finally exploding in 1895 with the Second War for Independence. Thirty years after Cuba's first war for independence, the United States intervened, this time not to help give birth to its "sister republics" in the Caribbean but instead to replace Spain as the imperial ruler of its Caribbean and Philippine colonies.[75]

PART III

Europe's Democratic Reveille

FIGURE 30. *Manhood Suffrage Riots in Hyde Park*, a painting by Nathan Hughes. On July 23, 1866, the Hyde Park Riot set the police and military against Reform League demonstrators and led British officials to fear the choice might be between democratic reform or grave social unrest. Smith Archive/Alamy Stock Photo.

CHAPTER 7

British Democracy

America is a standing rebuke to England. Her free institutions, her prosperity, the education of her people, the absence of a privileged class, are in too glaring contrast with our own condition to be forgiven. . . . Our opponents told us that Republicanism was on its trial. They insisted on our watching what they called its breakdown. They told us plainly that it was forever discredited in England. Well we accepted the challenge. . . . They may rely upon it that a vast impetus has been given to Republican sentiments in England, and that they will have to reckon with it before long. . . . The tottering edifice of English society may be shaken by other means than the six-pound franchise.

—EDWARD BEESLY, RADICAL REFORMER AND
HISTORY PROFESSOR, APRIL 29, 1865

The withdrawal of European powers from the American hemisphere coincided with the contagious flurry of democratic reforms, revolutions, and emancipation movements that spread across the Atlantic. In the American hemisphere, liberals understood the contest of the 1860s as one between republicanism and monarchy. European reformers generally sought to advance democracy within constitutional monarchies rather than press for "pure republicanism." "Red republicans" who favored the revolutionary overthrow of monarchies remained a small minority. In

France, the liberal opposition to Napoleon III remained haunted by the violence of the French Revolution. Democracy, the expansion of voting rights, governments responsible to the people, and fundamental freedoms of speech and assembly were the widely agreed upon goals of what they called "the European Democracy." These became the accepted standards of modern civilized nations.[1]

The following four chapters take up democratic upheavals in Britain, Spain, France, and Italy. These events were, in varying degrees, connected to the United States and the impact of the Civil War and Reconstruction. Americans generally applauded what they chose to see as the march of human progress toward a democratic future. As European liberals and radicals predicted, the Union's victory, the achievement of emancipation, Abraham Lincoln's role as a global icon of democratic self-rule, and the example of Radical Reconstruction influenced how European reformers envisioned the future and gave reformers a practical example of democratic success. In each site, it was internal political tensions and local leaders and organizations that actually produced democratic change.

European democrats imagined themselves citizens of a transatlantic democratic republic in the making. Most held up the United States and sometimes Switzerland as models for the kind of government they wanted for Europe. Though most worked toward reform within their own countries, more cosmopolitan voices, like Victor Hugo, Giuseppe Mazzini, and many others, projected their future as the "United States of Europe." The idea went back to the 1840s and gained new life during the American Civil War when the European left became infatuated with America, Lincoln, and the promise of democracy as a path to social justice and peace within and between nations, at least after the Confederate insurrection was defeated and slavery abolished.[2]

Britain's Tory (Conservative Party) leaders had at first welcomed America's civil war as final proof that "the bubble of democracy had burst," and they hoped its collapse would silence British Radicals advocating the "Americanization" of Britain. Four years later, that smug mood of satisfaction gave way to utter fear. The Union's victory and Abraham Lincoln's ascendance as a global hero were infecting the British working and middle classes with an impatient demand for democracy in Britain.

Americans inside Britain were alert to the new democratic mood. Charles Francis Adams, U.S. minister to Britain, wrote to the home office in July 1865: "I cannot resist the belief that this period marks an era in the political movement of Great Britain." He sensed that "old-fashioned conservatism has so far lost its hold" and would diminish further with the coming wave of democratic reform. America, he advised, must promptly reconstruct the Union and reaffirm its role as a global model of democratic success. "The progress of the liberal cause, not in England alone, but all over the world, is, in a measure, in our hands."[3]

Astute British observers understood that the American Civil War had helped reawaken their country's impatience for reform. John Morley, a leading Liberal spokesperson, proposed that the two countries were going through similar ordeals. British "partisanship" in the American Civil War acted as "the veil of a kind of civil war here," and the former's victory "was the force that made English liberalism powerful enough to enfranchise the workmen."[4]

The effect of the American contest on Britain's dormant reform movement was palpable as early as March 1863 at a mass meeting of trade unionists at St. James Hall in London. The hall was full of workers, men and women, an array of reformers, and a few revolutionaries. Among them were Karl Marx, who helped organize the meeting, John Bright, John Stuart Mill, and Henry Fawcett, the latter all prominent members of the Liberal Party. The speakers that day repeatedly linked the Union cause to that of British reform while blasting aristocratic Tories for siding with the slaveholders' rebellion.

Edward Beesly, a professor of history and leading spokesman for workers' rights, went further, comparing British workers to enslaved Blacks in the South. If the upper classes had their way, he told the audience, "you would differ from negro slaves in nothing except the colour of your skin."[5]

When news of Lincoln's assassination reached Britain two years later, workers wasted no time making the fallen leader a martyr to their cause of political empowerment. Thomas Bayley Potter, a Radical MP, told an audience of workers: "Let us not forget that he was a working man. . . . It was to emancipate slavery and to elevate labour, Abraham Lincoln lived and died. We lament his loss, and we hope and trust that his martyrdom will be the death knell of slavery and oppression throughout the world."[6]

British workers admired Lincoln for ending slavery and winning the war, yet there was more to it than that. His rise from his family's hardscrabble beginnings to the highest office in the nation was unimaginable in Britain's class-bound society. As the workers of Brighton explained, they "sympathize the more deeply" with Lincoln because "he was the first President elected from the working classes to the high position of ruler of one of the mightiest nations of the globe."[7]

Karl Marx, a German socialist living in exile in London since 1849, had taken a keen interest in the Civil War, especially in Lincoln, whose Emancipation Proclamation awakened Marx to the extraordinary potential for a revolutionary democracy taking a similar form in Britain and western Europe. Marx took a leading role in the International Working Men's Association (IWMA), known to history as the International or First International after reorganizing in 1889. Marx and other labor leaders inaugurated the International in late 1864 in London to unify workers across national boundaries and steer them from striking for higher wages to gaining political power. Marx authored the inaugural address, which drew revealing connections between European oppression and American democracy. After the Revolution of 1848 was "crushed by the iron hand of force . . . the most advanced sons of labour fled in despair to the Transatlantic Republic [America] . . . leaving an irreparable void in the ranks of the British proletariat," which had descended to the equivalent of "political blacks."[8]

Marx explained that the present task before the working classes was to "conquer political power," to turn away from the "temporary bribe" of better wages and working conditions and instead gain political power within the state. Political consciousness among workers, he noted, was evident in their "heroic resistance" in keeping the "ruling classes" from taking sides with the slaveholders' rebellion in America. The American war has "taught the working classes the duty to master themselves the mysteries of international politics. . . . Proletarians of all countries, Unite!"[9]

Marx's call to "conquer political power" signified an important, though for him temporary, turn toward democratic socialism, the non-revolutionary use of electoral politics to legislate socialist reforms into being. The International's first step was to help organize the Reform League, a coalition of middle- and working-class reformers whose sole purpose was to enfranchise workers and middle-class males excluded by property qualifications.[10]

Workers dominated the Reform League's leadership, rank, and file, and members of the International were foremost among them. Several aging veterans of the old Chartist movement, which had pushed for suffrage reform after the Reform Act of 1832, also played key roles. The Reform League borrowed from the Chartist tactics of mass meetings and enormous orderly processions to make a show of strength. The British democracy also made the most of international events to link their movement to the broader struggle for reform. Garibaldi's march on Rome, Poland's revolt against Russia, and, above all, America's stand against the slaveholders' rebellion aroused Europe's democracy and created a vivid sense of international solidarity in a common cause.[11]

There was also the horrifying massacre of Black protestors at Morant Bay, Jamaica, in October 1865 demanded a reexamination of Britain's much-prized reputation as the champion of emancipation. Though Britain had ended slavery in Jamaica and all its colonies in 1833, the primary beneficiaries were slaveholders who received handsome compensation for their losses, while the freed people were left without political power or resources to make the most of their freedom. The Morant Bay Rebellion prompted a widely publicized parliamentary investigation that featured several of the leading figures of the recent pro-Union party in Britain: John Bright, John Stuart Mill, Thomas Potter, Goldwin Smith, and Edmond Beales. Morant Bay also became a warning to America and Britain of the dangers of emancipation without enfranchisement, which did not go unnoticed by Radicals in both countries.[12]

Among the ranks of the Reform League, many had gained experience and political education supporting the Union cause. They learned how to organize large meetings and exert pressure on the government through their massive show of support. George Howell, the Reform League's industrious secretary, confirmed that "the one event which knit us together more than any other was the American Civil War. For years one test of a man's Liberalism was—What was he on the American question?"[13]

The Reform League's president Edmond Beales praised America's "magnificent example" of democracy. Though mired in civil war, the United States had carried out the reelection of Abraham Lincoln in "the most peaceful and orderly way" and, taking a dig at the British elite, "without any of the disgraceful scenes of drunkenness and riot" which constantly shame our nation. Britain's working classes are imbued with a "self-denying love of freedom and hatred of oppression," as demonstrated by their support of the "late American conflict between free institutions and slave institutions." Beales noted such qualities were not always present among those thought to be of "rank higher in the social scale." Extending the right to vote to workers may be the "surest preservative against discord, violence, and revolution," he added, perhaps as an ominous warning.[14]

Karl Marx was enormously pleased with the success of the League and its reception among workers. "The Reform League is our work," he wrote his close collaborator, Frederick Engels, in May 1865. "If we succeed in re-electrifying the political movement of the English working class, our Association will already have done more for the European working class . . . than was possible in any other way."[15] The League, Marx predicted, had potential beyond suffrage reform, he told Engels. "When the next revolution comes, and that will perhaps be sooner than might appear, *we* (i.e., you and I) will have this mighty ENGINE at *our disposal*."[16]

The launch of Britain's movement for manhood suffrage in the spring of 1865 coincided with hundreds of public demonstrations in response to Lincoln's assassination. In eulogies, resolutions of condolence, and newspaper articles, reform-minded authors took the occasion to issue shots at those who questioned Lincoln's qualifications or doubted America's ability to survive. The elevation of Lincoln as a hero of the democratic age and the depiction of the Civil War as a contest between aristocratic oppression and democratic freedom set the stage for the reform movement ahead.[17]

Britain's governing classes were not about to accept Lincoln's death nor his emancipation of four million enslaved as a mandate for reform. Parliament, though it included middle-class MPs, remained a bastion of the upper class who saw the rising tide of democracy as a threat to their traditional dominance in the House of Commons. Except for its Radical faction, the Liberal Party was no more willing to accept genuine democracy than were hidebound Tories.

Their contempt for the working class was blatant. Benjamin Moran, secretary to the U.S. legation in London, sat in the galleries of the House of Commons to watch the debate over a bill that would have increased the number of voters by a mere two to seven thousand. He wrote in his journal, "Some of the would be liberals spoke of the English workmen as if they were beasts. . . . The tories cheered like a rabble in a pit whenever anything sharp was said to degrade their fellow laboring countrymen . . . they looked upon mechanics as dogs."[18]

At the end of 1865, Parliament's resistance to reform eroded suddenly with the death of Lord Palmerston, who had obstructed even the slightest measure of reform. It was as though a stone wall blocking political reform had cracked, if not fallen. Not only has Lord Palmerston died, one journal noted, an entire "cycle of political history . . . has come to a termination." The Liberal Party formed a new government with John Russell as prime minister and William Gladstone as Chancellor of the Exchequer. In March 1866, they placed a reform bill before Parliament. Though Russell took a hand in crafting the legislation, it became known as the Gladstone Bill. Their purpose, however, was not to fling open the door to universal manhood suffrage but to selectively extend voting rights to "respectable artisans," excluding unskilled workers and the "residuum" of the unemployed poor. The favored device was a property and income qualification, which the bill set at £7 rent per annum.[19]

British fears of American democracy traced back to Alexis de Tocqueville's *Democracy in America*, the first volume appearing in French in

1835 and English the same year. A British journalist, Henry Reeve, did the translation and took some liberties that annoyed Tocqueville because he highlighted everything negative the author had to say about democracy. In 1862 Reeve issued a new introduction in which he claimed with more certainty than evidence that Tocqueville, who died in 1859, "would have mourned over the destruction of another of the noblest experiments ever made in human society." Reeve added that Tocqueville "was of the opinion that the democratic element is by its nature of so inconstant and destructive a character, that it is extremely doubtful whether a permanent, regular, and free government can be established and maintained on purely democratic principles." Reeve's timely spin on Tocqueville's widely respected work found a welcome place among those opposing democratic reform in Britain. He deftly transformed the author's prediction of democracy's inevitable ascent into a grim prophecy of doom.[20]

For advocates of democratic reform, Radicals like Richard Cobden, John Bright, and the Reform League leadership generally saw the United States, especially one cleansed of slavery, as a powerful model of democratic success. The exodus of British workers to America proved their point best. After 1865, a new generation of British intellectuals, many of whom had traveled and lived in America, provided a more temperate view of American politics and society than their predecessors. Oxford University's Goldwin Smith, James Bryce, Albert V. Dicey, and Leslie Stephen, to name a few, put aside the tiresome tradition of British snobbery and condescension to highlight what they saw as valuable lessons America's democracy might offer Britain.[21]

Gladstone's moderate bill brought a ferocious reaction from MPs in both parties who loathed even the slightest change in voting qualifications for fear it would open the floodgates to "extreme democracy" American style. The debate over reform was nothing less than a continuation of the referendum on American democracy that occupied Parliament during the Civil War.[22]

Opposition to democratic reform coalesced predictably around a defense of ancient English traditions, fears of social leveling, and disdain for America. Sir Edward Horsman, a Liberal MP for Stroud (one of the remaining rotten boroughs), led off with a furious attack against the insidious influence of America on reform leaders. Admiration of the United States had so infected John Bright, Horsman charged, that "his political principles, I say, are the principles, not of an Englishman, but of an alien." It was not the British people, he charged, but the Radicals in Parliament like Bright who were pushing for reform. The people he purported to speak for had no interest in transforming the "old tree of English liberty . . . into the brazen image of ignorance and intolerance which the worshippers of Trans-Atlantic equality wanted to set up."[23]

In April 1866, the debate resumed with the Tory opposition leader, Benjamin Disraeli, prophesying what democracy would bring to England: "You would have the rule of mobs in great towns, and the sway of turbulent multitudes. If a dominant multitude were to succeed in bringing the land of England into the condition of the land in America . . . England, from being a first-rate Kingdom, would become a third-rate Republic." England's "charm of tradition" and "families of historic lineage" would give way to a nation with "no statesmanship, no eloquence, no learning, no genius," only "a horde of selfish and obscure mediocrities, incapable of anything but mischief, and that mischief devised and regulated by the raging demagogue of the hour."[24]

What killed Gladstone's reform bill was not the hidebound High Tories Disraeli spoke for; it was a faction of anti-democratic and anti-American reactionaries within the Liberal Party. They became known as the "Adullamites" or "the Cave," an arcane biblical reference John Bright tagged them with to imply a sulking rebel minority seeking refuge in one another's company. The Adullamites' strength, in fairness, arose from concerns many moderate Liberals and Tories shared about the ills of democracy.[25]

The Adullamite opposition to Gladstone's bill launched a no-holds-barred assault on democracy, America, the ignorant masses, and what they saw as the "sentimental" and "philanthropic" nonsense reformers spouted in their effort to destroy all that was good in English society. Their leading spokesmen were Horsman and Liberal MP Robert Lowe, First Viscount Sherbrooke, MP from Calne, another rotten borough.

Lowe was an albino whose pale skin and pure white hair made a striking appearance. His weak eyesight had ruined his ambitions for a career in law and academics. He lived abroad for some time in Australia and visited America enough, at least, to allow him to speak knowingly about the failings of democracy. One wag speculated that Lowe's grudge might be due to "the accident of having been hit over the head during an [American] election riot in 1860."[26]

Lowe was fed up with what he derided as sentimental praise of the commoner. On March 13, 1866, he rose in Parliament to "say exactly what I think" of the whole lot of them. He then let loose with a blast of disparaging language against the poor that would echo through the press, parliamentary debates, and Reform League speeches for weeks to come. "If you want venality, if you want ignorance, if you want drunkenness, and facility for being intimidated; or if, on the other hand, you want impulsive, unreflecting, and violent people, where do you look for them in the constituencies?" Lowe's question, at least among the minds inside the Cave of Adullam, required no answer.[27]

Lowe was equally impatient with the idea that the so-called Great Republic in America had anything worth recommending to England: "Look at *America*. A section of the American democracy revolted and broke up the Union, the rest fought to preserve it." Now they are ready to go to war again to prevent another rebellion. He also blasted the low quality of American politicians. They "do not send honest, hardworking men to represent them in Congress"; they send corrupt men "who have lost their character and been driven from every respectable way of life, and who take up politics as a last resource." The House of Commons, in contrast, had produced some of the greatest statesmen in history. Why should England want to Americanize such proven greatness?[28]

The Adullamite rebellion was the kiss of death to Gladstone's Reform Bill. The Tories promptly welcomed the Adullamites to join forces in defeating the Reform Bill in June 1866, and Gladstone's government fell. The Liberal Party, in power for seventeen years, now watched in astonishment as the Tories stole its reform thunder. The Conservative Party formed a new government, led by Lord Derby as prime minister and

Benjamin Disraeli as Chancellor of the Exchequer. Suffrage reform appeared to be dead only to rise again as a Tory project.

While Parliament was fulminating about America and the ills of democracy, the popular reform movement was gaining force outside Westminster. Lacking the power of the ballot, the unenfranchised sought to create what Marx called "pressure from without" on Parliament. In the public squares of London and other cities, the British people made their demands for reform known; Parliament, in effect, merely acceded to them.

After Robert Lowe's insulting speech and the failure of Gladstone's bill, the Reform League took to the streets. In John Bright's words, the new Tory government had declared "war against the working classes." Workers had been tepid in supporting Gladstone's halfway step toward democratic reform. The League now demanded nothing less than full-out manhood suffrage with no property qualification, and they wanted a secret ballot to avert the intimidation of employers.[29] Whatever the shortcomings of Gladstone's weak reform bill, its failure aroused the Reform League to take democracy to the public square. They would vote with their feet, indeed their whole bodies, and demand respect from those in Parliament who had slandered them with accusations of ignorance, drunkenness, and violence.

Beginning in the summer of 1866 and continuing for more than a year, the Reform League staged spectacular demonstrations in London and other cities. In the order and discipline of their processions and the eloquence of their speeches was an indignant claim for respect as human beings. The demonstrators took pains to don their best clothing, march in precise military order, and in every way behave as "respectable," "moral" people, not the venal, drunken, ignorant roughs of the Tory and Adullamite imagination.[30]

Within days of Gladstone's fall from power, the Clerkenwell Branch Society of the Reform League, known to be among the more militant chapters, organized a meeting for the evening of June 17, 1866. It drew upwards of twenty thousand demonstrators to Trafalgar Square, with brass bands playing and flags flying. It was, by all accounts, "one of the largest political gatherings . . . in London for many years." Though a large contingent of police stood by, the demonstration proceeded with nothing but "the greatest order." Benjamin Lucraft, a cabinet maker, venerable Chartist, and member of the International, served as chair for the rally. Lucraft set the tone in a blunt opening address. "We have been 'diddled' again" and "will be 'diddled' to the end of time unless workers obtain their political rights." A formal resolution, enthusiastically endorsed by the crowd, raised the stakes by insisting that "no reform bill can now prove satisfactory short of registered and residential manhood suffrage." Other speakers threatened to drive the Tory government out. An ugly mood of frustration with hints of violence and revolution seemed to take hold as the "spirit of liberty" ran loose in the streets outside Parliament.[31]

Five days later, another meeting at Trafalgar Square surrounded Nelson's Column, the symbol of Britain's imperial greatness, with a boisterous crowd, this one estimated at fifty thousand strong. They began assembling at six in the evening as neighborhood groups arrived, marching in order behind bands and banners in "an orderly and quiet manner." The crowd listened to speeches for an hour and a half, then endorsed a resolution denouncing "the injurious and insulting language used toward the working classes," a reference to Robert Lowe's scurrilous slander. After dispersing, different groups fanned out, one to heckle Tory MP Lord Elcho in front of his home on St. James's Street. Another went back to the Tories' favorite gentlemen's club, the Carlton, this time to hiss and groan but also to charge up the steps and smash a few windows, an alarming new sign of violence. Then they marched to the Reform Club, called for Gladstone, and sang, "He's a jolly good fellow, and so say us all." The rowdy crowd next marched to Gladstone's home to pay respects before retiring for the evening.[32]

Up to this point, the government had done nothing to interfere with the Reform League demonstrations. Their massive size, angry rhetoric, and the habit of taunting politicians at their clubs and homes were causing alarm in upper-class circles. Their uneasiness grew after the Reform League announced plans for a more massive demonstration in Hyde Park in three weeks. Under pressure from Tory constituents, Home Secretary

Spencer Walpole issued a ban on public meetings in the park, explaining that political demonstrations were "entirely opposed to the purpose for which the parks are open to the public." Liberal Party leaders gave Walpole their support.

To Police Commissioner Sir Richard Mayne fell the unhappy duty of enforcing the ban. He was an Irish Protestant, strict disciplinarian, and staunch defender of middle-class Victorian morality. During the previous decade, Mayne had raised, organized, and trained a small army of some seven thousand men, whose duties included ensuring order at the growing number of "great public gatherings."[33]

The government's ban on political demonstrations played perfectly into the Reform League's hands. The League now wrapped suffrage reform in the hard-earned rights of freeborn Englishmen to enjoy free speech. Walpole's ban also handed the League a powerful pretext to confront the government with a massive show of civil disobedience. The League's leaders announced they were going forward with their plans to meet at Hyde Park on Monday evening, July 23, 1866.[34]

The Hyde Park demonstration reportedly drew two hundred thousand demonstrators and untold thousands of police and soldiers; crowd estimates varied according to the political sympathies of different newspapers. The Reform League's procession to Hyde Park began with League president Edmond Beales riding with an Anglican priest and other dignitaries in an open carriage, the very picture of respectability. Behind them followed a long procession of men carrying banners and marching in order through the streets of London. Beales led the procession past St. Martin's Church and Waterloo Place to Oxford Circus from League headquarters at Adelphi Terrace. There they converged with a large contingent of the League's Holborn Branch, "preceded by a brass band and a large tricolour of red, green, and blue," while the rowdy Clerkenwell Branch had their own band. "Banners of all hues fluttered in the air," one demonstrator recorded, and "the men tramped steadily to the music of the bands, and the whole scene, except for the absence of glittering arms and uniforms, resembled . . . a disciplined army." They came down Oxford Street in Chartist fashion, five-abreast, arm-in-arm, marching in "triumphal" spirit toward the park. "As far as the eye could reach in every direction," one newspaper reported, "there was a compact mass of people to be seen."[35]

The procession made its way to the Marble Arch at the entrance to the park, where they met an army of sixteen to eighteen hundred police on foot and horseback, their truncheons drawn and ready. When Beales arrived at the arch, he demanded entrance to the park and challenged the authority of Commissioner Mayne to obstruct a peaceable assembly in what was "the property of the people." A tall policeman thrust his truncheon in Beales's chest and "pushed him with more rudeness than was necessary a foot or two back." Police then "collared" Beales and tore his coat. One of the League leaders managed to get past the police cordon, and "then a melee ensued" as other demonstrators started pushing their way through. Mounted police came up behind the foot constables to form a second line of resistance, and police "threatened to use their staves if the people did not desist."[36]

Having stated his objection to the police ban, Beales returned to his carriage and led the procession away from Hyde Park toward Trafalgar Square. Some ten to fifteen thousand followed him in what by this time had become a ritual as they passed through St. James's Street and along Pall Mall, pausing in front of the Tory gentlemen's clubs to issue "a perfect roar of hooting and groaning." After arriving at Trafalgar Square, Beales addressed the crowd: "You have been robbed of your rights by a parliamentary faction." Do not stop, Beales implored, "until you have made the House of Commons cease to be what it is now, a mere mockery, . . . and have made it what it ought to be, a representative body of the Commons of the United Kingdom."[37]

Back at Hyde Park, the demonstrators stood their ground, demanding entrance. They began pushing at the iron fencing along Park Lane, led by the reliably militant Clerkenwell Branch. Under pressure from the heaving crowd, portions of the iron railings bordering the park gave way; then, they fell along Park Lane. The demonstrators rushed over the fallen fencing in a tide far too great to turn back. The police battered the first wave with their truncheons "but were swept aside like flies before the waiter's napkin" by the next onslaught. The crowd gathered at a large oak tree that soon became known as "the Reformers' Tree," where male and female

FIGURE 31. "The Mob Pulling down the Railings in Park Lane." The Reform League was a massive direct-action reform movement organized in early 1865 by the International Working Men's Association and middle-class reformers. Its purpose was to exert pressure on Parliament to broaden the franchise through a massive show of popular support. Many held up America as a model for British democracy and had come together earlier in support of the Union. *London Illustrated News*, August 4, 1866. Hathitrust.

speakers held forth. Later this place would become a revered site of democratic free speech known as Speakers' Corner.[38]

One of the orators told those gathered they were there "to assert their rights as Englishmen." Their defiance of the ban proved that "they had not yet given up that right. ('Hear, hear.')." The police and army were servants of the public, and freeborn "'Englishmen' were not to be ruled by their own servants." When an imposing force of Foot Guards and mounted soldiers approached them, the crowd welcomed "the people's Guards" and shouted, "Hurrah for our brothers in the red coats." When the police arrived, however, the demonstrators hissed, and some boys hurled stones. Then the crowd formed a procession and marched out of

Hyde Park, boisterously singing American Civil War songs cleverly adapted to insult Commissioner Mayne.

> We'll hang Sir Richard on a sour apple tree
> We'll hang Sir Richard on a sour apple tree
> As we go marching on
> Glory! Glory! Hallelujah![39]

From Hyde Park, the crowd marched in rough formation, still singing "Glory, Glory, Hallelujah!" as they traversed the streets of London to Trafalgar Square, where they met up with the Beales contingent. A sea of humanity filled the square surrounding Nelson's Column and stayed on into the evening, cheering the people's victory over the police and soldiers in what the press called the Battle of Hyde Park.[40]

At the time of the Hyde Park Riot, Karl Marx was busy finishing the first volume of his magnum opus, *Das Kapital*. Naturally, he saw glimmers of a workers' revolution in the works and immediately connected it to the American Civil War. In the preface to *Das Kapital*, he wrote: "As in the 18th century, the American War of Independence sounded the tocsin for the European middle class, so in the 19th century, the American Civil War sounded it for the European working class." Then, referring to the Reform League violence in the streets outside, he added: "In England the progress of social disintegration is palpable. When it has reached a certain point, it must re-act on the Continent."[41]

Marx gave Engels his take on the Hyde Park Riot in late July: "The government has almost caused a mutiny here." "If the railings had been used—and it almost came to that—for offence and defence against the police, and some score of the latter killed, the military would have had to 'step in,' instead of merely parading. And then things would have got quite jolly." Marx seemed to be fluctuating between "conquering political power" through peaceful suffrage reform and storming the barricades.[42]

Reformers and police continued to clash over the next three days. The demonstrators' astounding defiance completely stunned Spencer Walpole, who had imposed the Hyde Park ban. Walpole was a Tory favorite who was serving as home secretary for the third time. As a descendant of a long line of aristocratic members of England's governing class, he was the perfect embodiment of the privileged aristocracy abusing downtrodden workers. He realized that enforcing the ban would now require a massive show of force from police and soldiers.

Furthermore, they must be prepared to use their truncheons, swords, bayonets, and rifles. The press began referring to dark memories of the Peterloo Massacre in 1819, which started with a monster meeting in Manchester's St. Peters Field for suffrage reform and ended with a full-out British cavalry charge, mounted soldiers slashing and trampling unarmed men and women. The tag "Peterloo" was a disturbing allusion to the Battle of Waterloo. Was this what lay ahead for Britain?[43]

Two days after the Hyde Park Riot, Walpole sat down with a delegation of Reform League officers, who came to offer him a deal. If the government ordered all police and military from the park, the League would "use its influence" to ensure peace. The harried secretary responded immediately to the League leaders, gushing with warm appreciation for their conciliatory disposition. Afterward, rumors spread that Walpole had been moved to tears.

That evening, July 25, 1866, a crowd of forty to fifty thousand demonstrators came through the Marble Arch into Hyde Park in high spirits. Hawkers sold small vials of "Walpole's tears" to the joyful demonstrators. Beales greeted the crowd with "glad tidings of peace" and, at the end of an evening of speeches, led them out of the park in a "quiet and orderly manner." The Reform League had won its right to peaceable assembly, yet they were no closer to gaining political power.[44]

Until the debacle at Hyde Park, John Bright had been skeptical about universal manhood suffrage, despite his reputation as a flaming Radical. After July's violence, he was alarmed by the potential for violence and repression and became an outspoken prophet of British democracy. Bright was a Quaker textile mill owner whose long career as MP was devoted to reform causes to help the poor. During the American Civil War, he stood, almost alone, as an outspoken defender of England's "brethren beyond the Atlantic" and the "transatlantic English nation" that bound the two countries. Bright was in his mid-fifties, portly, with a kindly round face framed by bushy white sideburns. When he spoke, sometimes for hours, the crowds were mesmerized.[45]

Beginning in August 1866, Bright started a speaking tour that would take him through the major industrial cities of the Midlands, Scotland, and Ireland. His oratorical skills were in top form, and the public responded enthusiastically. He spoke with unusual freedom, skewering the Tory and Adullamite opponents of reform with malicious pleasure and casting them as enemies of the people.[46]

At Birmingham, more than 150,000 came out to hear him speak at a Reform League meeting. Bright spoke of other countries, including Canada and the United States, enjoying the practice of democracy without any of the social calamities predicted by British conservatives. He hailed Cyrus W. Field, inventor of the transatlantic cable, as "the Columbus of our time" who has brought the "two English nations" closer together. America's English heritage bestowed upon it a "broad and generous freedom"; now, its former mother country must establish its freedom on "a broad and generous representation of the people."[47]

At Glasgow, Bright took the argument beyond the numbers eligible to vote to expose the badly skewed system of representation that allowed half of the MPs to be elected by one-seventh of the electorate voting in tiny districts. Bright explained that of the more than 254 boroughs in the United Kingdom, only 54 had more than 2,000 electors. Over one-third (225) of MPs were entitled aristocrats, and the Liberal Party had only slightly fewer than the Tories. One-fifth of Parliament descended from thirty-one aristocratic families. No wonder they despised the very idea of democratic reform.[48]

Bright also pointed out that 84 out of 100 grown British men have no vote, adding they "might as well live in Russia, where there is no system of electoral government." Parliament does not represent the nation, Bright summarized. It represents a narrow and selfish class that "has failed miserably." "It revels in power and wealth, whilst at its feet, a terrible peril for its future lies—the multitude which it has neglected. If a class has failed, let us try the nation. That is our faith, that is our purpose, that is our cry—Let us try the nation."[49]

FIGURE 32. "The Brummagem Frankenstein." Artist John Tenniel depicted John Bright cowering in fear before a colossal rough-looking worker sporting a liberty cap and mocking Bright's claim in Birmingham that he had no fear of manhood suffrage. *Punch*, September 8, 1866. Hathitrust.

At nearly every stop, Bright recited the insulting language of Robert Lowe, which never failed to bring groans from the crowd. Lowe's views of them, Bright made clear, "are in the main the doctrines upon which the Tory party has acted for generations back."[50] Bright effectively turned the Tories' accusation against the Reform League for inciting class warfare back at them. In his last speech at St. Martin's Hall in London, he compared the situation in Britain to a massive volcano, with dense black smoke rising from its top and the trickling of molten lava oozing from its crevices, about to become a "river of fire." In case any should miss the point, he said, "history tells us dynasties and aristocracies have passed away and their name has been known no more for ever." Am I to blame for issuing a warning to the people below? "I did not build the mountain, or fill it with explosive materials. I merely warned the men that were in danger." The Tory party is "the turbulent element in English political society."[51]

While Bright and the Reform League campaigned to win popular support for reform, the Tory leadership waited out the game. Disraeli explained to Lord Derby that the longer the House of Commons delays a decision, "the more likely it will be in favor of moderation and postponement."[52] Disraeli failed to understand that Bright was transforming Robert Lowe and his Liberal Party Adullamites into Tory villains.[53]

Disraeli also tried to reassure Queen Victoria that the public was indifferent to reform and that the violence at Hyde Park was nothing more than "pure frolic by a knot of laughing boys." The queen was not convinced. There were disturbing signs that support for the monarchy was waning among the British people. Some of this was due to her long absences from London, tending to what critics called her "inappropriate" relationship with her servant, a Scotsman named John Brown. "Mrs. Brown," as some wags took to calling her, was being booed and hissed in public. Republicanism was suddenly more popular in Britain, and some in the press were stirring up the hostility toward the monarchy. The queen was concerned that the Tory government must do something in the way of reform, or "their supporters would become very angry and dissatisfied, so that much mischief might be done."[54]

Derby agreed. He explained to the queen that he wanted to bring
moderates in both parties together and exclude the "extreme
tic party" from shaping a new reform bill. He also enlisted the
d by asking her to come in person to open Parliament in Feb-
and endorse reform. The queen reluctantly agreed and gave
eech expressing her hope that Parliament would pass a bill
ely extend the Elective Franchise."[55]

nd Disraeli were doing their best to silence the "extreme
rty," the Reform League, joined by the trades unions,
voices were heard. Beales and the leadership deter-
d their right to stage another mass meeting in Hyde
y set was Monday evening, May 6, 1867.[56]
Spencer Walpole and the Tory government decided
eir ban on public meetings in the park and posted
on to that effect. The League responded by defacing
and putting up their own yellow placards telling
vernment ban. "Come as loyal, peaceful, and or-
of all riot and tumult," the League's summons to
nalterably fixed and resolved in demanding and
are entitled to." Beales made it clear that this
request admission and turn away if denied; he
that admittance if required."[57]
iberal MP and reform advocate, feared that
seemed impending."[58] Charles Francis Adams
n that the Hyde Park melee had so "alarmed the
r classes" that "there was last week a very general
fearful struggle, ending in more or less of confu-
odshed." There were also concerns that the Irish
a common cause with the Reform League and incite
against the government. Gustave Paul Cluseret, a
ner officer in the Union Army, was operating as an
n Brotherhood. In London, some alleged he was
ts of the Reform League to build an alliance. The
ers down the spines of Britain's governing classes.[59]

Cluseret's plot to join Fenians with the Reform League was one of a stream of rumors circulating at the time—most involved dangerous revolutionaries about to descend on London and, by some accounts, storm Parliament. "There was complete preparation for a grand street fight," one reform sympathizer recalled. "I know of men of good position who travelled up to London from the North to fight, and that clerks ii business houses had their rifles beside their desks." Whatever the validit of such rumors, there was no denying that "a new and ugly temper wa at work in the people," which terrified the English establishment.[60]

Blood was up in the Reform League, to be sure. Earlier, reformers h strained to portray themselves as respectable, peaceable petitioners Her Majesty's government. Now one heard cries for martyrdom revolution. "Let but a single drop of blood be shed on Monday n the League's journal, *The Commonwealth*, advised. If so, "the word go forth that such blood must be avenged" and signal "the reign of t has commenced and must be played out."[61]

The revolutionary tenor of Reform rhetoric escalated rapidly confrontation at Hyde Park drew near. Charles Bradlaugh, the pub of the *National Reformer*, a radical secularist weekly, came out v incendiary pamphlet titled *Reform or Revolution* and addressed nously to Parliament. "We gather on the green sward . . . as a I Parliament." "You are a House of Common in name, but not in fa if you prevent reform, "you will provoke a revolution." Older veterans were astonished by the revolutionary tone that had take

As the appointed hour approached, the government recruit to 15,000 special constables to supplement Mayne's army of also called in a regiment of Hussars and detachments of Life G Horse Guards. Ten thousand soldiers stood ready to move oi onstrators at a moment's notice.[63]

About six in the evening of May 6, 1867, the radical C Branch Reform League approached the park gates, brand flag with a red cap of liberty atop its staff, iconic symbols o Revolution and socialism. Within half an hour, somewh 100,000 and 150,000 (some claimed as high as 500,000) pe at the park. Walpole had issued threats of severe governr against any who defied the ban. And then, Walpole caved. He allowed the demonstrators to enter the park without even a truncheon drawn. Speakers addressed the crowds from no less than ten separate platforms. Music sounded from "ballad singers without number" hailed the coming triumph of reform.[64]

Walpole resigned in disgrace. Thomas Carlyle, England's supreme curmudgeon, mocked him bursting into tears while England humiliated itself by trembling before "Beales and his Roughs." Prime Minister Derby had to admit that his government had "subjected themselves to some slight humiliation in the public mind." The problem was not any want of police and military power sufficient to the task; it was the terrifying prospect of the government assailing thousands of unarmed citizens gathered in what no one could deny was an orderly assembly. Beales proclaimed May 6 "a great moral triumph—a triumph greater than any language of his could express."[65]

Disraeli had already been quietly at work on a new Reform Bill in a scheme to turn the Liberal Party's failure into a Tory victory. Disraeli's Reform Bill focused on the careful admission of new voters by adjusting how much property or rent would qualify men for the franchise. His main concern was to craft a Tory Reform Bill that would win voters to his party and throw Liberals on their back feet.

The odd result was a Tory bill far more expansive than the Gladstone Bill that failed in 1866. Instead of adding 400,000 voters, as Gladstone's bill would have done, Disraeli's bill enfranchised close to one million additional voters. The Reform Act of 1867 more or less doubled the electorate to about two million men, approximately one-third of the adult male population. In industrial cities, the effect of reform was far more pronounced. In Leeds, a northern textile city, the vote between 1866 and 1868 increased almost five times.[66]

The more incredible irony was that MPs of both parties viewed the 1867 Reform Act as a necessary bulwark against the advance of democracy, not a disastrous breach in the thick walls of privilege. The goal, one Conservative put it, was a bill "so large and liberal in its admissions to the franchise, that it shall be a settlement of the question."[67] Disraeli expressed the prevailing sentiment when he reassured the House: "We do not . . . live—and I trust it will never be the fate of this country to live—under a democracy." Reform would acknowledge the profound changes in British society since 1832, he admitted, but only "with a due deference to the traditions of an ancient State."[68]

Disraeli's prophecy was soon proved wrong. Instead of settling the reform question and curbing the advance of full-scale democracy, what became known as the Second Reform Act of 1867 opened the door to a series of relentless steps toward precisely that end. The Radical agenda after 1867 included the secret ballot, an attempt to end electoral bribery and intimidation. Radicals also sought to extend household suffrage from the boroughs to the countryside and redistribute seats based on population to make Parliament more representative of the British voting public.[69]

John Stuart Mill, the leading voice of British liberalism, wrote to the illustrious American author Ralph Waldo Emerson in the summer of 1867: "To me it seems that our two countries, on the whole the two most advanced countries of the world, have just successfully emerged from a crisis essentially similar, though by much the gravest and most trying in the US; which has shaken up and dislocated old prejudices, set the stagnant waters flowing, and the most certain consequence of which is that all the fundamental problems of politics and society, so long smothered by general indolence and apathy, will surge up and demand better solutions than they have ever yet obtained."[70]

The Reform Act of 1867 also gave birth to a far more inclusive vision of democracy—the enfranchisement of women. John Stuart Mill broached the matter of woman suffrage for the first time in Parliament when he proposed substituting the word "person" for all references to "male" in the Reform Bill. "Can it be pretended," Mill asked the House of Commons, "that women who manage an estate or conduct a business . . . are not capable of a function of which every male householder is capable?" Is it feared, he also asked, that "we should have worse laws, or be in any way whatever worse governed through the effect of their suffrages?" The House voted Mill's amendment down amid the "braying and brainless hilarity" of opposing MPs, but the question of women's political rights was now a subject of public debate and action.[71]

FIGURE 33. "Mill's Logic." John Stuart Mill became a leading public intellectual and political activist for liberalism in the 1860s. As a Member of Parliament, he introduced an amendment to the Reform Bill of 1867, proposing the word "person" be substituted for "male" by reason that by every criterion of education, property, and competence women were as qualified to vote as men. Mill's effort accelerated an explosion of woman suffrage activity across Britain. John Tenniel's cartoon shows him with Lydia Becker, one of the leading forces in the movement. *Punch*, March 30, 1867. Hathitrust.

Mill and his wife, Harriet Taylor Mill, had been deeply committed to the idea of female equality, and after her death, Mill stood for election to Parliament with women's rights a feature of his campaign. In 1866 he led a petition drive to present to Parliament to support woman suffrage. Out of this petition drive, dozens of new female suffrage societies emerged in London, Manchester, Edinburgh, Bristol, and Birmingham. More followed, and a flurry of pamphlets on the subject marked the beginning of a national movement for female suffrage and equal rights. Young Emmeline Pankhurst, future champion of the British Suffragettes, remembered as a child in Manchester her parents being caught up in the cause of Black freedom in America, something she thought "made a permanent impression on my brain and my character." Women took the lead in demanding the vote based on the same property qualifications as men by challenging local election laws. Though the idea of women's equality emerged decades earlier, in the latter half of the 1860s, an organized woman suffrage movement began simultaneously in Britain and the United States. The idea of women's political equality had entered the public square. In both countries, efforts to extend the vote to unenfranchised males sparked the first organized movements to enfranchise women. However, in both countries, women would wait for a half century before succeeding in winning the vote.[72]

As Britain moved toward democracy, the habitual prejudice and uninformed stereotypes about America and its democratic ills no longer went unchallenged. A group of Oxford Radicals led the way with a book, *Essays on Reform*, in 1867. The essay by Goldwin Smith, a notable friend of the Union during the war and great admirer of Lincoln, mocked the predictions from Britain's upper classes that America's democracy would fall apart and "anarchy and military despotism would ensue." Though their prophecies proved "utterly falsified," the privileged classes continued to assail America's democracy to thwart reform in Britain.[73] By the 1880s, Britain's Liberal Party showed its eagerness to catch up with the democratic tide by adopting Lincoln's "government of the people, by the people, and for the people" as its unofficial motto. Albert V. Dicey, one of the Oxford Radicals of '67, wrote of the "Americomania" taking hold in some quarters of the British mind. With democracy "all but established in England," he wrote, America's former detractors now turn their eyes to the United States for lessons in "guiding democratic progress in an orderly and conservative direction."[74]

Britain's democratic turn in the 1860s resulted from the convergence of social unrest among workers and a reluctant Parliament eager to concede just enough political power to stem the rising tide of democracy. Instead of stemming the tide, the reform movement of the 1860s awakened the lower classes to their miserable condition and the urgent need to conquer political power. The role of the United States, first as an example

of democratic failure for conservatives and then as a model of democratic success for reformers, played a significant role in the debate.
Americans, in turn, welcomed their mother country into the modern
age of democracy with a mix of pride and condescension. John Lothrop
Motley, U.S. minister to London, called the Reform Act of 1867 "the
fruit of the Appomattox apple tree." "Who imagined in 1862," he asked,
"that power would be transferred, in England so soon from land to
people, without bloodshed, and that it would be done by the Tories?"
Britain's "vast revolution," Motley thought, was "destined to place her
where she ought ever to be—side by side, in full friendship and in generous rivalry of freedom and the arts of peace with this Republic."[75]

CHAPTER 8

Spain's Democratic Moment

Tell me how it was; inspire my mind.
Tell me, how, to the admiration of the world
did you wipe away the black stain
that vilely tarnished your brilliant crest? . . .
Tell me how, since centuries past,
were the unfortunate sons with faded stars
stolen from Africa and
the virgin lands ravished?
And tell me, how were they later liberated
by the tenacious heroes of America

—CAROLINA CORONADO, SPANISH POET,
"THE REDEEMING EAGLE," MAY 1865

Britain's cautious step into the democratic future in 1867 was in keeping with its centuries-long tradition of constitutional monarchy, strong Parliament, and celebrated freedom of speech and assembly. Despite the fracases at Hyde Park and pervasive fears of revolutionary violence, as usual, Britain followed a peaceful parliamentary path to democratic reform.

In contrast, Spain's path to liberal democracy was fraught with traumatic reversals from the 1810s to the 1970s, including forty years of fascist rule. Queen Isabella II's Bourbon dynasty, which had ruled Spain since 1700, had reached its nadir in the 1860s. A court cabal of Jesuit neo-Catholic reactionaries and ultra-monarchists convinced Isabella to exclude the Progressives, a moderate left-of-center faction. It was an act of political suicide that led to the democratic revolution of 1868.[1]

Spain's "Glorious Revolution" was part of the contagious wave of democratic upheavals that spread across the Atlantic world in the wake of the Union's victory in 1865. Its costly and fruitless imperialist ventures during the American Civil War—Santo Domingo, Mexico, Peru, and Chile—had set the stage for revolution by opening fissures in the fragile coalition supporting the Bourbon throne.

The American Civil War shook Spain's stubborn complacency on slavery. During the war rumors of slave uprisings flashed through Cuba, Puerto Rico, and Brazil, the last bastions of American slavery. The example of the immediate, uncompensated emancipation of four million African Americans (two-thirds of all enslaved people in the Americas) forced discussion of abolition into the public square. From 1862 through the 1870s, the United States, formerly the protector of the transatlantic slave trade and slavery itself, played an unsung role in compelling Spain to abolish slavery, the last European nation to do so.[2]

It was telling that the first successful initiative for a Spanish antislavery organization came from the Caribbean. Julio Vizcarrondo, a Puerto Rican abolitionist, arrived in Madrid sometime in 1863 to organize an antislavery movement in Spain. Born to a wealthy slaveholding family in Puerto Rico, Vizcarrondo went to Madrid and Paris for education and returned filled with liberal ideas, particularly on the evils of slavery, which he set about broadcasting in his chosen vocation as a journalist. The Spanish governor of Puerto Rico, finding such publications incendiary, deported him to the United States in 1850, where he spent four years studying, writing, and contacting American abolitionists. Vizcarrondo also met and married Harriet Brewster, an American abolitionist who became a vital partner in his mission to end Spanish slavery. After returning to Puerto Rico in 1854, they moved to Madrid in 1863, determined to agitate the antislavery cause at the heart of the empire. They enlisted many of the leading figures of liberal Spain, including prominent Spanish women who joined the cause. In December 1864, the Spanish Abolitionist Society, the first organized antislavery movement in Spain's history, was founded. On April 2, 1865, it held its inaugural meeting.[3]

Another leading figure in Spain's nascent abolitionist movement was Cuban-born Rafael María de Labra, who came to Spain as a child and became an energetic voice for democracy, women's rights, and abolition. Labra edited the Society's newspaper, *El Abolitionista*, and wrote antislavery articles for *Revista Hispano-Americana: Política, Científica y Literaria*, a Madrid journal that advocated liberal reform. Known as the "Wilberforce of Spain," Labra admired Lincoln for his bold decision to end slavery immediately and without compensation, a model Labra proposed for Spain. He also applauded America's commitment to "reconstruct" instead of "restore" the republic and guarantee all citizens civil equality regardless of race.[4]

The timing of Spain's new abolitionist movement could not have been better. Within days of its first meeting, news of the Union's victory reached Europe, and Abraham Lincoln, El Gran Emancipador, became a global hero of freedom. In early May, deputies in the Cortes dared to break a code of silence on the slavery question that had been in place for nearly thirty years. The American Civil War had decided that slavery is finished, not only in the United States but also "in the whole American continent," Antonio María Fabié told the Cortes. "Now, will it be possible for them to keep those Spanish provinces, in the midst of the general emancipation of the slaves, will it be possible for them to keep this institution in their domains? I believe that it is not. . . . The question is urgent."[5]

Isabella II, Reina de los Tristes Destinos (Queen of Sad Destinies), was proclaimed queen in 1833 when she was only three. Her father, King Ferdinand VII, having no male heir, arranged to set aside the Salic Law forbidding the throne to pass to a female. His brother, Carlos, was enraged that a woman would occupy a Bourbon throne and instigated three Carlist Wars, as they were known, aimed at overthrowing her. Ferdinand's fourth wife, Maria Christina, served as Spain's autocratic regent until the young queen turned thirteen in 1843, though behind the scenes, she continued to play a dark role in Spanish politics.

From the beginning, Isabella's reign was assailed from the right by reactionary Carlistas and from the left by those who wanted Spain to join Europe's liberal democratic future. Moderates wanted a constitutional monarchy and an electorate restricted to men of substantial property, close to the British Tory ideal. Progressives were Anglophiles who wanted to keep the monarchy but only with radical suffrage reform along the lines of Britain's Reform Act of 1867. On the far left were Democrats, Republicans, and some socialists who wanted to abolish the monarchy and create a pure democratic republic based on universal manhood suffrage, akin to the American model. The political fissures worked to protect the throne, at least until Queen Isabella II drove the Progressives from power.[6]

All factions sought power by winning favor with their fickle queen. Her limited education, spare knowledge of politics and international affairs, and a weakness for male attention made her an easy target for flattery. At sixteen, against her will, she married a distant cousin whom she complained was "effeminate." She enjoyed an impressive array of lovers ranging from Spanish generals and political leaders to young courtiers, even foreign diplomats, and two U.S. ministers to Madrid if rumors count for anything. She became pregnant no less than twelve times, though only five children survived to adulthood. Her amorous adventures left gossipers to speculate as to the paternity of her children.[7]

By the 1860s, Isabella's youthful beauty was fading. One unkind observer described her figure as more "bulky" than "stately." Gustave Koerner, America's minister to Spain, first saw the queen standing "in the middle of the audience-chamber in full regal dress blazing with diamonds." He was struck by her "enormous *embonpoint* [fatness], though she was only a little over thirty years." To be fair, monarchs were often the target of cruel ridicule, and women with power generally paid a higher price than males when it came to appearances—and adultery.[8]

Isabella was neither educated nor especially curious about the world of politics and diplomacy. Her ignorance left her vulnerable to sycophantic courtiers who flattered and manipulated their way to power.

Her favorites were ambitious generals who had defended the Crown against domestic revolutionaries or won imagined glory for Spain in imperialist adventures abroad. Most were ambitious parvenus whose noble titles came from military glory, not aristocratic birth. General Leopoldo O'Donnell, First Duke of Tetuán and leader of the Liberal Union party, had championed the expansion of Spanish territory in Northern Africa. General Ramón Narváez had defended the throne against the Carlistas to win his title as 1st Duke of Valencia. He was an unscrupulous, cruel reactionary who served the queen three times as prime minister. General Juan Prim, leader of the Progressive faction, bore no less than three titles as count, rewards for his glories in Morocco. When the queen appointed him commander of Spanish forces in Mexico, rumors spread that Prim would become Mexico's new monarch, that is, until Prim pulled Spain out of the alliance in protest against the French plot to install Maximilian as monarch.[9]

Obsequious courtiers and journalists began referring to her as Queen Isabella La Catolica, a flattering reference to her namesake, Isabella I, whose triumphs included sponsoring Christopher Columbus's voyages to the New World and launching the Spanish Empire in America. It was the ambition of Spain's imperialists to reclaim their country's historic role as leader of the "Hispanic race." The term had gained currency by the 1860s in answer to Napoleon III's claim for French leadership of the "Latin race." Both imperialist ventures in the Americas ended more in humiliation than glory and eroded support at home.[10]

Juan Prim tried to light the fuse of revolution in an abortive barracks revolt in January 1866. He and his rebel band were forced to flee to Portugal and then go into exile in Europe. A few months later, in June 1866, a second revolt erupted at the San Gil barracks inside Madrid. When loyal officers resisted, rebel soldiers shot them on the spot. Civilians threw up barricades inside Madrid, and 1,200 insurgents took up posts throughout the capital. "The mutineers fought with the desperation of men with ropes round their necks," one observer noted. The rebellion was defeated and loyalists executed sixty-six rebel officers. Liberal army officers and civilians fled the country. From exile in Europe, Juan Prim issued a manifesto "to the nation," denouncing the reactionary government in Spain as "an insult to humanity" and calling for revolution.[11]

The queen blamed the brutal executions at San Gil on her prime minister, O'Donnell, whom she summarily sacked, thus ending the Liberal Union coalition that had held Spain together for the previous decade. His successor, Ramón María Narváez, was a thorough reactionary. He promptly suspended the Cortes, silenced the press, and ruled by executive decree. When students in Madrid protested the firing of Professor Emilio Castelar, an outspoken republican, for publishing an article mocking the queen, Narváez unleashed the police on them. The government banned all public activities of the Spanish Abolitionist Society, persecuted its members, and drove its leader, Julio Vizcarrondo, into exile. Spain had entered the most draconian phase of Queen Isabella II's reign. Narváez died suddenly in April 1868. On his deathbed, he famously said, "I don't need to forgive my enemies—I have had them all shot." It might have served as an epitaph for Isabella's reign as well.[12]

Soon after the failed San Gil revolt, on August 16, 1866, Prim and forty to fifty liberal opposition leaders met secretly in Ostend, Belgium. Their purpose was to create a revolutionary coalition united against the Bourbon throne and the Moderate government. Progressives wanted a British-style constitutional monarchy but a constitution closer to the U.S. model and a government elected by universal manhood suffrage. Republicans wanted to pitch the throne out the window, as their leader, Emilio Castelar, proposed. Most wanted to do away with the privileged nobility and remove the Catholic Church's stranglehold on education and religious freedom. The Ostend Pact of 1866 bound men of conflicting political ideologies by little more than disgust with the rotten Bourbon monarchy and the reactionary government sustaining it.[13]

Historians have missed a fascinating exchange that unfolded in the shadows about the same time as the Ostend meeting. In August 1866, U.S. minister to France, John Bigelow, was in Biarritz, an aristocratic seaside resort near the Spanish border and a favorite of Napoleon III during the summer heat. Bigelow received a message from a mysterious man who had served as an informant during the Civil War. "Monsieur

X," as Bigelow then referred to him, had proved a valuable informant by betraying Napoleon III's nefarious plan to build ships for the Confederacy. A Frenchman "of the Gascon type, small of stature, with glittering black eyes, and thick, coarse, jet-black hair," as Bigelow described him, Monsieur X now adopted as his nom de guerre "Viscount P. Trement." Trement wrote Bigelow on August 4 with an urgent request: "Have the goodness to let me know *immediately* if you can enter into relations with General Prim, who is now at Geneva. He *wants money*. In exchange he is ready, if he succeeds in Spain, to engage to abandon the island of Cuba to your government. I await your answer by *return of mail*."

Bigelow did not answer and instead forwarded the letter to Seward, explaining that he had "not thought it proper to make any reply to this note." The United States, having staked its entire foreign policy on the principle that foreign interference in a country's domestic insurrection was a violation of international law, could hardly turn around and conspire with Spanish rebels. Bigelow later learned that Prim and his collaborators had already communicated their plan to Seward, who also made no answer. The offer also made its way to Charles Sumner, chair of the Senate Foreign Relations Committee, and was later leaked to the press and used to embarrass Prim, who denied having made any such offer.[14]

Bigelow was still at Biarritz a few weeks later when another mysterious conspirator arranged to meet with him secretly. The Infante of Spain, Antoine, Duke of Montpensier, was the youngest son of the late "King of the French," Louis Philippe, the last Bourbon monarch of France, deposed in 1848. Montpensier married Queen Isabella II's younger sister, Luisa Fernanda, the Infanta (successor to the throne), making him an Infante. Montpensier, a lifelong conspirator, was supposedly operating in collusion with Prim's band of revolutionaries, but he also had his own agenda.

Bigelow listened carefully as this Bourbon prince "proposed darkly to make Cuba the price to us of such assistance as the United States might render to [Prim and] the Spanish *Emigrès* to overthrow the government." Montpensier came to Bigelow, rather than the U.S. minister, John Hale, in Madrid, as he explained, because the legation secretary, Horatio Perry, was married to Carolina Coronado, a brilliant poet and a favorite of the queen. Montpensier thought the legation could not be entrusted to keep his plot secret. To summarize, Montpensier wanted to conspire with the United States to acquire money for a revolution that would overthrow his sister-in-law and place him on the Bourbon throne in her place. He left Bigelow with a warning: the "revolution is ready to break out any moment." Now was the time for America to act.[15]

Prim and the Spanish revolutionaries were nothing if not persistent. At the end of October, Bigelow received a second note from Trement. This one warned Bigelow that "a secret treaty is being elaborated at this moment between a European power and General Prim" by which "the General will receive three and a half millions to continue the Spanish insurrection, and some supplies of arms, powder and material of war. On his side the general engages that, as soon as he succeeds, he will abandon all the Spanish Antilles." Was your government, Trement put the question, "not disposed to occupy itself with this matter?"[16]

Bigelow did not answer immediately. To be involved in aiding a revolutionary coup d'état was dangerous business. For the United States to even consider secretly buying a European colony in the Caribbean would put it in the company of the empires it denounced for violating the Monroe Doctrine. Such a scheme offended every principle of American republicanism. Bigelow finally responded tersely to Trement, saying he had no instructions from his government to allow him "to negotiate for the dismemberment of the territory of any friendly power." He was dismayed that Trement was even "making such a proposal to me in writing instead of seeking a personal interview." More to the point, neither Bigelow, Seward, nor his successor, Hamilton Fish, had any interest in acquiring Cuba or Puerto Rico, which was part of the offer. "Next to a civil war," Bigelow thought, "one of the greatest calamities that could befall the United States would be the acquisition of the Spanish Antilles."[17]

Seward agreed. The acquisition of Cuba had been the obsession of Southern slaveholders in the 1850s, and to acquire it now amounted to a reward to the South. The enthusiasm of the Southern press for annexation reinforced this concern.[18] Seward later confided to Bigelow that he had received the same offer "from the same quarter at the same time it reached you." "Would the United States want Cuba without slavery?"

FIGURE 34. Queen Isabella II in Exile. The Revolution of 1868 deposed Queen Isabella II, the monarch of the Spanish Bourbon dynasty that had ruled Spain since 1700. During the 1860s, her rule had reached new lows of unpopularity, aggravated by vainglorious imperialist adventures in the Americas. Napoleon III granted her asylum in France, where this picture was taken in 1870. Wikimedia Commons.

he asked Bigelow. "You know the history of Santo Domingo," alluding to the troubled economy and social strife afflicting the Dominican Republic. "Would the United States now want Cuba with slavery?" Both questions answered themselves.[19]

Prim and the Ostend Pact liberals did not wait for foreign aid to launch their revolution. On September 18, 1868, generals Juan Prim and Francisco Serrano, along with others in the coalition, proclaimed the new government, deposed Queen Isabella II, and established a provisional

FIGURE 35. Spain's Revolutionary Provisional Government. This photograph shows the two main leaders of the revolution, Juan Prim y Prats, minister of state, and Francisco Serrano, president, standing second and third from the left. J. Laurent photographer, Wikimedia Commons.

government in Madrid. "To arms, citizens, to arms!" Prim's pronunciamento proclaimed. "Let all Liberals during the contest blot out their former differences and make upon the altar of their country the sacrifice of painful recollections." Prim promised a government based on universal manhood suffrage to guarantee liberties and safeguard all citizens' rights. Though vague, it played well. The Spanish people hailed their new government immediately, and the revolution rolled across the Iberian Peninsula from Cadiz to Madrid with crowds cheering the advancing armies.[20]

The Bourbon dynasty that had ruled Spain for nearly 170 years, and the queen who had filled the throne since 1833, collapsed suddenly and with virtually no resistance from the military or populace, except for a brief battle at Alcolea. Spain's revolutionary armed forces entered Madrid on September 29 without firing a shot.[21]

When news of the revolution reached her, Queen Isabella II was with her entourage at the Hotel d'Angleterre in San Sebastian, a fashionable seaside resort on Spain's northern coast near the French border that served as the queen's summer residence. She was enjoying her family's company and that of her current lover, Carlos Marfori, an Italian singer in his former life, whom many considered the queen's lowest dive.[22]

Once she realized the revolution had succeeded, Queen Isabella II crossed into France late at night on September 30. A crowd outside the hotel witnessed her in disguise as she made her way to the royal railway car flanked by guards in medieval garb carrying pikes with ax blades. A band played the Bourbon March as onlookers watched in silence. She arranged to meet secretly with Napoleon III, taking in the sea air nearby at his summer residence in Biarritz. Queen Isabella hoped her fellow monarch might intervene on her behalf. Napoleon's wife, Empress Eugénie, after all, was Spanish. She was also a stern Catholic, fiercely antidemocratic, and known to be influential with her feckless husband.

The two monarchs met at one in the morning at the Biarritz train station. As the French emperor greeted the distressed Spanish queen, a train from Paris to Madrid suddenly roared into the station filled with Spaniards returning from exile to welcome the revolution. They shouted insults at the flustered queen and chanted, ¡Fuera, ¡Fuera! (Out! Out!).

Napoleon III offered the queen of Spain nothing more than safe passage to exile in France. "The parting was brief, silent, and mournful," one observer noted. "I never was present at a funeral where the grief of the mourners was more profound. . . . It was the funeral procession of a dynasty two hundred years old, which had breathed its last sigh in the Biarritz station. The signal is given. The train is put in motion. Everybody bows; and all is over."[23]

John P. Hale, U.S. minister to Spain, described the events in Spain to Seward with undisguised glee as though the revolution was another victory for American democracy abroad. The people of Madrid "pronounced enthusiastically for the insurgents" on September 29, and the "news swept over Spain like wildfire . . . marked in every instance and in all places with the same general characteristics of popular enthusiasm,

FIGURE 36. "Allegory of Spain's Glorious Revolution, 1868." Juan Prim y Prats, a
leader of the Glorious Revolution of 1868, carries the flag of Spain emblazoned
with the words "Viva La Libertad." Note, the female angel with the trumpet
does not wear the red republican cap of liberty and the soldier whose banner
calls for "Down with the Bourbons" is in keeping with the democratic but not
republican spirit of the revolution of 1868 in its first phase. *La Flaca*, 1873.
Album/Alamy Stock Photo.

peaceful execution, and thorough completeness." Hale later updated Seward to tell him, "the people of Madrid made their first essay in the exercise of sovereignty, electing by universal suffrage" a government. It was a provisional government with Francisco Serrano serving as president and Juan Prim as de facto prime minister. The exact form of government was to be decided later and only after accomplishing the main objective of dethroning Queen Isabella.

Once the provisional government was in place, Hale wasted no time in awarding it recognition by the United States. He delivered a fulsome speech in his practiced Spanish welcoming Spain into the democratic age. "A government claiming to be founded on divine right has been overthrown, and a government founded on a right still more divine, the right of the people, has been established in its place."[24]

Democrats across Europe, Mazzini, Victor Hugo, Garibaldi, and Alexandre Dumas, hailed the Spanish revolution. Élie Reclus, a prominent French radical, spoke as a "citizen of the Universal Republic" in welcoming the Spanish revolution. "Make the Federal Republic establish itself in Spain, and you will have contributed at the same time to the prosperity of your country and to the progress of the whole world. *Vivent les Républicains espagnols.*"[25]

Many Americans felt gratified to see Spain taking a democratic path to the future and possibly leading liberal Europe forward. John Hay, secretary to the U.S. legation in Madrid, gushed over the democratic spirit of 1868. "It is courageous and aggressive. It speaks every morning in the press denouncing the old infernal rule of violence and of superstition. It attacks the slavers of Cuba and the thought-stranglers of the Vatican. It is heard in the clubs, in the widespread committees of the people, who are laboring to prepare themselves to administer their own affairs. Its voice rings out in the Cortes in strains of lyric beauty, that are only heard in the fresh and dewy dawn of democracies."[26]

Though Prim and other revolutionaries favored the British model of constitutional monarchy, many admired the United States as a model republic and an example of democracy's success. While the revolutionary government was preparing to draft its constitution, a Spanish translation of the U.S. Constitution appeared with introductory notes by

Agustín Santayana (father of Spanish philosopher George Santayana). Santayana explained, "for the Spanish Nation, this knowledge is useful and interesting, but indispensable." In the U.S. Constitution, he added, are "the principles on which is founded the great republic today, whose powerful moral influence is spreading unconsciously throughout the world." At the same time, a Spanish translation of a two-volume history of the U.S. Constitution appeared, authored by Édouard Laboulaye, a professor in Paris who was Europe's leading expert on the subject.[27]

The Spanish constitution of June 1869 did reflect essential elements of the U.S. model, including a bicameral congress with an elected senate and legislature. The preamble, one republican deputy admitted, was "so similar that it could almost be said that it is a translation of the United States' constitution." Another deputy proposed that the government simply translate the entire U.S. Constitution and make it Spain's. The first article of the 1869 constitution safeguarded the freedom to associate, assemble, and petition, along with freedom of religion and the press. Terms such as "inalienable rights," "universal suffrage," and "self-government" suddenly became part of Spain's new democratic vocabulary.[28]

When it came to the head of state, Spain departed from the U.S. model of a president elected for fixed terms and launched a novel experiment in what Prim styled a "democratic monarchy." Prim, the architect of this bizarre concept, wanted to appease conservative monarchists yet ensure Spain's democracy that their new government would be responsible to the people. The new monarch must come from outside Spain and be free of ties to the Bourbon dynasty, including French Bourbons, which excluded Montpensier. The Infante Montpensier had already damaged his prospects in a classic affair of honor. One of the queen's cousins published an inflammatory letter calling Montpensier a "Jesuit conspirator" and "bloated French pastry cook" (an allusion to his earlier career). The offended Montpensier challenged him to a duel typically settled by one or two harmless shots to preserve honor. After several missed attempts, however, Montpensier shot his offender dead, a breach of etiquette that doomed his dream of ascending to the throne.[29]

Europe had a good supply of unemployed princes from which Spain might select its monarch, and Prim first proposed Prince Leopold of the

FIGURE 37. "Republican Demonstration in Madrid." Spain's democratic revolution involved a coalition of various liberal parties whose fractious relationship to one another led to the assassination of Juan Prim, the abdication of King Amadeo, and the creation of a Spanish republic and finally ended with the restoration of the Bourbon dynasty, and Isabella II's son, Alfonso, serving as king. *London Illustrated News*, December 20, 1868. Hathitrust.

German Hohenzollern dynasty. He was thirty-five years old, a distant relation to Prussia's King Wilhelm I, and married to Antónia de Braganza, the Infanta of Portugal's ruling dynasty. These impressive family connections added luster to Leopold's royal pedigree and would enhance the new Spanish regime's stature in Europe. Also, in Leopold's favor, Otto von Bismarck, the Prussian chancellor, actively lobbied Spain's leaders to engage the young prince. However, once news of Leopold's candidacy and Bismarck's meddling surfaced, Napoleon III was furious at the thought of two Hohenzollern monarchs flanking France on the east and south. King Wilhelm deftly engineered the withdrawal of Leopold's candidacy, but the insult to France, which Bismarck undoubtedly relished, was not forgotten. Indeed, it set the stage for the Franco-Prussian War and the fall of Napoleon III.

The birth of Spain's new government between September 1868 and June 1869, when the constitution was completed, coincided with the advent of Ulysses S. Grant's first term as president. The Johnson administration had already recognized Spain's new government, the first nation to do so. This was a "new Spain," President Grant told his cabinet, a modern democratic government. Secretary of State Hamilton Fish shared Grant's conviction that the United States must stand by Spain's liberal government and do nothing to undermine it by aiding the rebellion in Cuba.

In Congress, Nathaniel Banks of Massachusetts put forth a joint resolution that began with an expression of American enthusiasm for "the patriotic people of Spain in their efforts to establish the liberties of the Spanish nation." Banks's resolution also expressed America's support of "the people of Cuba in their efforts to secure their independence." Charles W. Willard, a Republican from Vermont, rose to point out the contradiction: "The Liberalists in Spain would not thank us for sending them friendly greetings on their success, if we at the same time expressed . . . a wish that they might be robbed of the fairest jewel in their possession." He then explained that recognizing the Cuban rebellion would violate everything the Union stood for during the Civil War when it warned Europe that any effort to aid the Confederate rebellion would be an act of war. Willard had put his finger right on the dilemma posed by the dual revolutions in Spain and Cuba.[30]

Hamilton Fish had already determined he would not negotiate with or even receive emissaries from the Cuban revolution. Instead, he would deal exclusively with Spain, beginning with an offer to mediate peace in Cuba. The Cuban crisis created an opportunity for the United States to carry out the central objectives of U.S. foreign policy after the Civil War: ridding the hemisphere of European empires and slavery.

Grant decided to appoint Daniel Sickles as U.S. minister to Madrid. He was another of Grant's wartime friends who had further earned the president's gratitude by delivering fiery campaign speeches for Grant. Sickles had some successful diplomatic experience but little to recommend him for the critical mission in Spain. A New Yorker with previous ties to the Democratic Party's Tammany Hall ring, Sickles had served

briefly as secretary to the U.S. legation in London. While there, he involved himself in the Ostend Manifesto, a reckless, unauthorized proclamation in 1854 that threatened war with Spain if it did not sell Cuba
to the United States. Sickles also had a reputation for fast living combined with a habit of indiscretion. He was a poor choice for such an
important post.[31]

There were howls of protest against Sickles's appointment inside the
cabinet, not least from Hamilton Fish, who thought him wholly unsuit-
able. The press piled on, and the Senate delayed confirmation, but Grant
stood by his friend. Sickles may have viewed his mission in Spain as a
negotiator sent to work out a "Cuba for cash" deal veiled as peace negotiations, but that was not what Fish had in mind. Fish questioned Cuba's
fitness for membership in the Union, referring mainly to its alien language and customs and its lack of experience with democratic government.
Also, the postwar Monroe Doctrine, with its "America for Americans"
slogan, might cast a U.S. takeover of Cuba as a kind of colonial transfer,
something out of keeping with republican ideals and, in any case, unnecessary to American commercial interests in Cuba.[32]

Much to Fish's annoyance, Sickles dallied for most of the summer,
tending to his personal business affairs in New York. Fish enlisted Paul
Forbes as a special envoy to Madrid to get things moving. Forbes was
from a venerable Boston Brahmin dynasty with deep interests in
European commerce with America, particularly Spain and its Caribbean
colonies, and was acquainted with Juan Prim and other leaders of Spain's
new government. At Fish's direction, Forbes met with Prim in May 1869
to discuss terms of peace in Cuba. "Spain accepts mediation," Forbes
telegrammed on July 20, 1869. "Prim asks hundred fifty million for Cuba
and Porto Rico. U. S. to guarantee. . . . Prim wishes to negotiate himself
alone through me only." This "turn," he added, was important.[33]

Though Fish was no more willing to annex Cuba than Seward had
been, he understood that Spain's desperate need for money might give
him leverage in negotiating terms for mediation. Fish set down a terse
four-point summary of the terms by which the United States was willing
to mediate: Cuba was to be independent, slavery was to be abolished,
Cuba would pay Spain no more than $100 million in compensation, and

the United States would guarantee payment. Both parties in Cuba were to lay down their arms during negotiations.[34]

The Cuban rebels were delighted to learn of Fish's plan for peace, and the New York Cuban Junta, acting as representatives of the rebel republic, immediately endorsed it. Fish's peace plan promised almost everything the insurgents had hoped for during the recent Guáimaro Assembly. In Fish's view, his peace plan would be a brilliant diplomatic solution for all parties: peace and independence for Cubans; one more European empire out of the American hemisphere; Spain to replenish its treasury; and instead of a war-torn slave colony, Cuba would be independent, free of slavery, and a grateful neighbor to the United States. Cuba's payments to Spain would come from $32 million in annual revenues from trade with the United States. As guarantor of what amounted to a mortgage, the United States could take possession of Cuba should it default on payments. That was not Fish's aim; he wanted to keep America out of a war with Spain and create a friendly, independent, republican, free-labor neighbor, a plan fully in keeping with Seward's vision of sturdy "buttresses" surrounding the United States.[35]

Sickles finally arrived in Madrid on July 21, 1869, and seemed in no hurry to get about his business with Prim, which involved nothing less than ending a bloody war in Cuba and emancipating almost 400,000 human souls. Utterly exasperated with Sickles's dithering, Fish sent him a cable on July 29. "An early decision on the proposition to mediate is extremely important. Hasten it."[36] Three days later, on August 1, Sickles sat down for an informal meeting with Prim, whose first question was how much money Cuba *and Puerto Rico* "would give" to Spain. Prim's desperation for money was a good sign in Sickles's view. Forbes reported over a month earlier that Prim had thrown Puerto Rico into the deal without prompting. Given that addition, Sickles felt authorized to raise the price. He casually estimated that the two islands might fetch US$125 million. Prim promised he would immediately present these terms to the Spanish government.[37]

Twelve days passed before Prim returned to Sickles, who by then was irritated with what he saw as stalling. After exchanging routine diplomatic civilities with platitudes about the long friendship between their two nations, Sickles launched into a blunt warning that the American people felt "deep sympathy with the Cuban people." The Cubans, after all, were "fighting for the same principles of self-government we had ourselves adopted." Sickles added that Spain and all other European powers would have to accept the eventual independence of all their American colonies as part of the new post-1865 reality.

Prim cut him off "as if he thought I had gone quite far enough," Sickles reported to Fish. Prim then confessed to the embarrassment caused by the contradiction of a revolutionary democratic, antislavery government in Spain now having to fight their brethren in Cuba who wanted the same thing. But he explained to Sickles that Spain could not surrender to rebels still at arms without suffering unacceptable disgrace to its national honor.[38] The rebels must lay down their arms before Spain could make any concessions. As for abolishing slavery, Prim told Sickles, "That is your glory in America, the reward of your philanthropy, and we do not wish to deprive you of it." Prim was being disingenuous, Sickles suspected. In truth, the Spanish government was up against a strong phalanx of *esclavistas* who wanted nothing to do with selling Cuba or abolishing slavery. Prim was happy to let the Cubans—or the United States—deal with the slavery question.[39]

Prim soon came back with new peace terms requiring that Cuba's rebels lay down their arms and allow Spain to conduct a plebiscite to determine whether the Cuban people wanted independence. If independence were their choice, Cuba would pay Spain a satisfactory amount, and the United States would guarantee payment. Prim's counteroffer made no mention of slavery or abolition.[40]

Fish answered promptly with a demand that Spain must agree to immediate disarmament on both sides. He warned Spain that the destruction of property and lives was rapidly escalating, and if Spain did not accept U.S. terms by October 1, 1869, his offer would expire.[41]

After receiving Fish's aggressive warning, Prim took off for France to take the waters at Vichy, apologizing to Sickles for his "sudden departure" and promising to return in about three weeks. Sickles was left to negotiate with Manuel Becerra, Spain's overseas minister. In a written memo, he warned Becerra that time was running out and President Grant would feel compelled to recognize Cuba's rebel government if Spain did not agree to U.S. terms.[42]

Becerra decided to blow things up by sending copies of Sickles's confidential memo to the press and several European governments. Becerra's blatant defiance of the diplomatic protocol was intended to inflame Spain's prickly sense of national honor and arouse disgust toward American arrogance. It had a predictable effect. Sickles reported to Fish that the press was pouring forth "extravagant reports" depicting the United States trying to bully Spain. The Spanish government announced plans to send more troops to Cuba. Becerra informed Sickles that Spain hoped to hold onto Cuba "because she trusts that a majority of the islanders regard it is still an honor and a privilege to be Spaniards."[43]

The Cuban uprising and Spain's exaggerated sense of its cost in national honor gave Spain's conservatives a potent weapon to derail the revolution and thwart the rebellion in Cuba. Cuba, the historian Raymond Carr ruefully observed, was the fatal cancer that sapped the Glorious Revolution's vitality. Sickles realized Prim did not dare give up Cuba without risking a counterrevolution from diehard monarchists and *esclavistas*. John Hay chronicled La Gloriosa's empty promises: a free, democratic society, the abolition of slavery, the emancipation of Cuba and Puerto Rico, and many others, all betrayed by "an attitude of tyranny and repression which recalls the worst days of the banished race." "Unless the situation changes for the better," he dolefully predicted, "the Revolution of September will pass into history merely as a mutiny."[44]

Above all, Hamilton Fish wanted to avoid war with Spain, and though he continued to threaten Spain with recognition of the Cuban rebels, he hoped not to have to back that up. So long as Spain feared U.S. intervention, he had leverage. Furthermore, if he failed to persuade Spain to give up Cuba, he might succeed in pressuring it to give up slavery.

Spain's government had been quietly working on a plan for gradual emancipation after the Cuban rebels proclaimed the immediate end of slavery in their Guáimiro constitution of April 1869. The following

FIGURE 38. "Effect of Mediation." President Grant appointed Daniel Sickles, a colorful Union war hero who had lost a leg at Gettysburg, as U.S. minister to Madrid. He was to mediate peace in Cuba on terms of independence and emancipation. However, Spain's prickly sense of national honor put Sickles in a firestorm of controversy and mediation efforts fell apart. After the Cuban rebels proclaimed the abolition of slavery, Hamilton Fish instructed Sickles to demand that Spain enact a plan of emancipation or the United States would recognize Cuban rebels. *Harper's Weekly*, October 23, 1869. Hathitrust.

month, the new overseas minister, Segismundo Moret y Prendergast, an author and ardent abolitionist, made the details known. All children born to enslaved mothers in Cuba and Puerto Rico since September 18, 1868 (the inception of the Glorious Revolution), were declared free, and no more slaves would be born in the Spanish Empire. However, those born to "free wombs" would work as apprentices (*patronatos*) to their mother's owners until age eighteen (fourteen for females), then for half wages until twenty-one. The Moret Law also granted freedom to slaves sixty or older, a provision more cruel than philanthropic since it relieved slaveholders from caring for their elderly workers. Moret's bill also promised emancipation to those who fought under the Spanish flag in Cuba. The law, Moret admitted, was "a compromise between the conservative elements and the revolutionary elements . . . that made the Revolution of September possible."[45]

Moret cut an impressive figure. John Hay described him as handsome, "six feet high, built like a trapeze performer, with a classical, clear-cut face," who spoke with a "fluency and ease of diction." Moret told the Cortes that the Cuban rebels, being "familiar with North American customs and language," had effectively presented their rebellion before the world as "the flag of liberty against the flag of tyranny." Spain must answer this with "definite proof . . . slavery is dead, and is finished forever in Spanish dominions."[46]

Slavery was not dead yet. The Moret bill stalled in the Cortes for over a year. The excuse was that Spain could make no concessions so long as the rebels were at arms. In truth, proslavery interests in Spain and Cuba were mounting a vigorous campaign against emancipation. Fish got fed up with the stalling. In early 1870 he let Spain know that emancipation was the "sine qua non" for further negotiations. "It becomes more apparent every day that this contest cannot terminate without the abolition of slavery," he instructed Sickles to tell Prim. "This government regards the government at Madrid as committed to that result."[47]

Debates on the Moret bill began in the Cortes in the spring of 1870 and dragged into the summer. Emilio Castelar, a devoted republican and abolitionist, disparaged Moret's gradualist approach. It was one of his more magnificent displays of oratory. Castelar "never writes a speech," John Hay marveled, "yet every sentence even in a running debate when all the government hounds are yelping at him at once, is as finished and as elegantly balanced as if he had pondered all a rainy Sunday over it."[48]

Castelar viewed America as the model for republicanism, advocated for a "United States of Europe," and idealized Abraham Lincoln as the embodiment of republican virtue. Sickles noted a small statue of Lincoln on Castelar's desk. Speaking before the Cortes, Castelar invoked Lincoln and America's bold path to complete and immediate emancipation. "Pause a moment to consider the man who wiped out this terrible stain which blotted out the stars of the American banner," he implored the Cortes. He reviewed Lincoln's humble Kentucky origins and ascent as "a new Moses, in the solitude of the wilderness." "A man of wisdom

FIGURE 39. Emilio Castelar y Ripoll. Spain's eloquent voice for pure republicanism and the full and immediate abolition of slavery. He greatly admired Abraham Lincoln and hailed Radical Reconstruction as the apotheosis of America's democracy. *La Ilustración de Madrid*, November 12, 1870. Wikimedia Commons.

and political prudence," Lincoln realized that "all hope of compromise was gone, that gradual steps are impracticable in reforms demanded by justice and humanity." Borrowing a page from Lincoln's book, Castelar proposed that Spain declare the end of slavery on the anniversary of the Emancipation Proclamation, January 1, 1872.[49]

Moret interrupted Castelar's passionate plea to point out that Lincoln had initially hoped for the very kind of gradual abolition his bill proposed. Had he succeeded, "the great evils such as the terrible war that cost the United States so much" might have been prevented. He drolly reminded Castelar, "the great Lincoln did not want to abolish slavery till 1900."[50]

Undaunted, Castelar praised American Reconstruction as an inspiring example of the successful enfranchisement of a once-downtrodden race: "The United States, having converted its slaves into men, have devoted themselves to turning those men into citizens." Then he took it further. "And today, gentlemen, those beings who were formerly not even men, are freer than the first of the sons of Europe. . . . Those men who were like beasts of burden, wretched as the reptiles that crawled among the cotton and the cane, are free men, are American citizens; they sit in the Congress and the Senate of Washington." Castelar's speech went on for hours yet failed to win the day. Castelar's Lincoln, the champion of immediate abolition, did not carry the Cortes, yet Moret's Lincoln, the sage advocate of gradual emancipation, prevailed.[51]

Hamilton Fish was not impressed with Spain's plodding steps toward abolition and wanted it known. "I can scarcely believe that it will command the support of the liberals of Spain, under whose auspices the revolution of 1868 was made. The total emancipation it contemplates is postponed far toward the middle of the next century." The law "may rather be called a project for relieving the slave owners from the necessity of supporting infants and aged slaves, who can only be a burden, and of prolonging the institution as to able-bodied slaves." Spain was violating a tacit agreement "to cordially co-operate with us in the extirpation of this blot on the civilization of America" (meaning the American hemisphere). This law must not be the end of the matter, only "the entering wedge for the eventual destruction of a pernicious system of labor."[52]

The Moret Law, Sickles agreed, was nothing more than "the beginning of the end." Meanwhile, he continued, Spain "has now for the first time distinctly and practically committed itself to the policy of emancipation." From the outset of the Cuban revolution, whichever side "proclaimed

FIGURE 40. "The Slaves Will Be Free." On July 4, 1870, Spain enacted the Fourth of July or Moret Law granting gradual emancipation of children born to enslaved mothers. Here Liberty, an angel wearing a red Phrygian cap, frees the slaves, while a Spanish flag flies in the distance. The tributes in the ribbon below are not to Spanish leaders but to Christ, Spartacus, George Washington, and Abraham Lincoln. *La Flaca*, 1873. Album/Alamy Stock Photo.

emancipation to the slaves, and gave civil and political rights and arms to the freedmen" would prevail. Spain once kept Cubans cowering in fear that "when Cuba ceased to be Spanish she would be African— never American. . . . But all this changed after our war, when so large a portion of the Cuban population yielded to the inevitable force of the example of the United States, and accepted the abolition of slavery as the indispensable condition of their unchanged desire for annexation to the American Union."[53]

The Cortes finally approved the Moret Law on June 23 and formally decreed the law on the Fourth of July 1870. Whether or not the name Ley de 4 de julio de 1870 (aka the Moret Law) was intended to appease the United States, it owed much to the American secretary of state who relentlessly pressured Spain into its noble humanitarian act. From Madrid, Daniel Sickles congratulated Hamilton Fish and President Grant: "In this step toward freedom, it must be a source of just satisfaction to the President that the influence of the United States has been conspicuous and benificent [*sic*]."[54]

The Moret Law, by whatever name, was not enough to mollify critics in America's Congress or the press. Moret and other Spanish officials worried that influential American politicians were denouncing Spain's emancipation law and claiming it to be a nefarious scheme to perpetuate slavery. The American press was also coming to a boil over the Cuba question, and mass meetings in several cities riled up public sentiment. Reports of Spanish atrocities in Cuba, some involving U.S. citizens, did not help. In May 1870, *Harper's Weekly* ran a chilling story on the summary execution of Cuban rebel General Goicouria. *Harper's* included an illustration showing the elderly general, with his long white beard, a priest administering last rites, the executioner ready to turn the screw that would slowly strangle him, and the crowd of soldiers, clergy, and cheering onlookers. Moret feared the Americans were whipping up a storm that would give President Grant an excuse to intervene in Cuba.[55]

Spain's foreign office had anticipated as much and instructed its minister to Washington to explain that the Moret Law was the best Spain could do, given the circumstances of the Cuban rebellion. Brazil, after all, was lagging behind Spain, and, he dared to suggest, it took decades for the United States to end slavery. "No one," Moret protested, "can justly formulate a charge against the Government of Spain because it had not instantly realized this reform."[56]

Cuba's slaveholders held public meetings to denounce the weak emancipation law and raised money to lobby for its repeal. For weeks the Spanish Volunteers in Cuba prevented the Moret Law from being published, let alone enforced. Their obstinance incited a storm of protest from abolitionists in Spain, the United States, and Britain. There was also talk of Charles Sumner leading Congress to endorse U.S. intervention in Cuba. Spanish officials finally published the Moret Law in Cuba at the end of September 1870, yet managed to delay enforcement of its provisions.[57]

The American press joined in shaming Spain for dragging its feet. The *New York Times* correspondent in Madrid ridiculed the moral pretensions of Spain's antislavery law: "Something is accomplished in snatching thousands of children and old men from this condition of servility, . . . but this law does not respond to the aspirations of the revolution, I was about to say to the cry of humanity entire."[58] Cuban rebel Juan Manuel Macías adroitly exposed Spain's feeble gesture in a pamphlet published in English. Spaniards in Cuba, he wrote, openly laugh at the law, which might "be called an Act for the abolition of slavery at some future time, thereby not only cheating the present generation of slaves of their rights, but giving the slaveholding class ample time to conspire against a moral revolution which it is their passionate desire to prevent."[59]

Spain's government spoiled what should have been an ideal opportunity to redeem the Glorious Revolution's promise of emancipation. In 1873, immediately after Spain proclaimed its First Republic, the government abolished slavery in Puerto Rico immediately. Even if enforced to the letter, the Moret Law would have taken more than a lifetime to end slavery. Practically, however, slavery in Cuba was rapidly withering beginning in the 1860s. It started in 1862 when the United States joined Britain in suppressing the African slave trade and pressuring Spain to follow suit. The number of enslaved in Cuba fell from almost 370,000 in 1862 to about 288,000 by 1871, below 200,000 by 1877. In the latter year, Spain also signed a treaty with China to end the traffic of Chinese coolies whose migration to Cuba had offset the decline of slavery. Spain's Emancipation Law of 1880 mandated staged emancipation for the remainder. In 1886, when Spain abolished slavery completely, only 25,000 remained in chains. The slow death of slavery was hastened by the upheaval of the Cuban revolution from the inside and growing international pressure from the outside. Against this, the stubborn efforts of the pro-slavery forces in Cuba and Spain did their best to impede emancipation.[60]

Meanwhile, following Grant's election to a second term in November 1872, Fish ramped up pressure on Spain to speed the end of slavery and reform the governance of Cuba. In response, Spain decided to appease abolitionists at home and abroad by bringing slavery in Puerto Rico to an end altogether in 1873. Emilio Castelar, who championed the bill in the Cortes, generously credited the United States. "We are brethren with the Americans in the cause of abolition," and this Cortes is the first to be freely elected by universal suffrage, Castelar reminded his fellow deputies. "Yesterday, we were unknown, today we are immortal. We belong to the race of Christ, Washington, Spartacus, and Lincoln because we have fearlessly pronounced the word liberty and the definitive redemption of the slaves." The Cortes answered with "great and prolonged applause" and shouts of *¡Viva España!*[61]

Brazil watched Spain give way to the antislavery tide. Lincoln's Emancipation Proclamation had shaken confidence in slavery's future at the highest levels of Brazil's government. It was not until after Spain acted, however, that Brazil's Senate finally confronted slavery's future. Speaking in favor of abolition, Senator Zacarias admitted that so long as the United States sustained slavery, "the issue could be ignored." "We were shielded," another senator interjected. Now, "with Brazil alone as the only slave country in America," Zacarias continued, "it was impossible to keep such an institution alive. . . . There was no need for a war against us to push us toward emancipation; the world laughing at us was enough; becoming the scorn of all nations . . . was enough." Brazil promulgated a similar plan for gradual emancipation in 1871, followed by total abolition in 1888. With the demise of slavery in its last two American bastions, the Spanish Caribbean and Brazil, an institution that for nearly four centuries had been the source of great wealth and shame finally ended.[62]

The two revolutions launched in 1868, instead of hurling Spain and Cuba into the modern age of democracy, failed after a few years. Prim's dream of a "democratic monarchy" died painfully when conspirators, suspected to be republicans, assassinated him in the streets of Madrid. His murder happened the same day Amadeo, the second son of King Victor Emmanuel II of Italy, arrived in Spain after being chosen to serve as Spain's democratic monarch. His brief reign was fraught with the ongoing war in Cuba, a Third Carlist War, republican uprisings, and opposition from monarchists who clamored for Queen Isabella's thirteen-year-old son, Alfonso, to take the throne. After two years, Amadeo abdicated in utter disgust, calling Spain a "madhouse," and returned to Italy. Spain quickly proclaimed its First Republic in February 1873.

The new republican government invited U.S. minister Daniel Sickles to recognize the Republic of Spain in an unusual public ceremony. Dressed in full military uniform, Sickles was escorted to the presidential palace in a state coach. Two military battalions received him with military honors while bands played American national airs. In his best Spanish, Sickles delivered his address to the president. Americans cannot be unmoved by the "spectacle of the Empire of Ferdinand and Isabella transformed into a Republic. The American people rejoice to see Spain imitating their example."[63]

Sadly, Spain's First Republic did not fare well. During its short life, Spain witnessed a succession of four presidents struggle with another Carlist rebellion from the right, anarchist uprisings from the left, and the seemingly endless war in Cuba. In December 1874, Spain's Sexenio Democratico (Six-year Democracy) came to a humiliating end when a military coup invited Alfonso, the son of Queen Isabella II, to serve as king and restore the Bourbon dynasty. The various political factions came to terms with a plan to rotate conservative and liberal governments. They were united only in their fear and hatred of the revolutionary left, socialists, anarchists, and Communists. Alfonso XII's descendants still occupy Europe's last Bourbon throne.[64]

John Hay, listening to a Spanish don speak of his admiration for the liberal governments of Britain and America, mordantly prophesied Spain's democratic future. "We shall have it here finally, I suppose," he told the young American, drolly adding, "The only trouble will be for the first five or six hundred years."[65]

CHAPTER 9

The Last Monarch of France

The people have come of age, as in the United States, and they intend
to govern themselves. . . . A new age has begun, the age of the worker,
novus ordo seclorum, as the Americans say. For a new age, a new flag, . . .
the red flag.

—*JOURNAL OFFICIEL*, PARIS COMMUNE, MARCH 31, 1871

The collapse of France's Second Empire in September 1870 and the civil
war in the Paris Commune the following spring was Europe's most dramatic crisis in this period of democratic reform and revolution. This
episode also marked the end of the century-long Age of Revolution,
during which the forces of democracy in Europe and the Americas
sought to create new nations based on freedom, equality, and self-rule
and overthrow the Old Regime based on autocratic rule, hereditary
privilege, Church domination, and unfree labor.

France's Second Empire originated in a bloody coup d'état that Louis
Napoleon, the elected president, instigated in December 1851. Within a
few days, he overthrew the democratic republic born in the Revolution
of 1848. The coup took place on December 2, the anniversary of the 1804
coronation of his uncle, Napoleon I. One year later he crowned himself
Emperor Napoleon III and returned France to an autocratic Bonapartist

monarchy that endured for eighteen years, albeit with some concessions to political freedom in the 1860s.[1]

France's Second Empire distinguished itself by stunning public improvements, including Baron Haussmann's glittering "City of Light" in Paris. It also boasted ambitious projects overseas, among which was the Suez Canal in Egypt and, not least, the Grand Design in Mexico, which also entailed plans for an interocean canal. The regime was also notorious for harsh repression of political freedom at home. French subjects (the term *citoyen* was banned) could not meet in gatherings of twenty or more without government permission in advance. The empire censored the press and public speech of all kinds. Even singing "La Marseillaise," the anthem of the French Revolution, was forbidden. Though the empire maintained universal male suffrage, Napoleon III's regime made it nearly impossible for the opposition to speak freely, organize campaigns, or voice objections to the government if elected to the Corps Législatif. Despite the draconian censorship, the left (a term of French invention, incidentally), which ranged from "Red" republicans on the far left to liberal constitutional monarchists on the center-left, was determined to restore France to its historical role in the leadership of European democracy.[2]

As with Britain's democratic reform of 1867 and Spain's Glorious Revolution of 1868, the United States took no direct part in the fall of Napoleon's Second Empire in 1870. Indirectly, however, Napoleon III's disastrous intervention in Mexico during the U.S. Civil War became a powerful weapon for the opposition. Once France faced a triumphant Union across the Mexican border in 1865, the fate of Napoleon's Grand Design was sealed. After Maximilian's execution in 1867, Lucien-Anatole Prévost-Paradol, a leading opponent of the empire, depicted the Mexican fiasco as a prime example of the disasters that result from an impulsive dictator operating without counsel from advisors, let alone popular consent. The emperor had expected what he hoped for, the suicide of the Great American Republic. Instead, it came out of the Civil War determined to rid Mexico of its so-called empire, by war if necessary. "Never was a more moving spectacle given to the world," Prévost-Paradol wrote, "never did France receive a livelier or clearer lesson; may this lesson at least not be useless!"[3]

Apart from the Mexican lesson, the American Civil War played a vital role in galvanizing the French opposition to the Second Empire. Though previously cynical about what La Grande République américaine had to teach them, during the Civil War, many on the French left came around to embracing Lincoln and the Union as champions of their common cause. They learned they could avoid imperial censorship by hailing Lincoln and the Union's struggle against the Slave Power, accomplished, as one tribute poignantly expressed, without "veiling the statue of liberty."[4]

One indication of how the American Civil War stirred the French left was the revival of their antislavery movement. France had long since abolished slavery, once in 1794, which Napoleon I rescinded, and again in 1848. Sainte-Suzanne Melvil-Bloncourt, a journalist in Paris, born in Guadeloupe to Creole (mixed-race) parentage, was a proponent of France's emancipation act of 1848 who viewed Lincoln's turn toward abolition as something animated by the wonderful force of "moral electricity." When news of Lincoln's assassination came, he composed a letter signed by 150 fellow Guadeloupeans, which was later included in the State Department's *Tributes of the Nations*. At the same time, he wrote to Frederick Douglass, inviting his interest in raising money through a subscription drive to promote the cause of emancipation across the Americas. Douglass responded warmly, "The cause of justice and liberty is as big as the world . . . I welcome your friendly letter and I reach out my hand to you across the Ocean." The Union may have conquered the slaveholders' rebellion, but both men recognized slavery and racial inequality yet lived in the Americas.[5]

Other veteran abolitionists in France saw the Union victory as a summons to aid the freed people in the United States and those still enslaved in Latin America. Augustin Cochin, Édouard Laboulaye, and several others organized the Comité français d'émancipation sometime before May 1865 to collect money for America's freed people and arouse international opinion against the remaining bastions of slavery in the empires of Brazil and Spain. The committee sent a lengthy message of support to President Johnson, urging him to "finish the work" that Lincoln "began so nobly." In late August 1867, the French Committee of Emancipation hosted an international antislavery conference in Paris at which Laboulaye, Cochin, William Lloyd Garrison, and several other leading abolitionists spoke, including a former slave from Georgia and a Black abolitionist from Haiti. "Let us strive to establish a moral exchange upon the far-off continents of Brazil and America," Laboulaye told the crowd. "Let it be constant" and never "cease until the last slave has been emancipated."[6]

Some in the French delegation were not content with the congratulatory tone of the resolutions the conference endorsed and submitted some scathing counterresolutions. Élisée Reclus, an outspoken anarchist, denounced the Empire of Brazil for holding one-third of its population in slavery, condemned the vile human traffic in Asian coolie labor as worse than slavery, and scolded the British for their massacre of Jamaican Blacks in 1865. He applauded Americans for admitting four million enslaved people into the human family but called on them to now grant full equality and abolish all forms of discrimination. He closed his oration with an astonishing salute to Nat Turner and John Brown.[7]

In April 1867, Emperor Napoleon III welcomed the world to the Exposition Universelle, to which all nations sent exhibits of their industrial and artistic achievements. It was the second such exposition staged by the Second Empire and by far the most extravagant. The city of Paris was itself the most glittering exhibit. Fourteen years earlier, Napoleon III had assigned Georges-Eugène Haussmann, prefect of the Seine, the enormous task of opening the city's dense medieval streets to light and air and arranging the city's boulevards, parks, and public buildings in a grand new design. Baron Haussmann, as he became known, demolished block after block of narrow, dark streets. He built in their place a grand design of wide diagonal boulevards adorned with spectacular public buildings, including the Palais Garnier and the Grand Hotel. He lined the streets with his signature buildings, shops below and apartments above, all designed with a pleasing uniformity of height and architectural features, mansard roofs, iron-railed balconies, and similar window arrangements. Thousands of new gaslights illuminated what became known as the "City of Light."[8]

FIGURE 41. "Napoleon III Receives the Sovereigns at Universal Exhibition of 1867." The Exposition Universelle was a world's fair designed to stun the world with the success of the Second Empire. Paris, the "City of Light," newly renovated by Baron Haussmann, provided the backdrop to the exhibits of industrial progress. Wikimedia Commons.

The emperor envisioned the exposition as a triumphal display of all he had done to revive Bonapartisme, the spirit of French imperial leadership in Europe and the world under the auspices of a powerful dictator. Napoleon invited all the royalty and heads of state in Europe, the Middle East, and Asia to witness the glory of the Second Empire on display in Paris.[9] Because the Mexico dispute had strained relations between the two countries, the United States came close to boycotting the exposition. Republican congressman Nathaniel Banks, though a fierce critic of the French intervention, made a persuasive speech favoring U.S. participation in the Paris Exposition Universelle. Here was the chance, he argued, to give "the democracy of America . . . an opportunity to speak face to face with the democracy of Europe." When the exposition opened in April 1867, the demoralized French troops from Mexico were arriving at the same time Americans came to Paris with their industrial wares and democratic pride.[10]

The crowned heads of Europe flocked to the exposition. One reporter counted no less than "twelve emperors and kings, six reigning princes, nine heirs apparent, a viceroy and countless 'highnesses'" who had descended on Paris. The *New York Times* headlines exclaimed it was "The Most Magnificent Show of the Century."[11] Malakoff, the *Times* correspondent in Paris, reported that thirty to sixty thousand people visited the exhibition daily. "The Champs Elysees is in a state of permanent *fête*; the Bois de Boulogne shows more rolling wealth and more fashion than ever before."[12]

On July 1, 1867, the exposition "cast its most brilliant blaze," and with "the sovereigns of the greatest nations assembling in Paris as though to render solemn homage to the moral influence of France." That morning, however, reports had confirmed rumors that Maximilian, the deposed emperor of Mexico, had been executed by a Mexican firing squad on June 19. Napoleon instinctively forbade French newspapers from printing anything about the execution and carried out his duties to all appearances unperturbed. Of course, the news got out, and the emperor quickly suspended all festivities planned for the visiting dignitaries. The *New York Times* reported the "fate of Maximilian hangs like a black cloud over all these splendors of royalty" and "has sent all the Courts of Europe into mourning, for there is scarcely a royal personage to whom he was not a blood relation."[13]

The French left was not mourning Maximilian's demise. From exile in America, young Georges Clemenceau, a thorough radical republican, scorned all the sentimental attention to the fallen monarch. "I have no pity for those people; to pity the wolf is to commit a crime against the lamb. His wife is mad, you say. Nothing more just: this almost makes me believe in Providence."[14]

In Paris, the empire's critics quickly seized the execution as an occasion to rub salt in Napoleon III's wounds. A few days after news of the execution arrived, Adolphe Thiers, an eloquent opposition leader, rose to speak in the Corps Législatif. In what one observer described as the "greatest speech" of the session, Thiers dragged the chamber through a litany of disastrous decisions on Mexico to lay them all "at their proper door." The government's feeble response to Thiers only encouraged more lacerating criticism. The session ended with the imperialists shouting *Vive l'empeur!* only to excite the left into exclaiming, *Vive la liberté! Vive la France!* A widely read pamphlet, *The Rise and Fall of Emperor Maximilian* (published outside of France in French and English), took readers through the entire Mexico debacle, treating it as a harsh lesson on the foibles of Napoleon's "personal government."[15]

Malakoff reported that "the opposition was never more active than now" in assailing the Second Empire. "In the liquidation of the Mexican question before the Legislature . . . we have seen the last coal of fire heaped upon the Ministerial back." He added, the "growing greatness of the United States is the phantom that is doing the work" by forcing France to retreat from Mexico. Napoleon III, whose Grand Design was to stem the advance of American republicanism into Latin America, now resorted to suggesting in a public letter that the best thing Mexico could do was "to fall into the arms of the United States."[16]

Though only fifty-nine years of age, Napoleon III had been in power for almost twenty trying years. Never robust in physical appearance, corpulent, limping, and deformed by short legs and a barrel chest (John Bigelow noticed he walked like a duck), by 1867, there were unmistakable signs he was failing.[17] The emperor suffered chronic rheumatism for years and now depended on a cane. He smoked cigarettes incessantly and tired quickly. "He looked so listless, so lifeless, so distrait, so broken," one observer at the exposition noted, "as if his thoughts were upon a distracted kingdom, a hostile Europe, a sick boy, and Maximilian in peril of his making!" Doctors had discovered a large kidney stone lodged in his bladder, which caused tremendous pain and severe urinary tract infections, indicated by oozing pus and blood. He took unhealthy doses of opium to relieve the pain and regularly visited Vichy to take water cures. Naturally, he was secretive about his ailments, which only encouraged rumors that he was at death's door. Courtiers and gossip hounds whispered as to what would follow his death.[18]

FIGURE 42. Napoleon III. He suffered deteriorating health, notably a large kidney stone that caused extreme pain, which led many to speculate when and how he would step aside. His plan was to hold on or appoint Empress Eugénie as regent until his son, Louis Napoleon, was old enough to take the throne. *Vanity Fair*, September 4, 1869. Wikimedia Commons.

As though putting his dynastic affairs in order, at the beginning of 1867 Emperor Napoleon III deliberately turned to accelerating progress toward his promised "Liberal Empire" and the eventual succession of his young son, Prince Louis Napoleon, to the throne. France would learn to "govern itself," the emperor announced. Deputies in the Corps Législatif would be allowed to pose questions to the government. Workers had been permitted to organize and engage in strikes since 1864, a right they began exercising more readily. In May 1868, laws censoring the press and restricting public meetings and political speech were relaxed, though not abandoned.[19]

If Napoleon III expected a grateful opposition singing his praises for their liberty to criticize the empire, he was in for a rude awakening. Victor Lanjuinais, a cynical elder statesman, prophesied that once Napoleon lifted the lid on free speech, the French people "would sweep him away in three months." The army "would fight for him reluctantly the first day, negotiate on the second, and turn against him on the third." His mordant predictions proved prophetic.[20]

As soon as the new press law allowed access to licenses, the sheer number of journals exploded, including radical journals that gamely aimed their cruel satire and bombastic polemics against the empire. Victor Hugo, an outspoken critic of the man he satirized in his book *Napoleon le Petit*, launched a daily named *Rappel*. Eugène Pelletan, a republican deputy and good friend of America, launched the *Tribune*. Aimé Malespine, a republican journalist who had sided with the Union, brought out *Réforme*. There were many more. The floodgates suddenly opened, and the opposition rushed in to feed a long-suppressed French appetite for irreverent criticism of their rulers.[21]

No journalist was more outrageous than Henri Rochefort, the weekly *La Lanterne* publisher. Rochefort was a writer of popular musical comedies with a well-honed talent for mocking the empire, especially Empress Eugénie, who came in for more abuse than her husband. Malakoff thought Rochefort said aloud what many "had been so long ruminating over themselves but dared not utter," and he "said it in such a superior style." In the inaugural issue of *La Lanterne*, Rochefort set the tone by professing to be a thorough Bonapartist. His favorite, however, was not Napoleon I or III but Napoleon II, a nonexistent monarch. "What a reign! My friends, what a reign! Not one tax, no useless wars with their ensuing levies; none of these distant expeditions [alluding to Mexico] through which we expend six hundred million in order to recover fifteen francs."[22]

Among the "new liberties" Napoleon III handed down from the throne was more freedom of public speech and assembly. The term *citoyen*, no longer banned, suddenly became a signifier of the new democratic spirit. Malakoff described a hilarious scene involving the venerable republican opposition leader, Jules Favre, speaking before a gathering of his constituents in the seventh arrondissement. Favre opened by addressing the crowd as *Messieurs! Non! Non!* they shouted in protest. Then he tried *concitoyens* (fellow citizens), "which met with a universal roar of '*Non! mille fois non!*'" (No! a thousand times no!) Finally, he used the "magic word, '*Citoyens!*' and the storm was appeased at once." "Imagine," Malakoff mused, "the ragamuffins of the Rue Mouffetard giving lessons in democracy to the old war-horse of the party!"[23]

The Liberal Empire also lifted the ban on unlicensed public meetings of more than twenty people. Still, the government continued to censor political speech, and dissidents had to mind the boundaries of what was allowed. Malakoff described a public meeting in 1869 that drew seven thousand men and women. The occasion was a book talk by Augustin Cochin, author of a new biography of Abraham Lincoln. Professor Édouard Laboulaye, the darling of Parisian students, handled the introduction. Billed as a discussion of "Lincoln, Liberty, the Republic," it became what Malakoff described as "one of those feasts of liberty," made all the sweeter for being "held under the nose of a hostile authority." In his opening remarks, Laboulaye drew comparisons between the American government and the French regime, playfully flirting with derogatory comments on the empire and then turning just in time to avoid censorship. The crowd, of course, was in on the game and erupted in laughter each time, reveling in the "feast of liberty" they shared.[24]

The main speaker, Augustin Cochin, was known as the "Wilberforce of France" for his long efforts to end slavery. He praised Lincoln and America for two hours while the audience listened with rapt attention.

"Every mention of the Republic, of Washington, of Lincoln, of Mrs. Beecher Stowe," Malakoff marveled, "threw the audience into an excitement we have never before seen in France." The audience was also registering its defiance of the Second Empire.[25]

As the Liberal Empire gradually eased the dictatorship of the Second Empire, America was going through its own stormy political reconstruction. When Radical Republicans in America impeached President Johnson, French republicans witnessed a remarkable constitutional process for challenging the head of state and asserting the elected legislature's power without resorting to violence.[26]

Georges Clemenceau, the future leader of France, was a young medical student in Paris's Latin Quarter in the 1860s. He became caught up in radical politics and in 1862 served several months in Mazas Prison for daring to organize a public celebration of France's 1848 revolution. He was elected president of the Society of Medical Students, comprised of radical activists, and served as its publicist and scribe. He participated in the Lincoln demonstrations in April 1865 and was likely among the medical students who delivered the eloquent address to John Bigelow. After that emotional moment, Clemenceau needed to verify his commitment to republicanism. "I would like to go and see how it works" in America, he told his father, an ardent republican. "Go!" the father told his son. That September, young Georges Clemenceau sailed for New York.[27]

Clemenceau settled into an apartment near Washington Square in New York City and paid his rent by writing reports on American politics to *Le Temps*, a leading Paris republican newspaper. His *Nouvelles des États-Unis* were published unsigned or with various nom de plumes to protect himself and his family from Napoleon III's censors. He found the boisterous democracy of America enthralling, the torchlight parades, the robust public oratory, and the noisy quarrels and insults hurled between competing candidates and parties. All of this was unimaginable in France at the time. So was the impeachment of a sitting president, on which he reported with great detail. In the trial of President Johnson, French republicans witnessed a remarkable constitutional

FIGURE 43. Georges Clemenceau. The future leader of France was a medical student and radical activist in Paris in 1865 when this photograph was taken. He joined student demonstrations in favor of Abraham Lincoln and a few months later left for the United States to see how a democratic republic actually worked. His reports on U.S. Reconstruction to *Le Temps*, a prominent Paris daily, flowed into the growing sense of *Américomanie* taking hold in some quarters of France at the time. Wikimedia Commons.

process for asserting the power of democracy against a tyrannical head of state.[28]

For Clemenceau, America's Reconstruction amounted to nothing less than "one of the most radical revolutions known in history." He marveled at Thaddeus Stevens, who, at death's door, relentlessly pressed the case against President Johnson, "the fire smoldering in the depths of his piercing eyes" with "all the wrath of a Robespierre." What impressed Clemenceau is that this revolution emerged from the people's will, leaving presidents Abraham Lincoln and Ulysses S. Grant as "the instruments and not the promoters" of the amazing strides in human progress that had been inconceivable in Europe.[29]

Edouard Portalis, another radical French journalist, published an account of his extensive travels in the United States during the Reconstruction. By his lights, the Radical Republicans were nothing less than "the avant-garde of humanity in its march . . . towards that state of equality, liberty and union." France had much to learn from the example. "Our sons will be grateful to the Republicans of the United States for the blood which they have shed on behalf of human freedom, and for the intelligence which they have shown in their defense of free labor."[30]

In the eyes of French admirers, Ulysses S. Grant stood close beside Lincoln as an icon of democratic leadership. Léon Gambetta, a brilliant young lawyer and future leader of the Third Republic, wrote an essay, "Le général Grant," in June 1868 that pointed out lessons in the future president's rise from military fame to political power. In Europe, such a figure might become a Cromwell or Bonaparte, yet "in the radical democracy of America . . . he can only be a great citizen, a Washington or a Grant, obliged to respect the law. . . . There, democratic institutions condemn genius to virtue."[31]

Jules Michelet, a prominent historian who had earlier belittled America's coarse culture, came to see it as a guide to France's quest for liberty. He proudly wrote about France's role in giving birth to the American republic. "When we have the joy of seeing this great America rising so high in its immensity—the pride, the hope, the salvation of the world. . . . She opens and illuminates the future by her great examples" while "wavering Europe . . . cannot take a step without the earth crumbling beneath her feet." When one American admirer asked him to inscribe a copy of his book, Michelet wrote, "America, daughter of Europe, is today her mother in democracy. [America] gives birth to her in liberty."[32]

French republicans also took great interest in the idea of a United States of Europe that would emulate America in form and content. The expression gained currency during the Revolutions of 1848 when Victor Hugo called for a United States of Europe at the Paris Peace Conference. "A day will come," Hugo prophesied, "when bullets and bombs will be replaced by votes, by the universal suffrage of the people, by the venerable arbitration of a great sovereign senate." Hugo also prophesied an eventual union between the United States of Europe and America, which would have enormous influence. "The two worlds must form one single Republic," he wrote.[33]

Hugo's vision of a United Europe was an early version of today's democratic peace theory, the concept that democratic, liberal nations based on popular consent are inclined toward peaceful solutions of international conflicts. In contrast, autocratic rulers, the theory posits, resort to war without as much concern for public opinion. Though ironic in light of America's horrific civil war, French interest in the United States of Europe sprang back to life in 1867 after France and Prussia nearly came to blows over the Grand Duchy of Luxembourg. Charles Lemonnier, a French philosopher and republican, organized the League of Peace and Liberty and called on all nations to send delegates to its inaugural conference in Geneva, Switzerland, in September 1867. Over ten thousand attended, mainly from western Europe and a small contingent from the United States. Giuseppe Garibaldi served as honorary president; Russian anarchist Mikhail Bakunin was a featured speaker; Karl Marx attended as a delegate of the International Working Men's Association.[34]

The League of Peace and Liberty envisioned a supranational federation to arbitrate conflicts peacefully. Lemonnier launched a journal, *Les États-Unis d'Europe*, and appealed directly to the public rather than trying to convince government leaders, who would naturally be jealous defenders of national autonomy. The Geneva Peace Conference was a forerunner to the League of Nations, the United Nations, and the European Union, and it explicitly modeled a united Europe on the American federation of democratic states. "In order to better understand what the United States of Europe can become," Lemonnier proposed, "let us study the United States of America." He suggested that Europe simply adopt the U.S. Constitution, change names as needed, and create a second United States on its side of the Atlantic. "Who would not be moved by the power, the morality, the greatness of the results?"[35]

In their enthusiasm for America and the promise of a transatlantic United States, French radicals were holding up a distant model across the ocean as a concrete example of democratic success and using this idealized democracy to make invidious comparisons with the Second Empire. However imperfect their understanding of American realities might have been, the French left used the American ideal to envision France's democratic future. America, Victor Hugo said, had "become the guide among nations . . . pointing out to its sister nations the granite way to liberty and universal brotherhood."[36]

Meanwhile, Napoleon III was spooning out concessions to democratic freedom from the throne to appease the left and consolidate support for the empire. He called for elections in May 1869, the first since 1863. As he hoped, pro-imperial candidates won most seats in the Corps Législatif (216 of 293), but it worried him that the opposition received a much larger share of the popular vote than they did of seats. Emperor Napoleon understood that for the Liberal Empire to be accepted, its government (the ministry or cabinet advising the emperor) must include deputies from the opposition.

Napoleon dithered for months before finally calling the Corps Législatif to session in November 1869. He told the chamber, "France wants liberty with order; I answer for Order; help me, gentlemen, to save liberty." In early January, he asked Émile Ollivier, a former republican committed to the Liberal Empire, to form a coalition government that included opposition deputies. A delegation of liberal deputies pressured Ollivier to do more than add a few opposition deputies to the ministry. France's government under the new constitution must be responsible not solely to the emperor but also to the Corps Législatif. This was a direct challenge to Napoleon III's "personal government" and it marked a crucial turn toward a democratic France.[37]

To amplify the democratic intent of his reforms, Napoleon III called for a plebiscite on the Liberal Empire and its new constitution. The choice he put before the people of France was between the Liberal Empire and a plunge into the Red revolutionary sea. France chose the Liberal Empire. On May 8, 1870, voters overwhelmingly (83 percent) endorsed the constitutional referendum. This plebiscite, Napoleon boasted, would "banish the threat of revolution" and establish the empire on a firm foundation of order and liberty. The Bonaparte legacy, he felt assured, would live on.[38]

Four months after the May referendum, the French people deposed Emperor Napoleon III, liberals proclaimed the Third Republic, and Radicals in the Paris Commune refused to accept its authority, plunging France into a civil war. Napoleon's fall happened suddenly and with no serious resistance from any quarter, least of all from the French people. The growing voice of the left had eroded support for the empire within France, but its collapse came at the hands of Chancellor Otto von Bismarck of Prussia.

Bismarck was a larger-than-life figure, tall and portly, with the aristocratic bearing of Prussia's Junker aristocracy and imbued with heroic capacity for food and liquor and enormous ambitions for Germany. During the 1860s, while Abraham Lincoln struggled to maintain the American Union, Bismarck and Prussia's King Wilhelm I put together a powerful confederation of German-speaking states. Prussia was endowed with a formidable military armed with artillery manufactured by Alfred Krupp. Krupp's ferocious fifty-ton cannon was on display at the Paris Exposition of 1867 as though to warn Europe of what Alexandre Dumas, the famous author, named the "Prussian Terror."[39]

The two countries nearly went to war in 1867 over the Luxembourg question, only to come to blows three years later when Spain's Juan Prim invited Prince Leopold, a member of Prussia's Hohenzollern dynasty, to fill the Spanish throne. Secretly, Bismarck lobbied Prim to choose

Leopold, knowing that the prospect of being flanked by Prussian monarchs on two borders would vex the French emperor to no end. The ploy worked perfectly.[40]

Members of the French press rivaled one another in calls for vengeance against Prussia. No politician or journalist dared question the prevailing faith that France remained the dominant military power on the Continent. When opposition leader Jules Favre dared to doubt French capacity to thrash the Prussian Army, deputies shouted him down.[41] For a time, Napoleon resisted the clamor for vengeance. King Wilhelm was not eager for war either and withdrew Leopold's candidacy. Napoleon told Ollivier, "the country will be disappointed, but what can we do?"[42]

Bismarck knew what to do. King Wilhelm was taking the waters at Bad Ems, a resort spa in Germany, when a French diplomat interrupted his morning stroll to press for additional guarantees regarding the Spanish throne, which he politely declined to commit. When Bismarck received a telegram explaining the incident at Ems, he deftly edited the innocuous message into an insult to France. The German chancellor then released his version to the press and sent copies to all foreign embassies. He later mused it was like a red flag before a Gallic bull. The Ems telegram lit a fuse that exploded in Paris and led Emperor Napoleon to announce he would personally lead the French Army to glory against Prussia.[43]

Students, workers, and Red republicans who only recently were supporting Rochefort and cursing the Second Empire fairly burst with patriotic fervor in support of the war. It did not help that news of the Ems telegram arrived in Paris on July 14, Bastille Day. Huge, rowdy crowds filled the streets shouting "Down with Prussia," "Down with Bismarck," "On to Berlin," and *Vive la guerre!* Many defiantly sang out "La Marseillaise," banned under the Second Empire, and the police did nothing to stop them. The next day Napoleon III officially lifted the ban, and the streets came alive with the martial airs of the long-silenced republican anthem.

Arise, children of the Fatherland,
The day of glory has arrived!
Against us, tyranny's

Bloody standard is raised . . .
To arms, citizens,
Form your battalions,
Let's march, let's march!

In Paris, crowds stopped professional singers in the streets and begged them to perform the anthem, twice, three times, and more. Once an exercise in subversion, singing "La Marseillaise" became a cathartic manifestation of patriotic solidarity.[44]

Republicans were dismayed by the war's effect on France's people. As Napoleon anticipated, the giddy patriotism that filled the air muted the left's discontent. Georges Clemenceau, returned from America, was appalled that his fellow republicans were so caught up in the war fever, convincing themselves "that the enemy of European liberty is to be found in Berlin." Clemenceau, instead, understood that victory for the French Empire would be the doom of republican France. "Whatever happens," he told himself, "this war will be a terrible disaster."[45]

Once news of the war reached America, General Philip Sheridan rushed overseas to act as an observer and embedded with the Prussian Army. Bismarck and King Wilhelm welcomed the American hero as an honored guest. He rode with Bismarck to the western front and, on September 1, arrived outside Sedan, near Belgium's border. A French Army of some 100,000 soldiers under General Bazaine (Sheridan's former rival in Mexico) was besieged by Prussian forces and prepared to surrender.[46]

The following day, September 2, Sheridan was outside reminiscing with a German soldier who had served in the Union Army when a carriage approached carrying Emperor Napoleon III, smoking a cigarette and dressed in full uniform. Bismarck, on horseback, came thundering down the road, dismounted, walked up to the French emperor, and gave him a sharp salute. Sheridan watched at a distance as the two European leaders sat on a bench outside a humble weaver's cottage, discussing the fortunes of war.[47] As the Prussian guard took Emperor Napoleon III away, Bismarck remarked, "There is a dynasty on its way out."[48]

FIGURE 44. Napoleon III Surrenders to Bismarck. The French emperor hoped a war would consolidate the nation's support of the Second Empire and he led the army onto the field of battle in the Franco-Prussian War. In early September, Napoleon III met with German chancellor Otto von Bismarck to surrender and later went into exile in England. The new government of France refused to surrender until January 1871, following the grueling siege of Paris. Wikimedia Commons.

The damage to the French military and public morale was devastating, but the war was not over. Prussian forces continued their march to Paris. Inside Paris, news of the surrender at Sedan ignited a revolution. Remarkably, after eighteen years in power, the Second Empire collapsed with almost no resistance, least of all from the French masses who seemed to feel nothing but disgust toward the emperor. Even the empress expressed contempt. "A Napoleon does not capitulate. Why did he not get himself killed?"[49]

Republicans seized the opportunity to turn French outrage to their advantage. Huge crowds poured into the streets, shouting *Vive la République!* and *A bas l'Empire!* (Down with the Empire!). Juliette Adam, a republican writer, described the scene on the evening of September 3: "Around ten, the boulevards from the rue Montmartre to the new Opera, resembled an immense forum. . . . Hatred, violence overwhelmed every heart; threats, abuse, recriminations, piled up on Bonaparte." A thick column of people marched toward the Bastille, gathering more as they went, then turned back to Montmartre chanting *Déchéance! Déchéance!* (Depose! Depose!)[50]

Within the Corps Législatif, no ministers were willing to defend the empire, yet few were ready to proclaim a republic for fear of revolutionary violence. Republicans in Lyon proclaimed the republic immediately, and the massive street demonstrations in Paris intensified the rebellious mood of France. Most deputies realized "it was essential for the Chamber to take power if it does not want [the government] to fall into the street." On the night of September 3, Favre introduced a motion to depose the empire. Even the Bonapartist deputies sat in sullen silence. Not one rose to defend the Second Empire.[51]

The following day, September 4, at the Palais Bourbon the deputies of the Corps Législatif engaged in an intense debate among republicans demanding an end to the empire, conservatives pushing for a Council of Regency, and centrists calling for a Council of National Defense. During the discussion, the mob surged into the chamber, and all decorum broke down amid deafening shouts of *Vive la Republique!* Léon Gambetta, the flamboyant republican leader, tried to mollify the crowd by reading out the motion the deputies approved to depose the empire. Jules Favre made himself heard above the din, calling for the crowd to assemble at the Hôtel de Ville, Paris's city hall, by tradition the proper place to declare France's new republic. Favre led a noisy procession almost two miles through the streets of Paris. The National Guard escorted the men, women, and children in the crowd, all in a festive, carnival spirit with flowers sticking out the end of the Guards' rifle barrels.[52]

The scene at the Hôtel de Ville was chaotic. A group of Reds had already commandeered the building and demanded a radical republican government. Favre seized the moment to propose that all the republican deputies currently seated in the Corps Législatif be hereby appointed to the new government. Léon Gambetta boldly took things in hand

FIGURE 45. Léon Gambetta Proclaims the Third Republic. Two days after Napoleon III's surrender, the streets of Paris filled with people chanting *Déchéance! Déchéance!* (Depose! Depose!). Gambetta, an ardent republican and admirer of America, took the lead in proclaiming the Third French Republic on September 4, 1870. *Illustracion Española*, September 25, 1870. Hathitrust.

and, in a booming voice, proclaimed the Third French Republic to the ecstatic crowd. Several "elected" deputies then set off on a mad scramble to claim cabinet offices and control the buildings associated with those offices.[53]

At the Corps Législatif Favre and other deputies hammered out plans for a provisional Government of National Defense to serve until circumstances allowed a fair election. At six in the evening, September 4, a telegram, signed by Gambetta, announced the Corps Législatif had deposed the empire, proclaimed the Third Republic, and established a provisional Government of National Defense. An autocratic empire that had ruled France for eighteen years was suddenly swept away. As Prussian troops approached Paris, preparing to begin a grueling siege, Gambetta, the new minister of the interior and war, made a spectacular escape by hot-air balloon to join the provisional government at Tours. In the maelstrom of war, siege, and famine, France was about to begin its third experiment in government by the people.[54]

Meanwhile, the Empress Regent Eugénie had been holed up in the Tuileries Palace royal residence, peering out the windows as the crowds roamed the streets shouting *Déchéance!* A delegation of centrist deputies came to ask her to abdicate as Empress Regent. She refused. Then her advisors implored her to flee Paris and set up a government in some remote site. "I will never run away in a cab like Charles X and Louis Philippe," she replied sharply. "I will never fly from the Revolution." She was about to do just that.[55]

Many blamed Eugénie for prodding her fickle husband into war and France's fury after Sedan was about to turn on her. The crowd was moving through the elegant streets of the Rue de Rivoli, tearing down symbols of the empire that adorned shops and public buildings. At one point, thinking that an eagle and coat of arms above the door of the U.S. legation was a French imperial symbol, men scaled the walls to tear it down. Realizing their mistake, they backed away and hailed their sister republic, shouting *Vive la République Américaine!*[56]

Late in the afternoon on September 4, the street crowds began responding to shouts of *Aux Tuileries!* They massed in front of the Tuileries

Palace's ornate iron gates, banging on them, ripping the gilt imperial eagles from atop the gateposts while rhythmically chanting *Dé-ché-ance! Dé-ché-ance! Dé-ché-ance!* Inside the palace, Eugénie's distraught advisors were about to give up on persuading her to flee when—the sound of the mob roaring outside the windows—she suddenly stood up and announced she was leaving, put on her coat, covered her face with a dark veil, and left with jewelry boxes strewn across the floor.[57]

Officials took down the Bonapartist flag atop the palace to appease the crowd, which was now shouting *À mort!* (To death!) Fearful of being seen by the rioters, the empress made her way out of the palace through the galleries of the Louvre lined with all the paintings she had come to love. She stopped but a moment to gaze at *The Wreck of the Medusa*, Théodore Géricault's famous painting of desperate shipwrecked refugees crowded onto a raft with sharks swarming about them. "How strange," she thought, that this would be her last memory of the Louvre.[58]

On impulse, Empress Eugénie decided to throw her fate into the hands of Dr. Thomas Evans, an American dentist and confidant to the imperial family. She and a woman attending her hired a cab and made their way unrecognized through the violent streets of Paris. Dr. Evans had witnessed the demonstrations outside and immediately understood she must escape to safety. He escorted the empress by carriage to Normandy and arranged a boat to take her across the channel to England and exile. Eugénie would eventually be joined by her husband, the last monarch of France.[59]

The provisional Government of National Defense, despite strong support for carrying on the war from French republicans, finally accepted Bismarck's harsh peace terms on January 28, 1871. Bismarck lifted the siege and sent trains filled with food into the starving city. On March 1, in a humiliating gesture of domination, Bismarck led the Prussian Army down the Champs-Élysées in an unwelcome victory march. Parisians draped the buildings in black and left the streets empty except for a few who looked on in sullen silence. Peace with Prussia was accomplished, but not peace within France.[60]

On February 8, 1871, elections for the permanent government returned demoralizing results for republicans. Monarchists won 62 percent of the seats, and the republican opposition won only 35 percent, most of those going to moderate republicans. On September 4, a determined minority had declared a republic, then France elected monarchists to govern it. Some were even talking about restoring the Bourbon monarchy with the Legitimist pretender, Comte de Chambord, taking the throne. The heavily working-class Red republicans of Paris, Lyon, and other urban centers feared the new government would attempt to restore some form of monarchy. They prepared for civil war.[61]

The *citoyens* of Montmartre began fortifying Butte Montmartre, the hill that gave the neighborhood its ominous name (Mount of Martyrs). Adolphe Thiers, elected prime minister of the new government, insisted the artillery belonged to the provisional Government of National Defense and demanded its surrender. Georges Clemenceau, representing the arrondissement surrounding Montmartre both as mayor and deputy in the National Assembly, frantically tried to reach a peaceful resolution. Though an ardent republican, Clemenceau came back from his years in America with a firm lesson: a republic *must* accept the will of the majority.[62]

Before sunrise on Saturday, March 18, on orders from Thiers, four thousand government troops entered Montmartre to confiscate the cannons. They were not strong enough to cow the Reds of Montmartre. Crowds of men and women, whose courage astonished everyone, faced down the soldiers trying to take possession of the cannons. The soldiers began fraternizing with the working-class residents of Montmartre, and General Lecomte ordered them to shoot anyone obstructing them and threatened to execute any who refused to fire. Women challenged Lecomte, "Are you going to fire on us? On your brothers? On our husbands?" A non-commission officer "placed himself before his company and yelled, louder than Lecomte, 'Turn up your rifle butts!' The soldiers obeyed. . . . The Revolution was made." The emboldened Communards then seized Lecomte and another general, took them aside, and began an impromptu trial. An angry group of men and women broke up the proceeding, pulled the two generals outside, and summarily executed them on the spot. An ugly scene followed, with executioners firing rounds into the bodies and women squatting and urinating on the bloodied corpses.[63]

FIGURE 46. The Barricade at Chaussée Ménilmontant. When the new French government decided to make peace with Prussia, radical Parisians in effect seceded and proclaimed the Paris Commune an independent government. The National Guard took their side as barricades went up and mobs ran amuck setting fire to buildings and tearing down all symbols of the deposed Second Empire. Ménilmontant was a republican stronghold northeast of the city center. Wikimedia Commons.

The March 18 violence set the tone for the bloodletting about to play out over the next nine weeks. Thiers, realizing his forces were far out-numbered, ordered all government troops to withdraw from the city. The city's National Guard took sides with the Parisian rebels and took control of the Hôtel de Ville. The Radicals of the Commune of Paris planned for elections of their own government, a true republic. The Communards quickly erected barricades in the streets, the iconic French emblem of rebellion. Paris was theirs.[64]

The Paris Commune left many puzzled by the explosion of murder and the nihilistic destruction of public monuments and buildings of a city most considered the world's capital of art, culture, gaiety, and pleasure. Beneath the City of Light, however, were growing pressures on working-class families. Paris doubled its population, from one to two million, during Napoleon III's reign. Haussmann's reconstruction of the center forced thousands of working-class families out of their apart-ments and hiked rents up in the increasingly crowded slums where they could find housing—the cost of living, especially housing, far outpaced wages. Haussmann's Paris accentuated the growing divide between the prosperous bourgeoisie on the Right Bank of the Seine and the squalid slums of neighborhoods like Montmartre and the Northeast People's Paris or the Latin Quarter filled with low-rent housing for students, artists, and workers.[65]

Among the main targets of wrath was the Catholic Church. French radicals, intellectuals, and many working-class families felt alienated from the Church and its priests. They saw Pope Pius IX's *Syllabus of Errors* as a symbol of Catholic reaction and resented the Church's traditional role as a buttress to monarchical legitimacy. During the upheaval of 1871, the Communards seized Church properties, converted them to public use, imprisoned priests, and took the Archbishop of Paris hostage.[66]

Despite the loosening of restrictions on public speech and organization, Parisians still lived in a police state where they were subject to harassment, imprisonment, or worse if they ran afoul of the law. Despite the empire's best efforts, a cynical, defiant culture of resistance persisted inside the Masonic Lodges, a refuge for republicans, and the bohemian cafés of the Latin Quarter, where socialism and republicanism found audiences among the intellectuals, students, and workers. Many would blame the International for the revolutionary violence. Journalists referred to the "Communists" to identify the Paris Commune government and the International Working Men's Association, whose cofounder, Karl Marx, was the author of the 1848 *Communist Manifesto*. "No," objected Malakoff in the *New York Times*, "the germs of the Commune belong to Paris: the socialism which was its basis and its essence, was French and Parisian."[67]

Elihu Washburne, U.S. minister to Paris, was among the few diplomats who did not evacuate Paris. He had been among the founders of the Republican Party in Illinois, an old friend of Lincoln, a congressman from Illinois, a veteran of the Union Army, and a staunch supporter of Radical Reconstruction. He left for Paris in March 1869, the high tide of Radical Reconstruction in America, and arrived in Paris to witness revolutionary violence and civil war unlike anything he had seen.[68]

In late March 1871, Washburne reported to Washington that the Communards had hoisted their red flag instead of the tricolor and that fighting between them and the government had begun. The national government withdrew to Versailles, once the refuge of King Louis XVI, until Parisian republicans hauled him to the guillotine in 1793. The nation was at war with itself, and the "spirit of insurrection and revolution is spreading over all France," Washburne wrote to Hamilton Fish in Washington.[69]

For days the Versaillais army lobbed artillery shells into the city, turning parts of Haussmann's sparkling City of Light into smoldering ruins. Adding to the damage was the deliberate destruction at the hands of the Communards, who set out to destroy symbols of imperial power. An army of *pétrolleuses*, female arsonists roamed the city with kerosene setting fires to government buildings. Washburne learned some eight thousand arsonists were at work in Paris, and "of all this army of burners, the women were the worst." Children also helped torch buildings and spread the fires. Communards sacked and burned dozens of buildings along the Rue de Rivoli and other posh streets in the heart of Haussmann's Paris. They set ablaze the Tuileries Palace, the Hôtel de Ville, and a portion of the Louvre Museum, where hundreds of irreplaceable art treasures were at risk. In a spectacular event on May 16, Vendôme Column, which exalted Napoleon I's victories, a boisterous crowd of twenty thousand sang revolutionary songs as a team of Communards pulled the monument to the ground.

Further orders were happily not carried out: one to burn the Louvre because its works of art glorified gods, kings, and priests; another to demolish Notre Dame Cathedral, a symbol of religious superstition. The Communards sacked and burned the home of Adolphe Thiers, leader of the French government. The destruction of public buildings, monuments, and religious buildings was an exorcism of anything that honored the old order. The purpose was to erase the past and clear the way to begin the world over with the Red Republic of Paris. In the words of "L'Internationale," the poem written at the time that became the new anthem of the socialist left:

No more tradition's chains shall bind us, Arise ye slaves no more in thrall.
The earth shall rise on new foundations, We have been naught, we shall be all.

T'is the final conflict. Let each stand in their place.
The Internationale shall be the human race.[70]

Commanding the Commune's armed forces was none other than Gustave Paul Cluseret, whom we last met conspiring with the British Reform League on behalf of the Fenians to foment violent uprisings in Ireland and Britain. His peripatetic career had taken him from Paris as a young military cadet and officer fighting on the conservative side of King Louis Philippe at the barricades in 1848 to the American Civil War as a Union officer. By then, Cluseret was a zealous international republican, abolitionist, and author of a polemic inciting all peoples of the Americas to join in solidarity against the monarchies of the Old World. He collaborated with Radical Republican leader Charles Sumner, whose recommendation helped secure his employment with the Fenians. Four years on, this soldier of fortune was back in Paris at the head of the Commune's National Guard, avowing devotion to socialism and claiming membership in the First International. Cluseret cut an impressive figure with his "coarsely handsome face" and impressive credentials. Still, his command was marked by what one observer described as "perpetual improvisation, fundamental incoherence, . . . a mob-scene where everyone commands and no one obeys." Alas, much the same could be said of the Commune at large.[71]

Communards converted Catholic churches and convents into social gathering places for political clubs and community assemblies, their members in red sashes while someone pounded out "La Marseillaise" and other "patriotic airs" on the organ. Other churches became barracks for the National Guard. Raoul Rigault, only twenty-five and easily the most vindictive and brutal of the Commune's leaders, issued orders to take as hostage "citizen [Georges] Darboy, calling himself Archbishop of Paris" with the idea of using him in a prisoner exchange. Darboy was a liberal priest who had stayed on to care for the starving Parisians during the siege and was very popular among most Parisians. He was a frail man in his late fifties and was left languishing in a dark, tiny cell for over two weeks before U.S. minister Elihu Washburne went to Commander Gustave Paul Cluseret on a humanitarian mission to plead for his release. When that failed, Rigault gave grudging permission for Washburne to visit Darboy in his cell. Then, on May 24, during the onslaught of the French Army, the Communards ordered Darboy and several other priests to be executed.[72]

The upheaval in Paris in the spring of 1871 signaled the rise of a socialist revolutionary movement that departed radically from the liberal republican ideology that had guided most democratic revolutions during the previous century. Clemenceau stood between the two fires. He remained an ardent republican but firmly opposed the violent rebellion against a popularly elected government. Revolutionary violence was justified against the tyrannical regime of the Second Empire. He insisted that the citizens of France had freely elected their government, and the majority will must be respected. Majority rule was the essential premise of democratic self-rule, and aggrieved minorities must accept the people's will or win popular support in the next election. Democracy allowed constant rivalry among political parties, leaders, and ideologies, but it rendered violent revolution unnecessary so long as free and fair elections assured government by the people. That basic idea had been the heart of Lincoln's objection to secession, and now Clemenceau was watching the Commune flout the same principle.[73]

In May 1870, government forces began closing in on the Commune. The civil war in France ended in Semaine Sanglante (Bloody Week), starting Sunday morning, May 21, when the French Army entered Paris. Vicious combat, block by block, continued through the day, from one barricaded neighborhood to the next. Both sides brutally executed those they captured. It culminated one week later at Père Lachaise Cemetery, one of the Commune's last holdouts. The Versaillais troops broke down the iron gates and stormed into the cemetery, fighting the Communards with rifles and bayonets amid the tombs. They captured dozens and lined them up in two rows against a wall next to a deep ditch, not sparing the many women and children. Clemenceau later recalled that machine guns fired openly for thirty minutes without pausing and mowed them down as they fell into a ditch. More prisoners were brought to the wall at Père Lachaise on Sunday in groups of 150 to 300, where they were lined up and shot, many falling into the mass grave the others lay in from the day before. It seemed, in retrospect, a perverse way of compensating for the humiliation Prussia had visited on the French Army the previous year.

The Mur des Fédérés or Communards' Wall marking the massacre came to serve as a Valhalla for other martyrs in the next century's struggles against fascist and authoritarian enemies of democracy. It also served as a monument marking the passage of a century-long Age of Revolution marked by the contest between democracy and autocratic monarchy and a new era in which the democratic left would be divided between democratic liberalism and revolutionary socialism.[74]

The Paris Commune left a deep impression on the political landscape on both sides of the Atlantic. It signaled the coming of a yawning chasm between liberals who sought reform through electoral politics and socialists committed to violent revolutionary change. The violence and destruction obscured the Communards' political vision of a radical, secular, democratic society organized as a federation of autonomous communes with governments directly controlled by the people.

As monarchists and aristocrats gave way to the advent of democracy, the fissure on the left between revolutionary socialism and bourgeois reformers continued to widen going forward. The split on the left was aggravated from the beginning when critics of the Commune laid blame for its excesses on the Communists of the First International.[75]

The American press and political leaders were disturbed by the revolutionary violence of the Commune, which they saw as a tragic departure from the forward march toward a stable government being born in the European cradle of republicanism. Elihu Washburne had quickly come to despise the Second Empire and, on September 5, described the peaceful celebration of the Third Republic. "In a few brief hours of a Sabbath day I had seen a dynasty fall and republic proclaimed, all without the shedding of one drop of blood." Two days later, on behalf of his government, Washburne recognized France's new government and welcomed it to the family of republics. "Enjoying the untold and immeasurable blessings of a republican form of government for nearly a century, the people of the United States can but regard with profound-

est interest the efforts of the French people . . . to obtain such free institutions as will secure to them and to their posterity the inalienable
rights of 'life liberty, and the pursuit of happiness.'"[76]

Washburne's sunny mood darkened during the long siege that followed, then descended into horror after the war began between the
Commune and the government. When other foreign diplomats fled to
safety near the Versailles government, Washburne stayed at his post. On
March 25, he wrote to Fish, "We see nothing but 'grim-visaged war,' barricades, regiments marching and counter marching, the beating of the
rappel, the mounting guard, . . . then there are the numerous arrests,
the mock trials, and the executions. . . . There is no power to be appealed
to for protection of life, liberty or property. Anarchy, assassination, and
massacre hold high carnival."[77]

The American press strained to understand what was happening
in their newborn sister republic. Most Americans believed France had
thrown off the yoke of monarchy to join what they saw as the march of
human progress to republican self-rule, peace, and stability. The sudden
lurch into revolutionary violence, nihilistic destruction, and anarchy
seemed another example of the "fickleness of her hot-headed populace"
and the incapacity of the "Latin race" to govern itself. The American
press reported and opined on events in Paris readily, though often with
sensationalist accounts of the violence. Some led American readers to
view the rampage of the Commune as another Reign of Terror, others
to a sinister new brand of terror coming from socialism and "Communism," a term that found currency as a word that referred in confusing
ways to the government of the Paris Commune and the Communist
movement identified with the International Working Men's Association
and Karl Marx's *Communist Manifesto* of 1848. The term "Reds," long
associated with France's *rouge républicains*, was now applied to the socialist extreme left. Headlines flashed images of Red Flags over Paris and
Reds committing horrific atrocities in Paris.[78]

Harper's Weekly could not do enough to feed the public appetite for
illustrated news of the mayhem in Paris. In one cartoon, Thomas Nast
compared New York of the Tweed Ring to Paris of the Communists,
depicting Versailles soldiers shooting civilians in the streets.[79]

One blistering *New York Times* editorial titled "The Commune and Liberty" assailed the "socialistic Democracy" of the Commune for attacking a government that "was the choice of the people" and, "at least nominally, a Republic." "For many years to come, the crimes of the Parisian socialistic Democracy will be charged upon liberty, and the first demands of the laboring classes and the cities of the Continent will be confused with the wild ideas and savage crimes of the French Communists. . . . the war-governing power in Paris declared war, not only against their bleeding country, but against art, property, and religion—against civilization itself."[80]

In a boastful Fourth of July editorial, the *New York Times* summarized what may have been the essential lesson Americans took from the Commune: "The people of Europe today are divided between those who dread and those who long for progress toward popular government. . . . The Commune has revealed to all parties at once the strength of the feelings by which its constituency was driven on to its terrible excesses, and the difficulty in Europe of gaining any indulgence for those feelings except by revolution." Admitting that New York may "have the material of a bloody Commune among us," there will be "no need of a siege of New York City . . . to drive it out." The American people, its government tested by rebellion, "are more fit than ever for self-government."[81]

CHAPTER 10

The Fall of Rome

The Romans still hope for that liberty which the Americans so largely
enjoy. You have fought and conquered, we struggling still suffer. May
this antique stone be the augury of the perpetuity of your freedom and
the advent of ours.

—THE NATIONAL ROMAN COMMITTEE,
TRIBUTE TO LINCOLN, JUNE 20, 1865

The reveille of democracy in Europe had no more formidable opponent
than Pope Pius IX, Bishop of Rome and Supreme Pontiff of the Universal Church. When elected pope in 1846, young Giovanni Maria Mastai
Ferretti was awake to the spirit of liberalism sweeping Europe. The
Revolutions of 1848 changed all that. Giuseppe Mazzini and Giuseppe
Garibaldi seized control of Rome, proclaimed it a republic, and promoted a radically new secular society in which the civic creed of nationalism and democracy took precedence over religion. The pope fled for
his life and would return to Rome an enemy of the Revolution.

The Roman Republic ended in the spring of 1849. French soldiers
garrisoned Rome, part of a bargain Napoleon III made in exchange for
Catholic support. From inside Rome's ancient walls, Pio Nono, as the
Italians called him, railed against the rise of the liberal state and the ideology of the democratic age. During the American Civil War, the pope

used his pulpit to issue public letters denouncing the Union for permitting Union soldiers to defile Catholic churches. He urged American bishops to call for peace at a time when peace meant separation, and privately he expressed strong sympathies with the South. The Confederacy sent envoys to enlist Pio Nono in their cause and came away boasting the most powerful pontiff in Europe had recognized the Confederacy. The pope said nothing to refute such claims, nor did he disavow Confederate propagandists who warned Catholics they would be excommunicated if they fought for the Union.[1]

Pius IX's 1864 *Syllabus of Errors* was a list of eighty "errors" or heresies afflicting modern society, including the belief that "the will of the people, manifested by what they call public opinion . . . constitutes the supreme law, independent of all divine or human right." The *Syllabus* also denounced such heresies as rationalism and tolerance of Protestants and all religions other than the "true Church of Christ." Of course, he listed communism, socialism, and other "pests of this kind" among the forbidden errors. The *Syllabus of Errors* put the Church in firm opposition to the Italian state and the entire modern world. The final heresy said it all: it was in error for any Catholic to believe that "the Roman Pontiff can and ought to reconcile and harmonize himself with progress, with liberalism, and with modern civilization." One cheeky Italian newspaper felt moved to ask when the pope might ban trains, telegraphs, steam engines, and gaslights.[2]

Until 1860, the Papal States encompassed Rome eastward to Umbria and Marche and northward toward Bologna. In addition to the French garrison, Rome was flanked by friendly Catholic monarchies to the north and south. That changed between 1859 and 1861 when Victor Emmanuel II, king of Sardinia, wrested Lombardy from Austria in 1859 (ruled by Austrian archduke Maximilian, incidentally) and annexed the duchies of Parma, Modena, and Reggio and the Grand Duchy of Tuscany in central Italy.

In 1860, Giuseppe Garibaldi and his celebrated army of volunteers, I Mille (The Thousand), invaded Sicily and, to an astonished world, conquered the Kingdom of the Two Sicilies, which added the Italian peninsula below Naples and the Island of Sicily to the united Kingdom of Italy. At the same time, united Italy took over most of the Papal States outside of Lazio, the region surrounding Rome. This left Pio Nono with the rump of his once vast temporal realm, but not for long. The new Italian nation proclaimed Rome its future capital and moved the government from Turin to Florence in 1865 to prepare for that day. Pio Nono took his stand in Rome against the Risorgimento and the godless Revolution.[3]

Papal Rome operated like a medieval theocracy. For centuries, Jews had been required to live within a walled ghetto and even to wear yellow badges at one time. Earlier in his career as pope, Pius IX opened the gates of the ghetto and granted Jews their freedom. Jews generally sided with the Risorgimento, and to Pio Nono, they threatened the Church. He punished them by enclosing the ghetto again. The emancipation of Rome's Jews became a central theme of the Risorgimento's vision of a secular liberal state. Giuseppe Verdi's "Chorus of the Hebrew Slaves," from his opera *Nabucco*, became Italy's unofficial anthem. Italians still rise and sing along with the chorus at public performances. In September 1870, Italians gave a Jewish officer the honor of blowing open the gates at Porta Pia; another led the first troops into Rome.[4]

The pope, alone among European heads of state, remained silent as Italy and Europe sang Lincoln's praises. *L'Osservatore Romano*, the semi-official daily organ of the Papal States, had vilified Lincoln during the war and issued a terse report that Lincoln had been shot in a theater, a place of sin, by its lights. Rufus King, America's minister to Rome, reported that "loyal Americans" wore "the usual badges of mourning, as a slight manifestation of their sorrow." Roman citizens, in contrast, dared not publicly demonstrate sympathy for Lincoln or the liberal secular republic in America without consequences.[5]

There was, however, one remarkable exception to the silence. The National Roman Committee, partisans of Italian unification with Rome, took it upon themselves to make their respect for Lincoln and dislike of papal Rome known to the world. They approached William J. Stillman, U.S. consul at Rome, rather than his superior, Rufus King, with a letter of condolence. They must have sensed, as did Stillman, that King was much too friendly to the pope and his right-hand man, Cardinal Antonelli, to be trusted. The Roman Committee convinced Stillman they were not revolutionaries, and Stillman assured Seward they were "an association of the most liberal, most estimable and influential citizens of Rome" whose purpose was to express "that public sentiment which is repugnant to the existing order of things." While all of Europe was "struck with a sorrow and indignation almost as great as that of America itself at the sad news of the death of Abraham Lincoln," their letter read, "the Romans alone, still separated from the great Italian family, have not had in the theocratic power which now governs them, the interpreter of the sorrow they have felt in learning of that horrible crime." The last point was a dig at the pope's stony silence in response to Lincoln's death.[6]

The letter itself was otherwise unexceptional, but the gift that came with it was spectacular. Sometime that summer, in the dark of night, the committee had appropriated a three-hundred-pound volcanic tufa stone from the ruins of an ancient agger (wall or ramparts) built during the reign of ancient Rome's sixth emperor, Servius Tullius. The stone was one of many carelessly strewn about during the construction of the new railway station, Roma Termini, beside which a remnant of the Servian agger still stands.

Servius, the committee's letter explained, "resembled in many respects the great citizen whom America has lately lost." He "admitted the plebeians to the citizenship" and "facilitated the acquisition of liberty by the serfs and made the freedmen citizens." Not incidentally, Servius Tullius, like Lincoln, was assassinated. "It seems therefore to the Roman people that on a stone of the agger of Servius Tullius, venerated relic of one of the most ancient monuments of the Eternal city, it would be fitting to unite for posterity the names of Abraham Lincoln and of the Sixth King of Rome each in his own hemisphere with an interval of 24 centuries having labored for the well-being of the people committed to his care and the restoration of the slave to the dignity of manhood." On the face of the stone, the Romans had chiseled, in Latin, a dedication to "Abrahamo Lincolnio." In English translation, it read: "president for the second time of the American Republic, citizens of Rome present this stone from the wall of Servius Tullius by which the memory of each of those brave advocates of liberty may be associated." The Roman stone found its way to America and, eventually, to an honored place on Lincoln's tomb in Springfield.[7]

Protestant America nurtured a deep suspicion toward the Catholic Church during the Civil War, particularly Pius IX, whom Protestants regarded as the natural enemy of the American republic. His apparent sympathy with the Confederacy and his role in sanctifying Maximilian's Mexican empire fed long-standing rumors that the Catholic Church was plotting the ruination of the Great Republic. Talk of Catholic involvement in the assassination of Lincoln fed off these preexisting suspicions of the Church and its pontiff.[8]

Dark rumors of a Catholic conspiracy behind the assassination focused on Mary Surratt and her son, John Surratt, both devout Catholics. Mary Surratt was tried and hanged with Catholic priests by her side, administering the last rites. John Surratt escaped and found refuge among Catholic priests in Montreal who kept him in hiding for weeks and then arranged for his passage to Rome, where he enlisted in the Papal Army under an alias, John Watson.[9]

Surratt was part of the Papal Zouaves, one of the foreign legions protecting the Papal States; Pio Nono did not trust Italian soldiers to defend him. Zouave referred to their unique uniforms, which featured baggy grey Bedouin-style pantaloons bound by a bright red sash with smart-looking white gaiters over the boots, a short gray jacket embroidered with red braid, and topped off by a dashing Turkish fez with a tassel.

Most of the Zouaves were itinerant Catholic men from Europe and the Americas, just the place for a man on the run. No doubt, Pope Pius IX's sympathy for the Confederacy and the protection offered by Catholic priests all along his escape route assured him that he was as safe as he could be half a world away from the United States. Nonetheless, he constantly dreaded being found out and felt certain U.S. authorities were on his trail.

Then, one day sometime in early April 1866, a young man dressed in the same Zouave uniform approached him and asked: "What is your name?" John Watson, he replied. "No, your name is not John Watson, your name is John H. Surratt, and you were introduced to me by Louis J. Weichmann at Little Texas in Maryland, in 1863." It was Henri Beaumont de Sainte Marie, a Canadian who had taught school with Surratt in Maryland. Surratt nervously told him to keep his identity secret, not knowing that his old friend from Maryland had been trailing him from Montreal to Liverpool and Rome. Unaware that Secretary of War Edwin Stanton had rescinded the reward for information on Surratt, Sainte Marie was a bounty hunter who had enlisted in the Papal Zouaves, the better to track down his prey.[10]

Surratt was either too naive or too full of himself to keep from spilling tales of his exploits to Sainte Marie. "I have done the Yankees as much harm as I could," he boasted. "We have killed Lincoln, the niggers' friend."[11] More surprisingly, Surratt regaled his wide-eyed friend with tales of how he took part in some way in the assassination and escaped Washington the next day disguised as an English tourist. Some thought Sainte Marie to be a blowhard and an unscrupulous bounty hunter, but his testimony on Surratt's bragging aligned with that of others.[12]

Sainte Marie quickly went to Rome to meet with Rufus King, U.S. minister to Rome, to tell him what he knew about Surratt. King was a former Union general, a New Yorker who had worked with Seward when he was New York's governor. King had ably served as commander of the Union's famed Iron Brigade and later as brigadier general in the Army of the Potomac. He suffered epileptic seizures and, in 1863, gave up his command for the post in Rome. Now General King confronted what was to be the most exciting episode of his diplomatic career. Sainte Marie told King what he knew, but he insisted on absolute confidentiality because he feared his life was imperiled. Sainte Marie felt certain Surratt had powerful connections in Europe and that men in the Papal Army were protecting him. "He says he can get money in Rome at any time," he wrote in his affidavit. "I believe he is protected by the clergy, and that the murder is the result of a deep-laid plot, not only against the life of President Lincoln, but against the existence of the republic, as we are aware that priesthood and royalty are and always have been opposed to liberty."[13]

King wrote to Seward, advising him of what he learned. Seward arranged for a background check of Sainte Marie, which confirmed his account. King had Sainte Marie sign an affidavit, which he sent to Washington. Seward handed all the documents to Secretary Stanton, who would decide whether to request Rome to extradite Surratt.[14]

Meanwhile, Seward instructed King to ask Cardinal Antonelli whether Rome would approve extradition if the United States wished to proceed. Rome and the United States had no extradition agreement between them. More vexing still, the Church opposed capital punishment and might object to handing over someone whose crime was punishable by death. To King's pleasant surprise, Cardinal Antonelli was agreeable. He admitted capital punishment "was not exactly in accordance with the spirit of the Papal government" but "in so grave and exceptional a case . . . the surrender of Surratt would be granted."[15]

What happened next reads in equal parts like an opera buffa or some sinister drama of dark conspiracy. It began when Cardinal Antonelli, or perhaps the pope, decided to order the immediate arrest of Surratt without waiting for King to get back to them with a formal request for extradition from the United States or even confirmation of Surratt's identity. From there, the mix of comic farce and deceit became murkier still. Surratt learned about his impending arrest after King sent a letter to Sainte Marie, which wound up in the hands of a Zouave trumpeter who bore the same last name. Because the hapless trumpeter did not read English, he asked one of his comrades to tell him what was in the letter. He turned for help to one of his English-speaking comrades, who else but "John Watson," alias John Surratt.

Surratt must have been shocked to realize that Saint Marie, his supposed friend, had betrayed him. Surratt headed off to escape arrest, and Papal Army officers caught up with him on the run a few miles from his post. They arrested him and brought him to a prison in Vitrelli, a small fortress town. At about four in the morning, the army officers woke Surratt up to take him to Rome. On their way out of the prison, surrounded by six guards, Surratt asked to visit the privy before the long day's journey to Rome. They were on a platform perched on the edge of a steep precipice. According to the officer in charge, Surratt walked toward the outhouse, "seized the balustrade, made a leap, and cast himself into the void, falling on uneven rocks, where he might have broken his bones a thousand times." The leap was twenty to thirty feet to the rocks and another hundred feet to the ravine below. Some speculated that "the filth from the barracks accumulated on the rock" might have softened the impact of his fall.

The "escape of Watson savors of a prodigy," one Papal Army officer marveled, with a strong hint of disbelief. "Incredible as the details of the story [appear]," King reported to Seward, "the cardinal [Antonelli] spoke of them as verified beyond all question, and expressed very great and apparently sincere regret at Surratt's escape." King seemed to take the story at face value, leaving many questions about the arrest and the escape unanswered.[16]

The pursuit of Surratt ended once he crossed from the Papal States into the Kingdom of Italy. Surratt sought medical treatment for arm and back injuries at a military hospital in Sora, just inside the Italian border. From Sora, the fugitive somehow made his way to Naples, 140 kilometers to the south. Once in Naples, Surratt put his charm and youthful looks to work by persuading British officials that he was a Canadian citizen seeking refuge from the despotic discipline of the Papal Army. U.S. officials learned of this too late to apprehend him before he boarded the *Tripoli*, bound for Alexandria, Egypt. The chase continued.[17]

Back in Rome, Rufus King was frantic. Telegraph and mail service to Alexandria was fraught with breakdowns and interruptions, and King went to extraordinary lengths to alert Charles Hale, the U.S. consul in Alexandria. Hale was waiting at the dock in Alexandria as the *Tripoli* arrived. He boarded the ship and soon identified Surratt among a crowd of itinerant laborers in steerage. "It was easy to distinguish him," Hale wrote, "by his Zouave uniform, and scarcely less easy by his almost unmistakable American type of countenance." The last of the Lincoln assassination conspirators, on the run for close to twenty months since April 1865, was finally in U.S. custody.[18]

Catholic conspiracy theories found new fuel during the trial of Surratt in Maryland, where Catholic influence still ran high. The first trial ended with a hung jury, and the statute of limitations set Surratt free by the time a second trial could begin. The Surratt story at every step

FIGURE 47. The Pope Bans Protestant Worship from Rome. Thomas Nast depicted U.S. Minister to Rome, Rufus King, and American Protestant worshippers being banned by Pius IX. When word of the pope interfering in Protestant worship among Americans in Rome hit the news, the press and Congress exploded with indignation. Congress defunded the U.S. consulate in Rome and broke diplomatic relations with the Holy See for more than a century. *Harper's Weekly*, February 9, 1867. Hathitrust.

reinforced theories about the long arm of the Catholic Church and Pope Pius IX's sinister intentions to destroy the American republic.[19]

American relations with papal Rome intensified in January 1867 when Congress learned that Pio Nono had banned the American Protestant Church from conducting services inside the walls of Rome. The report set off a firestorm in the American press and Congress. In January, the *New York Times* lit the fuse with a brief account explaining that papal authorities had shut down a Scottish Presbyterian Church "and that they threaten to put a stop to the services held at the American chapel."[20]

The newspaper went into full attack mode in an editorial a short time later: "The only government in the world that recognized the rebel Confederacy was that of the Sovereign of Rome. . . . The only Government in the world that denies today the right of worship to American Protestants within its capital is that of the Sovereign of Rome." The editorial went on to denounce papal Rome itself. "One cannot well appreciate the audacity of this feeble, corrupt, dying remnant of despotic rulership—the very caricature and ghostly counterfeit of impotent tyranny—with its paralytic army of petticoated priests." The *New York Times* thundered, "It is humiliating for us to read of our representative being obliged to slink outside the walls of Rome, along with his fellow-countrymen and fellow-religionists, like so many conspirators" while in America, Catholics raise "gorgeous Roman Catholic edifices, surrounded with all the appendages and endowments of a recognized Romish hierarchy."[21] Other intemperate editorials and letters to the editors gleefully piled on. "It is about time that this Roman nonsense of driving Protestant worshippers into the stinking suburbs of the Papal capital should be put a stop to. . . . The world has outgrown the influence of priestly curses."[22]

Back in Rome, Rufus King did not catch wind of the controversy until he read about it in the *New York Times*. He immediately wrote Seward to try to clear up what he thought was simply a misunderstanding. King explained that papal Rome had always forbidden Protestant churches and services of all non-Catholic religions within the walls of Rome. After all, Rome was a theocracy, not a tolerant liberal state. For years, American Protestants gathered in rooms at the U.S. legation to worship, which Rome tolerated. Having outgrown this space, the congregation chose to meet in a U.S. legation property in Trastevere, an old neighborhood across the Tiber River but well within the walls of Rome. King had the cheek to suggest that if Congress was so concerned with keeping the American Chapel as it was, it should consider appropriating sufficient funds for larger quarters worthy of its citizens.[23]

Before King's dispatch even reached Washington, Congress had already decided to cut diplomatic relations with papal Rome. Democrats were beholden to Catholic voters and objected to such hasty action. They tried to explain the whole affair as a misunderstanding, but few were in the mood for apologies. Congress voted overwhelmingly to defund the U.S. legation at Rome as of the end of June 1867, days after the execution of Maximilian and the signal defeat of Church and Crown in Mexico.[24]

It was as though the American government was anticipating the fall of Rome to the Risorgimento by withdrawing recognition of what it considered a relic of medieval times. Rufus King was left to close the office and return home at the end of 1867. The consulate in Rome carried on as the only United States diplomatic presence in Rome. More than a century would pass before President Ronald Reagan and Pope Paul II agreed to resume diplomatic relations in 1984.[25]

Italians viewed Rome as the crowning achievement of the Risorgimento, the ultimate realization of Italy as a resurgent, unified, liberal nation. Giuseppe Mazzini, the intellectual architect of the Risorgimento, prophesied in 1849 the "Third Rome." After the Rome of the emperors and the Rome of the popes would come the "Rome of the people."[26] Mazzini's dream of the Third Rome as the capital of Italy could never be realized so long as the French garrison remained in Rome.

That changed in September 1864 when Napoleon III struck a deal with the Italian government. According to the September Convention, France would withdraw its forces from Rome over the next two years if Italy agreed not to attack Rome.[27] In December 1866, the last French troops left Rome, and the French flag that had flown over Castle St. Angelo since 1849 was lowered. "Good God," Cardinal Antonelli asked, "what is to become of us? The revolution triumphs again, and the enemies of order, justice and morality carry the day!"[28]

Rufus King paid his annual New Year's visit to the pope in early January 1867, finding him in good spirits, but he was determined not to give an inch to the Revolution. "They tell me the Republicans are coming to Rome, *coute qui coute* [cost what it may]," the pope told King. They also say that "Garibaldi, Mazzini, are coming and mean to make Rome the capital of Italy. Well, we will wait and see." Then, pointing to a crucifix on the table, Pio Nono said: "This is all my artillery."[29]

After the French evacuated Rome, Giuseppe Garibaldi sounded the call to arms. *Roma o Morte!* (Rome or Death), the slogan of his heroic but

FIGURE 48. Giuseppe Garibaldi at Mentana. Rome was to be the capital of the reunited Italy, and Giuseppe Garibaldi and his red shirt army made *Roma o Morte!* (Rome or Death) the slogan for this final phase of the Risorgimento. In early November 1867, the Garibaldini nearly met death at the hands of French troops defending Rome at nearby Mentana. Museo del Risorgimento, Genoa, Wikimedia Commons.

failed campaign in 1862 rang across Italy. His army of red shirts materialized almost magically in response to their leader's call. They pushed back the Papal Army and advanced to Mentana, northeast of Rome. Napoleon III was furious at the Italian government for betraying the September Convention and ordered French troops back to Rome. They came armed with deadly new Chassepot rifles, with which they cut Garibaldi's ill-equipped army to ribbons. The Battle of Mentana left Garibaldi broken in spirit and the world in shock.[30]

After Mentana, French troops returned to their Roman garrison. Their presence added to the oppressive spirit of a city besieged. With the French garrison keeping the modern world at bay, Pius IX sought new ways to fortify his spiritual kingdom. "Our strongest argument against *Rome capital of Italy*," Pio Nono pronounced, "is *Rome capital of Catholicism*."[31]

The pope decided that Rome would host a massive international conclave known as the First Vatican Council. It brought all the world's bishops

FIGURE 49. The Ecumenical Council of the Vatican. On December 8, 1869, Pope Pius IX summoned cardinals and bishops from the Catholic world to gather in Rome. They were to ratify the *Syllabus of Errors*, the pope's 1864 epistle against liberalism, and consecrate his doctrine that the pope, as God's leader of the Church, was infallible. Lithograph by unknown artist, published by John Walsh and printed by J. F. Smart and Kahlmann, New York, 1870. Library of Congress.

and cardinals to the home of the holy mother church and reminded the world of Rome's spiritual power. The official purpose of the Vatican Council was to ratify the *Syllabus of Errors* and consecrate the doctrine of papal infallibility. The modern world was much in error, so the *Syllabus* told the world; the pope never was. Pope Pius IX was determined to rally the Catholic world to defend his temporal kingdom.

In December 1869, an impressive crowd of nearly eight hundred entered St. Peter's Basilica on opening day. Once the delegates assembled, Pope Pius IX appeared on a sedan chair at the entrance. He then walked down the center aisle to take his throne, where each member of the Council approached, the cardinals kissing his hand, bishops his knee, the others his foot, all according to ancient ritual.[32]

Several among those assembled opposed sanctifying the infallibility doctrine, especially the French, who were cold to the pope's argument against the liberal world. One dissenter, an Italian cardinal no less, dared to speak against the infallibility doctrine as contrary to Church tradition. The pope flew into a rage and called him into his private apartments for a complete dressing down. "It is an error," he fumed, "because I, I am the tradition, I, I am the Church!" After that, the Vatican Council approved the doctrine of infallibility with only two dissenting votes. From the spectators' gallery came cries of, "Long live the infallible pope!"[33]

The First Vatican Council was still in session when the Franco-Prussian War broke out in the summer of 1870. The pope and some of the Church hierarchy hoped a war might somehow save Rome by disrupting the Italian state. Napoleon III was embarrassed by the pope's reactionary pronouncements, which alienated France's liberal clergy. When war broke out in July, he quickly informed the pope by telegram that he would pull his troops out of Rome to fight the Prussians. All that stood between the pope and the Risorgimento was the poorly equipped Papal Army, which consisted entirely of foreign mercenaries because Italian soldiers could not be trusted. How far the pope's foreign legion would go in defending Rome was uncertain.[34]

King Victor Emmanuel II wrote a polite but disingenuous letter to Pio Nono, informing him he planned to order the Italian army into Rome because he feared republican revolutionaries might seize the opportunity to impose a "red republic" on Rome. "Nice words, but ugly deeds," Pio Nono muttered as he read the king's letter.[35]

There were no apparent signs of revolutionary plots among the inhabitants of Rome. There had been efforts to incite uprisings, but they went nowhere. The fall of Rome would be Italy's doing.[36] Italian forces assembled around the walls of Rome in September 1870. At five in the morning of September 20, 1870, they opened artillery fire at six different points along Rome's walls while infantry forces prepared to breach the gates at Porta Pia and Porta del Popolo.

The London *Times* reporter described the fall of Rome as though reviewing a spectacular opera: "I do not believe that so impressive a

FIGURE 50. "I am now infallible." Thomas Nast, well-practiced in anti-papal satire, lampooned Pius IX for convening the First Vatican Council, spurning the modern world, and consigning the Church to the Dark Ages. *Harper's Weekly,* July 30, 1870. Hathitrust.

drama has ever before been performed by more artistic actors, or on a grander scene, than that which I was this day a spectator; but then we must bear in mind that the spectacle was the fall of the temporal power of the Roman Pontiffs, the performers Italians, and the theatre Rome."[37]

The first Italian troops climbed over the rubble at Porta Pia by eleven that morning and entered Rome, the *Times* reported. Greeting them were "patriotic individuals bearing all sorts of queer, impossible weapons—long swords, pitchforks, sabers, staves," welcoming their liberators. There were also "crowds of men and women belonging to the Roman people of all classes and ages . . . in a frantic burst of enthusiastic applause, clapping their hands, embracing the national flag, and surrounding the Italian soldiers." "Loud cries of '*Roma Capitale!*' '*Viva la Libertà!*' '*Viva l'Italia!*' are to be heard on all sides." The Italian army had selected Roman soldiers, including several Jews, for the assault on Rome, and now they were "embracing old friends who have just recognized them, and altogether the scene is one of universal rejoicing."[38]

By half-past two that afternoon, they had made their way to Piazza Colonna, the center of historic Rome, where "the houses were bright with flags of all possible shapes, dimensions, and materials," which must have been distributed well before that day. Here, "in the very heart of the city . . . we found the most lively enthusiasm." "The whole population sang the Bersaglieri hymn, citizens preceding and following the troops." At four that afternoon, eight thousand papal soldiers capitulated to the Italians from their retreat at the Vatican and Castle St. Angelo. Though the Zouave officers had promised "to die the death of crusaders" and hold the Italian army at the gates for six days, they gave no resistance once the Italians entered the city. The fall of Rome was not an entirely bloodless affair; about one hundred Italians and fifty papal soldiers had been killed or wounded.[39]

Like Queen Isabella's Bourbon Spain and Napoleon III's Second Empire, Pope Pius IX's earthly kingdom rested on the suppression—not the support—of popular will. At the first sign that Rome was about to fall, the pope's political allies, mercenary armies, and the people of Rome threw the papal government over and embraced the Italians as liberators. The monarch of Rome became the prisoner of the Vatican.[40]

FIGURE 51. United Italy. Americans admired the Italian Risorgimento as a liberal, secular nationalist movement they hoped would eventually lead to a democratic republican state. Giuseppe Garibaldi, a global hero by this time, offered crucial support to the Union cause and at one point appeared ready to take command of the Union Army. This illustration by Thomas Nast appeared in *Harper's Weekly*, September 9, 1871. Hathitrust.

Americans greeted the fall of papal Rome to the Italian Risorgimento with glee, for the most part. The *New York Herald* applauded the "Emancipation of Rome" and "the extinction of the oldest dynasty in the world" following "a feeble resistance."[41] In New York City, a grand celebration at Apollo Hall, a glamorous new theater on Broadway, hailed the "Liberation of Rome" as another milestone for freedom. Flowers and flags filled the hall, and a pictorial representation of "free Italy, of colossal proportions" towered above the stage. Before the speakers took the podium, a band played "Viva l'America," a composition by Harrison Millard: "Throughout the world, our motto shall be: *Viva l'America*, home of the free!". The audience cheered several references to "the freeing of Rome from priestly influences and the unification of Italy." One speaker sounded a discordant note, denouncing the Savoy dynasty and vigorously insisting that "the thorough liberation of Rome would not be effected until a republican Government was secured for it." The Italian consul to New York protested, and a round of insults flew before another speaker deftly diverted attention by resorting to another "fiery denunciation of the priesthood." All ended well; singing, music, and dancing followed.[42]

Giuseppe Mazzini, the architect of Italian unification who envisioned the "Third Rome," lived to see the Rome of the Popes defeated but not long enough to see the Rome of the People, the republic he wanted for Italy. Between the futile assault on Rome at Mentana and the fall of Rome three years later, Mazzini was moving back and forth from exile in London to Italy, trying to foment revolutionary uprisings. His age, sixty-five in 1870, years of heavy smoking, and a lifetime of labor on behalf of Italy's Risorgimento were catching up with him. Chronically ill from damaged lungs, he was breathless and barely able to climb stairs. In early 1872 he sought refuge with a friend in the warmer climate of Pisa. There he died in early March.[43]

For Mazzini, America seemed too vast and dispersed and too focused on individual liberties to be the kind of republic he idealized, a coherent people and culture that shared a common sense of duty. Yet, like other European visionaries, Mazzini also saw America as a viable model for the

"United States of Europe," an idea he helped nurture among the European democracy. He saw Italy's Risorgimento as part of an international movement toward the "Universal Republic," a constellation of democratic nations living in peace, each with its distinct historic mission.

Mazzini was also an admirer of Abraham Lincoln, whom he recognized as the champion of America's own Risorgimento, leading the battle against the slaveholding aristocracy at home and, he hoped, about to take on Maximilian's Mexico, the "outpost of Caesarism" France had planted on American soil.[44]

Mazzini's most eloquent tribute to Lincoln came after he died in 1872. His embalmed body traveled slowly by train from Pisa to his birthplace, Genoa, where he was entombed at the Staglieno Cemetery. Instead of taking the direct line up the coast by way of Spezia to Genoa, which was incomplete, Mazzini's funeral train took nearly three days on a more circuitous route through Lucca, Pistoia, Bologna, Reggio Emilia, Parma, Piacenza, Alessandria, and then into Genoa.

Before his death, Mazzini was a wanted man, a "red republican" and enemy of the state who carried a death sentence on his head from years of conspiring against the Kingdom of Italy. Italian authorities and police all along the route were on the watch for republican demonstrations, yet they had to be careful not to provoke violence. For the Mazzinians, the funeral procession through Italy would be an impressive demonstration of reverence for a national hero and his "proof of belonging" to the Italian people.[45]

On the evening of March 14, the body of Giuseppe Mazzini went by train to Pisa to begin its nocturnal journey to Genoa. News of the funeral train had spread across Italy. All along the route, crowds of people gathered, men, women, children, and even babies in arms. Some carried torches and stood vigil as the train passed. Police dutifully reported people shouting "Viva la Repubblica" at some train stations, but the crowds were orderly. One brave professor, a poet named Giosuè Carducci, prepared flyers to post on the walls that read: "Giuseppe Mazzini, after forty years of exile, passes freely through Italian land today because he died. Oh Italy, such glory, such meanness and such debt for the future."[46]

FIGURE 52. "Rome, Funeral Oration over the Bust of Mazzini." Giuseppe
Mazzini, the intellectual architect of the Italian Risorgimento, was eulogized in
Rome in 1872. Behind the bust of Mazzini is a gigantic statue representing Italy
holding a laurel wreath above his head. Engraving by William Bromley III,
The Graphic, April 13, 1872. Artokoloro/Alamy Stock Photo.

On Sunday morning, March 17, 1872, a large crowd of 15,000 gathered at Principe station in Genoa to meet Mazzini's train and join the funeral procession that climbed three miles up a steep hill to the cemetery. "It was like a black ribbon," one observer recorded, "mottled with hundreds of flags, which unfolded to the sound of funeral marches, in the midst of a throng of people never seen again. The magnificent chariot mounted by the figures of History and the Roman Fascist and with bas-reliefs representing Machiavelli, Dante, Cola di Rienzi, Savonarola, Colombo, Arnaldo da Brescia, was pulled by six black horses." The procession began at the train station in Genoa at 11:30 a.m. and arrived at the tomb at 4:00 p.m.[47]

On the same Sunday morning, masses gathered in Rome at the Piazza del Popolo, named in honor of Mazzini's Republic of Rome in 1848–49. Students, Masons, workers of various trades, and representatives of several political groups, all with banners draped in black crepe. The procession made its way down the Corso de Victor Emmanuel, an arrow-straight street, Italy's tricolor flag hanging from every balcony. A reporter for the *Times* of London watched from the Campidoglio, the ancient and now modern seat of municipal government. "And then, drawn by four white horses, there came a car, supporting a colossal statue of Italy, whose right hand held a laurel crown above Mazzini's bust, which stood on a pedestal by her side."[48]

At the center of the car, strewn with wreaths and flowers, was a bust of Mazzini. Benedetto Cairoli, "known and esteemed as one of the most respectable men of the Extreme Left," rose to address the crowd. "Romans, here where Cola di Rienzo fell [referring to the fourteenth-century foe of papal temporal power], Mazzini triumphs." After Cairoli's "fluently and energetically delivered" speech, men lifted the statue of Mazzini off the cart, carried it into the Municipal Hall, and placed it between the busts of Michelangelo and Christopher Columbus. Mazzini's dream of the Third Rome, the capital of liberal Italy, was finally realized.[49]

CODA

The Undoing

The slave went free; stood a brief moment in the sun; then moved back again toward slavery. The whole weight of America was thrown to color caste. The colored world went down before England, France, Germany, Russia, Italy and America. . . . Democracy died save in the hearts of black folk.

—WILLIAM E. B. DU BOIS,
BLACK RECONSTRUCTION IN AMERICA, 1935

The achievements of Reconstruction at home and abroad were, as William E. B. Du Bois claimed, an extraordinary step forward for world democracy. At the beginning of the 1860s, conservative Europeans held up the so-called Great Republic as proof the experiment in democratic self-rule had utterly failed and cheered the prospect of its collapse. By 1865, liberals and radicals hailed America as the premonition of a democratic future for all modern nations.

Under the banner of the muscular new Monroe Doctrine and its defiant slogan, "America for Americans," the United States and Latin American allies led France to retreat from Mexico, Russia to evacuate North America, Britain to decolonize Canada, and Spain to abandon Santo Domingo, South America, and, so it appeared, Cuba and Puerto Rico, the last of its American empire.

By the end of 1869, the high tide of Reconstruction at home and abroad, the American republics had expelled or blunted any threat from those European empires that aggressed in the American hemisphere during the Civil War. William Seward and his entourage were at the National Palace in Mexico City for a banquet President Benito Juárez was giving in his honor. Seward, now aging and in retirement, rose on unsteady legs to address an audience of four hundred Mexican and American officials, about to hear a cogent summary of his worldview.

"Every part of the continent must sooner or later be made entirely independent of all foreign control," Seward began, "and of every form of imperial or despotic power—the sooner the better." "The people of the United States have opened their broad territories . . . freely to the downtrodden and oppressed of all nations, as a republican asylum." To "all who shall come within that asylum," the Constitution guarantees, "they shall be forever governed only by republican institutions."

Then, evoking the Monroe Doctrine, Seward said, "This noble guarantee extends in spirit, in policy, and in effect to all other nations in the American Hemisphere, so far as may depend on moral influences." Some nations near the United States, "while they are animated like the American people, with a desire for republican institutions, . . . are yet by reason of insufficient territory, imperfect development, colonial demoralization, or other causes, incapable of independently sustaining them." Some (he listed "ancient Louisiana," Florida, Alaska, Santo Domingo, and St. Thomas) have been offered incorporation into the United States. Others, "matured and self-reliant," have "nobly assumed the position and exercised the powers of exclusive sovereignty." He listed Mexico, Venezuela, Colombia, the Central American states, Peru, Argentina, and Chile, all considered "fraternal republics and political allies" of the United States. Seward closed with a toast to "the health of President Benito Juarez—a name indissolubly associated with the names of Presidents Lincoln, Bolivar, and Washington, in the heroic history of Republicanism in America."[1]

In Europe, the liberals and radicals embraced America's triumph over the slaveholding aristocracy and the radical program of Reconstruction as harbingers of change in the Old World. The energy that had driven the Age of Revolution between the American and French revolutions of the late eighteenth century and the failed Revolutions of 1848 had lain dormant and been suppressed by censorship for nearly two decades. Then it came alive again in the late 1860s, as though the Union's victory, Lincoln's martyrdom, and other democratic stirrings in Italy, Poland, Mexico, and elsewhere awakened a contagious spirit of confidence and possibility.[2]

Spain's Glorious Revolution of 1868 toppled Queen Isabella II's throne and created a new democratic regime. Napoleon III's Second Empire fell two years later, giving way to France's Third Republic. Days later, the Italian army stormed the gates of Rome and made it united Italy's new capital. The fall of Rome was the culmination of the Italian Risorgimento, which had captured the imagination of Europe and the Americas. Pope Pius IX, the sworn enemy of the Risorgimento and democracy at large, was stripped of his once vast temporal kingdom and consigned to its last remnant, Vatican City.[3]

In Britain and most of Europe, democracy would grow within the husks of the old monarchical system rather than demand "pure republics" to take their place immediately. Emilio Castelar, a leading voice of European republicanism, assured his American audience that Europe's future was democratic and America was its guiding light. "Monarchical faith still shines, but only like those distant stars which the astronomers tell us are apparent to our retina long after they have become extinct and all trace of them in the heavens is lost." Despite all the "armies of kings" and excommunications by popes, "modern civilization is democratic."[4]

Historians are forever cursed with the knowledge of what follows. Castelar and Seward's forecast of human progress toward a future of democratic peace, justice, and freedom must seem naive and utterly utopian to all who know what lay ahead. What followed the Reconstruction Era seems especially tragic because America's example of democratic success had meant so much to the world then. The achievements of domestic and international Reconstruction were challenged from the outset but not undone until the 1890s. The promise of America's Reconstruction era gave way to a far worse world marked by brutal racial violence and injustice, imperialist wars of conquest, and outrageous betrayals of democracy's fundamental principles.

Many Americans still wring their hands about the tragedy of the Civil War, wishing it could have somehow been avoided. But that war gave the nation an extraordinary opportunity to rebuild the country on the principles of 1776, a genuinely democratic republic with liberty and justice for all. The undoing of Reconstruction after the 1870s is the truly tragic chapter in America's history, and not because Radical Republicans were too uncompromising or unrealistic. It was the counterrevolution mounted by white Southerners to deny African Americans political rights and the whole nation's moral surrender to the idea that the freed people were forever "unfit" to participate in government by the people. That is what made the Civil War and Reconstruction come to a tragic end.

One of the more disconcerting features of this counterrevolution was the role historians played in legitimizing the sabotage of Reconstruction and the reign of disfranchisement, segregation, and racial subjugation that followed. In 1901, Professor William Archibald Dunning of Columbia University wrote an article for the *Atlantic Monthly* titled "The Undoing of Reconstruction." By 1870, Dunning began, the main goals of Reconstruction had been accomplished. African Americans enjoyed equal political rights with whites; the Republican Party was "in vigorous life" in all Southern states; and "the negroes exercised an influence in political affairs out of all relation to their intelligence or property."

At first, he coolly explained, whites organized terrorist groups, the Ku Klux Klan and others, to intimidate and crush the Republican Party in the South. "Intimidation was illegal," Dunning winked to his readers, "but if an untraceable rumor that trouble was impending over the blacks was followed by the mysterious appearance of bodies of horsemen on the roads at midnight, firing guns and yelling at nobody in particular, votes again were lost, but no crime or misdemeanor could be brought home to any one." Dunning expressed unabashed admiration for the many "ingenious" methods of suppressing the Black vote by exploiting "the poverty, ignorance, credulity, and general childishness of the blacks" and "on occasion . . . deliberate and high-handed fraud."

The violence and corruption required in suppressing the Black vote caused white Southerners to seek some more permanent method of excluding them. Mississippi led the way in 1890 with a provision in its new constitution that required all qualified voters to have paid poll taxes for the previous two years and "be able to read any section in the constitution of this state, or . . . be able to understand the same when read to him, or give a reasonable interpretation thereof." Dunning pointed out that this "intelligence qualification" gave election officials "the power to disfranchise illiterate blacks without disfranchising illiterate whites." As he put it, "the white must be stupid indeed who cannot satisfy the official demand for a 'reasonable interpretation,' while the negro who can satisfy it must be a miracle of brilliancy."

Because they did not make race per se the criterion for voting, literacy tests did not violate the Fourteenth or Fifteenth Amendment. South Carolina followed in 1895 with similar provisions to exclude voters based on literacy or understanding of the law. By 1902, Dunning concluded that "the political equality of the negro is becoming as extinct in law as it has long been in fact, and the undoing of reconstruction is nearing completion."[5] Once stripped of their political power, whites imposed the horrific regime of Jim Crow, shorthand for the draconian program of segregation, lynching, harassment, and degradation that stood in mockery of America's once proud claim to be the leading example of democracy and civilization.[6]

The undoing of international Reconstruction, which had aimed at driving out European imperialism, creating republican peace in the American hemisphere, and fostering the spread of democratic republicanism abroad, was also overturned in the 1890s when the United States suddenly veered toward overseas imperialist conquest. In 1895, Cuban revolutionaries resumed their struggle for independence, which Spain, as before, met with fierce resistance. This time the United States recognized the Cuban rebels' belligerent rights but stood by, officially neutral as the Cubans fought for freedom. In February 1898, a suspicious explosion inside the USS *Maine*, while docked in Havana Harbor, sparked outrage in the American press and public. War fever gripped America, and the pressure compelled President William McKinley to declare war against Spain and call for 125,000 volunteers to fight for Cuba's freedom. Secretary of the Navy Theodore Roosevelt, a robust proponent of the war to free Cuba, led his brigade of "Rough Riders" to victory at San Juan Hill. This storied episode aroused great enthusiasm for what John Hay, by this time McKinley's secretary of state, called America's "splendid little war."

The Spanish-American War rapidly expanded from intervention in Cuba to an imperialist war of conquest and annexation that spread from Cuba and Puerto Rico to Spain's Pacific colonies, Guam and the Philippine Islands. The U.S. Navy seized possession of Cuba and Puerto Rico and sent Admiral George Dewey and the U.S. Navy squadron from its base in Hong Kong to the Philippines. On May 1, 1898, Dewey's squadron nearly annihilated the Spanish fleet moored in Manila Bay.

The peace conference in Paris in December 1898 required Spain to cede Puerto Rico to the United States and immediately evacuate Cuba, which would remain nominally independent but with a provision in its constitution allowing U.S. intervention. The Treaty of Paris also awarded the United States possession of Spain's colonies in Guam and the Philippines.

Filipino republicans began their war for independence from Spain in 1896. They proclaimed the Philippine Republic and chose as their president Emilio Aguinaldo, a young revolutionary Mark Twain dubbed the Philippines' George Washington. Admiral Dewey invited the Filipino leader, then in exile in Hong Kong, to accompany him as he sailed to Manila to seize the Philippines in 1898. Aguinaldo later caught up with the American admiral, only to learn that the republic he led was about to be handed from one imperial ruler to another.[7]

As the U.S. Congress was about to ratify the Treaty of Paris in early 1899, war broke out between Filipino republicans and U.S. forces occupying the islands. The conflict that began with the United States proclaiming the emancipation of Cuba from Spanish rule as its official mission had now transformed into an imperialist war for the new American empire. The American republic now replaced the Spanish Empire fighting a brutal war to deny the Filipino people the right to govern themselves.

While the Philippine-American War dragged on for over three years, it opened a vigorous debate in Congress, the press, and the American public square. The main issue was the annexation of the Philippines and the larger question of whether America should become an empire. Anti-imperialists argued that the takeover of Spain's former colonies betrayed everything America stood for, from the Declaration of Independence to Abraham Lincoln's Gettysburg Address. The underlying principle was that no government should rule people without their consent. Those favoring annexation argued it was America's mission as an emerging world power and leading exemplar of modern democracy and Christianity to help civilize the backward races of the world. At issue were fundamental questions about what America stood for as a nation, a republic, and what it meant to be a citizen of such a nation.

Beneath their disagreements over the immediate issue of annexation, there was surprising agreement on race, white supremacy, and the relations of race and culture to democratic self-rule. Proponents of the new imperialism did not hesitate in stating that the expansion and protection of America's overseas markets were foremost in their motives. But their justifications for the annexation of the newly acquired Spanish colonies typically drew on more cosmopolitan and humanitarian pretensions about the duty of Americans, with their Anglo-Saxon brethren in Britain, to take up "The White Man's Burden" and elevate backward colored races into modern civilization.

The idea of an Anglo-American people had blossomed in the late 1860s when several British intellectuals began cultivating the idea that America's democracy was not so frightening and that it might be a guide to their own country's future. British authors wrote about "Greater Britain" and the global "English-speaking nation." Journals in Britain and America helped create an Anglo-American "imagined community" spanning the globe.[8]

None was more important in promoting the idea of Anglo-American civilization, nor in linking it to democracy and white supremacy, than James Bryce, Oxford history professor, Member of Parliament, future ambassador to the United States, and author of *The American Common-*

wealth, the most influential publication on the subject since Alexis de Tocqueville's *Democracy in America* (1835). Bryce consciously discredited Tocqueville, arguing that as a Frenchman, he failed to understand that America's democracy stemmed from a long tradition of Anglo-Saxon and Teutonic local self-government and had nothing to do with the revolutionary violence and radical ideas that animated France and the Continent. America and Britain were part of a transatlantic Anglo-American civilization with a mature, proven tradition of stable representative government poised to guide the modern world toward its democratic future.[9]

Bryce descended from a family of Scottish dissenters, his father was a Presbyterian minister, and when he came to Oxford as a student in the 1860s, he found himself at odds with its prevailing aristocratic, antidemocratic sentiment. A brilliant student, he was admitted to the Oxford Union, the famed student debating society. Most members sided with the rebel South in America's Civil War, and when they discussed the proposition, "That this House deeply regrets the late successes of the Federal arms; and believes the triumphs of the Government of Washington to be fatal to the freedom of America," the vote fell Ayes, 37, Noes, 25. This was in May 1865.[10]

Bryce found more open minds in a circle of students and professors, including Goldwin Smith, a leading advocate of the Union cause. In 1867, Bryce joined Smith and other students by contributing to the volume *Essays on Reform*. Bryce's essay blasted European critics of democracy. They have "constructed a monster like the Chimera of Iliad, terrible in every part. . . . And this they have named Democracy." Democracy, they would say, "has often been tried, and wherever it has been tried it has failed." Nonsense, Bryce answered, "Democracy has never yet been tried, except in Switzerland and in America," perhaps in Norway. Since the Middle Ages, European history has tilted toward "an equalization of the conditions of men" and the repudiation of feudal deference. "The social progress of democracy," Bryce concluded, "has outrun its political progress." It was high time Britain caught up with its people and the modern era.[11]

In August 1870, Bryce headed for America, eager to learn from the world's foremost democracy. At thirty-two, Bryce had won a prized appointment as Regius Professor of History at Oxford. He was an out-going man of medium height with reddish hair and a full beard framed by piercing blue eyes. With a winsome knack for engaging people, he met Americans on their terms, always taking copious notes on everything he learned and the places he saw. After several more visits, he was unable to get America out of his head and thought of pulling his thoughts together in "a little book . . . to try to give my countrymen some juster views than they have about the United States." It seemed to Bryce that Britain "urgently needed a manual of instruction about America."[12]

The American Commonwealth appeared four years later, in 1888. His modest plan for a concise "manual of instruction" had grown into a massive three-volume tome. Reviewers immediately hailed the book as a masterpiece, and letters of praise poured in from British and American intellectuals and political leaders. Bryce's work seemed destined to displace Tocqueville's ambivalent view of an alien American force with an encouraging embrace of democracy as an Anglo-American project. It quickly became a handbook on the workings of democracy at all levels of government. Translations of *The American Commonwealth* followed in French, Italian, Spanish, Portuguese, Russian, and later German and Hungarian. By the time of its third edition (1895), *American Commonwealth* had become a handbook of "biblical authority" on America and modern democracy. More than that, it was a textbook for European empires whose governance at home and overseas was fraught with conflicting ideas about democracy, race, and empire.[13]

For the 1895 edition, Bryce added new chapters, "The South since the War" and the "Present and Future of the Negro," to address what critics felt was an oversight in the earlier editions. For these essays, Bryce relied heavily on historians, including Woodrow Wilson, a student at Johns Hopkins, and John W. Burgess, a Columbia University expert on Reconstruction. He also became acquainted with William A. Dunning, mentor to the Dunning School, and James Ford Rhodes, best-selling author of a multivolume history of the Civil War era. All reflected the accepted orthodoxy that Radical Reconstruction was a tragic experiment orchestrated by vindictive partisans who granted political rights to a race barely removed from generations of enslavement and ill-equipped for their role as citizens in a democratic society. These views reinforced Bryce's thinking on the unique affinities of the Anglo-Saxon race for self-government, views he now broadcast to a world audience.

At the prestigious Romanes Lecture at Oxford in 1902, Bryce delivered a speech titled "The Relations of the Advanced and the Backward Races of Mankind." He began by setting out the problem when "advanced" races come in contact with "backward" races in the modern world. In cases like the Russian Empire, British rule in India, and Hispanic rule over Latin American natives, "despotic methods" of governance are standard. Democracy poses more difficulties, however. Bryce turned to America's Reconstruction with the example of a young boy asked to drive a locomotive to illustrate "the risks a democracy runs when the suffrage is granted to a large mass of half-civilized men." Despotic methods of violence and fraud to deny Blacks their constitutional right to vote had soiled America's democratic principles. America's Southern states had invented the ingenious solution of using educational and property qualifications to eliminate the vast majority of Black voters without violating the U.S. Constitution.

In Bryce's view, the moral was that "however excellent your intentions and however admirable your sentiments," you must not "legislate in the teeth of facts." The "facts," as he saw it, were that most Blacks "were not fit for the suffrage," and to allow them to vote endangered democracy for all. "The general opinion of dispassionate men," Bryce summed it up, "has come to deem the action taken in A. D. 1870 a mistake."[14]

Theories about "backward races" being "unfit" to participate in democratic government had gained currency in America and Europe simultaneously, particularly in Britain, where rising expectations of democratic standards in the metropolis starkly contrasted with colonial practices overseas. A common language and logic permeated the transatlantic debate on race and democracy. Arguments used to justify voter suppression proved useful to arguments for and against the annexation of alien peoples. Those calling for immigration restriction in the United States or South Africa likewise employed similar vocabulary. Henry Cabot Lodge of Massachusetts personified the contradictions in play. He sponsored the

Federal Elections Bill to thwart Southern whites' efforts to exclude "unfit" Blacks from voting and, at the same time, organized the Immigration Restriction League to keep "unfit" immigrants out of the country. Later, Lodge became an outspoken defender of the wars against Spain and the Philippine Republic and a chief spokesman on behalf of America's duty to civilize the world.[15]

White, or Anglo-Saxon supremacy, permeated domestic and international debates in the United States in the 1890s. At the same time the United States denied political rights to African American citizens at home, Congress debated closing the door to "colored" and non-Anglo-Saxon immigrants from abroad and argued whether the inhabitants of their newly won territories should be left to their own devices, annexed as future citizens of the republic, or remain colonial subjects of the new American Empire.

Theodore Roosevelt, an enthusiastic advocate of American imperialism, saw America's duty in the Philippines as lifting the yoke of tyranny from the oppressed and guiding them on the path of human progress. He wanted a Monroe Doctrine that would insist "that ultimately every European power should be driven out of America, and every foot of American soil, including the nearest islands in both the Pacific and the Atlantic, should be in the hands of independent American states, and so far as possible in the possession of the United States or under its protection."[16] He had little patience for critics who pointed to the brutal torture and murder of Filipino prisoners. "The simple truth is that we rescued those islands from the hideous tyranny of the Spaniards and the anarchy of the corrupt and bloody insurgent chiefs. . . . we have already given to the natives such justice and liberty as neither they nor their forefathers have ever known throughout the ages."[17]

If those favoring the new American Empire embraced a racist ideology that would seem to nullify any claim of actually benefiting those they conquered, the anti-imperialists shared many of the same prejudices. Once a revolutionary German 48er, Carl Schurz had parted ways with Radical Reconstruction during the Grant administration, partly over differences on Black civil rights. At seventy, Schurz became an outspoken critic of America's new imperialism, which he saw as a dangerous departure from the America Abraham Lincoln had defended. Under Lincoln's leadership, the American republic had become a model of "government by the people" and "the guiding star of mankind." The nation had added vast territories to its domain since independence, but all these lands, Schurz emphasized, were thinly populated and (except for Alaska) geographically contiguous and temperate in climate. Millions of immigrants with different languages and beliefs sought refuge in the American republic and, by the "assimilating force of American life," became "good Americans."

The Spanish war, Schurz continued, presented Americans with the prospect of assimilating "utterly alien" peoples in distant tropical climes. These people were "Spanish creoles mixed with negroes in the West Indies, and Malays, Tagals, Filipinos, Chinese, Japanese, Negritos and various more or less barbarous tribes in the Philippines." Should America bring these territories into the republic "on an equal footing with the other states they will not only be permitted to govern themselves as to their home concerns, but they will take part in governing the whole Republic, in governing us."[18]

Among the leading opponents of America's new empire were also several Southern Democrats who claimed personal experience in the difficulties of governing the colored races. South Carolina's U.S. senator Benjamin Tillman, an outspoken white supremacist and leading force in the undoing of Reconstruction, warned of the dangers of taking on the governance of colored races abroad. In a lengthy speech during the debate over the Treaty of Paris, Tillman attacked those Northern Republicans who had recently vilified the South for denying African Americans their political rights by turning the same rhetoric against them.

Tillman read to his fellow senators the poem of Rudyard Kipling, "The White Man's Burden," which he suggested was planted in *McClure's Magazine* to inspire Congress to embrace its duty to elevate the Filipinos.

Take up the White Man's Burden—
    Send forth the best ye breed—

Go, bind your sons to exile
    To serve your captives' need;
To wait, in heavy harness
    On fluttered folk and wild—
Your new caught sullen peoples,
    Half devil and half child.

Kipling had indeed composed the poem to encourage Americans to live up to their duty and share with Britain the burden of lifting the colored races into the civilized world, whether they wanted it or not. For Tillman, however, Kipling's poem was instead a "prophecy" of the misery in store for Americans about to take up the white man's burden.[19]

"Every man in this Chamber who has had to do with the colored race in this country voted against the ratification of the treaty," he told the Senate. Not because we are Democrats, he insisted, but "because we understand and realize what it is to have two races side by side that can not mix or mingle without deterioration and injury to both and the ultimate destruction of the civilization of the higher."[20]

After a lengthy debate, the Treaty of Paris finally passed in the Senate, though by only one vote, as though to underscore the deep divisions, confusing logic, and ambivalent emotions the debate had brought forth. The simultaneous sabotage of Radical Reconstruction at home and the rise of American imperialism abroad contradicted all that Abraham Lincoln claimed to be the purpose of the Civil War in testing whether a nation "conceived in liberty, and dedicated to the proposition that all men are created equal . . . could long endure." If it met that test, Lincoln anticipated a "new birth of freedom" not only for America, that "new nation conceived in liberty, and dedicated to the proposition that all men are created equal," but also for "any nation so conceived, and so dedicated" in the world beyond. By the end of the nineteenth century, it seemed America and much of the world were instead experiencing a new birth of white supremacy and imperialist domination—the antitheses of liberty and equality.

Today we look back at the undoing of Reconstruction with regret. After a century and a half, the democratic revolution that began during

Radical Reconstruction in the 1860s remains unfinished. The Second Reconstruction that began in the 1950s overcame many of the legal obstructions to racial equality put in place around the turn of the twentieth century. More than a half century later, there are disturbing signs of a second undoing of the civil rights gains accorded Blacks and other minorities. As in the 1890s, the reaction in America is part of a more ominous international movement against racial equality and democracy. The unfinished revolution that was America's struggle to achieve democracy in the 1860s comes to us again as a summons to redeem Abraham Lincoln's promise of a new birth of freedom for America and the world.

ACKNOWLEDGMENTS

Though writing a book is a lonely endeavor, many helped me along the way. My first debt of gratitude is to Lisa Adams of the Garamond Agency. Lisa patiently worked with me as the project evolved and kept faith in it. I am enormously honored to be part of Princeton University Press's "America in the World" series and wish to thank the series editors, Sven Beckert and Jeremi Suri, for their confidence in my book. I am greatly indebted to Priya Nelson, who guided me through the final revisions and proposed the book's title. Emma Wagh, Morgan Spehar, Theresa Liu, Jenn Backer, Dave Luljak and all the Princeton University Press staff who have cheerfully shepherded the book and its author through each stage of production have earned my deep appreciation.

I have benefited immensely from several very helpful suggestions from the two anonymous reviewers the press asked to evaluate the book. Several other anonymous reviewers offered comments on essays I published earlier for three collections of essays edited by William Link, Adam Domby and Simon Lewis, and Vernon Burton and Brent Morris.

The cosmopolitan scope of this book compelled me to wade into many unfamiliar historical pools. I called on many friends and strangers who took time from their own work to share their insights and expertise with unstinting generosity. Jay Sexton gave an early draft a very helpful reading that kept me going. Erika Pani read an early draft of my Mexico chapter and gave me numerous beneficial suggestions. Patrick Kelly also read the Mexico chapter and shared several fruitful leads. Eric Van Young read a more seasoned version of the Mexico chapter with good results. For the chapter on Russia and Alaska, I am indebted to Victoria Zhuravleva, whose deep knowledge of Russian foreign relations proved valuable. I am very grateful to Philip Buckner, who patiently shared his vast expertise on the making of Canada.

For the chapters on Spain and Cuba, I thank several people. Few understand this subject better than Josep Fradera, who was immensely helpful in commenting on early drafts of these chapters. Andre Fleche also read an early draft of my chapter on Cuba, gave me excellent advice, and kindly shared his deep knowledge from his research. Samantha Payne gave me a smart and helpful reading of the entire manuscript and was especially helpful regarding details on slavery and abolition in Latin America. James Shinn read the entire manuscript and freely shared his remarkable knowledge of Cuba and the Ten Years' War. Samantha and James, now neighbors of mine, allowed me to read their freshly produced dissertations, from which I profited greatly.

For the chapters on Europe, I am deeply indebted to my dear friend, Stève Sainlaude, who read all the chapters with particular attention to those dealing with France and Mexico. His insights and advice were priceless. Robert Saunders, the leading historian of the British Reform Act of 1867, gave generously to me, a stranger in America, and he challenged some of my interpretations in helpful ways. Gareth Stedman Jones, whose work on Karl Marx so impressed me, took the time to help me work out some of my thoughts on Marx. August Nimtz shared his deep knowledge of Marx and his American connections in a helpful review of my chapter on Britain, for which I am most grateful.

Juliana Jardim de Oliveira e Oliveira, who studied with me at the University of South Carolina, showed me the online path to Brazilian state papers and sent a copy of her wonderful dissertation on Brazil and the U.S. Civil War. After I gave a talk to Enrico Dal Lago's graduate students in Galway, he offered several helpful comments, including his lead to Giuseppe Mazzini's funeral train. Peter Kolchin helped me understand how Russia and America's simultaneous abolition of unfree labor helped forge their friendship in the 1860s. David Prior, a pioneer in the global history of Reconstruction, forthrightly shared his opinions of an early book proposal. Whether or not I took all the advice offered, I am sincerely indebted to those who helped me along the way.

Due mostly to the Covid pandemic, the bulk of my research took place not in distant archives but at home in front of my computer, which became my portal to the world of the 1860s. Some days, I would burrow into the rich collections of the Bibliothèque Nationale in Paris. Others found me in Madrid witnessing speeches on Lincoln, America, slavery, and emancipation. The British Newspaper Archive allowed me to search in seconds millions of newspapers. Dozens of similar online sites allowed me to travel through space and time with an ease I could never have imagined when I began my career as a historian over half a century ago. I applaud the anonymous armies of digital archivists making this possible.

Not everything is online yet, however, and I depended on the able staff of the Thomas Cooper Library at the University of South Carolina and the Addlestone Library at the College of Charleston. Special thanks to Kathy Snediker, who always responded cheerfully to my requests for help. The staffs of both libraries were enormously helpful in scanning articles and tracking down books to loan.

I am also grateful to the archivists at the Bishopsgate Library in London who helped me during a day of research on the Reform League. One of the more unforgettable among those who helped me is Marco Pizzo, director of the Museo Centrale del Risorgimento di Roma, who tracked down numerous documents on the Roman Liberals' tribute to Lincoln. He also took time to give me and my extended family, including three wide-eyed grandchildren, a fabulous museum tour featuring the red shirt and cap belonging to Giuseppe Garibaldi.

In several instances, I hired research assistants to gather material. Daniel Richter spent hours at the National Archives harvesting reactions to Lincoln's assassination from U.S. consulates abroad. Alex Chapman copied much of the Gustav Mayer collection at the LSE in London. Rodrigo Moreno worked through hundreds of Mexican newspapers in Mexico City that were otherwise inaccessible.

Though I am a proud father of two daughters, this book is dedicated to my four sons. All four have come to me by way of marriage. Matt Baker married my older daughter, Carrie, the same summer Ned DeWitt married my younger daughter, Kelly. Matt and Ned have proven to be loving and patient husbands, truly admirable fathers, and outstanding people. My other two sons, Scott and Jesse Wheeler, came to me by my own marriage, to Marjorie Spruill. Since we married, I have watched them grow into brilliant young adults, launch exciting careers, and enrich my life in many ways. I am, therefore, delighted to dedicate this book to all my sons.

Marjorie deserves my deepest thanks for her enthusiasm and faith in this book, which is part of the passion we share for history, travel, and learning about the world. More than anything, I am grateful for her abiding love, which makes everything worthwhile and inspires me every day.

ABBREVIATIONS

FRUS   Foreign Relations of the United States, online at
           HeinOnline.org

Hansard   Hansard Parliamentary Debates, online at hansard.parliament
           .uk; HC, House of Commons; HL, House of Lords

HED   US House of Representatives Executive Document

MECW   Karl Marx, Friedrich Engels, *The Collected Works of Karl
           Marx and Friedrich Engels*, 50 vols. (London: Lawrence and
           Wishart, 1975–2010)

NYT   *New York Times*, online at nytimes.com

SED   U.S. Senate Executive Document

NOTES

INTRODUCTION

1. *Tributes of the Nations to Abraham Lincoln* (Washington, DC: GPO, 1867), 109–10.

2. Eric Foner, *Nothing but Freedom: Emancipation and Its Legacy* (1983; Baton Rouge: Louisiana State University Press, 2007); Mark W. Summers, *The Ordeal of the Reunion: A New History of Reconstruction* (Chapel Hill: University of North Carolina Press, 2014).

3. John David Smith and J. Vincent Lowery, eds., *The Dunning School: Historians, Race, and the Meaning of Reconstruction* (Lexington: University of Kentucky Press, 2013).

4. Eric Foner, *Reconstruction: America's Unfinished Revolution, 1863–1877* (New York: Harper and Row, 1988); Michael Perman, "Eric Foner's Reconstruction: A Finished Revolution," *Reviews in American History* 17, no. 1 (1989): 78 (quote). Foner later emphasized the democratic achievements of Reconstruction in *The Second Founding: How the Civil War and Reconstruction Remade the Constitution* (New York: W. W. Norton, 2019).

5. Heather Cox Richardson, *West from Appomattox: The Reconstruction of America after the Civil War* (New Haven: Yale University Press, 2007); Stacey L. Smith, *Freedom's Frontier: California and the Struggle over Unfree Labor, Emancipation, and Reconstruction* (Chapel Hill: University of North Carolina Press, 2013); Elliott West, "Reconstructing Race," *Western Historical Quarterly* 34, no. 1 (2003): 6–26. To Elliott West goes credit for coining the term "Greater Reconstruction."

6. Richard White, *The Republic for Which It Stands: The United States during Reconstruction and the Gilded Age, 1865–1896* (New York: Oxford University Press, 2017).

7. W.E.B. Du Bois, *Dusk of Dawn: An Essay toward an Autobiography of a Race Concept* (1940; New York: Oxford University Press, 2007), 172.

8. David M. Potter, "Civil War," in *The Comparative Approach to American History*, ed. C. Vann Woodward (New York: Basic Books, 1968), 135–45; the essay was reprinted in Potter, "The Civil War in the History of the Modern World: A Comparative View," in *The South and the Sectional Conflict* (Baton Rouge: Louisiana State University Press, 1968), 287 (quote). Another effort to engage U.S. historians in world history was Harold Hyman, ed., *Heard Round the World: The Impact Abroad of the Civil War* (New York: Knopf, 1969). This volume was to be one of a series called The Impact of the Civil War.

9. Thomas J. Brown, ed., *Reconstructions: New Perspectives on the Postbellum United States* (New York: Oxford University Press, 2006); see especially the essay by Mark M. Smith, "The Past as a Foreign Country: Reconstruction, Inside and Out," 117–40; Orville Vernon Burton

and Peter R. Eisenstadt, eds., *Lincoln's Unfinished Work: The New Birth of Freedom from Generation to Generation* (Baton Rouge: Louisiana State University Press, 2022); Orville Vernon Burton and J. Brent Morris, eds., *Reconstruction beyond 150: Reassessing the New Birth of Freedom* (Charlottesville: University of Virginia Press, 2023); Adam H. Domby and Simon Lewis, eds., *Freedoms Gained and Lost: Reconstruction and Its Meanings 150 Years Later* (New York: Fordham University Press, 2022); Gregory P. Downs and Kate Masur, eds., *The World the Civil War Made* (Chapel Hill: University of North Carolina Press, 2015); Don H. Doyle, ed., *American Civil Wars: The United States, Latin America, Europe, and the Crisis of the 1860s* (Chapel Hill: University of North Carolina Press, 2017); Brian Schoen, Jewel L. Spangler, and Frank Towers, eds., *Continent in Crisis: The U.S. Civil War in North America* (New York: Fordham University Press, 2023); Jewel L. Spangler and Frank Towers, eds., *Remaking North American Sovereignty: State Transformation in the 1860s* (New York: Fordham University Press, 2020); William A. Link, ed., *United States Reconstruction across the Americas* (Gainesville: University Press of Florida, 2019); Henry Louis Gates, *Stony the Road: Reconstruction, White Supremacy, and the Rise of Jim Crow* (New York: Penguin Press, 2019); Jörg Nagler, Don H. Doyle, and Marcus Gräser, eds., *The Transnational Significance of the American Civil War* (New York: Palgrave Macmillan, 2016); David Prior, ed., *Reconstruction in a Globalizing World* (New York: Fordham University Press, 2018); David Prior, ed., *Reconstruction and Empire: The Legacies of Abolition and Union Victory for an Imperial Age* (New York: Fordham University Press, 2022); Angela Zimmerman, "Reconstruction: Transnational History," in *Interpreting American History: Reconstruction*, ed. John David Smith (Ashland: Kent State University Press, 2016), 171–96.

10. Gregory P. Downs, *The Second American Revolution: The Civil War–Era Struggle over Cuba and the Rebirth of the American Republic* (Chapel Hill: University of North Carolina Press, 2019); Evan C. Rothera, *Civil Wars and Reconstructions in America: The United States, Mexico, and Argentina, 1860–1880* (Baton Rouge: Louisiana State University Press, 2022); Jeremi Suri, *Civil War by Other Means: America's Long and Unfinished Fight for Democracy* (New York: Public Affairs, 2022); David Prior, *Between Freedom and Progress: The Lost World of Reconstruction Politics, Conflicting Worlds* (Baton Rouge: Louisiana State University Press, 2019); Samantha L. Payne, "The Last Atlantic Revolution: Reconstruction and the Struggle for Democracy in the Americas, 1861–1912" (PhD diss., Harvard University, 2022); Juliana Jardim de Oliveira e Oliveira, "A Guerra Civil no espaço Atlântico: A secessão norte-americana nos debates parlamentares brasileiros (1861–1865)" (PhD diss., Universidade Federal de Ouro Preto, 2017); James M. Shinn, "The Cuban Question: The Ten Years' War and the Reconstruction of U.S. Foreign Policy, 1865–1878" (PhD diss., Yale University, 2020); James M. Shinn, "The 'Free Cuba' Campaign, Republican Politics, and Post–Civil War Black Internationalism," in *Revolutions and Reconstructions: Black Politics in the Long Nineteenth Century*, ed. Van Gosse and David Waldstreicher (Philadelphia: University of Pennsylvania Press, 2020), 176–97; Isadora Moura Mota, "On the Imminence of Emancipation: Black Geopolitical Literacy and Anglo-American Abolitionism in Nineteenth-Century Brazil" (PhD diss., Brown University, 2017); Isadora Moura Mota, "Other Geographies of Struggle: Afro-Brazilians and the American Civil War," *Hispanic American Historical Review* 100, no. 1 (February 1, 2020): 35–62; Isadora Moura Mota, "On the Verge of War: Black Insurgency, the 'Christie Affair', and British Antislavery in Brazil," *Slavery and Abolition* 43, no. 1 (January 2, 2022): 120–39.

11. Steven McGregor, "Seward's Corollary to the Monroe Doctrine, 1863–1866," *International History Review* 43, no. 5 (2021): 1–19; Seward to Bigelow, November 2, 1865 (Seward quote); Bigelow to de Luhys, November 22, 1865; Seward to Hale, December 14, 1865; Hale to Seward, Alexandria, January 18, 1866, all in *FRUS*, 1865, 3:481, 482, 259, 264; Arnold Blumberg, "William Seward and the Egyptian Intervention in Mexico," *Smithsonian Journal of History* (Winter 1967): 31–48.

12. Arthur Corwin is among the few historians to credit the United States for its role in hastening Spanish emancipation; *Spain and the Abolition of Slavery in Cuba, 1817–1886* (Austin: University of Texas Press, 1967), chap. 13.

13. Roger Daniels, *Guarding the Golden Door: American Immigration Policy and Immigrants since 1882* (New York: Hill and Wang, 2005); Faye E. Dudden, *Fighting Chance: The Struggle over Woman Suffrage and Black Suffrage in Reconstruction America* (New York: Oxford University Press, 2011).

14. White, *Republic*, 290–305; Francis A. Walker, "The Indian Question," *North American Review* 116 (April 1873): 341–400.

15. W.E.B. Du Bois, *Black Reconstruction in America*, ed. David L. Lewis (1935; New York: Free Press, 1998), 708.

CHAPTER 1. TRIBUTES OF THE NATIONS

1. For a superb treatment of responses to the assassination within the United States, see Martha Hodes, *Mourning Lincoln* (New Haven: Yale University Press, 2015).

2. Kathryn Canavan, *Lincoln's Final Hours: Conspiracy, Terror, and the Assassination of America's Greatest President* (Lexington: University Press of Kentucky, 2015), 104, 119.

3. Edward Steers, *Blood on the Moon: The Assassination of Abraham Lincoln* (Lexington: University Press of Kentucky, 2001), 125–29; Charles A. Leale, *Lincoln's Last Hours* (New York: n.p., 1909).

4. Canavan, *Lincoln's Final Hours*, 119; Steers, *Blood on the Moon*, 14.

5. Tom Standage, *The Victorian Internet: The Remarkable Story of the Telegraph and the Nineteenth Century's On-Line Pioneers*, 2nd ed. (New York: Bloomsbury, 2014); Simone M. Müller, *Wiring the World: The Social and Cultural Creation of Global Telegraph Networks* (New York: Columbia University Press, 2016).

6. Robin W. Winks, *Canada and the United States: The Civil War Years*, 4th ed. (Montreal: McGill-Queen's University Press, 1998), 363–64; Cheryl A. Wells, "Icy Blasts to Balmy Airs: British North America and Lincoln's Assassination," *Journal of the Abraham Lincoln Association* 36 (Summer 2015): 26–47.

7. "European News," *NYT*, May 9, 1865; "Nova Scotian, Allan Line," Norway-Heritage, http://www.norwayheritage.com/p_ship.asp?sh=nosco.

8. Originally published as an appendix to the annual diplomatic correspondence, *FRUS*, 1865, as Department of State, *The Assassination of Abraham Lincoln, Late President of the United States of America: And the Attempted Assassination of William H. Seward, Secretary of State, and Frederick W. Seward, Assistant Secretary, on the Evening of the 14th of April, 1865: Expressions of*

Condolence and Sympathy Inspired by These Events (Washington, DC: GPO, 1866); later expanded as *Tributes of the Nations to Abraham Lincoln,* from the title on the spine of the 1867 edition. Arrival dates are extrapolated from reports for each country.

9. *Tributes,* 149–50.

10. *Tributes,* 528–29, extract from the London *Daily Telegraph,* April 28, 1865.

11. Benjamin Moran, *The Journal of Benjamin Moran, 1857–1865,* ed. Sarah Agnes Wallace and Frances Elma Gillespie (Chicago: University of Chicago Press, 1948), 2:1419.

12. "The Assassination of the President," *NYT,* May 11, 1865.

13. "The Assassination of the President."

14. *Tributes,* 416.

15. *Tributes,* 221–22.

16. *Tributes,* 219–20.

17. "A Requiem for Abraham Lincoln: An Address to the Liberals of Europe," *Tributes,* 342–44, 344 (quote).

18. Fogg to Hunter, Berne, May 3, 1865, *Tributes,* 721; James H. Hutson, *The Sister Republics: Switzerland and the United States from 1776 to the Present* (Washington, DC: Library of Congress, 1991); Heinz Karl Meier, *The United States and Switzerland in the Nineteenth Century* (The Hague: Mouton, 1963), chap. 4.

19. "Address of the Polish Emigrants," Zurich, May 3, 1865, *Tributes,* 784.

20. Fogg to Hunter, Berne, May 4, 1865; Fogg to Seward, Berne, June 20, 1865, *Tributes,* 722–23; 715, 724–25 (total signatures); 715–87 (all Swiss messages).

21. Malakoff, "A Sensation in Paris," *NYT,* May 5, 1865; Michael Vorenberg, "Liberté, Égalité, and Lincoln: French Readings of an American President," in *The Global Lincoln,* ed. Richard Carwardine and Jay Sexton (New York: Oxford University Press, 2011), 95. Though Vorenberg asserts French interest in Lincoln was limited to a small group of intellectuals, the student demonstrations, medal drive, and ongoing publications about Lincoln suggest a much broader public enthusiasm for Lincoln and the Union victory; see Thomas Sancton, *Sweet Land of Liberty: The French Left Looks at America, 1848–1871* (Baton Rouge: Louisiana State University Press, 2021) for evidence that the French left embraced Lincoln and the United States with enthusiasm.

22. Henri Allain-Targé, *La république sous l'empire lettres, 1864–1870,* ed. Suzanne de La Porte (Paris: Grasset, 1939), 22–25, quoted in Sancton, *Sweet Land,* 105–6.

23. Édouard Laboulaye, *Paris en Amérique* (Paris: Charpentier, 1863); Édouard Laboulaye, *Paris in America,* trans. Mary L. Booth (New York: C. Scribner, 1863); Pierre Larousse, *Grand dictionnaire universel du XIXe siècle . . . ,* vol. 1, pt. 1 (Paris: Administration du Grand dictionnaire universel, 1866), s.v. "américomanie." See also Maike Thier, "The View from Paris: 'Latinity,' 'Anglo-Saxonism,' and the Americas, as discussed in the 'Revue des Races Latines,' 1857–64," *International History Review* 33, no. 4 (2011): 627–44.

24. Édouard Laboulaye, "Speech of Edouard Laboulaye: On the Death of Mr. Lincoln," in *Lincolniana: In Memoriam,* ed. William V. Spencer (Boston: William V. Spencer, 1865), 320–26; Laboulaye to Bigelow, April 29, 1865, *Tributes,* 119.

25. Malakoff, "Interesting from Paris: Eulogies of the Press on the Character of Mr. Lincoln," *NYT,* May 16, 1865. Due to censorship of the French press, Malakoff reliably provided the fullest account of the student demonstrations. For the English translation, see A. Rey to Citizen Am-

bassador [Bigelow], *Tributes*, 109–10. See also, Georges Clemenceau, *Clémenceau: Lettres d'Amérique*, ed. Patrick Weil and Thomas Macé (Paris: Passés Composés, 2020), 16; Philip G. Nord, *The Republican Moment: Struggles for Democracy in Nineteenth-Century France* (Cambridge, MA: Harvard University Press, 1998), 199; Taxile Delord, *Histoire du Second Empire*, vol. 4 (Paris: Libraire Germer Bailliere, 1873), 16–17.

26. Malakoff, "Interesting from Paris: Eulogies"; Malakoff, "Dr. Gwin's Return to Mexico," *NYT*, May 1, 1865; Nord, *Republican Moment*, 199; Thomas A. Sancton, "The Myth of French Worker Support for the North in the American Civil War," *French Historical Studies* 11, no. 1 (1979): 58–80; Hans-Jürgen Grabbe, "The Hidden Lincoln in French Opinion," *American Studies Journal* (blog), March 30, 2016, http://www.asjournal.org/60-2016/hidden-lincoln-french -opinion; Clemenceau, *Clémenceau*, 16.

27. Bigelow to Seward, Paris, April 28, 1865, John Bigelow, *Retrospections of an Active Life: 1863–1865*, vol. 2 (New York: Baker and Taylor, 1909), 523.

28. Malakoff, "Interesting from Paris: Eulogies."

29. Bigelow to Seward, Paris, May 31, 1865, Bigelow, *Retrospections: 1863–65*, 2:579.

30. Malakoff, "The Demonstrations in Regard to Mr. Lincoln's Death," *NYT*, May 18, 1865; Malakoff, "Continued Demonstrations," *NYT*, May 28, 1865.

31. Malakoff, "Interesting from Paris: Eulogies."

32. "French Exiles in Belgium," *NYT*, June 6, 1865.

33. *Tributes*, 75. For more on this letter, see Bryan LaPointe, "'Moral Electricity': Melvil-Bloncourt and the Trans-Atlantic Struggle for Abolition and Equal Rights," *Slavery and Abolition* 40, no. 3 (September 2019): 543–62.

34. Comité français d'emancipation, *Adresse au Président des États-Unis, Mai 1865* (Paris: Simon Racon et Compagnie, 1865); for an English translation of the Committee's address, see *Tributes*, 105–9; Cochin to Bigelow, May 17, 1865, and Bigelow to Cochin, May 19, 1865, *FRUS*, 1865 (Washington, DC: GPO, 1865), 3:292–96; William Edward Johnston, ed., *Memoirs of "Malakoff"* vol. 2 (London: Hutchison, 1907), 529.

35. Charles-Louis Chassin, *Le génie de la Révolution*, 2 vols. (Paris: Pagnerre, 1863); Benjamin Gastineau, *Histoire de la souscription populaire à la médaille Lincoln* (Paris: A. Lacroix, Verboeck-hoven, 1865), 10; Nord, *Republican Moment*, chap. 1.

36. Gastineau, *Souscription populaire*, 8, 5; for an example of advertising the subscription drive, see "Nouvelles du jour," *La Presse*, May 1, 1865; on the carriage makers, see "Nouvelles du Jour," *La Presse*, July 28, 1865; Olivier Fraysse and Laurance Grégoire, "The French Masonic Tributes to Abraham Lincoln," *American Studies Journal*, January 9, 2020, http://www.asjournal .org/60-2016/french-masonic-tributes-abraham-lincoln/.

37. John Bigelow, *Retrospections of an Active Life: 1865–1866*, vol. 3 (New York: Baker and Taylor, 1909), 54; Gastineau, *Souscription populaire*, 12. Gastineau gives the correct spelling for Rigollet, not Pigollet as Bigelow had it.

38. Montagnie to Bigelow, Nantes, April 25, May 30, 1865, John Bigelow, "John Bigelow Papers, 1839–1912," Manuscript and Archives Division, New York Public Library, Series IV, Consular Correspondence and Papers, 1861–1866. The Bigelow Papers are now online at: https:// digitalcollections.nypl.org; Bigelow to Consul at Nantes, Paris, June 2, 1865, Bigelow, *Retrospections: 1865–66*, 3:53–54, 57.

39. Gastineau, *Souscription populaire*, 16.

40. "The Gold Medal Presented to Mrs. Lincoln by the People of France," *NYT*, December 23, 1866; Jason Emerson, "A Medal for Mrs. Lincoln," *Register of the Kentucky Historical Society* 109, no. 2 (2011): 192; Andrew C. Zabriskie, "The Medalic History of Abraham Lincoln," *Proceedings of the American Numismatic and Archeological Society of New York City* (1901): 33–39.

41. Gastineau, *Souscription populaire*, 18–21; Emerson, "Medal," 191. The total, 40,000 francs, would have been approximately US$1,200 in 1865.

42. "Abraham Lincoln Papers: Series 4, Addenda, 1774–1948: Gold Medal Presented to Mary Todd Lincoln by the French Medal Committee, Manuscript/Mixed Material, Library of Congress" (1866), https://www.loc.gov/item/mal4500052.

43. Emerson, "Medal," 187, 197.

44. Charles Forbes Montalembert, *La victoire du nord aux États-Unis* (Paris: E. Dentu, 1865); Montalembert, *The Victory of the North in the United States* (Boston: Littell and Gay, 1865), 22 (quote); Bigelow, *Retrospections: 1865–66*, 3:4.

45. *L'Avenir National*, April 28, May 3, May 4, 1865, *Tributes*, 145–50.

46. Mazzini to E. C. Fisher, London, May 21, 1865, reprinted in "Letter from Mazzini: The War in the United States and Its Effect in Europe," *NYT*, June 15, 1865. Fisher was the London agent for the U.S. Sanitary Commission; Giuseppe Mazzini, *Address to the Friends of Republican Principles in America from the Friends of Those Principles in Europe* ([New York]: n.p., 1865); Howard R. Marraro, "Mazzini on American Intervention in European Affairs," *Journal of Modern History* 21, no. 2 (1949): 109–14.

47. Mazzini to Moncure Conway, London, October 30, 1865, "America as a Leading Nation in the Cause of Liberty (1865)," in *A Cosmopolitanism of Nations: Giuseppe Mazzini's Writings on Democracy, Nation Building, and International Relations*, ed. Stefano Recchia and Nadia Urbinati (Princeton: Princeton University Press, 2009), 219–21. Though Conway did not publicize this letter, Mazzini expressed similar sentiments elsewhere.

48. *Tributes*, 575–76.

49. *Tributes*, 582–83.

50. *Tributes*, 573–74.

51. M. B. Bird, *The Victorious: A Small Poem on the Assassination of President Lincoln* (Kingston, Jamaica: M. De Cordova, McDougall, 1866), 51. Note: Haiti was commonly spelled Hayti at this time.

52. Philip S. Foner, *A History of Cuba and Its Relations with the United States*, vol. 2 (New York: International Publishers, 1962), 133–34; Shufeldt to Seward, Havana, October 12, 1862, Consular Dispatches from Cuba, 45, NARA RG 59. I have taken the liberty of correcting Shufeldt, who recorded "Avanza a Lincoln!"

53. Foner, *History of Cuba*, 2:133–34 (on mourning behavior and badges); Emeterio S. Santovenia, *Lincoln* (Buenos Aires: Editorial Americalee, 1948), 464–65 (*El Siglo* quotes); Emeterio S. Santovenia, *Lincoln in Martí: A Cuban View of Abraham Lincoln* (Chapel Hill: University of North Carolina Press, 1953), 4, 64–65 (on Martí's feelings for Lincoln); Emeterio S. Santovenia, "Pasión Cubana por Lincoln," *Revista de la Biblioteca Nacional José Martí* 4, no. 1 (March 1953): 64, 66 (on official censorship); James W. Cortada, "Spanish Views on Abraham

Lincoln, 1861–1865," *Lincoln Herald* 76, no. 2 (June 1974): 84; Ada Ferrer, *Cuba: An American History* (New York: Scribner, 2021), 120–21.

54. Emeterio S. Santovenia, "Reaffirmation of the Colonial Regime," in *A History of the Cuban Nation: Break with the Mother Country, 1837–1868*, ed. Ramiro Guerra et al., trans. James J. O'Mailia, vol. 4 (Havana: Editorial Historia de la Nación Cubana, 1958), 33; Santovenia, *Lincoln*, 485; Cortada, "Spanish Views on Abraham Lincoln, 1861–1865," 84; *Correspondence between the Department of State and the United States Minister at Madrid and the Consular Representatives of the United States in the Island of Cuba, and Other Papers Relating to Cuban Affairs*, 41st Cong., 2nd Sess., HED 160 (Washington, DC: GPO, 1870), 112 (on images of Lincoln in 1868).

55. Mejicano, "From Mexico," *NYT*, June 13, 1865.

56. *Tributes*, 626–29.

57. "Meeting of Mexican Exiles at Cooper Institute," *NYT*, July 20, 1865; Speech of Colonel Manuel Balbontin, in *Proceedings of a Meeting of Citizens of New York, to Express Sympathy and Respect for the Mexican Republican Exiles* (New York: J. A. Gray and Green, 1865), 39 (quote).

58. Samantha Payne, "The Last Atlantic Revolution: Reconstruction and the Struggle for Democracy in the Americas, 1861–1912" (PhD diss., Harvard University, 2022), chap. 1; Isadora Moura Mota, "On the Imminence of Emancipation: Black Geopolitical Literacy and Anglo-American Abolitionism in Nineteenth-Century Brazil" (PhD diss., Brown University, 2017); Isadora Moura Mota, "Other Geographies of Struggle: Afro-Brazilians and the American Civil War," *Hispanic American Historical Review* 100, no. 1 (February 1, 2020): 35–62; Isadora Moura Mota, "On the Verge of War: Black Insurgency, the 'Christie Affair', and British Antislavery in Brazil," *Slavery and Abolition* 43, no. 1 (January 2, 2022): 120–39.

59. Roberto Saba, *American Mirror: The United States and Brazil in the Age of Emancipation* (Princeton: Princeton University Press, 2021), 82–84, 117–20, 124, 127.

60. Louis Agassiz and Elizabeth Cabot Cary Agassiz, *A Journey in Brazil* (Boston: Houghton, Mifflin, 1867), 79.

61. Saba, *American Mirror*, 116–17.

62. Saba, *American Mirror*, 107–9.

63. Agassiz and Agassiz, *Journey in Brazil*, 49; Harry Bernstein, "South America Looks at North American Reconstruction," in *New Frontiers of the American Reconstruction*, ed. Harold Melvin Hyman (Urbana: University of Illinois Press, 1966), 87–104; Saba, *American Mirror*, chap. 3.

64. Juliana Jardim de Oliveira e Oliveira, "A Guerra Civil no espaço Atlântico: A secessão norte-americana nos debates parlamentares brasileiros (1861–1865)" (PhD diss., Universidade Federal de Ouro Preto, 2017), 149, 149n358; Joaquim Nabuco, *Lincoln's Centenary: Speech of the Brazilian Ambassador Joaquim Nabuco at the Celebration in Washington of Lincoln's Centenary Organized by the Commissioners of the District of Columbia, February 12th, 1909* (Washington, DC: n.p., 1909).

65. *Tributes*, 9–14.

66. *Tributes*, 561–66, 619–20.

67. Nelson to Seward, Santiago de Chile, June 1, 1865, *Tributes*, 37–39.

68. Bigelow, *Retrospections: 1863–65*, 2:557–58.

69. *FRUS*, 1865, 3:296.

70. Marsh to Bigelow, Turin, May 2, 1865, Bigelow, *Retrospections: 1863–65*, 2:531. Marsh wrote "England" but clearly meant "Europe."

71. Bigelow to Seward, Paris, May 31, 1865, Bigelow, *Retrospections: 1863–65*, 2:578–79.

72. Seward to Bigelow, November 18, 1865, *FRUS*, 1865, 3:351.

73. *Tributes*; the resolution authorizing publication faces page i.

74. William H. Seward, *Seward at Washington as Senator and Secretary of State: A Memoir of His Life, with Selections from His Letters, 1861–1872*, ed. Frederick William Seward, vol. 2 (New York: Derby and Miller, 1891), 327–28.

CHAPTER 2. RETRIBUTION

1. Palmerston to Queen Victoria, January 20, 1865, quoted in Brian Jenkins, *Fenians and Anglo-American Relations during Reconstruction* (Ithaca: Cornell University Press, 1969), 41–42.

2. Arnold Blumberg, "Bancroft's Eulogy of Lincoln and British Reaction," *Lincoln Herald* 67, no. 4 (December 1965), 151; George Athan Billias, *George Bancroft: Master Historian* (Worcester: American Antiquarian Society, 2004), 510–11.

3. Robert Lytton to his father, April 14, 1869, Edward Robert Bulwer Lytton, *Personal and Literary Letters of Robert, First Earl of Lytton*, ed. Betty Balfour, vol. 1 (London: Longmans, Green, 1906), 248; also related in M. A. De Wolfe Howe and Henry C. Strippel, eds., *The Life and Letters of George Bancroft*, vol. 2 (New York: C. Scribner's sons, 1908), 174n1.

4. George Bancroft, *Memorial Address on the Life and Character of Abraham Lincoln* (Washington, DC: GPO, 1866), 6.

5. Bancroft, *Memorial Address*, 47–50.

6. Howe and Strippel, *Life and Letters*, 2:158–63.

7. "The United States," *The Times*, February 27, 1866; "Reception of Mr. Bancroft's Oration in England," *NYT*, March 12, 1866; Blumberg, "Bancroft's Eulogy," 153.

8. George Bancroft, *Éloge funèbre du Président Abraham Lincoln, prononcé en séance solennelle du Congrès des États-Unis d'Amérique*, trans. Gustave Jottrand (Bruxelles: A. Lacroix, Verboeckhoven, 1866); Eugèno Chatard, "Amérique: L'incident Bancroft," *La Presse*, March 3, 1866.

9. Gustave Isambert, "Bulletin du Jour," *Le Temps*, March 6, 1866. "Lucubration" implies a pedantic, pompous treatise.

10. "Correspondencia de La Iberia," *La Iberia*, March 9, 1866, 3; "Parte Estranjera," *El Pensamiento Español*, March 9, 1866; *La Soberanía Nacional*, March 13, 1866; *La Nacion*, March 9, 1866.

11. Arnold Blumberg, "The Diplomacy of the Mexican Empire, 1863–1867," *Transactions of the American Philosophical Society* 61, no. 8 (1971): 86–87; Arnold Blumberg, "George Bancroft, France, and the Vatican: Some Aspects of American, French, and Vatican Diplomacy: 1866–1870," *Catholic Historical Review* 50, no. 4 (1965): 480; Blumberg, "Bancroft's Eulogy," 157n40; William H. Seward, *Seward at Washington as Senator and Secretary of State: A Memoir of His Life, with Selections from His Letters, 1861–1872*, ed. Frederick William Seward, vol. 2 (New York: Derby and Miller, 1891), 323 (Seward quote).

12. Nathan L. Ferris, "The Relations of the United States with South America during the American Civil War," *Hispanic American Historical Review* 21, no. 1 (1941): 53–54. On Bancroft's

interest in the French intervention in Mexico and its effect on the Monroe Doctrine, see Dexter Perkins, *The Monroe Doctrine, 1826–1867*, vol. 2 (Baltimore: Johns Hopkins University Press, 1933), 436, 447–48.

13. James D. Richardson, ed., *A Compilation of the Messages and Papers of the Presidents, 1789–1897*, vol. 2 (Washington, DC: GPO, 1897), 217–19. On the history of the Monroe Doctrine, see Jay Sexton, *The Monroe Doctrine: Empire and Nation in Nineteenth-Century America* (New York: Hill and Wang, 2011); Perkins, *Monroe Doctrine,* 2:109–110n65 for an account of young George Bancroft and John Quincy Adams confirming the latter authored the passage known as the Monroe Doctrine.

14. Joshua Leavitt, *The Monroe Doctrine* (New York: S. Tousey, 1863); Sexton, *Monroe Doctrine,* 123–24.

15. Leavitt, *Monroe Doctrine,* 16–17.

16. Perkins, *Monroe Doctrine,* 2:443–48; Leavitt, *Monroe Doctrine,* 14.

17. Joshua Leavitt, "The Key of a Continent," *New Englander* 23, no. July (1864): 517–39.

18. *Proceedings of a Meeting of Citizens of New York, to Express Sympathy and Respect for the Mexican Republican Exiles* (New York: J. A. Gray and Green, 1865), 7–10.

19. Richardson, *Compilation,* 6:368–69.

20. Sexton, *Monroe Doctrine,* 85, 102, chap. 4; "The President's Interpretation of the Monroe Doctrine.," *NYT,* December 7, 1865.

21. Alfred J. Hanna and Kathryn A. Hanna, *Napoleon III and Mexico: American Triumph over Monarchy* (Chapel Hill: University of North Carolina Press, 1971), chap. 1; Stève Sainlaude, "France's Grand Design and the Confederacy," in *American Civil Wars: The United States, Latin America, Europe, and the Crisis of the 1860s,* ed. Don H. Doyle (Chapel Hill: University of North Carolina Press, 2017), 107–24.

22. Erika Pani, "Dreaming of a Mexican Empire: The Political Projects of the 'Imperialistas,'" *Hispanic American Historical Review* 82, no. 1 (2002): 1–31; Erika Pani, "Juarez vs. Maximiliano: Mexico's Experiment with Monarchy," in *American Civil Wars: The United States, Latin America, Europe, and the Crisis of the 1860s,* ed. Don H. Doyle (Chapel Hill: University of North Carolina Press, 2017), 167–84; Erika Pani, "The U.S. Civil War: Looking across the Southern Border," *Civil War History* 66, no. 2 (June 2020): 173–80.

23. Hanna and Hanna, *Napoleon III and Mexico,* xv, 67, chap. 1; Maike Thier, "The View from Paris: 'Latinity,' 'Anglo-Saxonism,' and the Americas, as discussed in the 'Revue des Races Latines,' 1857–64," *International History Review* 33, no. 4 (2011): 627–44; Sainlaude, "France's Grand Design." For an early and prescient analysis of Napoleon III's Grand Design, see R. H. Patterson, *The New Revolution, or, The Napoleonic Policy in Europe* (W. Blackwood and Sons, 1860).

24. Don H. Doyle, *The Cause of All Nations: An International History of the American Civil War* (New York: Basic Books, 2015).

25. Matías Romero, *Dinner to Señor Matias Romero, Envoy Extraordinary and Minister Plenipotentiary from Mexico, on the 29th of March, 1864* (New York: n.p., 1866), 26.

26. Perkins, *Monroe Doctrine,* 2:449–52; Matías Romero, *Correspondencia de la Legacion mexicana en Washington durante la intervencion extranjera, 1860–1868,* vol. 4 (Mexico City: Imprenta del Gobierno, 1871), 9, 20–21, 77–78, 122, and passim.

27. *Congressional Globe*, 38th Cong., 1st Sess. (April 4, 1864): 1408; George Fox Tucker, *The Monroe Doctrine: A Concise History of Its Origin and Growth* (Boston: George B. Reed, 1885), 102–3.

28. William Edward Johnston, ed., *Memoirs of "Malakoff,"* vol. 2 (London: Hutchison, 1907), 437; Malakoff, "France and Mexico," *NYT*, May 5, 1864.

29. Republican Party Platform of 1864, June 7, 1864, Political Party Platforms, The American Presidency Project, University of California, Santa Barbara, https://www.presidency.ucsb.edu/documents/republican-party-platform-1864.

30. William C. Harris, "The Hampton Roads Peace Conference: A Final Test of Lincoln's Presidential Leadership," *Journal of the Abraham Lincoln Association* 21, no. 1 (Winter 2000): 30–61.

31. "The Rebel Congress, the Monroe Doctrine in the Rebel House," *NYT*, February 3, 1865; Daniel C. Dejarnette, *The Monroe Doctrine: Speech of Hon. D. C. De Jarnette* (Chapel Hill: University Library, University of North Carolina, 1865); Harris, "Hampton Roads Peace Conference"; Doyle, *Cause of All Nations*, 275.

32. Adams to Seward, London, February 17, 1865, *FRUS*, 1865, part 1, 178 (quote on panic); Boilleau to Drouyn de Lhuys, New York, February 7, March 28, 1865, Stève Sainlaude, "La Politique Étrangère de La France à l'égard Des Etats-Unis d'Amérique de 1839 à 1867" (PhD diss., l'Université Paris XII, 2009), 1109, 1296 (second quote). I am grateful to Professor Sainlaude for sharing this source and his immense knowledge of Franco-American relations.

33. Seward, *Seward at Washington, 1861–72*, 2:282.

34. Monadnock, "The 'First Act' Ended: Dread of War with America," *NYT*, May 5, 1865.

35. Malakoff, "Our Paris Correspondence," *NYT*, November 16, 1865.

36. Giuseppe Mazzini, *Address to the Friends of Republican Principles in America from the Friends of Those Principles in Europe* ([New York]: n.p., 1865); "Letter from Mazzini," *NYT*, June 15, 1865; Howard R. Marraro, "Mazzini on American Intervention in European Affairs," *Journal of Modern History* 21, no. 2 (1949): 109–14; Joseph Rossi, *The Image of America in Mazzini's Writings* (Madison: University of Wisconsin Press, 1954), 137–48; Stefano Recchia and Nadia Urbinati, eds., *A Cosmopolitanism of Nations: Giuseppe Mazzini's Writings on Democracy, Nation Building, and International Relations* (Princeton: Princeton University Press, 2009), 219–23. For an earlier example of transatlantic revolutionary plans, see "Karl Blind, Joseph Mazzini, and Alexandre A. Ledru-Rollin to Abraham Lincoln, London," April 24, 1862, Abraham Lincoln Papers at the Library of Congress.

37. Henry Winter Davis, *Speeches and Addresses Delivered in the Congress of the United States: And on Several Public Occasions* [1856–1865] (New York: Harper, 1867), 564–84; "The Fourth of July: Oration of Hon. H. Winter Davis at Chicago," *NYT*, July 9, 1865.

38. Montgomery Blair, *The Monroe Doctrine: Speech of Hon. Montgomery Blair at Hagerstown, MD, on 12th July, 1865. Exposing the Alliance of the American Secretary of State with Louis Napoleon to Overthrow the Monroe Doctrine and Establish a Despotism on This Continent* (Washington, DC: H. Polkinhorn, 1865); Sexton, *Monroe Doctrine*, 151–56.

39. "America for Americans," *NYT*, January 7, 1866.

40. Vicuña Mackenna speech in, "America for Americans." See also Daniel J. Hunter, [Benjamín Vicuña Mackenna], *A Sketch of Chili* (New York: S. Hallet, 1866), 58; Benjamín Vicuña Mackenna, *Diez meses de mision a los Estados Unidos de Norte America como ajente confidencial*

de Chile, 2 vols. (Santiago, Chile: La Libertad, 1867). For more Latin American enthusiasm for pan-American solidarity, see *Publicaciones de la Sociedad Democrática de los Amigos de América* (New York: Julian M. Casamena, 1865).

41. On Pan-American solidarity, see Robert W. Frazer, "Latin-American Projects to Aid Mexico during the French Intervention," *Hispanic American Historical Review* 28, no. 3 (1948): 377–88; for overviews of the evolution of the Monroe Doctrine during the Civil War, see Perkins, *Monroe Doctrine*, 2:421–65; and Sexton, *Monroe Doctrine*, 123–58.

42. Joseph A. Fry, *Lincoln, Seward, and US Foreign Relations in the Civil War Era* (Lexington: University Press of Kentucky, 2019), 50.

43. Walter LaFeber, *The New Empire: An Interpretation of American Expansion, 1860–1898* (Ithaca: Cornell University Press, 1963), 37 (quote); Ernest N. Paolino, *The Foundations of the American Empire: William Henry Seward and U.S. Foreign Policy* (Ithaca: Cornell University Press, 1973), 118–28; Frederic Bancroft, "Seward's Ideas of Territorial Expansion," *North American Review* 167, no. 500 (1898): 87; Joseph Gerald Whelan, "William Henry Seward, Expansionist" (PhD diss., University of Rochester, 1959); Fareed Zakaria, *From Wealth to Power: The Unusual Origins of America's World Role* (Princeton: Princeton University Press, 1998), chap. 3.

44. Clayton R. Newell and Charles R. Shrader, *Of Duty Well and Faithfully Done: A History of the Regular Army in the Civil War* (Lincoln: University of Nebraska Press, 2011), 304; Nathan Miller, *The US Navy: A History* (Annapolis, MD: Naval Institute Press, 1997), 245–46.

45. Bigelow to William Cullen Bryant, Paris, May 16, 1865, John Bigelow, *Retrospections of an Active Life: 1863–1865*, vol. 2 (New York: Baker and Taylor, 1909), 558.

46. Christopher Wilkins, "'They Had Heard of Emancipation and the Enfranchisement of Their Race': The African American Colonists of Samaná, Reconstruction, and the State of Santo Domingo," in *The Civil War as Global Conflict*, ed. David T. Gleeson and Simon Lewis (Columbia: University of South Carolina Press, 2014), 211–34; Christopher Dirk Wilkins, "American Republic, American Empire: The United States, Post–Civil War Reconstruction, and the State of Santo Domingo, 1868–1871" (PhD diss., Stanford University, 2012).

47. Edward L. Godkin, "The Annexation Fever," *The Nation*, April 1869, 289 (quote); Allan Nevins, *Hamilton Fish: The Inner History of the Grant Administration* (New York: Ungar, 1936), 180, 194, 262, 313. For more on racial and cultural aversions to annexing Latin American colonies or nations, see Eric T. Love, *Race over Empire: Racism and U.S. Imperialism, 1865–1900* (Chapel Hill: University of North Carolina Press, 2004); Paul Frymer, *Building an American Empire: The Era of Territorial and Political Expansion* (Princeton: Princeton University Press, 2019); Wilkins, "American Republic, American Empire."

48. Seward, *Seward at Washington, 1861–72*, 2:316.

49. William Henry Seward and Frederick William Seward, *Seward at Washington, 1846–1861*, vol. 1 (New York: Derby and Miller, 1891), 369–70 (quote). See also Thomas D. Schoonover, *Dollars over Dominion: The Triumph of Liberalism in Mexican-United States Relations, 1861–1867* (Baton Rouge: Louisiana State University, 1978), 283.

50. Address to President Baez, January 14, 1866, Seward, *Seward at Washington, 1861–72*.

51. Post–Civil War foreign policy resembles today's democratic peace theory in many ways. See Carsten Rauch, "The Power of Perception: Democratic Peace Theory and the

American Civil War," *European Review of International Studies* 3, no. 1 (2016): 5–30; Michael E. Brown, Sean M. Lynn-Jones, and Steven E. Miller, eds., *Debating the Democratic Peace* (Cambridge, MA: MIT Press, 1996); Michael W. Doyle, *Liberal Peace: Selected Essays* (London: Routledge, 2012).

CHAPTER 3. THE MEXICAN LESSON

1. For more on the two civil wars in North America, see Guillermo Palacios and Erika Pani, eds., *El Poder y La Sangre: Guerra, Estado y Nación en la Década de 1860* (Mexico City: El Colegio de Mexico, 2014) particularly the essays by Thomas Bender, Pablo Mijangos y González Palacios, Erika Pani, Gerardo Gurza Lavalle, Marcela Terrazas, and Fabio Moraga Valle.

2. Michel Chevalier, *France, Mexico, and the Confederate States*, trans. William Henry Hurlbert (New York: C. B. Richardson, 1863); Stève Sainlaude, "France's Grand Design and the Confederacy," in *American Civil Wars: The United States, Latin America, Europe, and the Crisis of the 1860s*, ed. Don H. Doyle (Chapel Hill: University of North Carolina Press, 2017); Erika Pani, "Dreaming of a Mexican Empire: The Political Projects of the 'Imperialistas,'" *Hispanic American Historical Review* 82, no. 1 (2002): 1–31; Erika Pani, "Juarez vs. Maximiliano: Mexico's Experiment with Monarchy," in *American Civil Wars: The United States, Latin America, Europe, and the Crisis of the 1860s*, ed. Don H. Doyle (Chapel Hill: University of North Carolina Press, 2017), 167–84.

3. Matías Romero, *Dinner to Señor Matias Romero, Envoy Extraordinary and Minister Plenipotentiary from Mexico, on the 29th of March, 1864* (New York: n.p., 1866); *Proceedings of a Meeting of Citizens of New York, to Express Sympathy and Respect for the Mexican Republican Exiles* (New York: J. A. Gray and Green, 1865); Robert Ryal Miller, "Matías Romero: Mexican Minister to the United States during the Juarez-Maximilian Era," *Hispanic American Historical Review* 45, no. 2 (May 1, 1965): 228–45; Matías Romero, *Mexican Lobby: Matías Romero in Washington, 1861–67*, ed. Thomas D. Schoonover (Lexington: University Press of Kentucky, 1986); Matías Romero, *A Mexican View of America in the 1860s: A Foreign Diplomat Describes the Civil War and Reconstruction*, ed. Thomas David Schoonover (Teaneck, NJ: Fairleigh Dickinson University Press, 1991).

4. *Congressional Globe*, 38th Cong., 1st Sess. (April 4, 1864): 1408.

5. William C. Harris, "The Hampton Roads Peace Conference: A Final Test of Lincoln's Presidential Leadership," *Journal of the Abraham Lincoln Association* 21, no. 1 (Winter 2000): 30–61; Lynn Marshall Case and Warren F. Spencer, *The United States and France: Civil War Diplomacy* (Philadelphia: University of Pennsylvania Press, 1970), 564–66.

6. Seward to Bigelow, March 11, 1865, *FRUS*, 1865, 241–42; James Fred Rippy, *The United States and Mexico* (New York: AMS Press, 1971), 270–71.

7. Glyndon G. Van Deusen, *William Henry Seward* (New York: Oxford University Press, 1967), 411–17.

8. Romero dispatches for April 20, 24, 1865, Matías Romero, *Correspondencia de la Legacion mexicana en Washington durante la intervencion extranjera, 1860–1868*, vol. 5 (Mexico City: Im-

prenta del Gobierno, 1871), 237–38, 249–50, 259–61; Romero, *Mexican Lobby*, 54–57; Romero, *A Mexican View of America in the 1860s*, 194–95.

9. Richard Zuczek, "Foreign Affairs and Andrew Johnson," in *A Companion to the Reconstruction Presidents, 1865–1881*, ed. Edward O. Frantz (Hoboken, NJ: John Wiley, 2014), 97–99; Andrew Johnson et al., *The Papers of Andrew Johnson*, vol. 6 (Knoxville: University of Tennessee Press, 1983), 727; Dexter Perkins, *The Monroe Doctrine, 1826–1867* (Baltimore: Johns Hopkins University Press, 1933), 2:471n1; Miller, "Matías Romero," 2.

10. Romero, *Correspondencia*, 5:259–61; for English translations of extracts from this correspondence, see Romero, *Mexican Lobby*, 50, 55–57.

11. Ulysses S. Grant, *Personal Memoirs of Ulysses S. Grant* (New York: Charles L. Webster, 1885), 53.

12. Robert W. Delaney, "Matamoros, Port for Texas during the Civil War," *Southwestern Historical Quarterly* 58, no. 4 (1955): 473–87; James W. Daddysman, *The Matamoros Trade: Confederate Commerce, Diplomacy, and Intrigue* (Newark: University of Delaware Press, 1984).

13. *Message of the President of the United States, of March 20, 1866, Relating to the Condition of Affairs in Mexico*, 39th Cong., 1st Sess., HED 73 (Washington, DC: GPO, 1866), 225; Ulysses S. Grant, *Personal Memoirs of U. S. Grant*, vol. 2 (New York: C. L. Webster, 1885), 1:32; Philip Henry Sheridan, *Personal Memoirs of P. H. Sheridan*, vol. 2 (New York: Charles E. Webster, 1888), 358–59; Delaney, "Matamoros," 473. For Grant's alleged quotes, see Hamlin Garland, *Ulysses S. Grant: His Life and Character* (New York: Doubleday and McClure, 1898), 314, quoted in William B. Hesseltine, *Ulysses S. Grant: Politician* (New York: Dodd, Mead, 1935), 53.

14. Romero to Ministry of Foreign Relations, Washington, June 5, 25, 1865, Romero, *Correspondencia*, 5:360–61; Miller, "Matías Romero," 243; Charles Allen Smart, *Viva Juárez!: A Biography* (London: Eyre and Spottiswoode, 1964), 339 (last quote).

15. Major General P. H. Sheridan, "Report of Operations and General Information of the Condition of Affairs in the Military Division of the Southwest and Gulf, and Department of the Gulf, from May 29, 1865, to November 4, 1866," in *Supplemental Report of the Joint Committee on the Conduct of the War, in Two Volumes: Supplemental to Senate Report No. 142, 38th Congress, 2d Session*, 2 vols., 38th Cong., 2nd Sess., S. Report 142 (Washington, DC: GPO, 1866), 2:72–77; Sheridan, *Personal Memoirs*, 2:205–29; Robert B. Brown, "Guns over the Border: American Aid to the Juarez Government during the French Intervention" (PhD diss., University of Michigan, 1951), 231; Robert Ryal Miller, "Arms across the Border: United States Aid to Juárez during the French Intervention in Mexico," *Transactions of the American Philosophical Society* 63, no. 6 (January 1, 1973): 15. Sadly, Robert Brown died while finishing his dissertation. Miller produced a series of articles that built upon Brown's work. Throughout, I have credited both scholars.

16. Sheridan, "Report of Operations," 74–75.

17. Grant to Sheridan, July 25, October 13, 1865, Ulysses S. Grant, *The Papers of Ulysses S. Grant*, ed. John Y. Simon, vol. 15 (Carbondale: Southern Illinois University Press, 1988), 285–86, 367, 425, all spelling and grammar as in the original; Sheridan, *Personal Memoirs*, 2:205–29.

18. Grant to President Johnson, July 15, 1865, Grant, *Papers of US Grant*, 15:264–65; John McAllister Schofield, *Forty-Six Years in the Army* (New York: Century Company, 1897), 379–80. The proposed loan from the United States would open the door to claims on Mexican territory

as indemnity should Mexico default. This is what concerned Seward when he warned that a move to liberate Mexico might turn into the conquest of Mexican territory.

19. Grant to Sheridan, July 25, 1865, Grant, *Papers of US Grant*, 15:285–86; Schofield, *Forty-Six Years*, 336–38.

20. Grant to Johnson, June 19, 1865, Grant, *Papers of US Grant*, 15:156–58. Romero's account of the meeting is found in Romero, *Mexican Lobby*, 66–69; see also William S. Kiser, *Illusions of Empire the Civil War and Reconstruction in the U.S.-Mexico Borderlands* (Philadelphia: University of Pennsylvania Press, 2022), 242.

21. John Bigelow, *Retrospections of an Active Life: 1863–1865*, vol. 2 (New York: Baker and Taylor, 1909), 481ff., Favre speech, April 1865; John Bigelow, *Retrospections of an Active Life: 1867–1871*, vol. 4 (New York: Doubleday, Page, 1913), 464–65; Alfred J. Hanna and Kathryn A. Hanna, *Napoleon III and Mexico: American Triumph over Monarchy* (Chapel Hill: University of North Carolina Press, 1971), xv, 303, and passim; Stève Sainlaude, *France and the American Civil War: A Diplomatic History*, trans. Jessica Edwards (Chapel Hill: University of North Carolina Press, 2020); Sainlaude, "France's Grand Design"; Maike Thier, "The View from Paris: 'Latinity,' 'Anglo-Saxonism,' and the Americas, as Discussed in the 'Revue des Races Latines,' 1857–64," *International History Review* 33, no. 4 (2011): 627–44.

22. John M. Schofield, "The Withdrawal of the French from Mexico: A Chapter of Secret History," *Century Illustrated Monthly Magazine* 54, no. 1 (May 1897): 128–37; Frederic Bancroft, *The Life of William H. Seward*, vol. 2 (New York: Harper and Brothers, 1899), 442. Romero's account of the meeting, probably based on leaks from Grant, is found in Romero, *Mexican Lobby*, 66–69; Walter Stahr, *Seward: Lincoln's Indispensable Man* (New York: Simon and Schuster, 2012), 441–43.

23. Romero, *Mexican Lobby*, 66–69; John Bigelow, *Retrospections of an Active Life: 1865–1866*, vol. 3 (New York: Baker and Taylor, 1909), 3:255.

24. Gideon Welles, *Diary of Gideon Welles* (Boston: Houghton Mifflin, 1911), June 16, 1865, 2:317; Stahr, *Seward*, 442–44.

25. Bigelow to Seward, Paris, May 5, 1865, Bigelow, *Retrospections: 1863–65*, 2:535–39; Bigelow, *Retrospections: 1865–66*, 3:67–72; Margaret Antoinette Clapp, *Forgotten First Citizen: John Bigelow* (Boston: Little, Brown, 1947), 244–45.

26. Seward to Bigelow, August 7, 1865, and Bigelow to Seward, Dieppe, August 21, 1865, Bigelow, *Retrospections: 1865–66*, 3:143, 151–56; for Bigelow's answer, see *New York Tribune*, February 27, 1869, extracted in Bigelow, *Retrospections: 1867–1871*, 4:251–52. See also, C. G. Thomson, *Italian Unity and the Roman Question: Also, Mexico, Maximilian, and the Monroe Doctrine* (Rochester: Democrat Steam Printing House, 1865), 19–24.

27. Montgomery Blair, *The Monroe Doctrine: Speech of Hon. Montgomery Blair at Hagerstown, MD, on 12th July, 1865. Exposing the Alliance of the American Secretary of State with Louis Napoleon to Overthrow the Monroe Doctrine and Establish a Despotism on This Continent* (Washington, DC: H. Polkinhorn, 1865). Blair had switched to the Republican Party in the 1850s and served in Lincoln's cabinet, but switched back to the Democrats over disagreements concerning Reconstruction.

28. John Jay, *An Imperial Policy Not Fitted for an American Minister: A Letter to J. Bigelow* (Paris: E. Brière, 1866); John Jay, *Union League Club of New York: Address of the President, June 23,*

1866 (New York: n.p., 1866); John Jay, *The Political Situation in the United States: A Letter to the Union League Club of New York* (London: Rivington, Waterloo Place, 1866).

29. *Proceedings of a Meeting*, 3; Joshua Leavitt, *The Monroe Doctrine* (New York: S. Tousey, 1863); Teresa Van Hoy, "Mexican Exiles and the Monroe Doctrine, New York and the Borderlands, 1865," *Camino Real: Estudios de Las Hispanidades Norteamericanas* 7, no. 10 (2015): 39–60.

30. *Proceedings of a Meeting*, 33.

31. For a collection of such songs, see "Civil War Sheet Music Collection," Library of Congress, Washington, DC, https://www.loc.gov/collections/civil-war-sheet-music/. Cited songs include Joseph Philbrick Webster and E. B. Dewing, *Get Out of Mexico: Song and Chorus* (Chicago: Lyon and Healy, 1866); Bob Barkis and James Wrigley, *Oh! I Vants to Go Home, or, Maximilian's Lament* (New York: J. Wrigley, 1865); George Cooper and Tucker, *We'll Go with Grant Again: Song of the Sons of Monroe* (New York: Wm. A. Pond, 1866); Captain F.W.A., *Song of the Sons of Monroe!* (New York: Francis Hart, 1866). I am grateful to Ricardo Reséndiz for sharing a copy of his thesis on this subject: "¡Fuera de México! La doctrina Monroe en las representaciones estadounidenses sobre el Segundo Imperio Mexicano" (MA thesis, Universidad de Guanajuato, 2019).

32. Webster and Dewing, *Get Out of Mexico*.

33. "Crusaders for Saint Monroe," *NYT*, May 12, 1865; Brown, "Guns over the Border," 65–70; Miller, "Arms across the Border," 34; Robert Ryal Miller, "The American Legion of Honor in Mexico," *Pacific Historical Review* 30, no. 3 (1961): 230.

34. "The Slavery Question in Cuba," *New York Herald*, May 22, 1865.

35. "Crusaders for Saint Monroe," *NYT*, May 12, 1865; "Revival of Filibustering," *NYT*, May 9, 1865; Brown, "Guns over the Border," 69–70. On Ortega and his claim to Mexico's presidency, see Ralph Roeder, *Juarez and His Mexico: A Biographical History* (New York: Viking Press, 1947), 611–14.

36. Romero, *Correspondencia*, 9:929, entry for April 26, 1867; Lawrence Douglas Taylor Hansen, "Voluntarios Extranjeros en los Ejércitos Liberales Mexicanos, 1854–1867," *Historia Mexicana* 37, no. 2 (1987): 224; Brown, "Guns over the Border," 86; for estimates of U.S. volunteers for Maximilian, see Miller, "Arms across the Border," 229, on imperialist volunteers. When Charles Sumner told Matías Romero that the United States had forced the French out of Mexico, Romero answered that America's "moral influence had been one of several factors compelling Napoleon to withdraw"; see Romero, *Mexican Lobby*, 157.

37. Brown, "Guns over the Border," 57, 153, 154; Roeder, *Juarez*, 601; Michael Hogan, *Abraham Lincoln and Mexico: A History of Courage, Intrigue and Unlikely Friendships*, 2016, Kindle loc. 1807–13; Rippy, *The United States and Mexico*, 268; Perkins, *Monroe Doctrine*, 2:448–49.

38. Sheridan, *Personal Memoirs*, 2:215.

39. Roeder, *Juarez*, 606–11; M. M. McAllen, *Maximilian and Carlota: Europe's Last Empire in Mexico* (San Antonio: Trinity University Press, 2014), 207–8.

40. Sheridan to Grant, New Orleans, November 5, 1865, *War of the Rebellion*, ser. 1, vol. 48, part 2, 1252–53, spelling as in the original.

41. On Confederate colonization plans, see Hallie M. McPherson, "The Plan of William McKendree Gwin for a Colony in North Mexico, 1863–1865," *Pacific Historical Review* 2, no. 4

(1933): 357–86; Alfred J. Hanna and Kathryn Abbey Hanna, "The Immigration Movement of the Intervention and Empire as Seen through the Mexican Press," *Hispanic American Historical Review* 27, no. 2 (1947): 220–46; Hanna and Hanna, *Napoleon III and Mexico*, xvii, 170–81; Andrew F. Rolle, *The Lost Cause: The Confederate Exodus to Mexico* (1965; Norman: University of Oklahoma Press, 1992), 62–65; Todd W. Wahlstrom, *Southern Exodus to Mexico: Migration across the Borderlands after the American Civil War* (Lincoln: University of Nebraska Press, 2015); Jeremi Suri, *Civil War by Other Means: America's Long and Unfinished Fight for Democracy* (New York: Public Affairs, 2022), chap. 3; Sheridan to Grant, New Orleans, August 1, 1865, Dept. et al., *War of the Rebellion*, ser. 1, vol. 48, p. 1147.

42. Bigelow to Drouyn de Lhuys, Paris, July 26, 1865, Bigelow, *Retrospections: 1865–66*, 3:119–21.

43. Napoleon III to Bazaine, August 17, 1865, quoted in Paul Gaulot, *La vérité sur l'expédition du Mexique d'après les documents inédits de Ernest Louet*, vol. 2 (Paris: Ollendorff, 1890), 257–59.

44. Sheridan, *Personal Memoirs*, 2:215–17; Roeder, *Juarez*, 615–17.

45. Schofield, *Forty-Six Years*, 339–40, 378–98; Donald B. Connelly, *John M. Schofield and the Politics of Generalship* (Chapel Hill: University of North Carolina Press, 2006), 182–86; John Holladay Latané, *The United States and Latin America* (New York: Doubleday, Page, 1920), 225–26; Perkins, *Monroe Doctrine*, 2:474.

46. Schofield, *Forty-Six Years*, 385; Malakoff, "The Mystery of Gen. Schofield's Visit," *NYT*, December 31, 1865; Albert Joseph Griffin, "Intelligence versus Impulse: William H. Seward and the Threat of War with France over Mexico, 1861–1867" (PhD diss., University of New Hampshire, 2003), 120–21.

47. Schofield, *Forty-Six Years*, 378–98, banquet toast, 386–87; Connelly, *Schofield*, 183–86; Malakoff, "How Thanksgiving Day Was Kept in Paris," *NYT*, December 23, 1865; Malakoff, "Thanksgiving Day at the French Capital," *NYT*, December 24, 1865.

48. Bigelow to Seward, Paris, December 8, 1865, Bigelow, *Retrospections: 1865–66*, 3:265–67.

49. Seward told Bigelow Schofield's mission was a ruse to get him out of Grant's hands; see Bigelow, *Retrospections: 1867–1871*, 4:42. This view was amplified in Seward's biography, Bancroft, *Seward*, 2:435. For more convincing interpretations of Schofield's effectiveness, see Perkins, *Monroe Doctrine*, 2:500–501, and Henry M. Wriston, *Executive Agents in American Foreign Relations* (Baltimore: Johns Hopkins University Press, 1929), 780–81; Griffin, "Intelligence versus Impulse."

50. "Andrew Johnson: First Annual Message, December 4, 1865," http://www.presidency.ucsb.edu/ws/index.php?pid=29506; Stahr, *Seward*, 445, 450–51; Hans L. Trefousse, *Andrew Johnson: A Biography* (New York: Norton, 1997), 270; Miller, "Arms across the Border," 15.

51. Seward to Bigelow, December 16, 1865, *FRUS*, 1865, 429. For a full analysis of Seward's changing policy on Mexico, see James Morton Callahan, *Evolution of Seward's Mexican Policy* (Morgantown: West Virginia University, 1908); Frank Edward Lally, *French Opposition to the Mexican Policy of the Second Empire* (Baltimore: Johns Hopkins Press, 1931), 111, 147, 159; cf. Clyde Augustus Duniway, "Reasons for the Withdrawal of the French from Mexico," *Annual Report of the American Historical Association for the Year 1902* 1 (1903): 2:514–16.

52. Lally, *French Opposition*; Perkins, *Monroe Doctrine*, 132–38; Bigelow, *Retrospections: 1865–66*, 3:497–98, 497 (quote).

53. Arnold Blumberg, "The Diplomacy of the Mexican Empire, 1863–1867," *Transactions of the American Philosophical Society* 61, no. 8 (1971): 89–90; Robert Ryal Miller, "Lew Wallace and the French Intervention in Mexico," *Indiana Magazine of History* 59, no. 1 (March 1963): 31–50; Stanton to Seward, Washington City, January 19, 1866, and enclosures on the Bagdad raid, *FRUS*, 1866 (Washington, DC: GPO, 1866), 275–77; Cruz García, "La invasión al puerto de Bagdad en enero de 1866," *Relatos e Historias en México*, March 31, 2020, https:// relatosehistorias.mx/nuestras-historias/la-invasion-al-puerto-de-bagdad-en-enero-de-1866; Edward Shawcross, *The Last Emperor of Mexico: The Dramatic Story of the Habsburg Archduke Who Created a Kingdom in the New World* (New York: Basic Books, 2021), 203–4; Ernst Pitner, *Maximilian's Lieutenant: A Personal History of the Mexican Campaign, 1864–7* (Albuquerque: University of New Mexico Press, 1993), 105–8. I am grateful to Professor Stève Sainlaude for sharing correspondence from France's minister to the United States, Montholon, warning France that war with the United States might erupt and referring to the Bagdad incident as proof of France's fragile position in Mexico; he cites Montholon to Drouyn de Lhuys, August 24, 1866.

54. "Ouverture de la session legislative de 1866," *Gazette nationale ou le Moniteur universel*, January 23, 1866; English translation, "Speech of the Emperor at the Opening of the Legislature," *NYT*, February 8, 1866.

55. "Overture 1866"; "Speech of the Emperor"; Schofield, *Forty-Six Years*, 345; for diplomatic correspondence surrounding the French decision, see Malakoff, "The Mexican Question Thought to Be Settled," *NYT*, February 16, 1866.

56. Seward to Bigelow, October 8, November 8, 1866, and Seward to Bigelow, November 23, 1866, Bigelow, *Retrospections: 1865–66*, 3:571–73, 598–600, 609–11.

57. Sheridan, *Personal Memoirs*, 2:224–26.

58. Brown, "Guns over the Border," 156–207; Robert Ryal Miller, "Herman Sturm: Hoosier Secret Agent for Mexico," *Indiana Magazine of History* 58, no. 1 (1962): 1–15; Herman Sturm, *The Republic of Mexico and Its American Creditors* (Indianapolis: Douglass and Conner, 1869), 20. Wallace later became famous as author of *Ben-Hur: A Tale of the Christ* (New York: Harper and Brothers, 1880).

59. McAllen, *Maximilian and Carlota*, 246–47; Emilio Velasco, *Documentos relativos a la batalla de Santa Gertrudis* (Matamoros: Segura y Ambros, 1866), 1; Pitner, *Maximilian's Lieutenant*, 124–25, 130–37.

60. Benito Juárez, *Documentos, Discursos y Correspondencia*, ed. Jorge L. Tamayo, vol. 11 (México: Editorial Libros de México, 1972), 239.

61. Sheridan, *Personal Memoirs*, 2:224–26; Velasco, *Santa Gertrudis*, 4; Pitner, *Maximilian's Lieutenant*, 140–41.

62. Brown, "Guns over the Border," 171; Miller, "Lew Wallace"; Miller, "Herman Sturm"; McAllen, *Maximilian and Carlota*, 246–47; William Lee Richter, "The Army in Texas during Reconstruction, 1865–1870" (PhD diss., Louisiana State University, 1970), 72, on U.S. soldiers at Santa Gertrudis.

63. Hanna and Hanna, *Napoleon III and Mexico*, 277–78; McAllen, *Maximilian and Carlota*, 273.

64. McAllen, *Maximilian and Carlota*, 317–18.

65. Richard Hill and Peter Hogg, *A Black Corps d'Elite: An Egyptian Sudanese Conscript Battalion with the French Army in Mexico, 1863–1867, and Its Survivors in Subsequent African History* (East Lansing: Michigan State University Press, 1995), 29–53, 89–93.

66. Steven McGregor, "Seward's Corollary to the Monroe Doctrine, 1863–1866," *International History Review* 43, no. 5 (2021): 1.

67. Bigelow to de Luhys, November 22, 1865, Seward to Hale, December 14, 1865, Hale to Seward, Alexandria, January 18, 1866, all in *FRUS*, 1865, 482, 259, 264; Arnold Blumberg, "William Seward and the Egyptian Intervention in Mexico," *Smithsonian Journal of History* (Winter 1967): 31–48.

68. Seward to Bigelow, November 23, 1866, *FRUS*, 1866, 366; Edwin C. Fishel, "A Cable from Napoleon," *Studies in Intelligence* 2, no. 3 (September 22, 1993).

69. Seward to Bigelow, November 23, 1866, *FRUS*, 1866, 366–67; Bigelow to Seward, Paris, December 3, 1866, *FRUS*, 1866, 368–69; Perkins, *Monroe Doctrine*, 2:534–36.

70. Seward to Bigelow, November 23, 1866, *FRUS*, 1866, 366–67; Bigelow to Seward, Paris, December 3, 1866, *FRUS*, 1866, 368–69; Perkins, *Monroe Doctrine*, 2:534–36.

71. McAllen, *Maximilian and Carlota*.

72. McAllen, *Maximilian and Carlota*, 321–22; Seaton Schroeder, *The Fall of Maximilian's Empire, as Seen from a United States Gun-Boat* (New York: G. P. Putnam Sons, 1887), 22–24.

73. Green's account is found in "A Complimentary Banquet," *Daily Alta California*, February 28, 1885; Mexican accounts of Maximilian's surrender do not mention any U.S. personnel involved; see Juan de Dios Arias, *Reseña histórica de la formación y operaciones del cuerpo de Ejército del Norte durante la intervención francésa, sitio de Querétaro y noticias oficiales sobre la captura de Maximiliano, su proceso íntegro y su muerte* (México: N. Chávez, 1867). Other accounts verify the Legion of Honor or some other American presence at the surrender: Ethel Alec-Tweedie, *Mexico as I Saw It* (London: Hurst and Blackett, 1901), 269–70; Albert S. Evans, *Our Sister Republic: A Gala Trip through Tropical Mexico in 1869–70* (Hartford: Columbian Book Co., 1871), 232; Jasper Godwin Ridley, *Maximilian and Juárez* (New York: Ticknor and Fields, 1992), 262; Elizabeth Wormeley Latimer, *France in the Nineteenth Century, 1830–1890*, 6th ed. (Chicago: A. C. McClurg, 1898), 208; Miller, "American Legion," 238.

74. For letters from Garibaldi, Hugo, Seward, and others, see Benito Juárez, *Documentos, discursos y correspondencia*, ed. Jorge L. Tamayo, vol. 12 (México: Editorial Libros de México, 1974), 182–98; Ridley, *Maximilian and Juárez*, 272–73; Schroeder, *Fall of Maximilian's Empire*, 92–102; "Victor Hugo's Address to Juarez," *NYT*, July 9, 1867.

75. Benito Juárez, *Manifiesto justificativo de los castigos nacionales en Querétaro*, ed. Isaí Tejeda Vallejo (Mexico City: M. Á. Porrúa, 2010), 34, 35 (quotes); Brian R. Hamnett, *Juárez* (London: Longman, 1994), 194.

76. "Manifiesto de Benito Juárez al volver a la capital de la república," July 15, 1867, in Juárez, *Documentos*, 12:272–74.

77. Brian R. Hamnett, *A Concise History of Mexico* (New York: Cambridge University Press, 2006), 170–71. For a detailed description of the execution, see McAllen, *Maximilian and Carlota*, chaps. 21, 22.

78. Evans, *Our Sister Republic*, 237. In 1900, Mexico permitted the Austrian government to memorialize the execution site with a small stone chapel and a portrait of Maximilian.

79. "Mexico: The Legion of Honor and Mexican Gratitude," *NYT*, January 19, 1868.

80. Evans, *Our Sister Republic*, 278.

81. William H. Seward, *Seward at Washington as Senator and Secretary of State: A Memoir of His Life, with Selections from His Letters, 1861–1872*, ed. Frederick William Seward, vol. 2 (New York: Derby and Miller, 1891), 455–56.

82. Evans, *Our Sister Republic*, 280–82.

CHAPTER 4. RUSSIA EXITS

1. "The Reform Struggle in Russia," *NYT*, March 9, 1865; see also "The Good Understanding with Russia," *NYT*, March 3, 1865. On U.S.-Russian relations, see Albert A. Woldman, *Lincoln and the Russians* (Cleveland: World Publishing Company, 1952); Norman E. Saul, *Distant Friends: The United States and Russia, 1763–1867* (Lawrence: University Press of Kansas, 1991), chap. 6; and David E. Shi, "Seward's Attempt to Annex British Columbia, 1865–1869," *Pacific Historical Review* 47, no. 2 (1978): 217–38.

2. "St. Petersburgh and Cherbourg: A Transatlantic Echo from Our War," *NYT*, November 26, 1865; "Russia and the United States," *NYT*, June 14, 1865; "What Russians Think of an Alliance with the United States," *NYT*, October 13, 1866; Saul, *Distant Friends*; Peter Kolchin, "Reexamining Southern Emancipation in Comparative Perspective," *Journal of Southern History* 81, no. 1 (2015): 7–40. On Seward's foreign policy, see Joseph A. Fry, *Lincoln, Seward, and US Foreign Relations in the Civil War Era* (Lexington: University Press of Kentucky, 2019), 25–27.

3. More recent studies of the Alaska Purchase have moved beyond this script but rarely situate it within the larger geopolitical shift that challenged the presence of European empires in the Americas. See Lee A. Farrow, *Seward's Folly: A New Look at the Alaska Purchase* (Fairbanks: University of Alaska Press, 2016); Michael A. Hill, "Myth of Seward's Folly," *Western Historical Quarterly* 50, no. 1 (Spring 2019): 43–64; Saul, *Distant Friends*; Ronald J. Jensen, *The Alaska Purchase and Russian-American Relations* (Seattle: University of Washington Press, 1975); Richard Emerson Neunherz, "The Purchase of Russian America: Reasons and Reactions" (PhD diss., University of Washington, 1975).

4. John Bigelow, *Retrospections of an Active Life: 1867–1871*, vol. 4 (New York: Doubleday, Page, 1913), 53.

5. Walter LaFeber, *The New Empire: An Interpretation of American Expansion, 1860–1898* (Ithaca: Cornell University Press, 1963), 28–31, 408; Ernest N. Paolino, *The Foundations of the American Empire: William Henry Seward and U.S. Foreign Policy* (Ithaca: Cornell University Press, 1973), chaps. 5, 6; Anthony G. Hopkins, *American Empire: A Global History* (Princeton: Princeton University Press, 2019), 305; Steven Hahn, *A Nation without Borders: The United States and Its World in an Age of Civil Wars, 1830–1910* (New York: Viking, 2016), 399.

6. Michael Knox Beran, *Forge of Empires, 1861–1871: Three Revolutionary Statesmen and the World They Made* (New York: Free Press, 2007), 155–56; Woldman, *Lincoln and the Russians*, 128–29.

7. S. A. Bent, "Gortschakoff," in *Familiar Short Sayings of Great Men*, 1887, https://www.bartleby.com/344/196.html. Note: English spellings of this Russian statesman's name vary.

8. Neunherz, "Purchase of Russian America," 59–60.

9. Frank Alfred Golder, "The American Civil War through the Eyes of a Russian Diplomat," *American Historical Review* 26, no. 3 (April 1921); Max M. Laserson, *The American Impact on Russia, Diplomatic and Ideological, 1784–1917* (New York: Collier, 1962), 169–72.

10. Frank A. Golder, "Russian-American Relations during the Crimean War," *American Historical Review* 31, no. 3 (1926): 464; Golder, "Russian Diplomat"; Woldman, *Lincoln and the Russians*, 18.

11. Saul, *Distant Friends*, 339–54; Jensen, *Alaska Purchase*, 30–33. For contemporary accounts of the visit, see "The Russian Banquet," *NYT*, October 20, 1863; "Our Russian Guests," *NYT*, October 2, 1863.

12. Saul, *Distant Friends*, 370.

13. *Tributes of the Nations to Abraham Lincoln* (Washington, DC: GPO, 1867), 679.

14. "Russia and the United States"; David Hecht, *Russian Radicals Look to America, 1825–1894* (New York: Greenwood Press, 1968); Saul, *Distant Friends*, 370n150; Ezekiel Lifschutz, "An English Letter by a Russian Jew Mourning the Death of Abraham Lincoln," *Publications of the American Jewish Historical Society* 50, no. 3 (1961): 248–50.

15. J. F. Loubat, *Narrative of the Mission to Russia, in 1866, of the Hon. Gustavus Vasa Fox, Assistant-Secretary of the Navy*, ed. John D. Champlin (New York: D. Appleton, 1873), 14; Saul, *Distant Friends*, 370–75.

16. Jensen, *Alaska Purchase*, 39–40; Loubat, *Mission to Russia*, 15–16 (resolution); "Thursday, May 3, 1866," *Congressional Globe*, 39th Cong., 1st Sess. (1866): 2353–78.

17. Laserson, *American Impact*, 187–90.

18. "Tuesday, May 8, 1866," *Congressional Globe*, 39th Cong., 1st Sess. (1866): 2443–81. Democratic senator Saulsbury of Delaware challenged Sumner's claim, but his motion to delete the words "by an enemy of emancipation" was voted down and the error remained in the message to Russia. The best account of this is Laserson, *American Impact*, 188–91.

19. Ari Arthur Hoogenboom, *Gustavus Vasa Fox of the Union Navy: A Biography* (Baltimore: Johns Hopkins University Press, 2008), 284–91. For accounts of the Fox expedition, see Laserson, *American Impact*; Edward Kasinec, "The Naval Mission to Russia of Gustavus Vasa Fox," in *The Tsar and the President: Alexander II and Abraham Lincoln, Liberator and Emancipator*, ed. Marilyn Pfeifer Swezey, trans. Robert H. Davis (Washington, DC: American-Russian Cultural Cooperation Foundation, 2008), 39–48.

20. For Welles's instruction to Fox, see Saul, *Distant Friends*, 370–78; Loubat, *Mission to Russia*, 18–19; Jensen, *Alaska Purchase*, 39–44.

21. Hoogenboom, *Fox*, 286; Jensen, *Alaska Purchase*, 40–41.

22. Hoogenboom, *Fox*, 286–87.

23. Department of State, *Russian Account of the Official Mission to Russia of Hon. G. V. Fox in 1866*, trans. S. N. Buynitzky (Washington, DC: GPO, 1867), 32. Fox's report to Welles, a diary of his activities in Russia, is included in this publication, 32–38.

24. Department of State, *Russian Account*, 7.

25. Department of State, *Russian Account*, 6–7; Hoogenboom, *Fox*, 286 (*Times* quote).

26. Department of State, *Russian Account*, 11.

27. Heinrich Fürstnow, *Miantonomoh-Galop* (New York: William A. Pond, 1867). Note: "galop" is a musical term for a fast-paced tune.

28. Department of State, *Russian Account; FRUS*, 1866, 404–22; Saul, *Distant Friends*, 370–71. For an interesting analysis of the toasts and speeches, see Laserson, *American Impact*, chap. 10.

29. Loubat, *Mission to Russia*; Department of State, *Russian Account*, 22, 29.

30. Hoogenboom, *Fox*, 288–89.

31. Loubat, *Mission to Russia*, 180; Laserson, *American Impact*, 194–95.

32. Department of State, *Russian Account*, 36; Hoogenboom, *Fox*, 288.

33. Jensen, *Alaska Purchase*, 43–44, 58–60.

34. David Hunter Miller, *The Alaska Treaty* (Kingston, Ontario: Limestone Press, 1981), 63–65, map in appendices. For an insightful account of the December 16 meeting, see Jensen, *Alaska Purchase*, 58–61.

35. Jensen, *Alaska Purchase*, 62–78; Glyndon G. Van Deusen, *William Henry Seward* (New York: Oxford University Press, 1967), 539–40; Paul S. Holbo, *Tarnished Expansion: The Alaska Scandal, the Press, and Congress, 1867–1871* (Knoxville: University of Tennessee Press, 1983), 104–9.

36. Jensen, *Alaska Purchase*, 77–78; Van Deusen, *Seward*, 539–40.

37. Jensen, *Alaska Purchase*, 73–74. For further details, see Ronald J. Jensen, "The Alaska Purchase and Russian-American Relations" (PhD diss., Indiana University, 1971), 78–79.

38. Jensen, *Alaska Purchase*, 74.

39. Jensen, *Alaska Purchase*, 75–76; Van Deusen, *Seward*, 540–41; Farrow, *Seward's Folly*, 46–47.

40. *Message of President Transmitting Correspondence on Russian America*, 40th Cong., 2nd Sess., HED 177 (Washington, DC: GPO, 1868), 119, quoting the *Washington Evening Star*, December 21, 1867.

41. William H. Seward, *Seward at Washington as Senator and Secretary of State: A Memoir of His Life, with Selections from His Letters, 1861–1872*, ed. Frederick William Seward, vol. 2 (New York: Derby and Miller, 1891), 367; James Morton Callahan, *The Alaska Purchase and Americo-Canadian Relations* (Morgantown: West Virginia University, 1908), 22.

42. Farrow, *Seward's Folly*, 53–70. Bribery played a role in some newspaper coverage; see Holbo, *Tarnished Expansion*.

43. *Correspondence on Russian America*, 44, quoting *New York Herald*, April 29, 1867.

44. *Correspondence on Russian America*, 40, quoting *Philadelphia North American and Gazette*, Friday, April 12, 1867

45. Holbo, *Tarnished Expansion*, 10; David Herbert Donald, *Charles Sumner and the Rights of Man* (1970; New York: Da Capo Press, 1996), 304–5 (quote).

46. Charles Sumner, *Speech of Hon. Charles Sumner, of Massachusetts, on the Cession of Russian America to the United States* (Washington, DC: Congressional Globe, 1867), 13, 16 (quotes).

47. Jensen, *Alaska Purchase*, 79–99, 92 (Senate vote), 100–101 (Sitka ceremony); Holbo, *Tarnished Expansion*, 47–49.

48. Jochen Wierich, *Grand Themes: Emanuel Leutze, Washington Crossing the Delaware, and American History Painting* (University Park: Pennsylvania State University Press, 2012).

49. "The Present Decade," *The Times*, April 2, 1867.

50. "Sale of Russian North America," *Diplomatic Review* 15, no. 5 (May 1, 1867): 68–70.

51. Kenneth Bourne, *Britain and the Balance of Power in North America, 1815–1908* (Berkeley: University of California Press, 1967), 302.

52. Jensen, *Alaska Purchase*, 94–95.

53. Neunherz, "Purchase of Russian America," 95.

54. "Our Relations with America," *NYT*, April 18, 1867, reprint from *Pall Mall Gazette*, April 4, 1867.

55. *Philadelphia North American and Gazette*, April 12, 1867, extract in *Message of President Transmitting Correspondence on Russian America*, 40th Cong., 2nd Sess., HED 177 (Washington, DC: GPO, 1868), 40.

56. Neunherz, "Purchase of Russian America," 207–41; see 166, 171, 248, 386, for examples of the sandwich metaphor.

57. *Message of President on Reciprocal Relations with British Provinces, and Condition of Fisheries*, 39th Cong., 2nd Sess., SED 30 (Washington, DC: GPO, 1867), 64, 19. Derby's report was published separately as E. H. Derby, *Letter to William K. Seward* (Washington, DC: GPO, 1867).

58. Neunherz, "Purchase of Russian America," 212–24.

59. Neunherz, "Purchase of Russian America," 228–29.

CHAPTER 5. HOME RULE FOR CANADA

1. Some of the leading works on Fenians are Lucy E. Salyer, *Under the Starry Flag: How a Band of Irish Americans Joined the Fenian Revolt and Sparked a Crisis over Citizenship* (Cambridge, MA: Harvard University Press, 2018); Christopher Klein, *When the Irish Invaded Canada: The Incredible True Story of the Civil War Veterans Who Fought for Ireland's Freedom* (New York: Doubleday, 2020); Patrick Steward, *The Fenians: Irish Rebellion in the North Atlantic World, 1858–1876* (Knoxville: University of Tennessee Press, 2013); Brian Jenkins, *The Fenian Problem: Insurgency and Terrorism in a Liberal State, 1858–1874* (Montreal: McGill-Queen's University Press, 2008); Niall Whelehan, *The Dynamiters: Irish Nationalism and Political Violence in the Wider World, 1867–1900* (Cambridge: Cambridge University Press, 2012); David Doolin, *Transnational Revolutionaries: The Fenian Invasion of Canada, 1866* (Oxford: Peter Lang, 2016). On British concerns of U.S. aggression after the war, see Palmerston's warning to Queen Victoria, Brian Jenkins, *Fenians and Anglo-American Relations during Reconstruction* (Ithaca: Cornell University Press, 1969), 41–42.

2. Donald F. Warner, *Idea of Continental Union: Agitation for the Annexation of Canada to the United States, 1849–1893* (Lexington: University of Kentucky Press, 1960), 58; John Boyko, *Blood and Daring: How Canada Fought the American Civil War and Forged a Nation* (Toronto: Vintage Canada, 2014), 248; Phillip E. Myers, *Dissolving Tensions: Rapprochement and Resolution in British-American-Canadian Relations in the Treaty of Washington Era, 1865–1914* (Kent: Kent State University Press, 2015).

3. John Darwin, *The Empire Project: The Rise and Fall of the British World-System, 1830–1970* (Cambridge: Cambridge University Press, 2009), 26, 149–59, 177–78, 395–98. Paine made constant use of the family metaphor; see Thomas Paine, *Common Sense* (1776; New York: Peter Eckler, 1922), 31, 32, 45.

4. Donald Creighton, *The Road to Confederation: The Emergence of Canada, 1863–1867* (1964; Don Mills, Ontario: Oxford University Press, 2012), 421–22; Adam Gopnik, *A Thousand Small Sanities: The Moral Adventure of Liberalism* (New York: Basic Books, 2019), 126, 185, 198–99.

5. Adam Mayers, *Dixie and the Dominion: Canada, the Confederacy, and the War for Union* (Toronto: Dundurn, 2003), 105.

6. Mayers, *Dixie and the Dominion*, 108.

7. Robin W. Winks, *Canada and the United States: The Civil War Years*, 4th ed. (Montreal: McGill-Queen's University Press, 1998), 299–301.

8. Boyko, *Blood and Daring*, 179–85.

9. Yves Roby, "The United States and Confederation," in *Roads to Confederation: The Making of Canada, 1867*, ed. Jacqueline D. Krikorian, vol. 2 (Toronto: University of Toronto Press, 2017), 338; Boyko, *Blood and Daring*, 191–92.

10. The diplomatic correspondence with Britain over the clandestine activities of Confederate agents in Canada fills nearly two hundred pages; see *FRUS*, 1865, 1–196; "The Hostility of Canada: The Anglo Rebel Alliance," *NYT*, December 16, 1864. See also, William A. Tidwell, *Come Retribution: The Confederate Secret Service and the Assassination of Lincoln* (Jackson: University Press of Mississippi, 1988), ch. 8.

11. "Hostility of Canada"; Winks, *The Civil War Years*, 318.

12. Roby, "United States and Confederation," 338.

13. William Howard Russell, *Canada: Its Defences, Condition, and Resources* (Boston: T.O.H.P. Burnham, 1865), 80, 200. The book was published in London and Boston as a final volume to Russell's highly influential account of the United States in the first year of war: William Howard Russell, *My Diary North and South*, 2 vols. (London: Bradbury and Evans, 1863).

14. Thomas Rawlings, *Emigration with Special Reference to Minnesota, U.S. and British Columbia* (London: Clayton, 1864), 11; see also George Donald Lillibridge, *Beacon or Freedom: The Impact of American Democracy upon Great Britain, 1830–1870* (Philadelphia: University of Pennsylvania Press, 1955), 62–63.

15. Monadnock, "Interesting Letter from Our London Correspondent," *NYT*, May 5, 1865.

16. Phillip Buckner, "'British North America and a Continent in Dissolution': The American Civil War in the Making of Canadian Confederation," *Journal of the Civil War Era* 7, no. 4 (2017): 512–40; Phillip A. Buckner, ed., *Canada and the British Empire* (New York: Oxford University Press, 2008), 66–86; Lester Burrell Shippee, *Canadian-American Relations, 1849–1874* (New York: Russell and Russell, 1970), 206–7; Bourne, *Britain and the Balance of Power in North America, 1815–1908*, 257.

17. Peter J. Smith, "The Ideological Origins of Canadian Confederation," *Canadian Journal of Political Science/Revue Canadienne de Science Politique* 20, no. 1 (1987): 26.

18. Creighton, *Road to Confederation*, chap. 4. Prince Edward Island sent delegates to the Quebec Convention but chose to stay out of the confederation after that.

19. "A History of the Vote in Canada," Elections Canada, https://www.elections.ca/content.aspx?section=res&dir=his/chap1&document=index&lang=e; Creighton, *Road to Confederation*, chap. 5.

20. P. B. Waite, *The Life and Times of Confederation, 1864–1867: Politics, Newspapers, and the Union of British North America*, Heritage (Toronto: University of Toronto Press, 1962), 323–24, 323 (quote); Creighton, *Road to Confederation*, 141–43. Peter Smith argues for deeper ideological underpinnings to the confederation movement: Smith, "The Ideological Origins of Canadian Confederation."

21. F. Y. Edgeworth and Fred E. Haynes, "The Reciprocity Treaty with Canada of 1854," *Publications of the American Economic Association* 7, no. 6 (November 1892): 7–70.

22. Winks, *The Civil War Years*, 253–54, 279, 293, 303–4, 317, 327, 336, 337, 340, 351–52; Roby, "United States and Confederation," 339, 342; Edgeworth and Haynes, "Reciprocity Treaty," 57.

23. J. G. Snell, "John F. Potter, Consul General to British North America, 1864–1866," *Wisconsin Magazine of History* 55, no. 2 (1971): 110–11.

24. Snell, "Potter," 110–11.

25. Warner, *Continental Union*, 47–48.

26. "Keep Cool," *NYT*, July 22, 1865; "The Provincials and Mr. Consul Potter," *NYT*, July 21, 1865; Snell, "Potter"; Warner, *Continental Union*, chaps. 2, 3, on annexation before and after 1865, 47–49, on Potter affair.

27. John Mitchel, *The Last Conquest of Ireland (Perhaps)* (Glasgow: R. and T. Washbourne, 1861), 219. The American Bishop John Hughes had developed the idea of British responsibility for the famine earlier; see *A Lecture on the Antecedent Causes of the Irish Famine in 1847: Delivered under the Auspices of the General Committee for the Relief of the Suffering Poor of Ireland* (New York: E. Dunigan, 1847). For useful overviews of the Fenian movement, see William D'Arcy, *The Fenian Movement in the United States, 1858–1886* (1946; Washington, DC: Catholic University of America Press, 1971); Salyer, *Under the Starry Flag*; Jenkins, *Fenian Problem*; Jenkins, *Fenians*; Wilfried Neidhardt, *Fenianism in North America* (University Park: Pennsylvania State University Press, 1975).

28. Don H. Doyle, *The Cause of All Nations: An International History of the American Civil War* (New York: Basic Books, 2015), 175. Estimates based on Benjamin Apthorp Gould, *Investigations in the Military and Anthropological Statistics of American Soldiers* (New York: Hurd and Houghton, 1869), 27, 574.

29. Susannah Ural Bruce, *The Harp and the Eagle: Irish-American Volunteers and the Union Army, 1861–1865* (New York: New York University Press, 2006), 54, 55, 80, 105, 148, 190.

30. Adams to Seward, London, September 22, 1865, *FRUS*, 1865, 561–63.

31. Salyer, *Under the Starry Flag*, 40.

32. Salyer, *Under the Starry Flag*, chaps. 1, 2; Steward, *The Fenians*, 76.

33. Salyer, *Under the Starry Flag*, 47; Jenkins, *Fenians*, 86–87.

34. On the U.S. Fenian movement, see Salyer, *Under the Starry Flag*; D'Arcy, *Fenian Movement*; Jenkins, *Fenian Problem*.

35. *Proceedings of the First National Convention of the Fenian Brotherhood Held in Chicago* (Philadelphia: James Gibbons, 1863); "The Irish Convention," *Chicago Daily Tribune*, November 7, 1863. See also, Caleb Richardson, "'The Failure of the Men to Come Up': The Reinvention of Irish-American Nationalism," in *Reconstruction in a Globalizing World*, ed. David Prior (New York: Fordham University Press, 2018), 121–44; for an overview of Irish nationalism, see Robert Kee, *The Green Flag* (London: Penguin, 2000).

36. *Proceedings of the Second National Congress of the Fenian Brotherhood, Held in Cincinnati, Ohio, January, 1865* (Philadelphia: James Gibbons, 1865), 5.

37. Richardson, "Failure," 128.

38. "The Fenian Brothers: Their Monster Gathering Yesterday," *NYT*, July 26, 1865; on Fenian picnics, see also Richardson, "Failure."

39. *The Fenians' Progress: A Vision* (New York: John Bradburn, 1865), 53, 68–91; cf. Richardson, "Failure"; Fenian Brotherhood, *Constitution of the Fenian Brotherhood: Adopted in General Congress at Philadelphia, Penn., October, 1865* (Philadelphia: James Gibbons, 1869); "The Fenian Congress," *NYT*, October 24, 1865.

40. D'Arcy, *Fenian Movement*, 86.

41. "The Fenian Congress: Announcement of the Unconditional Release of John Mitchel Uproarious Delight of the Fenians," *NYT*, October 21, 1865; "John Mitchel and the Fenians," *NYT*, October 24, 1865; Glyndon G. Van Deusen, *William Henry Seward* (New York: Oxford University Press, 1967), 500–501; Jenkins, *Fenians*, 56.

42. D'Arcy, *Fenian Movement*, 84–85; León Ó Broin, *Fenian Fever: An Anglo-American Dilemma* (New York: New York University Press, 1971), 52; Steward, *The Fenians*, 86; Jenkins, *Fenians*, 37–39, 134.

43. William Jenkins, "'Such Bastard Despotism': Fenian Views of Canadian Confederation," in *Globalizing Confederation: Canada and the World in 1867*, ed. Jacqueline D. Krikorian, Marcel Martel, and Adrian Shubert (Toronto: University of Toronto Press, 2017), 65; D'Arcy, *Fenian Movement*, 116, 117.

44. "Canada: The Expected Fenian Invasion," *NYT*, October 28, 1865; "The Fenian Scare in Canada," *NYT*, November 3, 1865; "A Fenian Plot in Canada Discovered," *NYT*, November 13, 1865; "From Canada: The Orangemen Moving," *NYT*, November 5, 1865; "The Fenian Flurry," *NYT*, March 14, 1866; Theodore C. Blegen, "A Plan for the Union of British North America and the United States, 1866," *Mississippi Valley Historical Review* 4, no. 4 (1918): 475.

45. "The Fenian Flurry."

46. "The Crusade against Canada," *The Nation* 2, no. 39 (March 29, 1866): 391–92; see also "The Good Side of Fenianism," *The Nation* 2, no. 36 (March 8, 1866): 295–96.

47. Robert Franklin McGee, *The Fenian Raids on the Huntingdon Frontier, 1866 and 1870* (Quebec: Canadian Gleaner, 1967), quoted in Buckner, "British North America," 524; "The Fenian Revolution," *NYT*, March 15, 1866.

48. Jenkins, "Bastard Despotism," 65–66.

49. D'Arcy, *Fenian Movement*, 136–42, 157–59; Hereward Senior, *The Last Invasion of Canada: The Fenian Raids, 1866–1870* (Toronto: Dundurn Press, 1991), chap. 4; J. G. Lorimer, *History of the Islands and Islets in the Bay of Fundy* (St. Stephen, New Brunswick: Saint Croix Courier, 1876), 83; *To the Fenian Brotherhood of America: Official Report of the Investigating Committee of the Department of Manhattan, Fenian Brotherhood* (New York: J. J. Duff and P. Daily, 1866).

50. D'Arcy, *Fenian Movement*, 153–57; Senior, *Last Invasion of Canada*, 45.

51. John O'Neill, *Official Report of Gen. John O'Neill* (New York: J. J. Forbes, 1870), 37–38; Richardson, "Failure."

52. Boyko, *Blood and Daring*, 271.

53. Neidhardt, *Fenianism in North America*, 61.

54. O'Neill, *Official Report of Gen. John O'Neill*, 39; Senior, *Last Invasion of Canada*, 59–89.

55. Senior, *Last Invasion of Canada*, 59, 88.

56. O'Neill, *Official Report of Gen. John O'Neill*, 40–41.

57. Disraeli to Darby, London, September 30, 1866, Benjamin Disraeli, *Benjamin Disraeli Letters*, ed. Michel Walter Parand, vol. 9 (Toronto: University of Toronto Press, 2013), 158–59.

58. Galt to his wife, London, January 14, 1867, quoted in Creighton, *Road to Confederation*, 430.

59. Creighton, *Road to Confederation*, 421–22; Darwin, *Empire Project*, 26, 149–59, 177–78, 395–98; Gopnik, *A Thousand Small Sanities*, 126, 185, 198–99.

60. Creighton, *Road to Confederation*, 422–23.

61. Warner, *Continental Union*, 65–66.

62. Creighton, *Road to Confederation*, 422–23.

63. "Wednesday, March 27, 1867," *Congressional Globe*, 1867, 372–98.

64. Queen Victoria, *The Letters of Queen Victoria*, ed. George Earle Buckle, vol. 4 (Cambridge: Cambridge University Press, 2014), 394; George Macaulay Trevelyan, *British History in the Nineteenth Century (1782–1901)* (London: Longmans, Green, 1922), 337.

65. *The Times*, April 2, 1867, "The Present Decade," 9; *Correspondence on Russian America*, 118–19.

66. Creighton, *Road to Confederation*, 422–24.

67. Hansard, HC, February 28, 1867 (Bright quote).

68. Warner, *Continental Union*, 57 (quote); "British North America Act 1867" (Queen's Printer of Acts of Parliament), https://www.legislation.gov.uk/ukpga/Vict/30-31/3/enacted.

69. Doris W. Dashew, "The Story of an Illusion: The Plan to Trade the Alabama Claims for Canada," *Civil War History* 15, no. 4 (1969): 335–37; Boyko, *Blood and Daring*, 295.

70. Warner, *Continental Union*, 70–73.

71. Dashew, "The Story of an Illusion," 343–44.

72. Dashew, "The Story of an Illusion," 344–46.

73. Dashew, "The Story of an Illusion," 348; Myers, *Dissolving Tensions*, chaps. 11, 12, 13; C. P. Stacey, "Britain's Withdrawal from North America 1864–1871," *The Canadian Historical Review* 36, no. 3 (1955): 185–98.

CHAPTER 6. AVANZA LINCOLN

1. Kinley J. Brauer, "Gabriel García y Tassara and the American Civil War: A Spanish Perspective," *Civil War History* 21, no. 1 (1975): 9; Dexter Perkins, *The Monroe Doctrine, 1826–1867*, vol. 2 (Baltimore: Johns Hopkins University Press, 1933), 301–302n62.

2. Anne Eller, *We Dream Together: Dominican Independence, Haiti, and the Fight for Caribbean Freedom* (Durham: Duke University Press, 2016); Alfred J. Hanna and Kathryn A. Hanna, *Napoleon III and Mexico: American Triumph over Monarchy* (Chapel Hill: University of North Carolina Press, 1971); Don H. Doyle, *The Cause of All Nations: An International History of the American Civil War* (New York: Basic Books, 2015), chap. 5.

3. William Columbus Davis, *The Last Conquistadores: The Spanish Intervention in Peru and Chile, 1863–1866* (Athens: University of Georgia Press, 1950), 9–12; Robert Ryal Miller, *For Science and National Glory: The Spanish Scientific Expedition to America, 1862–1866* (Norman: Uni-

versity of Oklahoma Press, 1968). For the text of the secret instructions, see Pedro de Novo y Colson, *Historia de la Guerra de España en el Pacífico* (Madrid: Fortanet, 1882), 86–87 (last quote); and Benjamín Vicuña Mackenna, *Historia de la guerra de Chile con España (de 1863 a 1866)* (Santiago de Chile: Victoria de H. Izquierdo, 1883), 16–17.

4. Davis, *Last Conquistadores*, 14–16, 21–24; F. E. Cerruti, *Peru and Spain* (London: Williams and Norgate, 1864).

5. Davis, *Last Conquistadores*, 9–12, 22, 54; Wayne H. Bowen, *Spain and the American Civil War* (Columbia: University of Missouri Press, 2011), 144, 147.

6. Davis, *Last Conquistadores*, 115–17; Robert W. Frazer, "The Role of the Lima Congress, 1864–1865, in the Development of Pan-Americanism," *Hispanic American Historical Review* 29, no. 3 (1949): 319–48. See also, M. Jenaro Carrillo, *Perú y España: Documentos relativos a los últimos sucesos ocurridos en el Perú* (Panama: Star and Herald, 1864); Ministerio de Relaciones Exteriores, *Cuestión entre el Perú y la España* (Lima: Imprenta del gobierno, 1864); *Publicaciones de la Sociedad Democrática de los Amigos de América* 1–4 (New York: Julian M. Casamena, 1864–65).

7. Davis, *Last Conquistadores*, 217–22, 304–6, chap. 13.

8. "The Monroe Doctrine: Meeting at the Cooper Institute," *NYT*, January 8, 1866. Note: Chili was the common spelling at this time. See also "'Traveler's Club' Lecture by Senor Don Benjamin Vicuna Mackenna," *NYT*, December 4, 1865; Daniel J. Hunter, [Benjamín Vicuña Mackenna], *A Sketch of Chili* (New York: S. Hallet, 1866).

9. Eller, *We Dream Together*, 221–28; Perkins, *Monroe Doctrine*, 2:307–8; "Advices from Santo Domingo and Hayti," *NYT*, July 4, 1865.

10. James W. Cortada, "Spain and the American Civil War: Relations at Mid-Century, 1855–1868," *Transactions of the American Philosophical Society* 70, no. 4 (1980): 30–41; Eller, *We Dream Together*; Frank Moya Pons, *The Dominican Republic: A National History* (Princeton: Markus Wiener, 1998), 197–218; Perkins, *Monroe Doctrine*, 2:306; David G. Yuengling, *Highlights in the Debates in the Spanish Chamber of Deputies Relative to the Abandonment of Santo Domingo* (Washington, DC: Murray and Heister, 1941), 6–12, 140, vote.

11. Eller, *We Dream Together*, 221–28; Perkins, *Monroe Doctrine*, 2:307–8; "Advices from Santo Domingo and Hayti."

12. Laurindo Lapuente, *Republicanas* (Buenos Aires: Mayo, 1865), 98 (my translation). This collection is filled with stirring poems expressing Latin American republican convictions.

13. Hovey to Seward, Lima, May 13, 1866, *FRUS*, 1866, 638–41. Note: torpedoes at this time meant underwater explosives fixed in place.

14. Seward to Hale, June 30, 1866, quoted in Davis, *Last Conquistadores*, 324–25.

15. Seward to Perry, August 22, 1865, *FRUS*, 1865, 552–53; Perry to Seward, Madrid, September 4, 1866, Davis, *Last Conquistadores*, 328, 331.

16. Hovey to Seward, Lima, May 13, 1866, *FRUS*, 1866 (Washington, DC: GPO, 1866), 638–41; Hovey to Fish, August 22, 1870, *FRUS*, 1870 (Washington, DC: GPO, 1870), 504–7; "The Bombardment of Callao: Spanish Barbarism," *NYT*, June 1, 1866; Cortada, "Spain and the American Civil War," 99–100; Davis, *Last Conquistadores*, chaps. 17, 18; 319–20, 330 (on Hovey).

17. Sickles to Fish, Madrid, June 26, 1870, *Presidential Message on Emancipation of Slaves in Cuba*, 41st Cong., 2nd Sess., SED 113 (Washington, DC: GPO, 1870), 16.

18. Emeterio S. Santovenia, "Reaffirmation of the Colonial Regime," in *A History of the Cuban Nation: Break with the Mother Country, 1837–1868*, ed. Ramiro Guerra et al., trans. James J. O'Mailia, vol. 4 (Havana: Editorial Historia de la Nación Cubana, 1958), 33 (quote); Roderick Hiram Conrad, "Spanish-United States Relations, 1868–1874" (PhD diss., University of Georgia, 1969), 25–26; Luis Martinez-Fernandez, *Fighting Slavery in the Caribbean: The Life and Times of a British Family in Nineteenth-Century Havana* (Armonk, NY: M. E. Sharpe, 1998), 40, 46; Arthur Corwin, *Spain and the Abolition of Slavery in Cuba, 1817–1886* (Austin: University of Texas Press, 1967), 115–21; Alexander von Humboldt, *The Island of Cuba*, trans. J. S. Thrasher (New York: Derby and Jackson, 1856), 86.

19. Santovenia, "Reaffirmation of the Colonial Regime," 33 (quote); Corwin, *Spain and Abolition*, 156 (population); Luis Martinez-Fernandez, "Political Change in the Spanish Caribbean during the United States Civil War and Its Aftermath, 1861–1878," *Caribbean Studies* 27, no. 1/2 (1994): 38–39.

20. Shufeldt to Seward, Havana, October 12, 1862, confidential, NARA, RG 59, Consular Dispatches from Cuba, T-20: 46. Shufeldt spoke Spanish and was, in accordance with Seward's instructions to all consuls and diplomats, able to report on popular sentiment. See Frederick C. Drake and R. W. Shufeldt, "Secret History of the Slave Trade to Cuba Written by an American Naval Officer, Robert Wilson Schufeldt, 1861," *Journal of Negro History* 55, no. 3 (1970): 220.

21. Savage to Seward, Havana, October 3, 1863, July 2, 1864, quoted in Dale T. Graden, *Disease, Resistance, and Lies: The Demise of the Transatlantic Slave Trade to Brazil and Cuba* (Baton Rouge: Louisiana State University Press, 2014), 199–202, 209.

22. Shufeldt to Seward, Havana, October 12, 1862, quoted in Martinez-Fernandez, "Political Change," 39–40; Assuntos Políticos, file 26, p. 13, Biblioteca Nacional, Havana, Cuba. Thanks to Aisnara and María de los Ángeles for their excellent research assistance.

23. Philip S. Foner, *A History of Cuba and Its Relations with the United States*, vol. 2 (New York: International Publishers, 1962), 135, quoting Carlos Rafael Rodriquez; see also Corwin, *Spain and Abolition*, 140.

24. Martinez-Fernandez, "Political Change," 46 (quote); see also Corwin, *Spain and Abolition*, 162–63.

25. Emeterio S. Santovenia, *Lincoln* (Buenos Aires: Editorial Amicalee, 1948), 465.

26. Santovenia, *Lincoln*, 465; Ada Ferrer, *Cuba: An American History* (New York: Scribner, 2021), 120–21.

27. Santovenia, *Lincoln*, 465–66; *Causa celebre: Asesinato del Presidente Lincoln, y atentados contra Mr. Seward y otros* (Habana: Diario de la Marina, 1865); see also James W. Cortada, "Spanish Views on Abraham Lincoln, 1861–1865," *Lincoln Herald* 76, no. 2 (June 1974): 84; Emeterio S. Santovenia, "Pasión Cubana por Lincoln," *Revista de la Biblioteca Nacional Jose Martí* 4, no. 1 (March 1953).

28. Corwin, *Spain and Abolition*, 154–61, 176; Christopher Schmidt-Nowara, *Empire and Antislavery: Spain, Cuba, and Puerto Rico, 1833–1874* (Pittsburgh: University of Pittsburgh Press, 1999), chap. 5; Christopher Schmidt-Nowara, "From Aggression to Crisis: The Spanish Empire in the 1860s," in *American Civil Wars: The United States, Latin America, Europe, and the Crisis of the 1860s*, ed. Don H. Doyle (Chapel Hill: University of North Carolina Press, 2017), 136; Harriet Beecher Stowe, *La choza del negro Tomás o vida de los negros, en el sur de los Estados Unidos*

(Madrid: José Marés, 1853); Harriet Beecher Stowe, *La Llave de la cabaña del tío Tom: Segunda parte de la célebre novela de Enriqueta Beecher Stowe,* trans. Gregorio Amado Larrosa (Barcelona: Vicente Castaños, 1855).

29. Corwin, *Spain and Abolition,* 154–61, 176; Schmidt-Nowara, *Empire and Antislavery,* chap. 5; Schmidt-Nowara, "From Aggression to Crisis," 136; Stowe, *La choza del negro Tomás;* Stowe, *Llave de la cabaña del tío Tom.*

30. A. Taylor Milne, "The Lyons-Seward Treaty of 1862," *American Historical Review* 38, no. 3 (1933): 511–25, 512 (quote); Seymour Drescher, *Abolition: A History of Slavery and Antislavery* (New York: Cambridge University Press, 2009), 328–29; Don E. Fehrenbacher and Ward McAfee, *The Slaveholding Republic: An Account of the United States Government's Relations to Slavery* (New York: Oxford University Press, 2001), 189–90; Arthur Corwin, *Spain and the Abolition of Slavery in Cuba, 1817–1886* (Austin: University of Texas Press, 1967), 147, 181, chap. 11; Leonardo Marques, *The United States and the Transatlantic Slave Trade to the Americas, 1776–1867* (New Haven: Yale University Press, 2016), 244–60; David R. Murray, *Odious Commerce: Britain, Spain and the Abolition of the Cuban Slave Trade* (Cambridge: Cambridge University Press, 1980), 244.

31. Corwin, *Spain and Abolition,* 162–63.

32. Corwin, *Spain and Abolition,* 185, 189–93. I have adopted Corwin's convenient appellation, the Colonial Reform Commission; see also Schmidt-Nowara, *Empire and Antislavery,* 106–8.

33. Corwin, *Spain and Abolition,* 190–93, 198–99, 287.

34. *Información sobre reformas en Cuba y Puerto Rico* (New York: Hallet and Breen, 1867), 2:249.

35. Corwin, *Spain and Abolition,* 202–5, 204 (quote).

36. J.C.M. Ogelsby, "The Cuban Autonomist Movement's Perception of Canada, 1865–1898: Its Implication," *The Americas* 48, no. 4 (1992): 445–61; Josep Maria Fradera, "Canadian Lessons, Roads Not Taken: Spanish Views on Confederation," in *Globalizing Confederation: Canada and the World in 1867,* ed. Jacqueline D. Krikorian, Marcel Martel, and Adrian Shubert (Toronto: University of Toronto Press, 2017), 143–58; *Información sobre reformas,* 1:198, 2:87, 110, 132; Corwin, *Spain and Abolition,* 206–14; Catherine Davies and Sarah Sánchez, "Rafael María de Labra and *La Revista Hispano-Americana* 1864–1867: Revolutionary Liberalism and Colonial Reform," *Bulletin of Spanish Studies* 87, no. 7 (November 1, 2010): 918, 922, 928–30.

37. Vidal Morales y Morales, ed., "Manifiesto de la junta revolutionaria de la isla de Cuba, dirigido a sus compatriotas de todas las naciones," in *Iniciadores y Primeros Martires de la Revolucion Cubana,* vol. 3 (Habana: Cultural, 1931), 501–10; Franklin W. Knight, "Colonial Response to the Glorious Revolution in Spain: The 'Grito de Yara,'" in *La Revolución de 1868: Historia, pensamiento, literatura,* ed. Clara E. Lida and Iris M. Zavala (New York: Las Américas, 1970), 196–206.

38. James J. O'Kelly, *The Mambi-Land* (New York: J. B. Lippincott, 1874), 242–43; Néstor Carbonell and Emeterio S. Santovenia, *Carlos Manuel de Cespedes: apuntes biograficos* (Havana: Seoane y Fernández, 1919), 8–9; Rafael Vidal Delgado and Ángel Guinea Cabezas de Herrera, *La sombra americana del general Prim* (Málaga: Rafael Vidal, 2014), 23–24.

39. Affidavit of William C. Tinker, December 11, 1869, *Correspondence between the Department of State and the United States Minister at Madrid and the Consular Representatives of the United*

States in the Island of Cuba, and Other Papers Relating to Cuban Affairs, 41st Cong., 2nd Sess., HED 160 (Washington, DC: GPO, 1870), 175. Note: Due to underfunding, Fish suspended publication of the annual state department publication known as *FRUS*. This is one of several congressional publications that substituted for the annual publication.

40. Santiago Perinat, *Las Guerras Mambisas* (Barcelona: Ediciones Carena, 2008), 141; "St. Domingo: Departure of Dominicans for the Cuban Army, the Annexation Movements," *NYT*, June 8, 1869; Ada Ferrer, *Insurgent Cuba: Race, Nation, and Revolution, 1868–1898* (Chapel Hill: University of North Carolina Press, 1999), 47–54.

41. O'Kelly, *Mambi-Land*, 221.

42. Ferrer, *Insurgent Cuba*, 25–28, 38–39.

43. Antonio Carlo Napoleone Gallenga, *The Pearl of the Antilles* (London: Chapman and Hall, 1873), 18 (quote); Antonio Pirala, *Anales de La Guerra de Cuba*, vol. 1 (Madrid: Felipe González Rojas, 1895), 385; Corwin, *Spain and Abolition*, 230; Jose M. Hernández, *Cuba and the United States: Intervention and Militarism, 1868–1933* (1993; Austin: University of Texas Press, 2013), 6–7.

44. "Cuban Prospects," *New York Tribune*, October 12, 1870.

45. *Presidential Message on Progress of Revolution in, and Political and Civil Condition of Cuba*, 41st Cong., 2nd Sess., SED 7 (Washington, DC: GPO, 1869), 20–21; Hernández, *Cuba and the United States*, 7; Corwin, *Spain and Abolition*, 230–32.

46. Néstor Ponce de León, *The Book of Blood: An Authentic Record of the Policy Adopted by Modern Spain to Put an End to the War for the Independence of Cuba (October, 1868, to December 1870)*, trans. Manuel M. Zarzamendi (New York: M. M. Zarzamendi, 1871).

47. Hall to Fish, Matanzas, June 3, 1869, *Progress of Revolution*, 26.

48. *Progress of Revolution*, 26–39, 58–61, 66, 95.

49. Nathaniel P. Banks, "Independence of Cuba," *Congressional Globe*, 41st Cong., 2nd Sess., Appendix (June 7, 1870): 454–65.

50. Céspedes to Seward, Bayamo, October 24, 1868, "Exposición al secretario de estado Norteamericano solicitando apoyo a la revolución y dejando entrever a posibilidad de la integración de Cuba en 'una sola nación' Americana," Carlos Manuel de Céspedes, *Escritos*, ed. Fernando Portuondo and Hortensia Pichardo Viñals (La Habana: Editorial de Ciencias Sociales, 1974), 2:10–13.

51. Céspedes, "Exposición," 2:10–13; Ferrer, *Insurgent Cuba*, 54, 197.

52. Céspedes to Grant, La Larga, Cauto River, February 18, 1869, and March 1, 1869, Camp Headquarters, Céspedes, *Escritos*, 2:28–29, 33–35.

53. "Decreto de Abolicion Condiconada de la Esclavitud," Bayamo, December 27, 1868, Céspedes, *Escritos*, 1:144–45.

54. Ferrer, *Insurgent Cuba*, 43–44.

55. Céspedes, *Escritos*, 1:150–51; Ferrer, *Insurgent Cuba*, 54; Vanessa Michelle Ziegler, "The Revolt of 'the Ever-Faithful Isle': The Ten Years' War in Cuba, 1868–1878" (PhD diss., University of California, Santa Barbara, 2007), 192.

56. Ramiro Guerra y Sánchez, *Guerra de los diez años, 1868–1878*, 2 vols. (Havana: Editorial de Ciencias Sociales, 1972), chap. 15, 247–49, on leaders; Guerra y Sánchez, *Ten Years War*, 5:54–56; *Progress of Revolution*, 11.

57. For descriptions of the delegates, see Guerra y Sánchez, *Guerra de los diez años, 1868–1878*, 247–48; Guerra y Sánchez, *Ten Years War*, 5:55–56, 74–76; Pirala, *Anales*, 1:580–89. See also Rebecca Jarvis Scott, *Slave Emancipation in Cuba: The Transition to Free Labor, 1860–1899* (Pittsburgh: University of Pittsburgh Press, 2007), 46–48, 63–64; Hernández, *Cuba and the United States*, 26.

58. For summaries of the debates, see Juan Pérez de la Riva, *En los días de Guáimaro, 9–12 de abril de 1869: Recortes de prensa, testimonios y documentos* (n.p., 1969), 107–12; Pirala, *Anales*, 1:580–89; Ziegler, "Revolt," 45–49.

59. Pirala, *Anales*, 1:581; Ziegler, "Revolt," 45–47; Herminio Portell-Vilá, *Historia de Cuba en sus relaciones con los Estados Unidos y España*, vol. 2 (Havana: Jesus Montero, 1939), 238–40. Portell-Vilá argues that Cuban enthusiasm for annexation quickly waned once it became clear U.S. aid was not forthcoming.

60. Pirala, *Anales*, 1:581n1.

61. Pirala, *Anales*, 1:581n1.

62. Robert E. May, *Manifest Destiny's Underworld: Filibustering in Antebellum America* (Chapel Hill: University of North Carolina Press, 2002); May, *The Southern Dream of a Caribbean Empire, 1854–1861*, 2nd ed. (Gainesville: University Press of Florida, 2002).

63. Pirala, *Anales*, 1:673; Antonio Zambrana, *La República de Cuba* (New York: N. Ponce de Leon, 1873), 45. See also the numerous tributes to López in *Publicaciones de la Sociedad Democrática de los Amigos de América*.

64. Guerra y Sánchez, *Ten Years War*, 5:81–82; on López and the role of the South in filibustering, see May, *Manifest Destiny's Underworld*; May, *Southern Dream*.

65. Raúl Cepero Bonilla, *Azúcar y abolición* (Habana: Editorial Cenit, 1948), 246.

66. Banks, "Independence of Cuba"; "Cuban Independence," *Congressional Globe*, 41st Cong., 1st Sess. (April 9, 1869): 652–715; Jay Sexton, "The United States, the Cuban Rebellion, and the Multilateral Initiative of 1875," *Diplomatic History* 30, no. 3 (June 2006): 342–43.

67. Allan Nevins, *Hamilton Fish: The Inner History of the Grant Administration* (New York: Ungar, 1936), 183–84, 231–48; Allen J. Ottens, *General John A. Rawlins: No Ordinary Man* (Bloomington: Indiana University Press, 2021); James M. Shinn, "The Cuban Question: The Ten Years' War and the Reconstruction of U.S. Foreign Policy, 1865–1878" (PhD diss., Yale University, 2020), 200–201 (on Rawlins); chaps. 5, 6 (public agitation). On African American support for Free Cuba, see James M. Shinn, "The 'Free Cuba' Campaign, Republican Politics, and Post–Civil War Black Internationalism," in *Revolutions and Reconstructions: Black Politics in the Long Nineteenth Century*, ed. Van Gosse and David Waldstreicher (Philadelphia: University of Pennsylvania Press, 2020), 176–97.

68. Frederick Douglass, *The Speeches of Frederick Douglass: A Critical Edition* (New Haven: Yale University Press, 2018), 255; Shinn, "'Free Cuba' Campaign," 179–81.

69. Shinn, "'Free Cuba' Campaign," 180, 197; John Mercer Langston, *Freedom and Citizenship: Selected Lectures and Addresses* (R. H. Darby, 1883), 159–60.

70. Shinn, "'Free Cuba' Campaign," 184.

71. Hamilton Fish, "Diaries," March 19, 1869, Hamilton Fish Papers, Library of Congress, Manuscripts; Nevins, *Fish*, 125, 129, 181–85; Stephen McCullough, *The Caribbean Policy of the*

Ulysses S. Grant Administration: Foreshadowing an Informal Empire (Lanham, MD: Lexington Books, 2018), chap. 1; Shinn, "Cuban Question," chap. 4.

72. Americus [Vine Wright Kingsley], *Spain, Cuba and the United States: Recognition and the Monroe Doctrine* (New York: C. A. Alvord, 1870). Kingsley, a prominent New York lawyer, laid out the full argument against recognition.

73. Nevins, *Fish*, 180, 194, 262, 313; on Radepont, see Alfred J. Hanna and Kathryn A. Hanna, *Napoleon III and Mexico: American Triumph over Monarchy* (Chapel Hill: University of North Carolina Press, 1971), chap. 2; and Nancy N. Barker, "The Factor of 'Race' in the French Experience in Mexico, 1821–1861," *The Hispanic American Historical Review* 59, no. 1 (1979): 64–80. Another influence was Michel Chevalier, *Society, Manners and Politics in the United States: Being a Series of Letters on North America* (Boston: Weeks, Jordan, 1839), introduction. See also, Maike Thier, "The View from Paris: 'Latinity,' 'Anglo-Saxonism,' and the Americas, as Discussed in the 'Revue des Races Latines,' 1857–64," *International History Review* 33, no. 4 (2011): 627–44; Thier, "A World Apart, a Race Apart?" in *America Imagined: Explaining the United States in Nineteenth-Century Europe and Latin America*, ed. Axel Körner, Nicola Miller, and Adam I. P. Smith (New York: Palgrave, 2012), 161–89; on racism and expansion, see Eric T. Love, *Race over Empire: Racism and U.S. Imperialism, 1865–1900* (Chapel Hill: University of North Carolina Press, 2004), 39–40, 48–49.

74. "Cuban Affairs," *NYT*, March 17, 1870 (quote); Portell-Vilá, *Historia de Cuba*, chap. 3.

75. Ferrer, *Insurgent Cuba*, chap. 4; Ferrer, *Cuba*, chap. 11.

CHAPTER 7. BRITISH DEMOCRACY

1. On the United States and the ascent of liberal democracy in this period, see David M. Potter, "The Civil War in the History of the Modern World: A Comparative View," in *The South and the Sectional Conflict* (Baton Rouge: Louisiana State University Press, 1968); John Dalberg-Acton, *Historical Essays and Studies*, ed. Reginald Vere Laurence and John Neville Figgis (London: Macmillan, 1907), chap. 4; Frank A. Ninkovich, *Global Dawn: The Cultural Foundation of American Internationalism, 1865–1890* (Cambridge, MA: Harvard University Press, 2009); Leslie Butler, *Critical Americans: Victorian Intellectuals and Transatlantic Liberal Reform* (Chapel Hill: University of North Carolina Press, 2007); Robert Lloyd Kelley, *The Transatlantic Persuasion: Liberal-Democratic Mind in the Age of Gladstone* (London: Routledge, 2020).

2. Angelo Metzidakis, "Victor Hugo and the Idea of the United States of Europe," *Nineteenth-Century French Studies* 23, no. 1/2 (Fall–Winter 1994–95): 72–84; Florencia Peyrou, "The Role of Spain and the Spanish in the Creation of Europe's Transnational Democratic Political Culture, 1840–70," *Social History* 40, no. 4 (November 2015): 512; Florencia Peyrou, "Des États Unis d'Europe à la Démocratie Latine: Les projets transnationaux des républicains espagnols au xixe siècle," *Cahiers de la Méditerranée*, no. 99 (December 15, 2019): 101–12; Edward Everett Hale, "The United States of Europe," *Old and New* 3, no. March (1870): 260–67; R. Laurence Moore, *European Socialists and the American Promised Land* (New York: Oxford University Press, 1970), especially chap. 1, "Marx and Engels Look to America."

3. Adams to Hunter, London, July 13, 1865, *FRUS*, 1865, 416–17. William Hunter was the acting secretary of state during William Seward's convalescence.

4. John Morley, "England and the War," *Fortnightly Review* 8 (October 1, 1870): 479; Brent E. Kinser, *The American Civil War in the Shaping of British Democracy* (Farnham: Ashgate, 2011).

5. *The Bee-Hive*, March 28, 1863, quoted in Paul Foot, *The Vote: How It Was Won and How It Was Undermined* (2005; London: Bookmarks Publications, 2012), 126–27. On Beesly and the turn toward working-class support of Lincoln and the Union, see Kevin J. Logan, "The *Bee-Hive* Newspaper and British Working Class Attitudes toward the American Civil War," *Civil War History* 22, no. 4 (1976): 337–48, and Gregory Claeys, "Professor Beesly, Positivism and the International: The Patriotism Question," in *"Arise Ye Wretched of the Earth": The First International in a Global Perspective*, ed. Fabrice Bensimon, Quentin Deluermoz, and Jeanne Moisand (Leiden: Brill, 2018), 332–42.

6. Gustav Mayer, *The Era of the Reform League: English Labour and Radical Politics, 1857–1872: Documents Selected by Gustav Mayer*, ed. John Breuilly, Gottfried Niedhart, and Anthony Taylor (Mannheim: J and J Verlag, 1995), 91.

7. *Tributes of the Nations to Abraham Lincoln* (Washington, DC: GPO, 1867), 221–22; Logan, "Bee-Hive."

8. Karl Marx, "Inaugural Address of the Working Men's International Association," September 28, 1864, *MECW*, 20:5–13. Note: the name of the International varied for no discernible reason; on Marx's role, see Marx to Engels, November 4, 1864, *MECW*, 42:11–19. For an excellent treatment of Marx's affinity with Lincoln, see Robin Blackburn, *Marx and Lincoln: An Unfinished Revolution* (London: Verso, 2011).

9. Marx, "Inaugural Address," *MECW*, 20:5–13. On the history of the First International, see the excellent essays in Fabrice Bensimon, Quentin Deluermoz, and Jeanne Moisand, eds., *"Arise Ye Wretched of the Earth": The First International in a Global Perspective* (Leiden: Brill, 2018).

10. Gareth Stedman Jones, "'Pressure from Without': Karl Marx and 1867," *Parliamentary History* 36, no. 1 (February 2017): 117–30; Gareth Stedman Jones, "Some Notes on Karl Marx and the English Labour Movement," *History Workshop*, no. 18 (1984): 124–37; Gareth Stedman Jones, *Karl Marx: Greatness and Illusion* (London: Penguin, 2017); Angela Zimmerman, "From the Second American Revolution to the First International and Back Again: Marxism, the Popular Front, and the American Civil War," in *The World the Civil War Made*, ed. Gregory P. Downs and Kate Masur (Chapel Hill: University of North Carolina Press, 2015), 304–36; August H. Nimtz, *Marxism versus Liberalism* (Cham, Switzerland: Palgrave, 2019), chap. 3.

11. Margot C. Finn, *After Chartism: Class and Nation in English Radical Politics, 1848–1874* (Cambridge: Cambridge University Press, 1993), 234–61; Mayer, *Reform League*, 54–111; Eugenio F. Biagini, *Liberty, Retrenchment and Reform: Popular Liberalism in the Age of Gladstone, 1860–1880* (Cambridge: Cambridge University Press, 2004), chap. 5; Ian Machin, *The Rise of Democracy in Britain, 1830–1918* (New York: St. Martin's Press, 2001), 56–70.

12. Christine Bolt, *The Anti-Slavery Movement and Reconstruction: A Study in Anglo-American Co-operation, 1833–77* (London: Oxford University Press, 1969), chap. 2, especially 36–40; Edward B. Rugemer, "Jamaica's Morant Bay Rebellion and the Making of Radical Reconstruction," in *United States Reconstruction across the Americas*, ed. William A. Link (Gainesville: University Press of Florida, 2019), 81–111; "Jamaica: A Warning to the United States," *NYT*, September 1, 1867.

13. George Howell, "Working Class Movements of the Century with Personal Reminiscences," *Reynolds's Newspaper*, November 29, 1896, 4; F. M. Leventhal, *Respectable Radical: George Howell and Victorian Working Class Politics* (London: Weidenfeld and Nicolson, 1971), 45, 47–48; see also Aldon D. Bell, "Administration and Finance of the Reform League, 1865–1867," *International Review of Social History* 10, no. 3 (1965): 385–409; Foot, *The Vote*, 135–36; Jane Rendall, "The Citizenship of Women and the Reform Act of 1867," in *Defining the Victorian Nation: Class, Race, Gender and the British Reform Act of 1867*, ed. Catherine Hall, Keith McClelland, and Jane Rendall (Cambridge: Cambridge University Press, 2000), 119–78.

14. Edmond Beales, *Speech of Edmond Beales* (London: James George Taylor, 1865), 9, 12 (quotes).

15. Marx to Engels, London, May 1, 1865, *MECW*, 42:150.

16. Marx to Engels, London, September 11, 1867, *MECW*, 42:424; Detlev Mares, "Little Local Difficulties?: The General Council of the IWMA as an Arena for British Radical Politics," in *"Arise Ye Wretched of the Earth": The First International in a Global Perspective*, ed. Fabrice Bensimon, Quentin Deluermoz, and Jeanne Moisand (Leiden: Brill, 2018), 44–46.

17. Enemies of democratic reform in Parliament and the press continued to use America as an example of democracy's dangers. See, for examples, Robert Saunders, "'Let America Be the Test': Democracy and Reform in Britain, 1832–1867," in *The American Experiment and the Idea of Democracy in British Culture, 1776–1914*, ed. Ella Dzelzainis and Ruth Livesey (London: Routledge, 2016), 79–92; also Michael J. Turner, *Liberty and Liberticide: The Role of America in Nineteenth-Century British Radicalism* (Lanham, MD: Lexington Books, 2014). Turner focuses on Thomas P. Thompson, a skeptic on democracy, yet the author admits (p. 187) that reformers continued to advocate America as a model for British reform. Anthony G. Hopkins, *American Empire: A Global History* (Princeton: Princeton University Press, 2019), 302, echoes Saunders and Turner. On the veneration of Lincoln among British liberals, see Adam I. P. Smith, "'The Stuff Our Dreams Are Made Of': Lincoln in the English Imagination," in *The Global Lincoln*, ed. Richard Carwardine and Jay Sexton (New York: Oxford University Press, 2011), 123–38; Adam I. P. Smith, "The 'Cult' of Abraham Lincoln and the Strange Survival of Liberal England in the Era of the World Wars," *Twentieth Century British History* 21, no. 4 (December 2010): 486; Biagini, *Liberty, Retrenchment and Reform*, 69–70, 77–81, 377–78.

18. Benjamin Moran, *The Journal of Benjamin Moran, 1857–1865*, ed. Sarah Agnes Wallace and Frances Elma Gillespie (Chicago: University of Chicago Press, 1948), 2:1425; note: all spelling and punctuation as in the original. The debate Moran witnessed is found in Hansard, HC, May 3, 1865.

19. Robert Saunders, *Democracy and the Vote in British Politics, 1848–1867: The Making of the Second Reform Act* (Burlington, VT: Ashgate, 2011), chap. 6 on the Gladstone bill, 189 (quote).

20. Alexis de Tocqueville, *Democracy in America*, trans. Henry Reeve, 2nd ed. (London: Longman, Green, Longman, and Roberts, 1862), xxxix–xl; Lucy Hartley, "Democracy at the Crossroads: Tocqueville, Mill, and the Conflict of Interests," in *The American Experiment and the Idea of Democracy in British Culture, 1776–1914*, ed. Ella Dzelzainis and Ruth Livesey (London: Routledge, 2016), 78n11; Saunders, "Let America Be the Test," 86; F. B. Smith, *The Making of the Second Reform Bill* (Cambridge: Cambridge University Press, 1966), 78–79.

21. Several of these men contributed to an important collection, *Essays on Reform* (London: Macmillan, 1867). See also Walter Bagehot, "The Reform Act of 1867, and the Function of the House of Peers," in *Essays on Parliamentary Reform*, vol. 1 (London: Kegan Paul, 1883), 183–248; Adam I. P. Smith, "Victorian Radicalism and the Idea of America: *Reynolds's Newspaper*, 1850–1900," and Anthony Howe, "John Bull and Brother Jonathan: Cobden, America, and the Liberal Mind," in *The American Experiment and the Idea of Democracy in British Culture, 1776–1914*, ed. Ella Dzelzainis and Ruth Livesey (London: Routledge, 2016); Smith, *The Making of the Second Reform Bill*, 230–31.

22. Saunders, *Democracy and the Vote*, 144; Saunders, "Let America Be the Test."

23. Hansard, HC, March 12, 1866.

24. Hansard, HC, April 27, 1866.

25. Saunders, *Democracy and the Vote*, 162. Bright's invention of this term is documented in Hansard, HC, March 13, 1866.

26. Robert Blake, *Disraeli* (London: Faber and Faber, 2012), 440–41.

27. Hansard, HC, March 13, 1866.

28. Hansard, HC, April 26, 1866; Leslie Stephen, "The Political Situation in England," *North American Review* 107, no. 221 (1868): 545.

29. Saunders, *Democracy and the Vote*, 226–30; Mayer, *Reform League*, chap. 3.

30. Biagini, *Liberty, Retrenchment and Reform*, 265; Keith McClelland, "England's Greatness: The Working Man," in *Defining the Victorian Nation: Class, Race, Gender and the British Reform Act of 1867*, ed. Catherine Hall, Keith McClelland, and Jane Rendall (Cambridge: Cambridge University Press, 2000), 71–118; Mayer, *Reform League*, chaps. 3, 4.

31. "Reform Meeting in Trafalgar Square," *London Evening Standard*, June 28, 1866; Mayer, *Reform League*, 171–73, quoting *The Commonwealth*, June 30, 1866.

32. "Reform Demonstration," *The Times*, July 3, 1866; "The Great Reform Demonstration," *The Times*, July 3, 1866; An Eye-Witness, "The Reform Demonstration in Trafalgar-Square," *London Evening Standard*, July 3, 1866; Mayer, *Reform League*, 178–84.

33. Foot, *The Vote*, 148; "Mayne, Sir Richard," in *Dictionary of National Biography*, vol. 37 (London: Smith, Elder, 1894), 165–66.

34. "Attempt of the Tory Government to Suppress the Right of Public Meeting," *Reynolds's Newspaper*, July 22, 1866.

35. Henry Broadhurst, *Henry Broadhurst, M.P.: The Story of His Life from a Stonemason's Bench to the Treasury Bench* (London: Hutchinson, 1901), 34–37; "The Reform Demonstration in Hyde Park," *The Times*, July 24, 1866; Mayer, *Reform League*, 178–81, quoting *The Commonwealth*, July 28, 1866.

36. Broadhurst, *Henry Broadhurst*, 36; "The Reform Demonstration in Hyde Park"; "The Hyde Park Demonstration," *London Daily News*, July 24, 1866; Mayer, *Reform League*, quoting *The Commonwealth*, July 28, 1866.

37. *The Commonwealth*, July 28, 1866, extracted in Mayer, *Reform League*; "The Reform Demonstration in Hyde Park."

38. "The Hyde Park Demonstration"; Amanda Foreman, "Park of Ages: Far More than Just an Urban Retreat, Hyde Park Is a Living Archive of British Culture and History," *American Scholar* 82, no. 3 (2013): 44–53; "Speakers' Corner," The Royal Parks, https://www.royalparks.org.uk/parks/hyde-park/things-to-see-and-do/speakers-corner.

39. Mayer, *Reform League*, 178–84, quoting *The Commonwealth*, July 28, 1866; Broadhurst, *Henry Broadhurst*, 39–40; F. B. Smith, *The Making of the Second Reform Bill* (Aldershot: Gregg Revivals, 1993), 121–33.

40. "The Great Reform Demonstration," *Reynolds's Newspaper*, July 29, 1866; Mayer, *Reform League*, 178–84, an account from *The Commonwealth*, July 28, 1866.

41. Marx, "Preface to the First German Edition," Karl Marx and Friedrich Engels, *The Collected Works of Karl Marx and Friedrich Engels*, vol. 35 (London: Lawrence and Wishart, 1996), 35:9.

42. Marx to Engels, London, July 27, 1866, *MECW*, 42:300; Derek Sayer, "Marx after Capital: A Biographical Note (1867–1883)," in *Late Marx and the Russian Road: Marx and the Peripheries of Capitalism*, ed. Teodor Shanin (New York: New York University Press, 1983), 143.

43. Foot, *The Vote*, 61–63, 148–49, 155. An online search of British journals for July 1866 through the following May reveals dozens of references to the Peterloo Massacre, British Newspaper Archive, https://www.britishnewspaperarchive.co.uk/; see also Broadhurst, *Henry Broadhurst*, 40. For a dramatic film on this event, see *Peterloo* (BFI Film Fund, Film4, Thin Man Films, 2019).

44. Moran to Seward, London, September 29, 1866, *FRUS*, 1866, 205; Mayer, *Reform League*, 184–87, quoting *Bee-Hive*, July 28, 1866; Royden Harrison, *Before the Socialists: Studies in Labour and Politics, 1861–1881* (London: Routledge and Kegan Paul, 1965), 91; Joseph McCabe, *Life and Letters of George Jacob Holyoake*, vol. 2 (London: Watts, 1908), 28; Foot, *The Vote*, 148–49.

45. George Macaulay Trevelyan, *The Life of John Bright* (Boston: Houghton Mifflin, 1913); William Cash, *John Bright: Statesman, Orator, Agitator* (London: I. B. Tauris, 2012); Philip S. Foner, *British Labor and the American Civil War* (New York: Holmes, 1981).

46. Trevelyan, *John Bright*, 363–69.

47. John Bright, *Speeches on Parliamentary Reform* (Manchester: John Heywood, 1867), 6.

48. Foot, *The Vote*, 139.

49. Bright, *Speeches on Parliamentary Reform*; Cash, *John Bright*, 118–19; Mayer, *Reform League*, 191–95.

50. Bright, *Speeches on Parliamentary Reform*, 3, 4, 13.

51. Bright, *Speeches on Parliamentary Reform*, 73.

52. Disraeli to Derby, November 18, 1866, Benjamin Disraeli, *Benjamin Disraeli Letters*, ed. Michel Walter Parand, vol. 9 (Toronto: University of Toronto Press, 2013), 198; Saunders, *Democracy and the Vote*, 231–32.

53. Disraeli to Queen Victoria, July 23, 1866, and Disraeli to Montague Corry, September 5, 1866, Disraeli, *Benjamin Disraeli Letters*, 9:114, 139.

54. Disraeli, *Benjamin Disraeli Letters*, 9:xv, 4155; Paula Bartley, *Queen Victoria* (London: Taylor and Francis, 2016), 173; N. J. Gossman and International Institute for Social History, "Republicanism in Nineteenth-Century England," *International Review of Social History* 7 (1962): 51–60; Queen Victoria, *The Letters of Queen Victoria*, ed. George Earle Buckle, vol. 4 (Cambridge: Cambridge University Press, 2014), 433–34, 449–50. For a film version of this story, see *Mrs. Brown* (BBC Scotland, Ecosse Films, Irish Screen, 1997).

55. Derby to Victoria, January 10, 1867, and Victoria to Derby, January 12, 1867, Queen Victoria, *Letters of Queen Victoria*, 4:388–91; Bartley, *Queen Victoria*, 173–74; Hansard, HC, February 5, 1867.

56. Harrison, *Before the Socialists*, 188–89, 188n5.

57. Harrison, *Before the Socialists*, 89–91.

58. John Stuart Mill, *Autobiography* (London: Longmans, Green, Reader, and Dyer, 1873), 290.

59. Adams to Seward, London, May 7, 1867, *FRUS*, 1867, 85–86; Harrison, *Before the Socialists*, 83; John Rutherford, *The Secret History of the Fenian Conspiracy, Its Origin, Objects, and Ramifications*, vol. 2 (London: C. K. Paul, 1877), 278–79; Gustave Paul Cluseret, "My Connection with Fenianism," *Fraser's Magazine*, n.s., 6 (July 1872): 31–46. See also Disraeli, *Benjamin Disraeli Letters*, 9:442n1, 444n1, on Fenian agents in London. Matthew Arnold made "Hyde Park anarchy-mongering" a symbol of the dangers of democracy in *Culture and Anarchy: An Essay in Political and Social Criticism* (London: Smith, Elder, 1869), 124–25, 193.

60. Frederic Harrison, *Order and Progress* (London: Spottiswoode, 1875), 183–184n1; Saunders, *Democracy and the Vote*, 227–28, argues the threats of violence and Conservative fears were exaggerated; Trevelyan, *John Bright*, 361 (quote on ugly temper).

61. *The Commonwealth*, May 4, 1867, extracted in Harrison, *Before the Socialists*, 93.

62. Charles Bradlaugh, *Reform or Revolution: An Address to the Lords and Commons of England, Etc.* (London: National Reformer, 1867), 6; Harrison, *Before the Socialists*, 93.

63. Harrison, *Before the Socialists*, 93–94.

64. Harrison, *Before the Socialists*, 94–95.

65. Harrison, *Before the Socialists*, 94, 95; Hansard, HL, May 9, 1867; Saunders, *Democracy and the Vote*, 250.

66. D. G. Wright, "Leeds Politics and the American Civil War," *Northern History* (June 1974): 122.

67. Saunders, *Democracy and the Vote*, 266.

68. Hansard, HC, March 18, 1867 (Disraeli quote); Saunders, *Democracy and the Vote*, chap. 8, covers the details of the Reform Act and its passage.

69. Machin, *The Rise of Democracy in Britain*, chap. 4; Foot, *The Vote*, 163–70.

70. Mill to Emerson, August 12, 1867, quoted in Butler, *Critical Americans*, 87.

71. Saunders, *Democracy and the Vote*, 258 (quotes); Hansard, HC, May 20, 1867; Rendall, "The Citizenship of Women and the Reform Act of 1867." For Mill's earlier views on woman suffrage, see John Stuart Mill, *On the Admission of Women to the Electoral Franchise Spoken in the House of Commons, May 20th, 1867* (London: Trubner, 1867); John Stuart Mill, *Considerations on Representative Government*, 2nd ed. (1859; London: Parker, Son, and Bourn, 1861), 184–86; John Stuart Mill, *The Subjection of Women* (London: Longmans, Green, 1869).

72. Emmeline Pankhurst, *My Own Story* (London: Vintage, 2015), 3–4 (quotes); Krista Cowman, "Female Suffrage in Great Britain," in *The Struggle for Female Suffrage in Europe: Voting to Become Citizens*, ed. Blanca Rodriguez Ruiz and Ruth Rubio Marín (Leiden: Brill, 2012), 274–75. On Mill and Taylor, see Adam Gopnik, *A Thousand Small Sanities: The Moral Adventure of Liberalism* (New York: Basic Books, 2019), 7; Rendall, "The Citizenship of Women and the Reform Act of 1867." See also Mrs. Stuart [Harriet Hardy Taylor] Mill, *Enfranchisement of Women* (London: Turner, 1868). On female suffrage in America, see Faye E. Dudden, *Fighting Chance: The Struggle over Woman Suffrage and Black Suffrage in Reconstruction America* (New York: Oxford University Press, 2011); Marjorie Julian Spruill, *One Woman, One Vote: Rediscovering the Woman Suffrage Movement*, 2nd rev. ed. (Tilamook, OR: NewSage Press, 2021).

73. Goldwin Smith, "The Experience of the American Commonwealth," in *Essays on Reform* (London: Macmillan, 1867), 217–37.

74. A. V. Dicey, "Americomania in English Politics," *The Nation* 42, no. 1073 (January 21, 1886): 52–53.

75. John Lothrop Motley, *Historic Progress and American Democracy* (New York: Charles Scribner, 1869), 61–63.

CHAPTER 8. SPAIN'S DEMOCRATIC MOVEMENT

1. Raymond Carr, *Spain, 1808–1939* (Oxford: Clarendon Press, 1966), 211–12, 290–99; Adrian Shubert, "Spain," in *War for the Public Mind: Political Censorship in Nineteenth-Century Europe*, ed. Robert Goldstein (Westport, CT: Greenwood, 2000), 175–209; Frank A. Ninkovich, *Global Dawn: The Cultural Foundation of American Internationalism, 1865–1890* (Cambridge, MA: Harvard University Press, 2009), 124–25.

2. Arthur Corwin, *Spain and the Abolition of Slavery in Cuba, 1817–1886* (Austin: University of Texas Press, 1967); Seymour Drescher, "From Empires of Slavery to Empires of Antislavery," in *Slavery and Antislavery in Spain's Atlantic Empire*, ed. Josep M. Fradera and Christopher Schmidt-Nowara, 1st ed. (New York: Berghahn Books, 2013), 291–316; Juliana Jardim de Oliveira e Oliveira, "A Guerra Civil no espaço Atlântico: A secessão norte-americana nos debates parlamentares brasileiros (1861–1865)" (PhD diss., Universidade Federal de Ouro Preto, 2017), chap. 5. See also Samantha Payne, "The Last Atlantic Revolution: Reconstruction and the Struggle for Democracy in the Americas, 1861–1912" (PhD diss., Harvard University, 2022), 38–39, for an informative review of scholarship on U.S. influence in Brazil and Spain.

3. Paloma Arroyo Jiménez, "La sociedad abolicionista española, 1864–1886," *Cuadernos de historia moderna y contemporánea* 3 (1982): 127–50; Corwin, *Spain and Abolition*, chap. 9, 177–79 (on Vizcarrondo).

4. Rafael M. de Labra, *La emancipacion de los esclavos en los Estados-Unidos* (Madrid: M. G. Hernandez, 1873), 40–43, 54; Rafael M. de Labra, *De la representación é influencia de los Estados-Unidos de América en el derecho internacional* (Madrid: A. J. Alaria, 1877); Corwin, *Spain and Abolition*, 153–71, 160 (on Wilberforce of Spain); Kate Ferris, *Imagining "America" in Late Nineteenth Century Spain* (New York: Palgrave Macmillan, 2016), 26; Catherine Davies and Sarah Sánchez, "Rafael María de Labra and *La Revista Hispano-Americana* 1864–1867: Revolutionary Liberalism and Colonial Reform," *Bulletin of Spanish Studies* 87, no. 7 (November 1, 2010), 915–38.

5. Corwin, *Spain and Abolition*, 176, 185; *Diario de Sesiones del Congreso de los Diputados*, Serie histórica, no. 79 (Madrid: Madrid Palacio del Congreso de los Diputados), May 6, 1865, 1701, https://app.congreso.es/est_sesiones/.

6. Charles J. Esdaile, *Spain in the Liberal Age: From Constitution to Civil War, 1808–1939* (Oxford: Blackwell, 2000), 95, 104–22; Florencia Peyrou, "The Role of Spain and the Spanish in the Creation of Europe's Transnational Democratic Political Culture, 1840–70," *Social History* 40, no. 4 (November 2015): 497–517; Florencia Peyrou, "A Great Family of Sovereign Men: Democratic Discourse in Nineteenth-Century Spain," *European History Quarterly*, no. 2 (2013); Mary Vincent, *Spain, 1833–2002: People and State* (Oxford: Oxford University Press, 2008), chap. 1;

Raymond Carr, "Liberalism and Reaction, 1833–1931," in *Spain: A History*, ed. Raymond Carr (Oxford: Oxford University Press, 2000), 211.

7. John Kiste, *Divided Kingdom: The Spanish Monarchy from Isabel to Juan Carlos* (Brinscombe: History Press, 2011), 22, 23, 34–36, 37–38, 73; Rachel Challice, *The Secret History of the Court of Spain during the Last Century* (New York: D. Appleton, 1909) chap. 12; Carl Schurz, Frederic Bancroft, and William Archibald Dunning, *The Reminiscences of Carl Schurz*, vol. 2 (New York: McClure, 1907), 251.

8. Julia Clara Pitt Byrne, *Cosas de España: Illustrative of Spain and the Spaniards as They Are* (London: Alexander Strahan, 1866), 7; Gustav Philipp Körner, *Memoirs of Gustave Koerner, 1809–1896*, ed. Thomas J. McCormack, vol. 2 (Cedar Rapids, IA: Torch Press, 1909), 267; Schurz, Bancroft, and Dunning, *Reminiscences*, 2:250–52. See also Isabel Burdiel's introductory essay to the published pornographic cartoons of the queen and various Spanish notables: Isabel Burdiel, ed., *SEM: Los borbones en pelota* (Zaragoza: Institucion Fernando el Catolico, 2012).

9. Carr, *Spain*, 295–96.

10. Dexter Perkins, *The Monroe Doctrine, 1826–1867*, vol. 2 (Baltimore: Johns Hopkins University Press, 1933), 286; John Ledding Phelan, "Pan-Latinism, French Intervention in Mexico (1861–1867) and the Genesis of the Idea of Latin America," in *Conciencia y Autenticidad Históricas*, ed. Juan Antonio Ortega y Medina (Mexico City: UNAM, 1968), 279–98.

11. "The Military Revolt in Spain," *NYT*, January 22, 1866; "Spain: Manifesto from Gen. Prim," *NYT*, July 30, 1868; Carr, *Spain*, 296, 297.

12. Carr, *Spain*, 239, 290–304, 297 (Castelar); Francis Henry Gribble, *The Tragedy of Isabella II* (London: Chapman and Hall, 1913), chap. 24; Davies and Sánchez, "Labra," 15; Jiménez, "La sociedad abolicionista española, 1864–1886," 130.

13. Peyrou, "Great Family," 238–39; Jorge Vilches García, *Emilio Castelar, la patria y la república* (Madrid: Biblioteca Nueva, 2001), 81; Henri Leonardon, *Prim* (Paris: Alcan, 1901), 113–14; Gribble, *Tragedy of Isabella*, 228–29; C.A.M. Hennessy, *The Federal Republic in Spain: Pi y Margall and the Federal Republican Movement, 1868–74* (Oxford: Clarendon Press, 1962), 33–35.

14. Viscount P. Trement to Bigelow, Geneva, August 4, 1866, in, Bigelow, *Retrospections: 1865–66*, 3:496, 497; John Bigelow, *France and the Confederate Navy, 1862–1868* (New York: Harper and Brothers, 1888), 1–7, 190–93; the Sumner connection is mentioned in "The Montpensier-De Bourbon Duel, Particulars of the Fatal Encounter," *NYT*, March 14, 1870. The idea of selling Cuba to finance revolution in Spain had a long history; see Peyrou, "The Role of Spain and the Spanish in the Creation of Europe's Transnational Democratic Political Culture," 504.

15. Bigelow, *France*, 191–92; James Morton Callahan, *Cuba and International Relations: A Historical Study in American Diplomacy* (Baltimore: Johns Hopkins Press, 1899), 355–56; "The Duke of Montpensier's Chances for the Crown," *NYT*, November 12, 1868; "Opposition to the Duke of Montpensier's Suppression of Republicanism," *NYT*, June 18, 1869.

16. Bigelow, *France*, 191; Trement to Bigelow, received October 25, 1866, John Bigelow, *Retrospections of an Active Life: 1865–1866*, vol. 3 (New York: Baker and Taylor, 1909), 591.

17. James W. Cortada, "Spain and the American Civil War: Relations at Mid-Century, 1855–1868," *Transactions of the American Philosophical Society* 70, no. 4 (1980): 30–41, 87–88; Bigelow, *France*, 192 (quotes).

18. "Cuba and the United States: The Cry for Annexation," *NYT*, November 18, 1868.

19. Seward to Bigelow, October 8, 1868, in John Bigelow, *Retrospections of an Active Life: 1867–71*, vol. 4 (New York: Doubleday, Page, 1913), 225.

20. Edward Henry Strobel, *The Spanish Revolution, 1868–1875* (Boston: Small, Maynard, 1898), 1–4.

21. Carr, *Spain*, chap. 8; Gribble, *Tragedy of Isabella*, chap. 25.

22. Elizabeth Wormeley Latimer, *Spain in the Nineteenth Century* (Chicago: A. C. McClurg, 1897), 326; Challice, *Secret History of the Court of Spain*, 206–10.

23. Gribble, *Tragedy of Isabella*, 262–64; Latimer, *Spain*, 326–28.

24. Hale to Seward, Madrid, October 9, 1868, *FRUS*, 1868 (Washington, DC: GPO, 1868), 19–20; Gribble, *Tragedy of Isabella*, 264–65; Strobel, *The Spanish Revolution, 1868–1875*.

25. Élisée Reclus, *Correspondance*, vol. 1, 3 vols. (Paris: Librairie Schleicher Freres, 1911), 307 (quoting his brother, Élie); Hennessy, *Federal Republic*, 49n1.

26. John Hay, *Castilian Days* (Boston: J. R. Osgood, 1871), 369–70.

27. Kate Ferris, "A Model Republic," in *America Imagined: Explaining the United States in Nineteenth-Century Europe and Latin America*, ed. Axel Korner and Nicola Miller (New York: Palgrave Macmillan, 2016), 54; Agustín Santayana, ed., *Constitución política de los Estados Unidos de América* (Avila: P. Vaquero, 1868); Édouard Laboulaye, *Estudios Sobre la Constitución de Los Estados-Unidos*, trans. Joaquín Guichot (Sevilla: E. Perié, 1869); Joaquín Oltra, *La influencia norteamericana en la Constitución Española de 1869* (Madrid: Instituto de Estudios Administrativos, 1972).

28. Ferris, "A Model Republic," 54–55; Ferris, *Imagining "America,"* chap. 1; for the text of the new constitution, see *Constitucion de la monarquia española, promulgada en Madrid el dia 6 de junio de 1869* (Madrid: Imprenta Nacional, 1869). For an English translation, see Arnold R. Verduin, "The Constitution of 1869," in *Manual of Spanish Constitutions, 1808–1931: Translation and Introduction* (Ypsilanti, MI: University Lithoprinters, 1941); James W. Cortada, *Two Nations over Time: Spain and the United States, 1776–1977* (Westport, CT: Greenwood Press, 1978), 142–43.

29. "The Montpensier-De Bourbon Duel, Particulars of the Fatal Encounter"; Robert Sencourt, *The Spanish Crown, 1808–1931: An Intimate Chronicle of a Hundred Years* (New York: C. Scribner's Sons, 1932), 233.

30. C. W. Willard, "Proposed Recognition of Cuba," *Congressional Globe*, 41st Cong., Special Session (April 9, 1869): Appendix: 18–21 (quotes on 18).

31. Garry Boulard, *Daniel Sickles: A Life* (Bloomington, IN: iUniverse, 2019), chap. 63; Edgcumb Pinchon, *Dan Sickles, Hero of Gettysburg and "Yankee King of Spain"* (Garden City, NY: Doubleday, Doran, 1945), 237.

32. Stephen McCullough, *The Caribbean Policy of the Ulysses S. Grant Administration: Foreshadowing an Informal Empire* (Lanham, MD: Lexington Books, 2018), 12–13; Stephen McCullough, "Avoiding War: The Foreign Policy of Ulysses S. Grant and Hamilton Fish," in *A Companion to the Reconstruction Presidents, 1865–1881*, ed. Edward O. Frantz (Hoboken, NJ: John Wiley, 2014), 313; Roderick Hiram Conrad, "Spanish-United States Relations, 1868–1874" (PhD diss., University of Georgia, 1969), 47–51; Callahan, *Cuba*, 376–77; Allan Nevins, *Hamilton Fish: The Inner History of the Grant Administration* (New York: Ungar, 1936), 189–90; Boulard, *Sickles*, 697, 704–5; Pinchon, *Sickles*, 226–28.

33. Nevins, *Fish*, 191–94; Conrad, "Spanish-United States Relations," 51–52; Forbes to Fish, Madrid, July 20, 1869, U.S. State Department, "Despatches from Special Agents, 1794–1906," https://catalog.archives.gov/id/213812201. Note: Porto Rico was the common spelling at this time.

34. Nevins, *Fish*, 193.

35. Nevins, *Fish*, 193–97; McCullough, *Caribbean Policy*, 1–23.

36. Fish to Sickles, July 29, 1869, *Correspondence between the Department of State and the United States Minister at Madrid and the Consular Representatives of the United States in the Island of Cuba, and Other Papers Relating to Cuban Affairs*, 41st Cong., 2nd Sess., HED 160 (Washington, DC: GPO, 1870), 18.

37. Correspondence between Fish and Sickles, July–August 1869, *Correspondence . . . Relating to Cuban Affairs*, 13–21. See also Javier Rubio, *Juan Prim: sus años de gobernante, su asesinato: una revisión necesaria*, Biblioteca diplomática española (Madrid: Ministerio de Asuntos Exteriores y Cooperación, 2017), 397–402.

38. Sickles to Fish, Madrid, August 12, 1869, *Correspondence . . . Relating to Cuban Affairs*, 19–21.

39. Sickles to Fish, Madrid, August 12, 21, 1869, *Correspondence . . . Relating to Cuban Affairs*, 19–22, 29–31.

40. Sickles to Fish, Madrid, August 13, 1869, *Correspondence . . . Relating to Cuban Affairs*, 23.

41. Fish to Sickles, August 24, September 1, 1869, *Correspondence . . . Relating to Cuban Affairs*, 31, 32.

42. Sickles to Fish, Madrid, September 5, 8, 1869, and Sickles to Becerra, Madrid, September 3, 1869, *Correspondence . . . Relating to Cuban Affairs*, 33–37.

43. Sickles to Fish, Madrid, September 8, 14, 1869, and Becerra to Sickles, Madrid, September 16, 1869, *Correspondence . . . Relating to Cuban Affairs*, 36–38, 39–41; Boulard, *Sickles*, 707–12.

44. Carr, *Spain*, 219, 306; Hay, *Castilian Days*, 392.

45. Corwin, *Spain and Abolition*, 245–57. The Moret Law essentially copied the proposal the Cuban delegation made to the Colonial Reform Commission two years earlier in 1867.

46. Hay, *Castilian Days*, 326–27; Corwin, *Spain and Abolition*, 245–57.

47. Fish to Sickles, January 26, 1870, *Correspondence . . . Relating to Cuban Affairs*, 69–70.

48. William Roscoe Thayer, *The Life and Letters of John Hay*, vol. 1 (Boston: Houghton Mifflin, 1916), 320–21; John Hay, *Letters of John Hay and Extracts from Diary*, ed. Clara L. Hay, vol. 1 (Washington, DC: n.p., 1908), 387. On Castelar as orator, see also Hennessy, *Federal Republic*, 84–85.

49. On Castelar's endorsement of the United States of Europe, see Emilio Castelar, *Discursos Parlamentarios y Políticos de Emilio Castelar en la Restauración* (Madrid: Angel de San Martín, 1885), 1:23; Emilio Castelar, *Discursos políticos de Emilio Castelar: Dentro y fuera del parlamento en los años de 1871 a 1873* (Madrid: L. López, 1873), 317, 441, 469. The full text of Castelar's speech is found in *Diario de Sesiones*, June 20, 1870, 8693–9002. The speech was also published separately: Emilio Castelar, *Abolición de la esclavitud* (Madrid: J. A. García, 1870). An extract, translated by John Hay to English, is found in *Presidential Message on Emancipation of Slaves in Cuba*, 41st Cong., 2nd Sess., SED 113 (Washington, DC: GPO, 1870), 16–17. On U.S. influence in Spanish debates on slavery, see Ferris, *Imagining "America,"* chap. 3.

50. *Diario de Sesiones,* June 20, 1870, 8999; Corwin, *Spain and Abolition,* 250; Ferris, *Imagining "America,"* 104.

51. For more on Castelar and abolition, see "Two Great Republican Speeches," *NYT,* July 7, 1870; *Emancipation of Slaves in Cuba,* 16–17. See also Castelar, *Abolición*; Corwin, *Spain and Abolition,* 249–51; Carolyn P. Boyd, "A Man for All Seasons: Lincoln in Spain," in *The Global Lincoln,* ed. Richard Carwardine and Jay Sexton (New York: Oxford University Press, 2011), 103ff.; Emilio Castelar, "Emilio Castelar (1832–1899): The Orator of the Cortes of Spain," in *Famous Orators of the World and Their Best Orations,* ed. Charles Morris (Chicago: J. C. Winston Company, 1902), 636–37.

52. Fish to Sickles, June 20, 1870, *Emancipation of Slaves in Cuba,* 12–17; Corwin, *Spain and Abolition,* chap. 13; cf. Gregory P. Downs, *The Second American Revolution: The Civil War-Era Struggle over Cuba and the Rebirth of the American Republic* (Chapel Hill: University of North Carolina Press, 2019), 116.

53. Sickles to Fish, June 26, 1870, *Emancipation of Slaves in Cuba,* 16–17.

54. Sickles to Fish, Madrid, June 26, 1870, *Emancipation of Slaves in Cuba,* 14–16; *Ley de 4 de julio de 1870 sobre abolicion de la esclavitud y reglamento para su ejecucion en las islas de Cuba y Puerto-Rico* (Havana: Imprenta del gobierno, 1872).

55. Corwin, *Spain and Abolition,* 259–61; Nevins, *Fish,* 344–50; "The Fate of Goicouria," *Harper's Weekly* 14 (May 21, 1870): 326, 380, 381.

56. Corwin, *Spain and Abolition,* 259–61, 261 (quote).

57. "Cuba, the Planters Strongly Opposed to Emancipation," *NYT,* July 8, 1870; Corwin, *Spain and Abolition,* 259–61; Christopher Schmidt-Nowara, "The End of Slavery and the End of Empire: Slave Emancipation in Cuba and Puerto Rico," *Slavery and Abolition* 21, no. 2 (August 1, 2000): 193; "Cuban Emancipation Pronounced a Fraud in Spain," *NYT,* October 10, 1870. Gallenga reported it was two full years before the Volunteers permitted publication of the Moret Law: Antonio Carlo Napoleone Gallenga, *The Pearl of the Antilles* (London: Chapman and Hall, 1873), 121.

58. "Affairs in Spain," *NYT,* July 11, 1870.

59. Juan Manuel Macías, *Cuba in Revolution: A Statement of Facts* (London: Head, Hole, 1871), 7 (quote from F. W. Chesson's introduction).

60. Seymour Drescher, *Abolition: A History of Slavery and Antislavery* (New York: Cambridge University Press, 2009), 346–48; Leonardo Marques, *The United States and the Transatlantic Slave Trade to the Americas, 1776–1867* (New Haven: Yale University Press, 2016), 255, 260, on the impact of the U.S. Civil War on slavery; David R. Murray, *Odious Commerce: Britain, Spain and the Abolition of the Cuban Slave Trade* (Cambridge: Cambridge University Press, 1980), 244 (on slave imports); Corwin, *Spain and Abolition,* on U.S. pressure to end slavery, 256, 276–77, 284; on U.S. example of abolition, 149, 193, 198, 209, 250; Conrad, "Spanish-United States Relations," 84–85. On the demise of Cuban slavery, see Rebecca J. Scott, "Explaining Abolition: Contradiction, Adaptation, and Challenge in Cuban Slave Society, 1860–1886," *Comparative Studies in Society and History* 26, no. 1 (1984): 86, 88; Schmidt-Nowara, "End of Slavery," 194–96.

61. Corwin, *Spain and Abolition,* 284–87; *Diario de Sesiones,* December 24, 1872, 2542–43.

62. Brazil Senate debates, September 4, 1871, *Annaes do Senado do Império, 3a Sessão em 1871 da 14a Legislatura de 1 a 30 de Setembro,* vol. 5 (Rio de Janeiro: Typographia do Diário do

Rio de Janeiro, 1871), 29–30. I am grateful to Rafael de Bivar Marquese for directing me to this; see Rafael de Bivar Marquese, "The Civil War in the United States and the Crisis of Slavery in Brazil," in *American Civil Wars: The United States, Latin America, Europe, and the Crisis of the 1860s*, ed. Don H. Doyle (Chapel Hill: University of North Carolina Press, 2016), 223–24. Strangely, most historians of Brazil seem to pay more attention to U.S. than Spanish influence on Brazilian emancipation; see Laird W. Bergad, *The Comparative Histories of Slavery in Brazil, Cuba, and the United States* (New York: Cambridge University Press, 2007); Drescher, *Abolition*, 348–71; Drescher, "From Empires of Slavery to Empires of Antislavery," 303; Jeffrey D. Needell, *The Party of Order: The Conservatives, the State, and Slavery in the Brazilian Monarchy, 1831–1871* (Palo Alto: Stanford University Press, 2006), 233–34; Robert Edgar Conrad, *The Destruction of Brazilian Slavery, 1850–1888*, 2nd ed. (Malabar, FL: Krieger Publishing, 1993), chap. 4; Robert Brent Toplin, *The Abolition of Slavery in Brazil* (New York: Atheneum, 1972); Leslie Bethell, "The Decline and Fall of Slavery in Brazil (1850–88)," in *Brazil: Essays on History and Politics*, ed. Leslie Bethell (London: University of London Press, 2018), 113–44.

63. "Republican Spain," *NYT*, February 16, 1873; Sickles to Fish, Madrid, March 11, 1873, *FRUS*, 1873, vol. 2 (Washington, DC: GPO, 1874), 928–30; Downs, *Second American Revolution*, 121.

64. Esdaile, *Spain in the Liberal Age*, chap. 7.

65. Hay, *Castilian Days*, 347.

CHAPTER 9. THE LAST MONARCH OF FRANCE

1. François Furet, *Revolutionary France, 1770–1880* (1988; Oxford: Blackwell, 2008), 429–65; Philip G. Nord, *The Republican Moment: Struggles for Democracy in Nineteenth-Century France* (Cambridge, MA: Harvard University Press, 1998), 1–14.

2. Roger Price, *The French Second Empire: An Anatomy of Political Power* (Cambridge: Cambridge University Press, 2001); Nord, *Republican Moment*, 34–37, 129–30, 190–91.

3. "France and Mexico, Prevost Paradol," *NYT*, December 16, 1867; Paradol, preface to E. de Kératry, *L'élévation et la chute de l'empereur Maximilien* (Paris: Libraire Internationale, 1867), xx (quote).

4. Thomas Sancton, *Sweet Land of Liberty: The French Left Looks at America, 1848–1871* (Baton Rouge: Louisiana State University Press, 2021); "Abraham Lincoln Papers: Series 4, Addenda, 1774–1948: Gold Medal Presented to Mary Todd Lincoln by the French Medal Committee, Manuscript/Mixed Material, Library of Congress" (1866), https://www.loc.gov/item/mal4500052/.

5. Frederick Douglass, "Une Lettre de Frederic Douglass," *New Orleans Tribune*, December 16, 1865, 554–55; Bryan LaPointe, "'Moral Electricity': Melvil-Bloncourt and the Trans-Atlantic Struggle for Abolition and Equal Rights," *Slavery and Abolition* 40, no. 3 (September 2019): 543–62.

6. Comité français d'émancipation, *Adresse au Président des États-Unis, Mai 1865* (Paris: Simon Racon et Compagnie, 1865); in English translation, *Tributes of the Nations to Abraham Lincoln*

(Washington, DC: GPO, 1867), 105–9; "Anti-Slavery Conference in Paris," *NYT*, September 13, 1867; *Special Report of the Anti-Slavery Conference: Held in Paris, in the Salle Herz, on the Twenty-Sixth and Twenty-Seventh August, 1867* (London: Committee of the British and Foreign Anti-slavery Society, 1867), 9 (Laboulaye quote).

7. *Special Report*, 12–15.

8. Éric Hazan, *The Invention of Paris: A History in Footsteps* (London: Verso, 2011).

9. Arthur Chandler, "Paris 1867 Exposition: History, Images, Interpretation," Ideas, http://www.arthurchandler.com/paris-1867-exposition/; Jasper Ridley, *Napoleon III and Eugénie* (New York: Viking, 1980), 528–33.

10. Nathaniel Prentiss Banks, *Speech of Hon. N. P. Banks, of Massachusetts, upon the Representation of the United States at the Exhibition of the World's Industry, Paris, 1867 Delivered in the House of Representatives March 14, 1866* (Washington, DC: Mansfield and Martin, 1866).

11. Monadnock, "The Monarchs in Paris," *NYT*, June 19, 1867.

12. Malakoff, "Affairs in France," *NYT*, May 30, 1867.

13. Ralph Roeder, *Juarez and His Mexico: A Biographical History* (New York: Viking Press, 1947), 673–77, 675 (first quote); Monadnock, "The Monarchs in Paris"; Monadnock, "The Shadow of Maximilian's Death in Europe," *NYT*, July 20, 1867 (last quote); Malakoff, "How the News of Maximilian's Death Is Received in Europe," *NYT*, July 5, 1867; "Maximilian's Fate," *NYT*, July 18, 1867; "European Intelligence: All European Courts in Mourning for Maximilian," *NYT*, July 6, 1867.

14. Clemenceau to Louise Jordan, New York, September 6, 1867, in Georges Clemenceau, Sylvie Brodziak, and Jean-Noel Jeanneney, *Correspondance: 1858–1929* (Paris: R. Laffont, Bibliothèque nationale de France, 2008), 125–27.

15. "France and Mexico," *NYT*, August 7, 1867; Frank Edward Lally, *French Opposition to the Mexican Policy of the Second Empire* (Baltimore: Johns Hopkins Press, 1931), 138–39 (Thiers and other quotes); Kératry, *L'élévation et la chute de l'empereur Maximilien*; for an English version, E. de Kératry, *The Rise and Fall of the Emperor Maximilian: A Narrative of the Mexican Empire, 1861–7*, trans. G. H. Venables (London: S. Low, Son, and Marston, 1868).

16. Malakoff, "Affairs in France: The Reception of the Sovereigns," *NYT*, July 26, 1867.

17. John Bigelow, *Retrospections of an Active Life: 1817–1863*, vol. 1 (New York: Baker and Taylor, 1909), 246–47.

18. Bigelow, *Retrospections, 1817–1863*, 1:246–47; Elizabeth Wormeley Latimer, *France in the Nineteenth Century, 1830–1890*, 6th ed. (Chicago: A. C. McClurg, 1898), 190; Ridley, *Napoleon III*, 492, 524–25, 546–47; Fenton Bresler, *Napoleon III: A Life* (New York: HarperCollins, 1999), 349, 353; Henry Morford, *Paris in '67, or, The Great Exposition, Its Side-Shows and Excursions* (New York: G. W. Carleton, 1867), 185 (quote on appearance); Price, *Second Empire*, 267.

19. Furet, *Revolutionary France*, 487; Price, *Second Empire*, 145–46, chap. 5; Ridley, *Napoleon III*, 524–25, 551, 555–57.

20. Nassau William Senior, *Conversations with Distinguished Persons during the Second Empire, from 1860 to 1863*, vol. 2 (London: Hurst and Blackett, 1880), 191.

21. Sancton, *Sweet Land*, 126–27; Price, *Second Empire*, 268–69.

22. William Edward Johnston, ed., *Memoirs of "Malakoff,"* vol. 2 (London: Hutchison, 1907), 519–25 (Rochefort quote); Roger Lawrence Williams, *Henri Rochefort, Prince of the Gutter Press* (New York: Scribner, 1966), 27–36; Roger L. Williams, "Unkindly Light: Henri Rochefort's

Lanterne," *French Historical Studies* 1, no. 3 (1960): 321 (Napoleon II quote). In 1815, Napoleon I tried and failed to impose his son as heir to the throne.

23. Johnston, *Memoirs of "Malakoff,"* 2:531.

24. Johnston, *Memoirs of "Malakoff,"* 2:529.

25. Johnston, *Memoirs of "Malakoff,"* 2:529; Augustin Cochin, *Abraham Lincoln* (Paris: Degorce-Cadot, 1869).

26. For French reactions to Reconstruction in America, see Sancton, *Sweet Land,* chaps. 14, 15, 16.

27. Georges Clemenceau, *Clémenceau: Lettres d'Amérique,* ed. Patrick Weil and Thomas Macé (Paris: Passés Composés, 2020), 10–11, 16–17.

28. Georges Clemenceau, *American Reconstruction 1865–1870 and the Impeachment of President Johnson,* ed. Fernand Baldensperger, trans. Margaret MacVeagh (New York: Dial Press, 1928)

29. David Robin Watson, *Georges Clemenceau: France* (London: Haus Publishing, 2009), 20–24; David Robin Watson, *Georges Clemenceau: A Political Biography* (London: Eyre Methuen, 1974), 28–30; Clemenceau, *Clémenceau,* 16–17; Clemenceau, *American Reconstruction,* 13–20.

30. Edouard Portalis, *Les États-Unis, le self-government et le césarisme* (Paris: A. Le Chevalier, 1869), 196, quoted in Sancton, *Sweet Land,* 128.

31. Léon Gambetta, "Le général Grant," *Revue politique* 1 (June 13, 1868): 33–35, quoted in Sancton, *Sweet Land,* 131.

32. Sancton, *Sweet Land,* 280, 208–9.

33. Sancton, *Sweet Land,* 104; Angelo Metzidakis, "Victor Hugo and the Idea of the United States of Europe," *Nineteenth-Century French Studies* 23, no. 1/2 (Fall–Winter 1994–95): 72–84. Giuseppe Mazzini advocated European union all during this period. See Stefano Recchia and Nadia Urbinati, eds., *A Cosmopolitanism of Nations: Giuseppe Mazzini's Writings on Democracy, Nation Building, and International Relations* (Princeton: Princeton University Press, 2009), chap. 9; C. A. Bayly and E. F. Biagini, eds., *Giuseppe Mazzini and the Globalization of Democratic Nationalism, 1830–1920* (Oxford: Oxford University Press, 2008).

34. *Les États-Unis d'Europe* (Berne) first appeared in January 1868. See also Charles Lemonnier, *Les États-Unis d'Europe* (Paris: Librairie de la Bibliothèque Démocratique, 1872); Charles Lemonnier, *La vérité sur le Congrès de Genève* (Berne: Vérésoff et Garrigues, 1867); Leon-Adrien de Montluc, *La vie de Charles Lemonnier* (Paris: Solsona, 1924); Anthony P. Campanella, "Garibaldi and the First Peace Congress in Geneva in 1867," *International Review of Social History* 5, no. 3 (1960): 459 (on attendance).

35. Lemonnier, *Les États-Unis d'Europe,* 127–29, quoted in Sancton, *Sweet Land,* 202–3.

36. Hugo, "My Fellow Citizens of the World," April 29, 1865, in Belle Becker Sideman and Lillian Friedman, eds., *Europe Looks at the Civil War: An Anthology* (New York: Orion Press, 1960), 307.

37. Price, *Second Empire,* 397 (quote); Alan Strauss-Schom, *The Shadow Emperor: A Biography of Napoleon III* (New York: St. Martin's Press, 2018), 368–69; Furet, *Revolutionary France,* 481–91; Johnston, *Memoirs of "Malakoff,"* 2:515.

38. Price, *Second Empire,* 397–401.

39. Alexandre Dumas, *La terreur prussienne* (Paris: Michel Lévy, 1868), serialized in *La Situation* the previous year; Ross King, *The Judgment of Paris: The Revolutionary Decade That Gave the World Impressionism* (2007; New York: Bloomsbury, 2009), 206–7.

40. J.A.S. Grenville, *Europe Reshaped, 1848–1878* (Oxford: Blackwell, 2000), 273–75.

41. Ridley, *Napoleon III,* 559.

42. Anna L. Bicknell, *Life in the Tuileries under the Second Empire* (New York: Century, 1895), 212–15; Alain Plessis, *The Rise and Fall of the Second Empire, 1852–1871*, trans. Jonathan Mandelbaum (Cambridge: Cambridge University Press, 1985), 69; Ridley, *Napoleon III*, 561 (quote); King, *Judgment of Paris*, 273–74.

43. David Wetzel, *A Duel of Giants: Bismarck, Napoleon III, and the Origins of the Franco-Prussian War* (Madison: University of Wisconsin Press, 2001), 151–52; Ridley, *Napoleon III*, 558–62.

44. Ridley, *Napoleon III*, 562.

45. Watson, *Clemenceau* (1974), 34–35.

46. Price, *Second Empire*, 445–46; Philip Henry Sheridan, *Personal Memoirs of P. H. Sheridan*, vol. 2 (New York: Charles E. Webster, 1888), 403–5.

47. Sheridan, *Personal Memoirs*, 2:406–8.

48. Theo Aronson, *The Fall of the Third Napoleon* (London: Thistle, 2014), 277–78.

49. Price, *Second Empire*, 452.

50. Price, *Second Empire*, 455.

51. Price, *Second Empire*, 454–55.

52. Aronson, *Fall of the Third Napoleon*, 298–99; J.P.T. Bury, "Gambetta and the Revolution of 4 September 1870," *Cambridge Historical Journal* 4, no. 3 (1934): 263–82.

53. Aronson, *Fall of the Third Napoleon*, 300; Bury, "Gambetta and the Revolution of 4 September 1870," 265–66.

54. Price, *Second Empire*, 455–56, 460–61.

55. Aronson, *Fall of the Third Napoleon*, 279–80, 281–82.

56. "France Republican," *NYT*, September 6, 1870.

57. Aronson, *Fall of the Third Napoleon*, 301–2; Thomas Wiltberger Evans, *Memoirs of Dr. Thomas W. Evans: The Second French Empire*, ed. Edward A. Crane, vol. 2 (New York: D. Appleton, 1905), 261–62, 303.

58. Evans, *Memoirs of Dr. Thomas W. Evans*, 2:261–74.

59. Evans, *Memoirs of Dr. Thomas W. Evans*, 2:279–310.

60. John M. Merriman, *Massacre: The Life and Death of the Paris Commune* (New York: Basic Books, 2014), 15; Alistair Horne, *The Fall of Paris: The Siege and the Commune, 1870–71* (1965; London: Penguin, 2007).

61. Furet, *Revolutionary France*, 500, 510–11.

62. Watson, *Georges Clemenceau: France*, 28.

63. Merriman, *Massacre*, 29–30; Horne, *The Fall of Paris*, Kindle loc. 5339–81.

64. Merriman, *Massacre*, 28–29; Watson, *Clemenceau* (1974), 47–49.

65. Merriman, *Massacre*, prologue.

66. Merriman, *Massacre*, chaps. 4, 7.

67. Merriman, *Massacre*, prologue, 37, 235, 251; Quentin Deluermoz, "The IWMA and the Commune: A Reassessment," *"Arise Ye Wretched of the Earth": The First International in a Global Perspective*, ed. Fabrice Bensimon, Quentin Deluermoz, and Jeanne Moisand (Leiden: Brill, 2018); Samuel Bernstein, "American Labor and the Paris Commune," *Science & Society* 15, no. 2 (1951): 144–62; "J" [Dr. William Edward Johnston, aka Malakoff], "European News by Mail," *NYT*, July 7, 1871. Malakoff left his job as correspondent to serve in the American Ambulance Brigade.

68. E. B. Washburne and Michael Hill, *Elihu Washburne: The Diary and Letters of America's Minister to France during the Siege and Commune of Paris* (New York: Simon and Schuster, 2012).

69. Washburne to Fish, Paris, March 27, 1871, *FRUS*, 1871, 316–17.

70. Horne, *The Fall of Paris*, part 2; Merriman, *Massacre*, 119–23; David G. McCullough, *The Greater Journey: Americans in Paris* (New York: Simon and Schuster, 2011), chap. 10; "The Internationale" (quote), https://www.marxists.org/history/erol/uk.secondwave/internationale.htm.

71. Gustave Paul Cluseret, *Mexico, and the Solidarity of Nations* (New York: Blackwell, 1866); Philip Mark Katz, *From Appomattox to Montmartre: Americans and the Paris Commune* (Cambridge, MA: Harvard University Press, 1998), 4–25; Merriman, *Massacre*, 44.

72. Merriman, *Massacre*, chap. 4; E. B. Washburne, *Recollections of a Minister to France, 1869–1877*, vol. 2 (New York: C. Scribner's Sons, 1887), chap. 6.

73. Watson, *Clemenceau* (1974), 28.

74. Merriman, *Massacre*, chap. 9.

75. Merriman, *Massacre*, chap. 11; Frank A. Ninkovich, *Global Dawn: The Cultural Foundation of American Internationalism, 1865–1890* (Cambridge, MA: Harvard University Press, 2009), 96–98; Katz, *Appomattox to Montmartre*, chap. 4.

76. Washburne and Hill, *Elihu Washburne*, 44–45.

77. Washburne and Hill, *Elihu Washburne*, 164.

78. On the "Latin race," see Maike Thier, "A World Apart, a Race Apart?" in *America Imagined: Explaining the United States in Nineteenth-Century Europe and Latin America*, ed. Axel Körner, Nicola Miller, and Adam I. P. Smith (New York: Palgrave, 2012), 161–89; Maike Thier, "The View from Paris: 'Latinity,' 'Anglo-Saxonism,' and the Americas, as Discussed in the 'Revue des Races Latines,' 1857–64," *International History Review* 33, no. 4 (2011): 627–44; for an excellent analysis of U.S. press coverage, see Katz, *Appomattox to Montmartre*, chap. 4. The Library of Congress database Chronicling America produced nearly 18,000 hits for mentions of Paris + Commune for all newspapers in 1871. For typical examples in the *New York Times*, see "Paris under the Communists," *NYT*, March 28, 1871; "The Revolt of the Communists," *NYT*, April 9, 1871; "A Communist Manifesto," *NYT*, April 21, 1871; "A Word for the Communists," *NYT*, April 26, 1871; "The Reds in Paris," *NYT*, April 15, 1871; Monadnock, "The Wretched Reign of the Reds in Paris," *NYT*, April 28, 1871; "The Socialistic Insurrection in Paris," *NYT*, March 21, 1871.

79. Thomas Nast, "Cartoon Comparing Tweed Ring and Paris Commune," *Harper's Weekly*, July 1, 1871; Thomas Nast, "The Madness of Paris, Illustration," *Harper's Weekly*, June 10, 1871; Thomas Nast, "The Exile's Victory," *Harper's Weekly*, June 17, 1871; Thomas Nast, "General Carnage on His High Horse, Illustration," *Harper's Weekly*, May 20, 1871; "Cartoon 'The Jumping Frog,'" *Harper's Weekly*, April 15, 1871; "Burning of Paris, Illustrations," *Harper's Weekly*, July 1, 1871; "The End of the Commune, Illustration of Petrolouse Executed by French Soldiers," *Harper's Weekly*, July 8, 1871.

80. "The Commune and Liberty," *NYT*, May 31, 1871.

81. "Our National Anniversary," *NYT*, July 4, 1871.

CHAPTER 10. THE FALL OF ROME

1. David I. Kertzer, *Prisoner of the Vatican: The Pope's Secret Plot to Capture Rome from the New Italian State* (Boston: Houghton Mifflin, 2004), 9–10; Pope Pius IX to Venerable Brother John [Hughes], October 18, 1862, *Official Records of the Union and Confederate Navies in the War*

of the Rebellion . . . Correspondence with Diplomatic Agents, ser. 2, 3:559–60; "A Letter from Pope Pius IX, to the Catholics of Chicago," *NYT,* November 28, 1862; Leo Francis Stock, "Catholic Participation in the Diplomacy of the Southern Confederacy," *Catholic Historical Review* 16 (April 1930): 16; David J. Alvarez, "The Papacy in the Diplomacy of the American Civil War," *Catholic Historical Review* 69, no. 2 (April 1, 1983): 237–38; Russell to Lord Russell, L'Arricia near Rome, July 30, 1864, Odo Russell, *The Roman Question: Extracts from the Despatches of Odo Russell from Rome, 1858–1870,* ed. Noel Blakiston (London: Chapman and Hall, 1962), 288, on the pope's Confederate sympathies. For an account of the Confederacy's relations with the Vatican, see Don H. Doyle, *The Cause of All Nations: An International History of the American Civil War* (New York: Basic Books, 2015), 257–70.

2. Kertzer, *Prisoner,* 23–24; Russell, *Roman Question,* 300–305; *Encyclical Letter of Pope Pius IX, and the Syllabus of Modern Errors,* English translation (Rome: n.p., 1864).

3. Kertzer, *Prisoner,* 107; Russell, *Roman Question,* 311.

4. Frank J. Coppa, "Pio Nono and the Jews: From 'Reform' to 'Reaction,' 1846–1878," *Catholic Historical Review* 89, no. 4 (2003): 671–95; Dan V. Segre, "The Emancipation of Jews in Italy," in *Paths of Emancipation: Jews, States, and Citizenship,* ed. Pierre Birnbaum and Ira Katznelson (Princeton: Princeton University Press, 1995), 232 (on Jews at Porta Pia); Mario Rossi, "Emancipation of the Jews in Italy," *Jewish Social Studies* 15, no. 2 (1953): 113–34. I profited from a tour and fascinating exhibit at the synagogue in Rome: "1849–1871 Ebrei di Roma tra Segregazione ed Emancipazione," Jewish Museum of Rome, April 5, 2022, https://museoebraico.roma.it/.

5. Anthony B. Lalli and Thomas H. O'Connor, "Roman Views on the American Civil War," *Catholic Historical Review* 57, no. 1 (1971): 21–41; *Tributes of the Nations to Abraham Lincoln* (Washington, DC: GPO, 1867), 685.

6. Stillman to Seward, Rome, June 25, 1865, Leo Francis Stock, ed., *United States Ministers to the Papal States: Instructions and Despatches, 1848–1868,* vol. 2 (Washington, DC: Catholic University Press, 1933), 300.

7. Stock, *Papal States,* 2:300, 356n.

8. William Hanchett, *The Lincoln Murder Conspiracies* (Urbana: University of Illinois Press, 1983); Michael J. Sobiech, "Chiniquy's Lincoln: Aiming Booth's Bullet at the Roman Catholic Church," *American Catholic Studies* 127, no. 4 (2016): 23–47.

9. *Trial of John H. Surratt in the Criminal Court for the District of Columbia,* vol. 1 (Washington, DC: GPO, 1867), 471–84; Andrew C. A. Jampoler, *The Last Lincoln Conspirator: John Surratt's Flight from the Gallows* (Annapolis, MD: Naval Institute Press, 2008), 72–87; "Arrest of John H. Surratt, Accomplice of Booth in Assassination of President Lincoln," *U.S. Congressional Serial Set* 1305 (1866): 13–14; Louis J. Weichmann and A. C. Richards, *A True History of the Assassination of Abraham Lincoln and of the Conspiracy of 1865,* ed. Floyd E. Risvold (New York: Knopf, 1975), 336–37.

10. Weichmann and Richards, *True History,* 339. Sainte Marie did not admit to pursuing Surratt for the reward; Jampoler, *Last Lincoln Conspirator,* 109–10.

11. Sainte Marie, affidavit, July 10, 1866, *FRUS,* 1866, 135–36.

12. Jampoler, *Last Lincoln Conspirator,* 104–5.

13. Sainte Marie, affidavit, July 10, 1866, *FRUS,* 1866, 135–36; Duane Koenig, "General Rufus King and the Capture of John H. Surratt," *Wisconsin Magazine of History* 25, no. 1 (1941): 43–50.

14. King to Seward, Rome, July 14, August 8, affidavits June 28, July 10, 1866, *FRUS*, 1866, 134–39; Holt to King, Washington, DC, May 19, 1866, Weichmann and Richards, *True History*, 340–41.

15. Seward to King, October 16, 1866, and King to Seward, Rome, August 8, 1866, *FRUS*, 1866, 139–41; Seward to King, October 16, 1866, Stock, *Papal States*, 2:383.

16. Reports from papal officers Allet and De Lambilly, November 8, 1866, and King to Seward, Rome, November 10, 1866, *FRUS*, 1866, 141–45; for an alternative account implying collusion among Zouave comrades, see Jampoler, *Last Lincoln Conspirator*, 114–15. The various accounts of Surratt's arrest are rife with variations of facts often as they relate to place-names and their spellings.

17. King to Seward, Rome, November 19, 1866, *FRUS*, 1866, 143–44.

18. Hale to Seward, Alexandria, November 27, 1866, *FRUS*, 1866, 148–49, 275.

19. Diplomatic correspondence on the Surratt affair is found in Howard R. Marraro, *L'unificazione italiana vista dai diplomatici statunitensi*, ed. Alberto Maria Ghisalberti, vol. 4 (Roma: Istituto per la storia del Risorgimento italiano, 1963), 380–89. See also *Trial of John H. Surratt in the Criminal Court for the District of Columbia*, 1:471–84 (quotes), 474, 480; Jampoler, *Last Lincoln Conspirator*, 72–87; "Arrest of John Surratt," 13–14; Weichmann and Richards, *True History*, 336–37.

20. "European News: Protestant Worship in Rome to Be Interdicted," *NYT*, January 12, 1867.

21. "Protestants and the Sovereign of Rome," *NYT*, January 25, 1867.

22. "To Correspondents," *NYT*, January 27, 1867; Jampoler, *Last Lincoln Conspirator*, 115–16.

23. King to Seward, Rome, February 11, 18, 1867, *FRUS*, 1867 (Washington, DC: GPO, 1867), 700–702.

24. Howard R. Marraro, "The Closing of the American Diplomatic Mission to the Vatican and Efforts to Revive It, 1868–1870," *Catholic Historical Review* 33, no. 4 (1948): 423–47. The full debate on the Roman Question is found in "Wednesday, January 30, 1867," *Congressional Globe*, 39th Cong., 2nd Sess. (1867): 851–89.

25. Marraro, "The Closing of the American Diplomatic Mission to the Vatican and Efforts to Revive It"; "Thursday, May 19, 1870," *Congressional Globe*, 41st Cong., 2nd Sess. (1870): 3628–35; Martin Hastings, "United States–Vatican Relations," *Records of the American Catholic Historical Society of Philadelphia* 69, no. 1/2 (1958): 20–55.

26. Spiro Kostof, "The Third Rome: The Polemics of Architectural History," *Journal of the Society of Architectural Historians* (1973): 239–50. On Mazzini, see Denis Mack Smith, *Mazzini* (New Haven: Yale University Press, 1996).

27. Malakoff, "Our Paris Correspondence," *NYT*, October 21, 1865.

28. Kertzer, *Prisoner*, 14–18; Russell to Clarendon, Rome, July 10, 1866, Russell, *Roman Question*, 330, 334–42.

29. King to Seward, Rome, January 14, 1867, Stock, *Papal States*, 2:411.

30. Kertzer, *Prisoner*, 13–14, 19–20; Smith, *Mazzini*, 181–83; Lucy Riall, *Garibaldi: Invention of a Hero* (New Haven: Yale University Press, 2007), 350–52.

31. Kertzer, *Prisoner*, 24–25.

32. Kertzer, *Prisoner*, 27.

33. Kertzer, *Prisoner*, 31.

34. Russell, *Roman Question*, 310–11; Frank J. Coppa, *Cardinal Giacomo Antonelli and Papal Politics in European Affairs* (Albany: SUNY Press, 1990), 156.

35. Coppa, *Antonelli*, 158.

36. Smith, *Mazzini*, 210–11; Coppa, *Antonelli*, 157, 158.

37. "The Italians at Rome," *The Times*, September 29, 1870.

38. "The Italians at Rome."

39. "The Italians at Rome."

40. Kertzer, *Prisoner*, chaps. 3, 4, especially 55–58.

41. "The Emancipation of Rome and the Pope," *New York Herald*, October 5, 1870; "The Papal Power," *New York Herald*, December 11, 1870.

42. "'The Liberation of Rome': Celebration in Apollo Hall Last Evening," *NYT*, October 29, 1870.

43. Smith, *Mazzini*, 223–25.

44. Stefano Recchia and Nadia Urbinati, eds., *A Cosmopolitanism of Nations: Giuseppe Mazzini's Writings on Democracy, Nation Building, and International Relations* (Princeton: Princeton University Press, 2009), 132–35, 219–23; Joseph Rossi, *The Image of America in Mazzini's Writings* (Madison: University of Wisconsin Press, 1954), 134–37; Howard R. Marraro, "Mazzini on American Intervention in European Affairs," *Journal of Modern History* 21, no. 2 (1949): 109–14; Smith, *Mazzini*, 167.

45. Sergio Luzzatto, *La mummia della Repubblica: Storia di Mazzini imbalsamato* (Turin: Einaudi, 2011), 27–35; Luzzatto, *1872: I funerali di Mazzini* (Rome: Laterza, 2013). I am grateful to Enrico Dal Lago for alerting me to this interesting story of Mazzini's funeral train.

46. Luzzatto, *Mummia della Repubblica*, 20.

47. Federico Donaver, *Vita Di Giuseppe Mazzini* (Firenze: Successori Le Monnier, 1903), 424–25; Luzzatto, *Mummia della Repubblica*, 21.

48. "A Mazzini Demonstration," *The Times*, March 22, 1872; Angelico, "Europe: Mazzini's Death," *NYT*, April 14, 1872.

49. Angelico, "Europe: Mazzini's Death"; Smith, *Mazzini*, 224–25; Gavin Williams, "Orating Verdi: Death and the Media c.1901," *Cambridge Opera Journal* 23, no. 3 (2011): 134–35.

CODA

1. Albert S. Evans, *Our Sister Republic: A Gala Trip through Tropical Mexico in 1869–70* (Hartford: Columbian Book Co., 1871), 283–86.

2. E. J. Hobsbawm, *The Age of Revolution, 1789–1848* (New York: Vintage Books, 1996); R. R. Palmer, *The Age of the Democratic Revolution: A Political History of Europe and America, 1760–1800* (Princeton: Princeton University Press, 2014); Adam Gopnik, *A Thousand Small Sanities: The Moral Adventure of Liberalism* (New York: Basic Books, 2019), 15; James E. Sanders, *The Vanguard of the Atlantic World: Creating Modernity, Nation, and Democracy in Nineteenth-Century Latin America* (Durham: Duke University Press, 2014), chap. 4.

3. J.A.S. Grenville, *Europe Reshaped, 1848–1878* (Oxford: Blackwell, 2000), part 3 describes the transformation of "authoritarian Europe."

4. Emilio Castelar, "The Progress of Democracy in Europe," *North American Review* 141, no. 348 (1885): 420 (quote); Emilio Castelar y Ripoll, "The Republican Movement in Europe, 5 Parts," *Harper's New Monthly Magazine* 45 (1872): 47 (quote); Frank A. Ninkovich, *Global*

Dawn: The Cultural Foundation of American Internationalism, 1865–1890 (Cambridge, MA: Harvard University Press, 2009), 80–81.

5. William Archibald Dunning, "The Undoing of Reconstruction," *Atlantic Monthly* 88, no. 528 (October 1901): 437–49.

6. Neil R. McMillen, *Dark Journey: Black Mississippians in the Age of Jim Crow* (Urbana: University of Illinois Press, 1990); Michael Perman, *Struggle for Mastery: Disfranchisement in the South, 1888–1908* (Chapel Hill: University of North Carolina Press, 2001); Eric Foner, *Reconstruction: America's Unfinished Revolution, 1863–1877* (New York: Harper and Row, 1988).

7. Susan K. Harris, *God's Arbiters: Americans and the Philippines, 1898–1902* (New York: Oxford University Press, 2011), 12–13.

8. Paul A. Kramer, "Empires, Exceptions, and Anglo-Saxons: Race and Rule between the British and United States Empires, 1880–1910," *Journal of American History* 88, no. 4 (2002): 1315–53.

9. James Bryce, *The American Commonwealth*, 3rd ed., 2 vols. (New York: Macmillan, 1895); James Bryce, "Historical Aspects of Democracy," in *Essays on Reform* (London: Macmillan, 1867), 239–78; Abraham S. Eisenstadt, "Bryce's America and Tocqueville's," in *Reconsidering Tocqueville's Democracy in America*, ed. Abraham S. Eisenstadt (New Brunswick, NJ: Rutgers University Press, 1988), 229–309; Edmund S. Ions, *James Bryce and American Democracy, 1870–1922* (London: Macmillan, 1968), 37; Bradford Perkins, *The Great Rapprochement: England and the United States, 1895–1914* (New York: Atheneum, 1968), 147; Leslie Butler, *Critical Americans: Victorian Intellectuals and Transatlantic Liberal Reform* (Chapel Hill: University of North Carolina Press, 2007), chap. 6.

10. Christopher Harvie, *The Lights of Liberalism: University Liberals and the Challenge of Democracy, 1860–86* (London: Allen Lane, 1976), 76, 87, 96, 98, 103, 105–6, 115, 132–33, 192–93; Hugh Tulloch, *James Bryce's American Commonwealth: The Anglo-American Background* (Woodbridge: Boydell Press, 1988), 19–25; H. A. Tulloch, "Changing British Attitudes towards the United States in the 1880s," *The Historical Journal* 20, no. 4 (1977): 825–40; Philip Alderton, "The Oxford Union Debates the American Civil War," *American Civil War Round Table UK*, http://www.acwrt.org.uk/uk-heritage_The-Oxford-Union-Debates-the-American-Civil-War.asp.

11. Bryce, "Historical Aspects of Democracy"; see also Harvie, *Lights of Liberalism*, 107. Harvie situates Bryce within a generation of pro-democracy and pro-American intellectuals.

12. Ions, *Bryce*, 120–21, 127–28; Eisenstadt, "Bryce's America and Tocqueville's," 235–37.

13. Ions, *Bryce*, 131, 314n18. My research on WorldCat.org reveals many additional foreign-language translations, some with multiple editions.

14. James Bryce, *The Relations of the Advanced and the Backward Races of Mankind, The Romanes Lecture, 1902* (Oxford: Clarendon Press, 1902), 39.

15. Henry Cabot Lodge, *National Supervision of National Elections: Speech of Hon. Henry Cabot Lodge . . . in the House of Representatives, Thursday, June 26, 1890* (Washington, DC: G. R. Gray, printer, 1890); Henry Cabot Lodge, "The Restriction of Immigration," *North American Review* 152, no. 410 (January 1891): 27–36; Henry Cabot Lodge, "Lynch Law and Unrestricted Immigration," *North American Review* 152, no. 414 (May 1891): 602–12.

16. "The Monroe Doctrine," in Theodore Roosevelt, *The Works of Theodore Roosevelt*, vol. 13 (New York: C. Scribner's Sons, 1923), 168–81, 169 (quote); Frank Ninkovich, "Theodore Roosevelt: Civilization as Ideology," *Diplomatic History* 10, no. 3 (July 1, 1986): 135–36.

17. Theodore Roosevelt, "Speech at Grand Rapids," September 7, 1900, *The Works of Theodore Roosevelt*, ed. Hermann Hagedorn, vol. 14 (New York: Scribner's Sons, 1926), 352–53; Christopher Lasch, "The Anti-Imperialists, the Philippines, and the Inequality of Man," *Journal of Southern History* 24, no. 3 (1958): 319–31.

18. Carl Schurz, "The Issue of Imperialism," University of Chicago, January 4, 1899, *Speeches, Correspondence and Political Papers of Carl Schurz*, ed. Frederic Bancroft, vol. 6 (New York: G. P. Putnam's Sons, 1913), 1–36.

19. Rudyard Kipling, "The White Man's Burden," *McClure's Magazine* 12, no. 4 (February 1899): 290–91; Patrick Brantlinger, "Kipling's 'The White Man's Burden' and Its Afterlives," *English Literature in Transition, 1880–1920* 50, no. 2 (2007): 172–91.

20. "Senate—Tuesday, February 7, 1899," *Congressional Record* 32 (1899): 1529–34.

INDEX

Note: Page numbers in italic type indicate illustrations.

abolition. *See* slavery: abolition of

Abolitionista, El (newspaper), 204

Adam, Juliette, 249–50

Adams, Charles Francis, 124–25, 133, 177, 195

Adams, John Quincy, 49

Adullamites, 183–85, 194

African Americans and Black peoples:
British workers likened to, 177, 178; and
Cuba, 167–70; Irish likened to, 133; at
Lincoln's death, 17; racist attitudes about,
4–5, 287, 292–97; Reconstruction and,
4–5, 287–88; suffrage for, 287–88, 293.
See also slavery

Agassiz, Louis, 36–37

Agramonte, Ignacio, 164

Aguinaldo, Emilio, 289

Alabama Claims, 119–21, 126, 144–46, 170

Alaska Purchase, 8, 63–64, 99–104, 112–19, 122

Alexander II, Tsar of Russia, 100, 102–8, 112

Alfonso XII, King of Spain, 230

Allain-Targé, Henri, 23

Allen, William H., 82–83

Amadeo, King of Spain, 229–30

American Anti-Slavery Society, 168–69

Americas: European imperialism in, 42,
49–51, 53; international Reconstruction
and, 7–8; Spanish imperialism in, 8, 50,
53, 59–60, 147–72, 206. *See also individual
countries*; British North America;
Monroe Doctrine; Pan-Americanism

Anglo-American, 102, 121, 127, 139, 205

Anglo-Saxon culture, 52, 63, 70, 171, 290–94

Anthony, Susan B., 11

Antonelli, Giacomo, Cardinal, 265, 269, 273

Argentina, 38

aristocracy: challenges to European, 4, 9,
24, 46, 100; democracy/republicanism
vs., 7, 53, 54, 70; in Russia, 100; Southern
slaveholders associated with, 2, 7, 24, 36,
46, 100

Army and Navy Gazette (newspaper), 108

Aubert, François, "Emperor Maximilian's
Firing Squad," 97

Avenir National (newspaper), 31

Aztecs, 96

Baez, Buenaventura, 64

Bagdad Raid, 88–89, *88*

Bakunin, Mikhail, 105, 244

Balbontin, Manuel, 79

Bancroft, George, 43–49, *44*, 51, 100; *History
of the United States of America*, 45

Banks, Nathaniel P., 143, 167, 217, 235

Battle of Mentana (1867), 274, *274*

Battle of Santa Gertrudis (1866), 91

Bazaine, François Achille, 84–85, 92, 94–95,
248

Beales, Edmond, 179, 180, 187–88, 191, 195,
197

Becerra, Manuel, 220–21

Becker, Lydia, *199*

Beesly, Edward, 175, 177

Bigelow, John, 2, 24–25, 27, 28, 31, 39–40, 59, 62, 77–79, 85–88, 94, 101, 107, 207–10, 237, 241

Bird, M. B. (Mark Baker), 33–34

Bismarck, Otto von, 216, 246–48, 253

Black Decrees, 83–84, 160, 163

Black peoples. *See* African Americans and Black peoples

Blair, Montgomery, 59, 79, 318n27

Blanc, Louis, 29

Blondeel, Edouard, 44

Bolívar, Simón, *96*

Book of Blood, The, 160

Booth, John Wilkes, 1, 2, 17, 72

Bourbon dynasty, Spanish, 10, 147, 203, 204, 207–16, 230

Bradlaugh, Charles, 196

Braganza, Antónia de (Infanta of Portugal), 216

Brazil, 9, 36–37, 227, 229, 233–34

Brewster, Harriet, 203–4

Bright, John, 144, 177, 179, 182–83, 185, 191–94, *193*

Bristol Reform Union, 22

Britain: American Northwest and, 101–2; and Anglo-American culture, 290; attitudes about America in, 181–84, 200; and Canada, 8, 55–57, 118–19, 121–29, 141–46; and democracy, 175–202; Irish animosity for, 131–33; and liberalism, 177, 198–99; and Lincoln, 16, 19–22, *20*, 123; monarchy in, 10, 194; Parliament in, 9, 116, 135, 142, 144, 179, 181–85, 192, 195–96, 198–200; reform efforts in, 3, 9, 22, 181–202; suffrage in, 179–82, 185–87, 191–95, 197–200; United States and, 20–21, 43, 46–48, 55–57, 100, 104, 108, 116–18, 123–26, 144–46, 175; workers in, 9, 19, 21–22, 177–86. *See also* British North America

British Columbia, 101, 117–20, 144, 146

British North America (1867), 8, 18, 62, 117–20, 122–23, 126–30

British North America Act, 123, 142, 144

Brown, George, 127

Brown, John (American abolitionist), 2, 25, 234

Brown, John (Queen Victoria's servant), 194

Bruce, Frederick, 43, 46, 47, 117–18, 143

Bryant, William Cullen, 53, 59

Bryce, James, 182, 290–93; *The American Commonwealth*, 290–92

Burgess, John W., 292

Cairoli, Benedetto, 283

Camagüey Revolutionary Committee, 163–65

Campbell, Lewis, 94

Campobello campaign, 139

Canada, 121–46; Britain and, 55–57, 118–19, 121–29, 141–46; British Columbia and, 101, 117–20, 146; confederation movement in / dominion of, 8, 118, 122–23, 127–30, 129, 142–46; and democracy, 122–23, 128–29; Fenian Brotherhood and, 43, 122, 131–33, 138–42, 144, 146; and Lincoln, 18; name of, 142–43; origins of, 127; Parliament in, 123, 128–29, 146; United States and, 121–27, 130–31, 143–46. *See also* British North America

capital punishment, 269

Carducci, Giosuè, 281

Caribbean: calls for U.S. annexation of, 62; Spanish imperialism in, 8, 50, 53, 147–72, 206; as troublesome region during Civil War, 61. *See also individual countries*

Carlistas, 204–6, 230

Carlos (brother of Ferdinand VII), 204

Carlota, Empress of Mexico, 91–92

Carlyle, Thomas, 197

Carr, Raymond, 221

Cartier, George-Étienne, 127

Carvajal, José, 90–91

Castelar y Ripoll, Emilio, 4, 207, 223–25, 224, 229, 286

Castro, Fidel, 167

Catholicism: Fenian distancing from, 135; and First Vatican Council, 274–76, 275; in France, 256, 258; in Ireland, 133; liberalism opposed by, 10, 263–64, 275–76; and Lincoln's assassination, 267–71; and Maximilian, 89–90; and papal infallibility, 275–76; Protestantism vs., 135, 264, 267, 271–72, 271; in Spain, 207; and U.S. Civil War, 47, 263–65, 267, 271. *See also* Papal States; Pius IX, Pope

censorship: in France, 2, 10, 23, 29, 31, 232–33, 239–41, 247, 256; in Spain, 48

Céspedes, Carlos Manuel de, 157–59, 161–65, 167

Chambord, Henri, Comte de, 254

Chandler, Zachariah, 145

Charles V, Holy Roman Emperor, 96

Chartists, 179, 187, 196

Chassin, Charles-Louis, 27–29

Chernyshevski, Nicholas, 105

Chicago Tribune (newspaper), 125

Chile, 8, 38–39, 53, 59–60, 149, 152

China and Chinese immigrants, 11, 47, 228, 234

Chincha Islands, 148, 151

Christ. *See* Jesus Christ

Civil War (United States): Brazil and, 36; Britain and, 46, 47, 55, 100–101, 104, 123–26, 141, 176–77, 291; Canada and, 123–24; Catholicism and, 47, 263–65, 267, 271; Cuba and, 153–54; Europe and, 43, 46–59, 123, 176; Fenian Brotherhood and, 131–33; France and, 23–24, 46–47, 55, 74, 100–101, 104, 208, 232–33; international effects of, 6, 9, 42; Italy and, 279; Mexico and, 8, 35; and Monroe Doctrine, 49–50, 53–55; retribution for, 43, 57–59, 61–62, 76, 121–22, 124, 144–46; Russia and, 99–104; Spain and, 147, 149. *See also* Confederates/Confederacy

Clemenceau, Georges, 236, 241, 242, 243, 248, 254, 259

Cluseret, Gustave Paul, 195–96, 258

Cobden, Richard, 182

Cochin, Augustin, 27, 233–34, 240

Colonial Reform Commission (Spain), 156–57

Columbus, Christopher, 206

Comité français d'émancipation. *See* French Committee of Emancipation

Commonwealth, The (British newspaper), 196

Communism/Communist, 230, 256, 260, 261, 262, 264. *See also* Paris Commune

Confederates/Confederacy: British support for, 46; Catholic support for, 47, 264, 267, 271; European support for, 42, 53, 55, 61, 69–70; French support for, 46, 74; Maximilian's relationship with, 8, 35, 74, 76, 83–85. *See also* Civil War

Conservative Party (Britain). *See* Tory Party

Conservatives (Church Party) [Mexico], 69–70, 89–90

Constantine, Grand Duke, 112

coolies. *See* China and Chinese immigrants

Cooper Union, New York City, 4, 36, 51, 79, 150

Corona (Mexican general), 95

Coronado, Carolina, 202, 208

cosmopolitanism, 6, 33, 45, 176, 290

Courrier des États-Unis (newspaper), 48

Crawford, R. Clay, 88–89

Crimean War (1853–56), 100–103

Cuba: Creoles in, 152–53, 156; flag for, 165–67, 166; independence movement in, 8, 34–35, 62, 157–72, 217, 219, 229–30, 288–89; and Lincoln, 34–35, 152–54, 158; slavery and enslaved peoples in, 8–9, 152–59, 162–64, 167–69, 220–29; Spain and, 8–9, 152–72, 208, 218–30, 288–89; Spanish atrocities against, 160–61, 169; Spanish reform ideas for, 156–57; United States and, 62, 63, 161–72, 168, 169, 208–9, 217–30; and U.S. annexation, 8, 62, 162, 164–65, 167, 171–72, 209, 226

Darboy, Georges, 258–59

Davis, Henry Winter, 42, 53–54, 57–59

Davis, Jefferson, 47

Defenders of the Monroe Doctrine, 83

democracy: Britain and, 175–202; Canada
and, 122–23, 128–29; democratic peace
theory, 244; Europe and, 176, 179, 281,
286, 291; France and, 31, 232, 259; goals of,
176; Lincoln as symbol of, 2; monarchy
and, 286; Spain and, 202–3, 214, 230; in
Switzerland, 22–23; Tocqueville and,
181–82; United States as model of, 31, 33,
105; violent revolution opposed by, 259;
white supremacy linked to, 290, 293.
See also republicanism

Democratic Party (United States): Andrew
Johnson's reliance on, 137; and Catholicism, 272; and Mexico, 59; opposition to
imperialism from Southern, 295–96; and
Russia, 106

democratic peace, 65, 123, 146, 244, 286, 316n51

Denmark, 63–64

Derby, Edward Stanley, Lord, 142, 184, 194–95,
197

Derby, Elias H., 119

Dewey, George, 289

Dicey, Albert V., 182, 200

Diplomatic Review (newspaper), 116

Disraeli, Benjamin, 141–42, 183, 185, 194, 197–98

Dix, John, 125

Dominican Republic, 53, 63–64, 147, 210.
See also Santo Domingo

Douglass, Frederick, 168–69, 233

Drescher, Seymour, 156

Drouyn de Lhuys, Edmond, 85

Du Bois, William E. B., 1, 4–6, 284; *Black
Reconstruction*, 4–5, 12

Dulce, Domingo, 160

Dumas, Alexandre, 214, 246

Dunning, William Archibald, 4, 287–88, 292

Dunning School, 4–5, 292

Egypt, 92

Elcho, Francis Charteris, Lord, 186

Emancipation. *See* slavery: abolition of

Emancipation Law (Spain, 1880), 228

Emancipation Proclamation (United States,
1863), 9, 37, 100, 123, 155, 178, 224, 229

Emerson, Ralph Waldo, 198

Ems telegram, 247

Engels, Frederick, 180, 190

Enlightenment, 10, 24, 129

Escobedo, Mariano, 91, 95

Espartero, Baldomero, 229

États-Unis d'Europe, Les (journal), 244.
See also United States of Europe

Eugénie, Empress of France, 92, 212, 238,
239, 252–53

Europe: and democracy, 176, 179, 281, 286,
291; imperialism in the Americas by, 8,
42, 47–48, 50, 53, 57–60; international
Reconstruction in, 8–10; Mexico and,
53–55; political left in, 176; reform efforts
in, 9–10, 16, 21; Russia and, 99–103; and
U.S. Civil War, 43, 46–59

European Union, 245

Evans, Albert, 97–98

Evans, Thomas, 252

Exposition Universelle (Paris, 1867), 234–36,
235, 246

Fabié, Antonio María, 156, 204

Favre, Jules, 77, 240, 247, 250, 252

Fawcett, Henry, 177

Federal Elections Bill (United States), 294

Fenian Brotherhood: and British reform
efforts, 195–96; and Canada, 43, 122,
131–33, 138–42, 144, 146; and the Civil
War, 131–33; Cluseret and, 258; in Ireland,
133–35, 146; Irish liberation as goal of, 43,
122, 133–42, 159, 258; membership of, 136;
origin of, 131, 132; picnics held by, 43,
136–37, 136; stereotypes of, 133–34, 134, 137

Ferdinand VII, King of Spain, 204–5

Ferreira, Felix, 37

Field, Cyrus W., 192

Fifteenth Amendment (U.S. Constitution),
288

First International. *See* International
    Working Men's Association
First Vatican Council (1869), 274–76, *275*
Fish, Hamilton: and *Alabama* Claims, 146;
    and Alaska Purchase, 63; American secu-
    rity as goal of, 219; background of, 170;
    and Cuba, 160, 163, 167, 170–72, 209, 218–20;
    and foreign policy, 3, 7; and France, 257,
    261; and Spain, 9, 160, 217–21, 223, 226–29
Fogg, George, 22, 23
Foner, Eric, *Reconstruction*, 5
Forbes, Paul, 218, 219
Forster, William E., 20–21
Fourteenth Amendment (U.S. Constitution),
    288
Fourth of July Law (Spain, 1870). *See* Moret
    Law
Fox, Gustavus Vasa, 107–12, *109*, *111*
France: attitudes about America in, 24, 107,
    233, 241–45, 252; and Catholicism, 256,
    258; censorship in, 2, 10, 23, 29, 31, 232–33,
    239–41, 247, 256; Corps Législatif in, 77,
    89, 232, 236, 239, 245–46, 250, 252; and
    democracy, 24–26, 29–32, 232, 259; Gov-
    ernment of National Defense, 252–54;
    Italy and, 273–74; and liberalism, 77, 176,
    240–41, 245–46; and Lincoln, 23–31, 39–40;
    Mexico and, 7, 8, 10, 40, 46–47, 52–54, 59,
    64, 67, 69–72, 74–95, 148, 206, 232, 235–37,
    281; Paris Commune, 10, 231, 246, 254–62,
    255; political left in, 10, 232–33, 236–37,
    245; and Prussia, 10, 88, 216, 244, 246–54,
    249, 276; reform efforts in, 3, 10, 23–31;
    republicanism in, 26, 236, 239–44, 246,
    248–55, 261; Second Empire, 2, 4, 10, 23,
    28–29, 231–32, 234–41, 245–50, 259, 260,
    286; and slavery, 27, 233–34; suffrage in,
    232; Third Republic, 246, 251, 252–53, 260,
    286; tributes to Lincoln from, 2; United
    States and, 23–24, 46–48, 57, 74–95, 100,
    104, 107, 232–33, 235–36, 260–62. *See also*
    French Revolution; Napoleon III; Paris,
    France
Francis, Allen, 120

French Committee of Emancipation, 27,
    233–34
French Medal, 27–31, *30*
French Revolution, 27, 30, 176, 196, 232
Fürstnow, Heinrich, "The *Miantonomoh*
    Galop," 108, *110*

Gaiffe, Adolphe, 19
Galt, Alexander, 142
Gambetta, Léon, 243, 250, *251*, 252
García Tassara, Gabriel, 147
Garibaldi, Giuseppe, 3, 32, 95, 179, 214, 244,
    263, 264, 273–74, *274*, 279
Garrison, William Lloyd, 234
Geneva Peace Conference, 244–45
Géricault, Théodore, *The Wreck of the
    Medusa*, 252
"Get Out of Mexico" (song), 80, *81*
Gladstone, William, 181–86
Gladstone Bill, 181–85, 197
Glorious Revolution (Spain, 1868), 10, 150,
    203, 210–14, *213*, 221–22, 228–30, 286
Godkin, E. L., 63
Goicouria, Domingo de, 227
Gorchakov, Alexander, 103, 105, 112
Grand Design, of Napoleon III for the
    Americas, 10, 51–52, 67, 70, 94, 171, 232,
    237. *See also* Latin race
Grant, Ulysses S.: and *Alabama* Claims,
    146; and Cuba, 62, 162, 167, 170, 221; and
    foreign policy, 3; French attitudes about,
    243; and Mexican-American War, 73, 90;
    and Mexico, 73–77, 84, 86; and Spain,
    217–18, 221, 227–29
Great Coalition (Canada), 127
Greater Reconstruction, 5
Green, George, 95, 98
Guadeloupe, 27, 233
Guam, 289
guarantee clause (U.S. Constitution), 7
Guerra Chiquita (Little War) [Cuba, 1879–80],
    172
Gustavus Fox Expedition, 107–11, *109*, *111*
Gwin, William, 84

Habeas Corpus Act (Britain), 135

Haiti, 33, 150, 157

Hale, Charles, 270

Hale, John, 208, 212, 214

Hall, Henry C., 160–61

Harper's Weekly (magazine), 227, 262

Harris, Robert, *The Fathers of Confederation*, 129

Haussmann, Georges-Eugène, Baron, 232, 234–35, 255–57, 256

Hawai'i, 102

Hay, John, 214, 221, 223, 230, 289

Herzen, Alexander, 105

Holmes, Oliver Wendell, 109

Holy Alliance, 50

Horsman, Edward, 182–83

Hovey, Alvin, 151

Howard, Elisa, 103

Howell, George, 180

Hugo, Victor, 15, 16, 29, 95, 176, 214, 239, 244, 245

Hyde Park riot (1866), 186–90, *189*

immigration, 294

Immigration Restriction League, 294

Inter-American Congress (1864), 148

International Working Men's Association, 4, 9, 178–79, 244, 256, 260, 261

Ireland, 131, 133–35

Irish Republican Brotherhood, 131

Isabella I, Queen of Castile, 206

Isabella II, Queen of Spain, 10, 147, 150, 154, 203–12, *210*, 214, 230, 286

Italy: France and, 273–74; Jews in, 265, 278; and liberalism, 32, 265–66, 273; and Lincoln, 32–33; nationalism in, 263, 279; and the Papal States, 10, 263–67, 273–83; reform efforts in, 16; republicanism in, 263, 281–83; Rome as capital of, 273–83, 286; unification of, 264–65, 273–74, 279, 280; United States and, 32–33, 279–81, *279*

Jamaica, 179, 234

Jay, John, 79

Jefferson, Thomas, 114

Jequitinhonha, Francisco Gê Acayaba de Montezuma, Viscount of, 37

Jerome Napoleon, Prince (France), 107–8

Jesus Christ, 226, 229

Jews, 105, 265, 278

Jim Crow regime, 288

Johnson, Andrew: and Alaska, 113–14; American security as goal of, 51–52; animosity toward, 64; annexation of territories opposed by, 8; and Bancroft's congressional speech, 43, 48–49; and Canada, 143; and foreign policy, 3; impeachment of, 241, 243; and the Irish, 137–38; and Mexico, 72, 74, 76, 87; as president, 15, 27; and Reconstruction, 114; and slavery, 233; and Spain, 217

Johnson, William Edward (nom de plume: Malakoff), 25–26, 54, 57, 236–37, 239–41, 256

Johnson-Clarendon Treaty, 144

Jordan, Thomas, 160

Journal Officiel, 231

Juárez, Benito, 35, 73, 82–85, 90, 94–97, *96*, 285

Karakozov, Dmitry, 105–6

Killian, Bernard Doran, 137–38

King, Rufus, 265, 268–70, 272–73

Kipling, Rudyard, "The White Man's Burden," 295–96

Kirk, Robert, 38

Koerner, Gustave, 205

Krabbe, Nikolay Karlovich, 112

Krupp, Alfred, 246

Ku Klux Klan, 287

Kung, Prince (China), 47

Laboulaye, Édouard, 24, 215, 233–34, 240

Labra, Rafael María de, 204

LaFeber, Walter, 61

Langston, John Mercer, 169

Lanjuinais, Victor, 239

Lanterne, La (newspaper), 239–40

Lapuente, Laurindo, "Republicanas," 151

Latin race, 52, 70, 79, 94, 171, 206, 261
League of Nations, 245
League of Peace and Liberty, 244
Leavitt, Joshua, 50–51, 69, 79; "The Key of a Continent," 51
Lecomte, Claude (French general), 254
left. See political left
Lemonnier, Charles, 244–45
Leopold von Hohenzollern (Prussian prince), 215–16, 246–47
Leutze, Emanuel, Signing the Alaska Treaty, 116, 117
liberalism: Britain and, 177, 198–99; Catholic opposition to, 10, 263–64, 275–76; European opposition to, 50; France and, 77, 176, 240–41, 245–46; Italy and, 32, 265–66, 273; Mexico and, 52, 69; socialism vs., 260; Spain and, 204, 207, 210–11, 217
Liberal Party (Britain), 177, 181, 183–84, 187, 194, 197, 200
Liberation Army (Cuba), 34–35, 158–60, 162–63
Lincoln (ship), 116
Lincoln, Abraham: Alexander II compared to, 104–6, 108; Catholic involvement in assassination of, 267–71; on Civil War outcome, 1; criticisms of, 16, 123, 265; Emancipation Proclamation, 37, 100, 123, 155, 178, 224, 229; and European imperialism, 53; Gettysburg Address, 16; and Mexico, 53, 70; news of assassination of, 1–2, 17–19, 21, 34–36, 38, 154, 177, 180, 233; as political symbol/model, 2, 3, 8, 13, 16, 21, 24–26, 31, 33–35, 37, 39, 60, 102, 105, 152–54, 158, 176–78, 180–81, 200, 204, 223–26, 233, 240–41, 281, 295; Second Inaugural Address, 16; Southern secession in response to election victory of, 69; and Spain, 149; tributes to, 1–4, 15, 18–42, 90, 96, 105, 155, 178, 180, 233, 240, 263, 265–67, 281–82
Lincoln, Mary Todd, 17; gold medal presented by the French to, 27–31, 30
literacy tests, 288

Lodge, Henry Cabot, 293–94
London Emancipation Society, 19
London Times (newspaper), 16, 48, 108, 116, 121, 126, 143–44, 276, 278, 283
López, Narciso, 165–67
Louisiana Purchase, 114
Louis Napoleon. See Napoleon III
Louis Napoleon, Prince (France), 238–39
Louis Philippe, King of France, 208, 258
Louis XVI, King of France, 257
Louvre, Paris, 252, 257
Lowe, Robert (First Viscount Sherbrooke), 183–84, 186, 194
Lucraft, Benjamin, 186
Luisa Fernanda, Infanta of Spain, 208
Luxembourg, 244, 246
Lyons, Richard, Lord, 117
Lyons-Seward Treaty (United States, 1862), 8, 155–56

Macdonald, John A., 122, 127–28
Machado, Eduardo, 165
Madison, James, 46
Magniadas, Franky, 29
USS Maine, 288
Malakoff. See Johnson, William Edward
Malespine, Aimé, 239
Mambises. See Liberation Army
Manet, Edouard, The Execution of Maximilian, 67, 97
Manifest Destiny, 8, 64
Marfori, Carlos, 212
Maria Christina (Spanish regent), 204–5
Maritime provinces, 128, 146. See also New Brunswick; Newfoundland; Nova Scotia; Prince Edward Island
"La Marseillaise" (song), 232, 247–48, 258
Marsh, George, 39
Martí, José, 34, 154
martyrdom, 17
Marx, Karl, vii, 4, 9, 177–80, 190, 244, 256; Communist Manifesto, 256, 261; Das Kapital, 190

Maximilian, Emperor of Mexico, 3, 8, 35, 47–48, 53–54, 67, 69–70, 74–77, 80, 82–85, 89–98, 93, 148, 206, 232, 236, 267, 273, 281

Mayne, Richard, 187–88, 190, 196

Mazzini, Giuseppe, 32, 55–57, 58, 176, 214, 263, 273, 280–83, 282

McClure's Magazine, 295

McKinley, William, 289

Meade, George, 139

Melvil-Bloncourt, Sainte-Suzanne, 233

Men of Action, 139–40

Mexico: American volunteers to fight in, 82–83; civil war in, 69; European aggression in, 53–55; France and, 7, 8, 10, 40, 46–47, 52–54, 59, 64, 67, 69–72, 74–95, 148, 206, 232, 235–37, 281; and liberalism, 52, 69; and Lincoln, 35–36; popular American songs about, 80–82; reform efforts in, 16; Reform War (1858–61), 69; Spain and, 147–48; United States and, 8, 35–36, 51, 70, 72–98

USS *Miantonomoh*, 107–8

"The *Miantonomoh* Galop" (song), 108, 110

Michelet, Jules, 29, 243–44

Midway Island, 63

Mill, Harriet Taylor, 199

Mill, John Stuart, 177, 179, 195, 198–99, 199

Millard, Harrison, "Viva l'America," 280

I Mille (The Thousand), 264

Mitchel, John, 131, 137–38

monarchy: in Britain, 10, 194; democracy and, 286; republicanism vs., 7, 10, 45, 49–54, 57, 59–60, 64–65, 78–80, 100, 115, 143, 150–52, 167, 171, 175, 194, 253–54, 261; in Spain, 10, 205, 215, 229–30, 286; U.S. antipathy toward, 7, 45–46

Monck, Charles Stanley, Lord, 125

Moniteur, Le (newspaper), 90

Monroe, James, 49, 53

Monroe Doctrine: bipartisan agreement on, 43, 51, 57, 80; calls for aggressive enforcement of, 43, 54–55, 79–83; Canada as

target of, 143; Civil War and, 49–50, 53–55; defense of republicanism as purpose of, 7, 49–54, 57, 59–60, 64–65, 78–80, 126, 151–52, 167; European fears of U.S. uses of, 55–59; Johnson and, 73; and opposition to slavery, 92, 94; origins of, 49, 99; protection of the Americas as purpose of, 7, 43, 51, 53, 59–60, 72, 76, 126, 150–52, 167, 284–85; Spain and, 147; U.S. adherence to, 209, 218

Monroe League, 83

Montagnie, John de la, 28

Montalembert, Charles Forbes, Comte de, vii, 31

Montpensier, Antoine, Duke of, 208–9, 215

Morales Lemus, José, 163

Moran, Benjamin, 20, 181

Morant Bay Rebellion (1865), 179, 234

Moret Law (Spain, 1870), 9, 222, 225–28, 226

Moret y Prendergast, Segismundo, 222–25

Morley, John, 177

Motley, John Lothrop, 201

Mur des Fédérés (Communards' Wall), 260

Nabuco, Joaquim, 37

Nadich, Abraham, 105

Nanaimo Tribune (newspaper), 120

Napoleon I, Emperor of France, 50, 231, 233, 240, 257

Napoleon II, 240

Napoleon III, Emperor of France: and the American Confederacy, 46–47; American criticism of, 48; and Franco-Prussian War, 10, 216, 246–49, 249, 253; French rule of, 2, 4, 10, 23, 28–29, 97, 107, 176, 206–8, 216, 231–32, 234–41, 235, 245–48, 255, 276, 286; health of, 237, 238; and Italy, 263, 273–74; Mexican goals and the Grand Design of, 10, 46–47, 51, 52, 67, 69–70, 73, 77, 80, 84–95, 93, 107, 171, 232, 237; and Spain, 210, 212

Narváez, Ramón María, 206–7

Nast, Thomas, 134, 262; "The British Lion Disarmed," *145*; "I am now infallible," *277*; "The Pope Bans Protestant Worship from Rome," *271*; "United Italy," *279*

Nation (magazine), 138

nationalism: Bancroft and, 45; Fenians and Irish, 131, 135; Italian, 263, 279

National Reformer (British newspaper), 196

National Roman Committee, 263, 265–66

Native Americans, 11

Nelson, Thomas, 38–39, 98

New Brunswick, 128, 139, 144

Newfoundland, 128, 144

New York Cuban Junta, 219

New York Herald (newspaper), 82, 115, 125, 280

New York Times (newspaper), 26, 54, 56, 59, 80, 82, 100, 125, 126, 131, 172, 236, 256, 262, 271–72

New York Union League Club, 79

Nicholas I, Tsar, 102

Nicolas, Grand Duke of Russia, 105

Nova Scotia, 128, 144, 146

Nova Scotian (ship), 18

O'Connell, Daniel, 132

O'Donnell, Leopoldo, 206, 207

O'Kelly, James, 159

Ollivier, Émile, 245, 247

O'Mahony, John, 136

O'Neill, John, 140

Ontario, 127, 129, 144, 146

Ortega, Jesús Gonzáles, 82–83

L'Osservatore Romano (newspaper), 265

Ostend Manifesto, 218

Ostend Pact (1866), 207, 210

Ottoman Empire, 102

Oxford Radicals, 200

Paine, Tom, 122

Pall Mall Gazette (newspaper), 118

Palmerston, Henry John Temple, Lord, 43, 47, 60–61, 181

Pan-African Congress, 6

Pan-Americanism, 7, 37, 38, 49, 59–60, 74, 79–80, 90, 98, 150, 167, 172

Pankhurst, Emmeline, 199–200

papal infallibility, 275–76

Papal States, 10, 263–83

Paris, France, 2, 10, 86–87, 232, 234–36, 247–57, 251

Paris Commune, 10, 231, 246, 254–62, 255

Paul II, Pope, 273

Pelletan, Eugène, 29, 31, 239

Perman, Michael, 5

Perry, Horatio, 152, 208

Peru, 8, 38, 53, 58, 59, 148–49, 151–52

Peterloo Massacre (1819), 191

Peyrat, Alphonse, 31

Phare de la Loire (newspaper), 28

Philippines, 102, 289–90, 294–95

Piña Mora, Aarón, mural featuring Lincoln, Juárez, and Bolívar, *96*

Pinzón, Luis H., 148

Pius IX, Pope (Pio Nono), 10, 47, 263–67, 271, 273–78, 277, 286; *Syllabus of Errors*, 10, 256, 264, 275

Poland, 23

political left: in Europe, 176; in France, 10, 232–33, 236–37, 245; liberalism vs. socialism in, 260; in Spain, 205, 230

poll taxes, 288

Portalis, Edouard, 243

Potter, David, 6

Potter, John Fox, 130–31

Potter, Thomas Bayley, 21, 177–78, 179

Preliti, Luigi, 32

Presse, La (newspaper), 48, 108

Prévost-Paradol, Lucien-Anatole, 232

Prim, Juan, 148, 158, 206–11, 213, 214–15, 218–21, 223, 229, 246

Prince Edward Island, 128, 144

Progressives (Spain), 203, 205, 206, 207

Protestantism, 135, 138, 264, 267, 271–72, 271

Prussia, 10, 88, 216, 244, 246–54, 276

Puerto Rico, 9, 156–57, 170, 172, 203, 209, 219, 222, 228, 229, 289

Quebec, 121, 122, 126–29, 142, 146

racism: anti-Black, 4–5, 287, 292–97; exhibited by Anglo-Americans, 63, 78–80, 171, 290, 292–97; theories underlying, 11, 293–94
Radepont, Aimé, marquis de, 171
Radical Reconstruction, 114, 176, 224, 256, 292, 294–95, 296
Radical Republicans (United States), 4, 5, 7, 53, 59, 100, 179, 241, 243, 256, 258, 287
Rappel (newspaper), 239
Rawlings, Thomas, 126
Rawlins, John, 167
Reagan, Ronald, 273
Reciprocity Treaty (1854), 130–31
Reclus, Élie, 214
Reclus, Élisée, 234
Reconstruction: contemporary relevance of, 11–12; contradictions and failures of, 11, 286–97; domestic and international, 7–11, 287–97; goals of, 7–8; international perspective on, 6; Radical, 114, 176, 224, 256, 292, 294–95, 296; scholarship on, 4–6; Second, 5, 296–97; as symbol and model for Europe, 225, 243
Reeve, Henry, 182
Reform Act (Britain, 1832), 179
Reform Act (Britain, 1867), 9, 197–98, 201, 205
Réforme (newspaper), 239
Reform League (Britain), 9, 22, 179–80, 182, 184–96, 258; Clerkenwell Branch, 185, 187, 188, 196; Holborn Branch, 187
republicanism: as check on imperialism, 63; European antipathy toward, 50; France and, 26, 236, 239–44, 246, 248–55, 261; Italy and, 263, 281–83; monarchy vs., 7, 10, 45, 49–53, 57, 59–60, 64–65, 78–80, 100, 115, 143, 150–52, 167, 171, 175, 194, 253–54, 261; United States as model of, 26; U.S. promotion of, 7, 45–46. *See also* democracy

Republican Party (United States): and Alaska Purchase, 114–15; animosity toward Andrew Johnson from, 64, 137; and Mexico, 54; Southern animosity toward, 69, 287. *See also* Radical Republicans
Reutern, Mikhail de, 112
Revels, Hiram, 169
Revista Hispano-Americana (journal), 204
Revolutions of 1848, 16, 32, 178, 244, 263
Revue des Deux Mondes (newspaper), 88
Rhodes, James Ford, 292
Rigault, Raoul, 258
Rise and Fall of Emperor Maximilian, The (pamphlet), 237
Risorgimento, 3, 16, 32–33, 265, 273–83, 286
Rivera, José, 79
Roberts, William R., 137
Robinson, Christopher, 38
Rochefort, Henri, 239–40
Rome. *See* Papal States
Romero, Matías, 35–36, 53, 70, 71, 72–75, 79, 83, 319n36
Roosevelt, Theodore, 289, 294
Rouher, Eugène, 78
Rush-Bagot Treaty (1817), 125, 130
Russell, Earl, 46
Russell, John, 181
Russell, William Howard, 126
Russia: and Alaska, 8, 99–104, 112–19; and Crimean War, 100–103; Europe and, 99–103; United States and, 47, 99–120; workers in, 100

Sainte Marie, Henri Beaumont de, 267–69
Santayana, Agustín, 215
Santayana, George, 215
Santo Domingo, 8, 58, 59, 62, 63, 150–51, 158, 210. *See also* Dominican Republic
Santovenia, Emeterio, 154–55
Savage, Thomas, 153
Schofield, John M., 75, 86–87
Schultz, Christian, *Fraternité Universelle*, 13
Schurz, Carl, 294–95

Second Reconstruction, 5, 296–97
Second Reform Act (Britain, 1867), 128, 198
self-rule, 96–97
September Convention (Italy and France, 1864), 273–74
serfdom, 100, 102, 106
Serrano, Francisco, 210, 214
Servius Tullius, Emperor of Rome, 266
Seward, Frances (Fanny), 55, 72
Seward, Frederick, 17, 72
Seward, William H.: and *Alabama* Claims, 119–20, 144; and Alaska Purchase, 63–64, 101–2, 112–18, *117*, 122; American security as goal of, 7, 50–53, 55, 57, 61, 63–65, 76–78, 101, 107, 172, 219, 285; and Asia, 102; attempted assassination of, 2, 17, 40, 72; belligerent rhetoric of, 60–61; and British Columbia, 119–20, 122; and Canada, 124–25, 130; and Cuba, 161–62, 172, 209; and the Irish, 133, 137–38, 139; and Italy, 266, 268–70, 272; and Mexico, 53, 70, 72–73, 76–79, 83–90, 92, 94, 95, 97–98; and slavery, 8–9, 155; and Spain, 151–52, 208, 212, 214; and United States as model for the world, 3, 25, 39–41, 48–49
Shelby, Joseph O. "Jo", 84
Sherbatoff, Prince (Russia), 111
Sherbrooke, First Viscount. *See* Lowe, Robert
Sheridan, Philip, 74–76, 83–85, 90, 248
Sherman, William Tecumseh, 94
Shufeldt, Robert, 153–54
Sickles, Daniel, 217–23, 222, 225–30
slavery: abolition of, 8–9, 27, 37, 92, 94, 100, 155–57, 162–64, 203–4, 220–29, 233–34; aristocracy associated with, 2, 7, 24, 36, 46, 100; Brazil and, 36–37, 227, 229, 233–34; in Cuba, 8–9, 152–59, 162–64, 167–69, 220–29; French opposition to, 27, 233–34; gradual approaches to abolition of, 9, 221–26, 229; Mexico and, 35; serfdom likened to, 100; Spain and, 9, 155–56, 203–4, 220–29, 233; United States and, 7, 21–22, 155, 227–28

Slidell, John, 86
Smith, Goldwin, 179, 182, 291; *Essays on Reform*, 200
Smith Edmund, Kirby, 74
socialism, 179, 256, 258–59, 261, 264
Society of Medical Students (France), 241
Society of the American Union (Chile), 38–39
Socrates, 13
Spain: censorship in, 48; the Cortes in, 4, 150, 156, 204, 207, 214, 223–26, 229; Cuba and, 8–9, 152–72, 208, 218–30, 288–89; and democracy, 202–3, 214, 230; First Republic, 228, 230; imperialism in the Caribbean and South America, 8, 50, 53, 59–60, 147–72, 206; Isabella II's reign in, 204–7; and liberalism, 204, 207, 210–11, 217; Mexico and, 147–48; monarchy in, 10, 205, 215, 229–30; political left in, 205, 230; rebellions in, 206–14, 213, 228–30, 286; reform efforts in, 3, 10, 150, 170; revolutionary provisional government in, *211*; and slavery, 9, 155–56, 203–4, 220–29, 233; suffrage in, 211, 229; United States and, 48, 147, 149, 151–52, 170–71, 208–10, 214–30, 288–89
Spanish Abolitionist Society, 155, 204, 207
Spanish-American War (1898), 289
Spanish Antilles, 209
Spanish Volunteers, 159–61
Spartacus, 226
St. Albans raid, 123–26, *125*, 130
Stanley, Frederick, Lord, 117
Stanton, Edwin M., 17, 268–69
Stanton, Elizabeth Cady, 11
Stephen, Leslie, 182
Stephens, Alexander, 55
Stevens, Thaddeus, 106, 243
Stillman, William J., 265–66
St. James Hall, London, 4
Stoeckl, Eduard de, 44, 103–4, 112–14, 116, *117*
Stowe, Harriet Beecher, 241; *La choza del negro Tomás*, 155
St. Petersburg Journal (newspaper), 105

St. Thomas, 62

Sturm, Herman, 90–91

Sudan, 92

Suez Canal, 232

suffrage: African American, 287–88, 293; in
    Britain, 179–82, 185–87, 191–95, 197–200;
    in France, 232; in Spain, 211, 229; in
    United States, 200, 287–88, 293; woman,
    11, 198–200, *199*

Sumner, Charles, 7, 99, 106, 109, 114–16, *117*,
    122, 144–45, 170, 208, 227, 258

Surratt, John, 267–71

Surratt, Mary, 267

Sweeny, Thomas, 139

Switzerland, 22–23

Tassara, Gabriel García, 43

Tavares Bastos, Aureliano Cândido, 36

Temps, Le (newspaper), 241, 242

Tenniel, John: "Britannia Sympathises with
    Columbia," *20*; "The Brummagem
    Frankenstein," *193*; "The Fenian Pest,"
    134; "Mill's Logic," *199*

Thiers, Adolphe, 236–37, 254–55, 257

Thirteenth Amendment (U.S. Constitution),
    155

Thornton, Edward, 146

Thurston, David, 18

Tillman, Benjamin, 295–96

Tinker, William C., 158

Tocqueville, Alexis de, 181–82, 291, 292

Tory Party (Britain), 176, 177, 181, 183–86,
    192, 194, 197, 201

Treaty of Paris (1898), 289, 295–96

Trement, Viscount P. (pseudonym of
    informant), 207–9

HMS *Trent*, 61, 123

Tribune (French newspaper), 239

Tributes of the Nations to Abraham Lincoln,
    40–41

Tripoli (ship), 270

Turner, Nat, 234

Twain, Mark, 289

United Nations, 245

United States: and Anglo-American, 102,
    121, 127, 139; and Anglo-Saxon culture, 52,
    63, 70, 171, 290–94; Britain and, 20–21, 43,
    46–48, 55–57, 100, 104, 108, 116–18, 123–26,
    144–46, 175; British attitudes toward,
    181–84, 200; Canada and, 121–27, 130–31,
    143–46; Congress in, 7, 43–48, 51, 53–54,
    63–64, 70, 90, 106–7, 112–14, 227, 271–72,
    289–90, 294; Cuba and, 62, 63, 161–72,
    168, 169, 208–9, 217–30; failures of
    Reconstruction in, 287–88, 293–97;
    foreign policy of, 7–8, 50; France and,
    23–24, 46–48, 57, 74–95, 100, 104, 107,
    232–33, 235–36, 260–62; French attitudes
    toward, 24, 107, 233, 241–45, 252; imperi-
    alism and anti-imperialism of, 55–57, *56*,
    63–64, 102, 172, 288–90, 294–96; Italy
    and, 32–33, 279–81, *279*; Mexico and, 8,
    35–36, 51, 70, 72–98; as model of democ-
    racy, 31, 33, 105; and papal Rome, 268–73;
    and the Philippines, 290; post–Civil War
    army of, 55, 61–62; Russia and, 47, 99–120;
    and slavery, 7, 21–22, 155, 227–28 (*see also*
    Emancipation Proclamation); Spain and,
    48, 147, 149, 151–52, 170–71, 208–10, 214–30,
    288–89; suffrage in, 200, 287–88, 293; as
    symbol and model for Europe and the
    world, 9–10, 12, 16, 21, 23–26, 31–33, 36,
    39–41, 45–46, 98, 176–77, 180, 189, 190,
    200–202, 214, 223, 231, 232–33, 241,
    243–45, 252, 280–81, 284–86, 295

United States of Europe, 176, 223, 244–45, 281

universal republic, 26, 32–33, 57, 176, 214,
    244, 281

U.S. Constitution, 214–15, 245

U.S. State Department, 39, 41, 109, 114

Valmaseda, Blas Villate de Herra, count of,
    160, 162–63

Valparaíso, Chile, bombardment of, 149, *149*

Vatican Council, 10

Vendôme Column, Paris, 257

Verdi, Giuseppe, "Chorus of the Hebrew Slaves," 265
Victor Emmanuel II, King of Italy, 32, 229, 264, 276
Victoria, Queen of England, 43, 123, 144, 194–95
Vicuña Mackenna, Benjamín, 59–60, 150
Villalobos, Joaquín, 79–80
Virgin Islands, 64
Vizcarrondo, Julio, 203–4, 207
voting rights. *See* suffrage; woman suffrage

Walker, Francis A., 11
Wallace, Lew, 89, 90–91
Walpole, Spencer, 187, 190–91, 195–97
War of 1812, 121, 130
Washburne, Elihu, 256–58, 260–61
Washington, George, 13, 37, 60, 226, 229, 241
Webb, James Watson, 36
Weed, Thurlow, 112

Weichmann, Louis J., 268
Welles, Gideon, 78, 107
West Indies, 63–64
White, Richard, *The Republic for Which It Stands*, 5
white supremacy, 4–5, 290, 293–96
Wilhelm I, King of Prussia, 216, 246–48
Willard, Charles W., 217
Wilson, Woodrow, 292
woman suffrage, 11, 198–200, *199*
Wydenbruck, Baron, 43

yellow fever/*vomito*, 92, 150
Young, Bennett, 124

Zacarias de Góis (Brazilian senator), 229
Zambrana, Antonio, 164–65
Zarco, Francisco, vii, 79
Zouaves, 267–70, 278

A NOTE ON THE TYPE

THIS BOOK has been composed in Arno, an Old-style serif typeface in the classic Venetian tradition, designed by Robert Slimbach at Adobe.